A Longman Cultural Edition

Oscar Wilde's

THE PICTURE
OF DORIAN GRAY

D0556840

Edited by

Andrew Elfenbein

University of Minnesota, Twin Cities

PEARSON
Longman

New York   Boston   San Francisco
London   Toronto   Sydney   Tokyo   Singapore   Madrid
Mexico City   Munich   Paris   Cape Town   Hong Kong   Montreal

Editor-in-Chief: Joseph P. Terry
Development Editor: Christine Halsey
Executive Marketing Manager: Ann Stypuloski
Production Coordinator: Scarlett Lindsay
Project Coordination, Text Design, and Electronic Page Makeup: Grapevine
    Publishing Services, Inc.
Cover Designer/Manager: John Callahan
Manufacturing Manager: Mary Fischer
Printer and Binder: Courier Corporation / Westford
Cover Printer: Coral Graphics Services, Inc.

Cover Image: *Portrait of Betsy Brown* © Michelle Puleo / SuperStock.

Library of Congress Cataloging-in-Publication Data

Wilde, Oscar, 1854–1900.
  [Picture of Dorian Gray]
  Oscar Wilde's The picture of Dorian Gray / edited by Andrew Elfenbein.
      p. cm. — (Longman cultural edition)
  Includes bibliographical references.
  ISBN 0-321-42713-0
    1. Conduct of life—Fiction. 2. Youthfulness—Fiction. 3. Portraits—Fiction.
I. Elfenbein, Andrew. II. Title.

  PR5819.A2E44 2007
  823'.8—dc22
                                                              2006025222

Copyright © 2007 by Pearson Education, Inc.

Please visit our Web site at www.ablongman.com

ISBN: 0-321-42713-0

2 3 4 5 6 7 8 9 10—CRW—09 08 07

Contents

List of Illustrations

Cover: *Portrait of Betsy Brown* © Michelle Puleo / SuperStock.

About Longman Cultural Editions

Reading always seems to vibrate with the transformation of the day—now, yesterday, and centuries ago, when the presses first put printed language into wide circulation. Correspondingly, literary culture has always been a matter of change: of new practices confronting established traditions; of texts transforming under the pressure of new techniques of reading and new perspectives of understanding; of canons shifting and expanding; of informing traditions getting reviewed and renewed, recast and reformed by emerging cultural interests and concerns; of culture, too, as a variable "text"—a reading. Inspired by the innovative *Longman Anthology of British Literature*, Longman Cultural Editions respond creatively to the changes, past and recent, by presenting key texts in contexts that illuminate the lively intersections of literature, tradition, and culture. A principal work is made more interesting by materials that place it in relation to its past, present, and future, enabling us to see how it may be reworking traditional debates and practices, how it appears amid the conversations and controversies of its own historical moment, how it gains new significances in subsequent eras of reading and reaction. Readers new to the work will discover attractive paths for exploration, while those more experienced will encounter fresh perspectives and provocative juxtapositions.

Longman Cultural Editions serve not only several kinds of readers but also (appropriately) their several contexts, from various courses of study to independent adventure. Handsomely produced and affordably priced, our volumes offer appealing companions to *The Longman Anthology of British Literature*, in some cases enriching and expanding units originally developed for the *Anthology*, and in other cases presenting this wealth for the first time. The logic and composition of the contexts vary across the series. The constants are the complete text of an important literary work, reliably edited, headed by an inviting introduction, and supplemented by helpful annotation; a table of dates to track its composition, publication, and public reception in relation to biographical, cultural, and historical events; and a guide for further inquiry and study. With these common measures and uncommon assets, Longman Cultural Editions encourage your literary pleasures with resources for lively reflection and adventurous inquiry.

SUSAN J. WOLFSON
General Editor
Professor of English
Princeton University

About This Edition

In *The Picture of Dorian Gray*, Oscar Wilde single-handedly perfected the decadent novel in English. No other work has ever come close in its ability to encapsulate and explore the multiple paradoxes invoked by the *fin de siècle*: the combination of intellectual adventurousness with intense soul weariness; the unsteady mixture of consumerism and defensive isolation from the world; the tonal uncertainty that veers from brilliant comedy to melodramatic sensationalism; the obsessive attention to realistic surfaces combined with a fantasy plot. This Longman Cultural Edition gives readers a variety of contextual information to illuminate these paradoxes and Wilde's ability to turn them in unexpected directions.

Wilde's novel exists in two versions, a first version published in *Lippincott's Magazine* in 1890 and a longer version published by Ward, Lock, and Co. in 1891, with a now famous preface. This edition is based on the 1891 version. In the "Textual Issues" section, readers can learn more about the differences between the two versions, which ended up playing a significant role in Wilde's trials for "gross indecency" (meaning, in this case, sex between men). In addition, I have included extra annotations for the notorious Chapter 11, which Wilde fills with a dazzling array of exotic and obscure details—their very unfamiliarity part of their allure, as well as a challenge to ordinary habits of comprehension.

The Picture of Dorian Gray occasioned a storm of controversy upon its first publication, and critics have never been quite comfortable with it since, accusing it of everything from indecency to dullness. In "Victorian Reactions to *The Picture of Dorian Gray*," I track this storm by reprinting much of Wilde's battle with one of his fiercest critics in the pages of the *St. James's Gazette*, a battle with wider stakes in Victorian debates about aesthetics, criticism, and the responsibility of the artist. A review by Wilde's informal mentor Walter Pater and brilliant parodies by Wilde's contemporaries are complemented by material reporting the more serious repercussions of Wilde's work: an edited version of the transcripts of one of Wilde's trials, in which *The Picture of Dorian Gray* served as evidence of Wilde's "sodomitical" propensities.

Although Wilde himself was tempted at times to dismiss his novel as a potboiler, it was the most ambitious work he had yet written, one that engaged major aesthetic and intellectual issues. The other selections in the Contexts materials show this territory. The "Aestheticism" section traces major influences on Wilde's philosophy of art. Wilde always acknowledged his debt to the leader of the Aesthetic movement, Walter Pater, though his prose style was more heavily influenced by cultural critic Matthew Arnold, and his philosophy by French sources, especially the notorious *À Rebours* of Joris-Karl Huysmans. Wilde's own critical works form some of the most memorable and challenging formulations of Victorian aesthetic philosophy.

Wilde has sometimes been underestimated as an intellectual: his work often seems too deliberately witty and blatantly trivial. Yet the publication of Wilde's notebooks in 1989 complicated this view. Rather than being a store of languid poetry or barbed one-liners, the notebooks hold page after page of quotations from the most advanced scientific thinkers of his day. We can see the effect on *The Picture of Dorian Gray*, which is everywhere engaged with post-Darwinian developments in evolution and scientific method. The "Science" section of the Contexts fills in this framework.

There are also personal frameworks, at once private and culturally potent. For many years, Wilde's homosexuality was either glanced at quickly or just evaded. Recent interest in the history of sexuality has turned Wilde into a key figure not only because of his trials but also because of his attempt in works like *The Picture of Dorian Gray* to develop a homosexual aesthetic. He was writing at the same time that sexologists in Germany and England, such as Havelock Ellis, were moving the discussion of sexuality from religious and legal terms to medical and psychological inquiry. Wilde's own understanding was heavily influenced by the representations of ancient Greek sexuality in writers such as John Addington Symonds, representations that disturbed some of his contemporaries.

In the footnotes for *The Picture of Dorian Gray*, I have often quoted from late nineteenth-century works; just a few words from Victorian sources can provide vivid information about details. I have also avoided the tendency of previous editors to note the many good lines and epigrams that Wilde later recycled in his society comedies. While this recycling is a significant aspect of Wilde's authorial practice, I find that pointing it out in footnotes is distracting.

I am grateful to the College of Liberal Arts at the University of Minnesota for a single-semester leave in which to complete this edition and to the many people who helped with my queries: James Eli Adams, Daniel Brewer, Philip Clausen, Christopher Cramer, Michael Hancher, Nita Krevans, Oliver Nicholson, Patrick Noon, Herbert Tucker, and the staff of the University of Minnesota's Wilson Library. I am also indebted to previous editors of this novel: Peter Ackroyd, Joseph Bristow, Donald Lawler, Isobel Murray, and Norman Page. Chrysta Meadowbrooke and Dianne Hall offered invaluable support in manuscript preparation. John and Dima Watkins were indispensable, as always. Above all, I'd like to thank Susan Wolfson, for her care and intelligence as an editor.

ANDREW ELFENBEIN
University of Minnesota, Twin Cities

Introduction

Oscar Fingal O'Flahertie Wills Wilde was born in Dublin to a respectably professional Protestant family. His father was a doctor; his mother, a leading writer for Irish nationalism. Wilde went to school in Ireland and then won a scholarship to study at Oxford, where he excelled in the classics, earning an enviable "double first" in his exams and the Newdigate prize in poetry. Here, too, he encountered Pre-Raphaelite art that was challenging mid-Victorian conventions and became a university celebrity for his ostentatious appearance and sharp wit.

When, despite his academic honors, Wilde was turned down for a position at the university, he found himself contending with straitened finances. The inheritance from his father was meager, and he had to find work. He moved to London and quickly formed an aesthetic cult around him. His brilliant conversation made him the darling of the social scene, and his poses produced caricatures in periodicals such as *Punch* and in Gilbert and Sullivan's operetta *Patience*. His early attempts at writing were less promising: his play *Vera, or The Nihilists* was unsuccessful, and his *Poems* were roundly condemned by the press. As his conversational brilliance might suggest, he found his talent instead in public lecturing and embarked on a profitable tour of the United States and Canada during which he visited virtually every major city.

Upon returning to London, he married Constance Lloyd, with whom he had two children, Cyril and Vyvyan (the namesakes of his dialogue *The Decay of Lying*). Needing to support them, he edited *The Woman's World*, through which he came into contact with most of the leading women writers of the day. Yet his desires increasingly turned to his own writing, and, during the late

1880s, to liaisons with men (homoerotic themes had long been present in his writings).

Giving up *The Woman's World*, he devoted himself to becoming a professional author. His initial ventures experimented with a variety of different modes: literary review, fairy tale, philosophical dialogue, short story, and novella. He hit the mark with drama. The triumph of *Lady Windermere's Fan* in 1891 was followed by *Salome* (so scandalous that it could not be produced in England), *A Woman of No Importance, An Ideal Husband*, and his masterpiece, *The Importance of Being Earnest*. His success occurred alongside a difficult affair with the beautiful, unstable Lord Alfred Douglas, sixteen years Wilde's junior. Douglas demanded Wilde's time, attention, and money, and Wilde became increasingly debt-ridden and estranged from his family. Moreover, Douglas's father, the Marquess of Queensberry, violently disapproved of their affair and eventually labeled Wilde (in peculiar spelling) a "posing somdomite."

Infuriated, Wilde accused Queensberry of libel. A trial ensued, bringing to light abundant evidence of Wilde's affairs with other men. Wilde lost his case and was immediately arrested on the criminal charge of "gross indecency" (less dire than sodomy, but easier to prove). This trial ended in a hung jury, but a second trial on the charge found Wilde guilty. He received the maximum sentence of two years' hard labor at Reading Gaol. Bankrupt and ostracized, Wilde endured a brutal prison term, during which he wrote *De Profundis* (published after his death), a long letter reviewing his life and castigating Douglas. Upon his release, he fled England for the Continent. Although he published the wrenching, bitter *The Ballad of Reading Gaol*, a poem based on his time in prison, he could not reignite his career. With his works unmarketable because of the scandal of his name, Wilde, sick, poor, and nearly friendless, died in Paris in 1900—though not without noting, "My wallpaper and I are fighting a duel to the death. One or the other of us has to go."

The Picture of Dorian Gray (1890, 1891)

The Picture of Dorian Gray was first published in 1890, in the American *Lippincott's Magazine*. As this venue may suggest, the tale was designed as popular magazine fiction, despite its elite high decadent aesthetics. On the page opposite the title, American read-

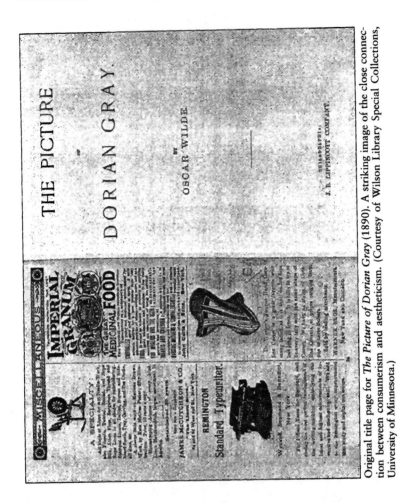

Original title page for *The Picture of Dorian Gray* (1890). A striking image of the close connection between consumerism and aestheticism. (Courtesy of Wilson Library Special Collections, University of Minnesota.)

ers encountered not abstruse aesthetic and philosophical discussions but advertisements for such items as Imperial Granum (the "Great Medicinal Food"), Remington typewriters, and Dr. Warner's Four-in-Hand Coraline Corsets. Aestheticism was not as far from consumer culture as it sometimes liked to pretend, as the novel's own abundance of luxury goods makes evident.

Already a celebrity, Wilde knew enough about the market not to offer a run-of-the-mill story, of the kind that would merely cater to respectable middle-class taste. Instead, he wrote *The Picture of Dorian Gray*, which ripples with every variety of scandalous behavior, especially homosexuality and its array of codes and coded scenes. Abuse poured from the reviewers: they found the novel "singularly unpleasant," "unclean," and "unmanly, sickening, vicious."[1] Britain's most prominent bookseller, W. H. Smith, even refused to stock it. But it sold well.

Wilde responded vigorously to his critics and developed plans to expand the magazine tale into a separate novel. Yet its notoriety was also a problem. Wilde had trouble finding a publisher and had to settle for Ward, Lock, and Co., the British distributors of *Lippincott's*. While the expanded version did not do as well as Wilde had hoped, probably because the magazine version had exhausted demand, the scandal did not die down. Both versions were repeatedly summoned into evidence in Wilde's libel trial against the Marquess of Queensberry.

The *furore* surrounding *The Picture or Dorian Gray* has never quite dissipated, and its excesses and secrets continue to unsettle its readers. Today, what may hit home most is not its homosexual coding but its reflection of fears of aging, even more prominent now than for the Victorians. A cultural obsession with youth makes everyone either gray or (Dorian) Gray, either openly aging or immobilizing the face into a mask of youth, while the interior decays. The more effort that goes into preserving the appearance of youth, the greater the sense of internal hideousness becomes. What Wilde imagined as the unappeasable force of conscience has become for us an embarrassing failure to conquer biology.

The battle against time permeates not only the novel's theme but also its structure. *The Picture of Dorian Gray* appeared at an interesting moment in the history of the novel, when an older mode of lengthy realistic fiction (the "triple-decker" novel) and a newer, shorter mode of detective stories and supernatural romances, such as Arthur Conan Doyle's *A Study in Scarlet* and Robert Louis Stevenson's *The Strange Case of Dr. Jekyll and Mr. Hyde*, were battling for readers' attention. Although Wilde owed much to traditional realistic fiction, his work falls more squarely in the second category. It's not even clear that *The Picture of Dorian Gray* should be called a novel: Wilde called it a "story" and didn't like "novelette." In its first

---

[1]Quoted from *Oscar Wilde: The Critical Heritage*, ed. Karl Beckson (London: Routledge, 1970), 71, 72, 82.

version it occupied only 98 pages; expanded, it still reads like a long short story. Some of the effect of abbreviation accrues from the odd chronology. Time is suspended in the first chapter, in which flowers that do not normally grow together are simultaneously in full bloom. Although the events in the novel unfold across about eighteen years, there is no reference to change in history and politics.[2] *Dorian Gray* is arranged into two halves with an interlude. The first half occupies a few weeks during the height of a London season; the second, a few weeks in November and possibly December, approximately eighteen years later, with a final scene the following May. In between stretches the long Chapter 11, during which Dorian runs through catalogues of unusual experiences and blithely corrupts every eligible young man in London. Short stretches of time take up many chapters, while a long time period is collapsed into only one.

Several characters intensify this odd pulsation of time by commenting that their lives do not follow ordinary chronological development of the kind perfected in the realistic Victorian novel. They seem to live in suspended animation until one critical encounter: Basil lives only after meeting Dorian; Dorian, after hearing Lord Henry; Sibyl, after falling in love with Dorian. Moreover, their lives end, become "gray," before they have really ended: Basil's art collapses without Dorian, and even Lord Henry ends up bored and solitary. Clock time and psychological time diverge: "What has the actual lapse of time got to do with it? It is only shallow people who require years to get rid of an emotion" (p. 108), Dorian protests to Basil; while waiting for Alan Campbell, Dorian finds that "suddenly, Time stopped for him" (p. 165); Lord Henry believes that the mere scent of "*lilas blanc*" causes him "to live the strangest month" of his life "over again" (p. 213).

Even at the level of rhetoric, the novel marks an uncomfortable relation to time. One of its favorite phrases is "from time to time," as if it were hardly worth being too specific. Characters punctuate their speeches with the phrase "That is all" or "That was all," as if compelled to end abruptly. The phrase clamps down on the unexpected ramifications of human events, as if simply announcing that a topic was finished could make it so.

---

[2] See John Sutherland, *Is Heathcliff a Murderer?: Great Puzzles in Nineteenth-Century Fiction* (Oxford: Oxford Univ. Press, 1996), 196–201.

The novel's odd organization of time reflects not only the breakdown of the older, realistic mode of Victorian fiction but also anxieties raised by Darwin's theory of evolution. Wilde filled his commonplace book with quotations from leading evolutionary thinkers, including Thomas Henry Huxley, Herbert Spencer, and W. K. Clifford. Darwin had proposed that man descended from primitive forms, whose traces were still latent in modern man. Modernity was therefore haunted by its lack of modernity. As Lord Henry claims, "The mutilation of the savage has its tragic survival in the self-denial that mars our lives" (p. 22). Throughout the novel, past histories erupt into the modern world, to gloss, even to ground, present action: "There were times when it appeared to Dorian Gray that the whole of history was merely the record of his own life, not as he had lived it in act and circumstance, but as his imagination had created it for him, as it had been in his brain and in his passions" (pp. 141–42).

The press of prior history suffuses the novel's rhetoric and imagery. For example, in his "Preface," Wilde declares, *"The nineteenth century dislike of Realism is the rage of Caliban seeing his own face in a glass"* (p. 3). The epigram (which equates Victorian readers with a monster from Shakespeare's *The Tempest* who had become an archetype of primitivism) collapses the present, the Renaissance, and a mythic, prehistoric past. Just as T. S. Eliot was to do in *The Waste Land, The Picture of Dorian Gray* creates elaborate networks of imagery that turn the present into an echo chamber of prior times. These networks surface both in the characters' ideas and in the objects around them, as if the novel's luxury antiques, which come from a wide range of historical periods, ironically accompanied the characters' dependence on the past.

The most ancient pattern draws on classical Greece, which provides multiple possibilities for understanding Dorian's life. Basil and Lord Henry see Dorian in terms of a gallery of Greek homoerotic icons: Adonis, Narcissus, Hylas, Ganymede, Hermes, the faun. Dorian's name, however, evokes not aesthetic languor but the Spartans, the famed Greek warriors. Dorian wishes to emulate "the gods of the Greeks" by being "fleet and strong and joyous." Another classical model comes from Dorian's mother, painted in her "loose Bacchante dress" (p. 141), who resembles Lord Henry's philosophy, which dances "like a Bacchante" (p. 44) during dinner.

Dorian may be a reincarnation of beautiful, doomed youths; a neo-Spartan, living an intensely physical life; or an ecstatic Bacchante, drunk with the worship of wine. Dorian is not just Greek: his experience is infused with medieval and Renaissance models as well, especially as understood by such Victorian writers as Walter Pater and John Addington Symonds. If Lord Henry tells Dorian that "mediæval art is charming, but mediæval emotions are out of date" (p. 80), he also gives Dorian the poisonous book that seems inspired by "the spiritual ecstasies of some mediæval saint" (p. 124) and that Dorian uses to recreate himself. The Renaissance is second only to the classics in the novel's imagery. Dorian loves Sybil Vane for bringing Shakespeare's heroines to life, as if the Victorian theater, no less than Darwinian man, sustained the past within itself. Basil compares his love for Dorian to famous Renaissance prototypes: it is "such love as Michael Angelo had known, and Montaigne, and . . . Shakespeare himself" (p. 118). Wilde's diction even draws on Renaissance English, as if to insist on its continuing presence. The sound of London is like a "bourdon" (p. 5); Sybil's voice is like an "hautbois" (p. 54); a wreath of smoke rises like a "violet riband" (p. 90). The European Renaissance is likewise everywhere in Dorian's tastes as a collector, though it exists less as Pater's vibrant site of illumination than as a dark world of secrets. The old schoolroom that houses Dorian's portrait features a "Flemish tapestry" and an "Italian *cassone*" (p. 153). In Dorian's "Florentine" cabinet lies his stash of opium. The Renaissance acquires guilt by association as a setting for Dorian's furtive, hidden life.

If contemporary history is mostly absent, contemporary London is not. Wilde describes it so precisely that one can trace on a map where each episode occurs, even how characters get from one place to another. (It is an upper-class London; the luxurious West End districts are more exactly realized than the dark recesses of the East End.) London clubs, restaurants, newspapers, and current events appear, along with references to contemporary musical celebrities like Adelina Patti and Anton Rubenstein, the modern music of Richard Wagner, and even current developments in chemistry.

This chronology that is both immediate and deeply historical is matched by spaces that are at once highly local and charged with a global network of peoples, objects, and experiences. In the first scene, Lord Henry thinks about Japanese artists while smoking Egyptian cigarettes and sitting on a divan covered with Persian saddlebags. Homes fill up with Dutch silver, German music, Venetian lamps, French books and book bindings, a Japanese table, the "small Chinese box" (p. 180) that holds Dorian's opium, a lamp "of Moorish workmanship" (p. 157), and "Algerian pastilles" (p. 180). James Vane makes a living in Australia and, later, plans to depart for India; Dorian encounters "Malays" and a "half-caste" (pp. 185, 186) in London's opium dens; and the United States is a storehouse of wealthy young heiresses.[3] In light of this temporal and spatial clutter, the notorious Chapter 11, which details Dorian's restless pursuit of sensations, seems less like a break from the action than an encapsulation of it. Its brilliant catalogues revise the surrounding chapters by subtracting the action and focusing on the props, adding even more historical periods (the Byzantine) and more geographical spaces (South America).

All these networks of spatial and temporal imagery converge on a single space: the attic corner where Dorian's picture hangs. Critic Eve Kosofsky Sedgwick proposes that Dorian's erotic relation to older men (like Basil and Lord Henry) is displaced onto his narcissistic relation to himself, embodied by his portrait.[4] Yet what exactly is this narcissism? The myth of self-love (Narcissus's fatal enchantment with his reflection) appears here as helpless dread: Dorian's fear at what he beholds taints all the pleasure of his life of sensation. His fear never compels him to spiritual reform, but to stasis and repetition.

Yet, on a practical level, Dorian has nothing to worry about, at least compared to active homosexuals in the Victorian era, who faced possible criminal prosecution, blackmail, public scandal and humiliation, and economic insecurity. Wilde was sentenced not just for "gross indecency" but for sex with "rent boys." The prosecution exploited their economic vulnerability by bribing them to testify against Wilde. Why didn't Wilde, when faced with the homophobic bullying of the Marquess of Queensberry, simply flee England? On the most practical level, he needed England, specifically London, for his living as a writer.

---

[3]Only Wilde's native Ireland seems conspicuously absent from the global catalogue.
[4]*Tendencies* (Durham: Duke Univ. Press, 1993), 151.

Money is no concern for Dorian Gray, however. His wealth is a golden shield against serious danger, and so his fears appear less like genuine torments than a privilege of luxury. At one point, Dorian confronts the worst that can happen: he is "very nearly black-balled at a West End club"—only "very nearly" (p. 139). Even if the picture were discovered, he would still be safe. As he knows, it

> would tell them nothing. It was true that the portrait still preserved, under all the foulness and ugliness of the face, its marked likeness to himself; but what could they learn from that? He would laugh at any one who tried to taunt him. He had not painted it. What was it to him how vile and full of shame it looked? Even if he told them, would they believe it? (p. 138)

But Dorian is still not safe from himself. The next paragraph begins, "Yet he was afraid." The sheer pointlessness of his fear is the point: the only fear worth having is a groundless one.

Wilde's plot reinforces the vanity of Dorian's terror. The second half of the novel contains several abortive attempts to shatter his self-sufficiency, all of which he easily overcomes. Dorian's imperviousness to danger allows him never to have to dissemble because wealth makes performance unnecessary. Those who do perform, especially on demand, suffer: Sybil and Mrs. Vane. If, as critic James Eli Adams has argued, sincerity and earnestness were the hallmarks of respectable Victorian masculinity, then Dorian is a fine role model. In his open expressions of his heartlessness and amorality, he is perfectly sincere.[5] The catastrophe comes about only when he tries acting by plotting his own reformation and abandoning his pastoral idyll with Hetty. In his eyes, the picture mocks this reform as hypocrisy, a poor piece of acting, much like that of Mrs. Vane. And so he tries to destroy it for giving his performance a bad review.

Yet how accurate is the picture as a moral monitor? After the first changes, Dorian wonders, "The vicious cruelty that marred the fine lines of the mouth had, no doubt, appeared at the very moment that the girl had drunk the poison, whatever it was. Or was it indifferent to results? Did it merely take cognizance of what passed

---

[5]See *Dandies and Desert Saints: Styles of Victorian Masculinity* (Ithaca: Cornell Univ. Press, 1995).

within the soul? He wondered" (p. 105). The novel never fully re-solves Dorian's question. At a critical moment, Dorian simply de-cides that "the picture, changed or unchanged, would be to him the visible emblem of conscience" (p. 92). Conscience was a much-debated topic among the Victorians, especially in light of Darwin-ian evolution. If conscience was not a product of Christian moral-ity, how did it originate? Darwinians argued that it arose in the struggle for existence: "The function of conscience is the preserva-tion of the tribe as a tribe," wrote W. K. Clifford (see pp. 228–29). *The Picture of Dorian Gray* argues a different case. Conscience is an exercise in luxury, its aesthetic instrument locked up in an old schoolroom and contemplated at leisure. And in this luxurious self-regard, the project may be more aesthetic than moral. The portrait changes in recording not only sin but also age, and this is a result of biology, not morality: "He would examine with minute care, and sometimes with a monstrous and terrible delight, the hideous lines that seared the wrinkling forehead or crawled around the heavy sensual mouth, wondering sometimes which were the more horri-ble, the signs of sin or the signs of age" (p. 127).

Nor are the supposed "signs of sin" unambiguous. After the first appearance of "lines of cruelty" around the picture's mouth, Dorian wonders, "Cruelty! Had he been cruel? It was the girl's fault, not his. He had dreamed of her as a great artist, had given his love to her because he had thought her great. Then she had disappointed him. She had been shallow and unworthy" (p. 91). Is this only Dorian's weak self-justification, a frail defense against incipient conscience? The portrait possibly simplifies what could be read as a complicated moral situation, with guilt on both sides, by too easily placing all the blame on Dorian. It at least raises the possibility that Sybil, if not entirely at fault, was not entirely blameless either.

Similarly questionable is the picture's judgment of Dorian for breaking off his affair with Hetty:

> For it was an unjust mirror, this mirror of his soul that he was looking at. Vanity? Curiosity? Hypocrisy? Had there been nothing more in his renunciation than that? There had been something more. At least he thought so. But who could tell? . . . No. There had been nothing more. Through vanity he had spared her. In hypocrisy he had worn the mask of goodness.

For curiosity's sake he had tried the denial of self. He recognized that now. (pp. 218–19)

In the 1890 version, this passage ended after "But who could tell?" Dorian confronts his mirror and accuses it of being "unjust": at least in his own opinion, he believed that his renunciation of Hetty was a genuine reformation. In the 1891 revision, Wilde added sentences to let Dorian decide that the picture was right, after all, because hypocrisy and curiosity motivated him to renounce Hetty. Yet the revision may only sharpen the original uncertainty about Dorian's motives. The new sentences sound defensive, as if Dorian were overdoing his own self-condemnation to hide his doubts about the picture's moral authority.

At its most haunting, *The Picture of Dorian Gray* proposes that Dorian's picture may bear only a tenuous relationship to him. The picture never speaks for itself. Dorian always has to interpret it, and his interpretations are not necessarily right. The more desperately Dorian tries to read the picture, the more it seems to have a secret plot of its own. Rather than being Dorian's double or copy, the picture may exist in a world with a logic that Dorian never grasps. Dorian's desire to see the picture as his conscience contains an element of wishful thinking, a narcissism to which the picture is oblivious or indifferent.

If *The Picture of Dorian Gray* tells us anything, it is that narcissism is not as easy as it looks: the self with whom you fall in love may not be the self you thought it was. It is an eerie parable of modernity, in which all prior historical moments and all the objects of the globe are available as frameworks for self-knowledge, only to prove partial and unsatisfactory. A supernatural force, in the form of the picture, appears to judge a sinner, but these judgments appear only as representations that are themselves subject to further interpretation. In Dorian's relationship to his picture, we find a model for our own relationship to *The Picture of Dorian Gray*, a temptation to the pleasures of narcissistic interpretation and a warning about its discontents.

Table of Dates

1859	Charles Darwin, *On the Origin of Species by Means of Natural Selection*; John Stuart Mill, *On Liberty*; Dickens, *A Tale of Two Cities*; George Eliot, *Adam Bede*; birth of Arthur Conan Doyle.
1859–60	Opium War with China.
1860	Dickens, *Great Expectations*; birth of Anton Chekhov.
	Essays and Reviews sparks controversy over the truth of religion; Abraham Lincoln becomes president of the United States.
1861	Eliot, *Silas Marner*.
	Prince Albert dies and Queen Victoria goes into a long period of mourning; beginning of the Civil War in the United States; Russia emancipates the serfs; unification of Italy.
1862	Mary Braddon, *Lady Audley's Secret*; John Ruskin, *Unto This Last*; Christina Rossetti, *Goblin Market and Other Poems*; George Meredith, *Modern Love*; Victor Hugo, *Les Misérables*.
1863	Mill, *Utilitarianism*.
1864	Wilde starts school at Portora Royal School, Enniskillen. The mistress of Wilde's father brings a libel suit against Wilde's mother, seriously damaging the reputation of Wilde's father.
	Dickens, *Our Mutual Friend*; John Henry Newman, *Apologia pro Vita Sua*.
1865	Matthew Arnold, *Essays in Criticism*; Ruskin, *Sesame and Lilies*; Lewis Carroll, *Alice in Wonderland*; Richard Wagner, *Tristan und Isolde*; birth of Rudyard Kipling.
	First transatlantic cable opened; Lincoln assassinated.
1866	Algernon Charles Swinburne, *Poems and Ballads*; Fyodor Dostoyevsky, *Crime and Punishment*.
	Hyde Park riots for extended franchise; Austro-Prussian War.
1867	Wilde's older sister Isola dies, eleven years old.
	Karl Marx, *Das Kapital*.

Second Reform Bill passes and leads to expansion of franchise; trial of Governor Eyre for role in violent suppression of uprising of black Jamaicans in 1865; revival of Irish Nationalist movement; foundation of the Independent Dominion of Canada.

1868 Morris, *The Earthly Paradise*; Louisa May Alcott, *Little Women*; Wilkie Collins, *The Moonstone*.

The conservative Benjamin Disraeli and the liberal William Ewart Gladstone both become Prime Minister for the first time.

1869 Mill, *The Subjection of Women*.

Disestablishment of the Irish Church; opening of the Suez canal; birth of Mohandas Gandhi; Dmitry Mendeleyev develops the periodic table of the elements.

1870 Ruskin's inaugural address as Slade Professor of Fine Art at Oxford; Dickens, *The Mystery of Edwin Drood* (published posthumously); D. G. Rossetti, *Poems*.

Forster Education Act makes schooling mandatory for children in England and Wales, ages 5–12; competitive civil service examinations instituted; Vatican proclaims papal infallibility; Franco-Prussian War; birth of Vladimir Lenin.

1871–74 Wilde at Trinity College, Dublin, where he studies classics and ancient history.

1871 Darwin, *The Descent of Man*; Eliot, *Middlemarch*.

Newnham College, Cambridge, founded for women's education; trade unions legalized; unification of Germany; Paris Commune.

1872 Samuel Butler, *Erewhon*.

Secret ballot adopted for national elections.

1873 Walter Pater, *Studies in the History of the Renaissance*; Leo Tolstoy, *Anna Karenina*.

1874–78 Wilde wins prize for Greek at Trinity. Leaves Ireland to enter Magdalen College, Oxford, with a scholarship; studies classics and ancient history.

1874 Trollope, *The Way We Live Now*; birth of Winston Churchill.

1875   Wilde begins to develop his lifelong fascination with Roman Catholicism.

W. S. Gilbert and Arthur Sullivan begin their collaboration.

1876   Wilde's father dies, leaving Wilde less money than expected. This critical moment for Wilde meant that he would not have an independent income and would have to work. Wilde takes a First Class (top honors) in Classical Moderations.

Eliot, *Daniel Deronda*; Stéphane Mallarmé, *L'Après-midi d'un faune*.

Alexander Graham Bell invents the telephone; Queen Victoria becomes Empress of India; Gladstone leads agitation against the Ottoman Empire in the wake of the Bulgarian massacres; Leopold II establishes the Belgian Congo.

1877   Wilde visits Greece and Rome and is temporarily expelled by Magdalen College for traveling when he should have been at Oxford; his half-brother dies and leaves him £100 a year on the condition that he remain a Protestant.

1878   Wilde wins the Newdigate Prize for his poem *Ravenna* and takes a First Class at Oxford in *Litterae Humaniores*. Despite his academic achievement, he is not elected a fellow, closing off for him the possibility of an academic career.

1879   Wilde moves to London to make a living.

Henrik Ibsen, *A Doll's House*.

First women's colleges at Oxford founded; births of Albert Einstein and Joseph Stalin.

1880   Wilde becomes a London celebrity as a leading aesthete, noted for his witty conversation and outrageous clothes.

Death of Eliot; Dostoyevsky, *The Brothers Karamazov*.

1881   Wilde's *Poems* published; reviews were generally bad; Wilde's aestheticism caricatured in *Punch* and Gilbert and Sullivan's *Patience*.

Henry James, *Portrait of a Lady*; death of Thomas Carlyle.

1882   Wilde embarks on an exhausting lecture tour to the United States and Canada, sponsored by D'Oyly Carte in connection with the New York production of *Patience*. Wilde lectures almost daily and earns $5,605.31.

Britain occupies Egypt; births of James Joyce and Virginia Woolf.

1883   Wilde visits Paris and lectures in England on his impressions of America. His play *Vera* fails in New York.

Friedrich Nietzsche, *Also Sprach Zarathustra*; Olive Schreiner, *The Story of an African Farm*.

1884   Wilde marries Constance Lloyd and takes a house in Chelsea.

Mark Twain, *Huckleberry Finn*; Johannes Brahms, *Symphony No. 3*.

General George Gordon and his troops massacred at Khartoum in the Sudan; Berlin Conference organizes the carving up of Africa by European powers; Social Democratic Federation and Fabian Society (both socialist organizations) founded; birth of Eleanor Roosevelt.

1885   Wilde becomes a regular contributor of reviews to the *Pall Mall Gazette*; his son Cyril is born.

Pater, *Marius the Epicurean*.

1886   Wilde's son Vyvyan is born; Ruskin is asked to be godfather, but refuses. Wilde meets Robert Ross, possibly his first male lover and later his literary executor.

Robert Louis Stevenson, *The Strange Case of Dr. Jekyll and Mr. Hyde*; Thomas Hardy, *The Mayor of Casterbridge*.

Crisis in Parliament over Irish Home Rule leads to the splintering of the Liberal Party and the consequent dominance of the Conservatives.

1887–89   Wilde edits *The Woman's World* (formerly *Lady's World*) and is active in soliciting contributions from many of Britain's major women writers.

1887	"Bloody Sunday" riot: clash in London between 20,000 marchers (including William Morris, George Bernard Shaw, and Marx's daughter Eleanor Aveling) and 2,400 soldiers and policemen.
1888	Wilde publishes a volume of children's stories, *The Happy Prince and Other Tales*; meets William Butler Yeats. Constance Wilde edits the *Gazette* of the Rational Dress Society, an important feminist organization, and begins to address pacifist organizations.
	Kipling, *Plain Tales from the Hills*; death of Arnold; birth of T. S. Eliot.
	London dock strike.
1889	Wilde publishes "The Portrait of Mr. W. H." in *Blackwood's*; J. M. Stoddart, the editor of the American *Lippincott's Magazine*, comes to London to solicit contributions and encourages both Wilde and Doyle at the same dinner; Wilde begins affair with John Gray.
	Pater, *Appreciations, with an Essay on Style*; Yeats, *The Wanderings of Oisin and Other Poems*.
	Naval Defence Act; birth of Adolf Hitler.
1890	First version of Wilde's *The Picture of Dorian Gray* appears in *Lippincott's* in Britain and America.
1891	Major year for the publication of Wilde's works: *Intentions* (critical essays), *Lord Arthur Savile's Crime and Others Stories*, "The Soul of Man Under Socialism," revised version of *The Picture of Dorian Gray*, *A House of Pomegranates* (fairy tales). His early play *The Duchess of Padua* is produced in New York. Begins relationship with Lord Alfred Douglas.
	George Gissing, *New Grub Street*; Ibsen's *Ghosts* produced in London; Hardy, *Tess of the d'Urbervilles*; Gustav Mahler, *Symphony No. 1*.
1892	*Lady Windermere's Fan* is produced and is successful; Sarah Bernhardt is refused a license to produce *Salome*; Wilde increasingly distances himself from his wife and children, partly because he needs space to

work and partly because of his involvement in London's gay subculture through a series of relationships, including one with Edward Shelley; Wilde aids Douglas, who is being blackmailed.

James Keir Hardie becomes first Labor candidate to win a seat in Parliament; death of Tennyson; "Michael Field" (Katharine Harris Bradley and Edith Emma Cooper), *Sight and Song*.

1893   *Salome* published (in French) in Paris. *A Woman of No Importance* produced and is successful; *Lady Windermere's Fan* published; Alfred Wood tries gay blackmail on Wilde; despite literary successes, Wilde is constantly in debt.

Yeats, *The Celtic Twilight*.

1894   *The Sphinx*, *Poems in Prose*, English translation of *Salome* (with illustrations by Aubrey Beardsley), *A Woman of No Importance*; Marquess of Queensberry (father of Douglas) threatens Wilde in Wilde's home.

Robert Hichens, *The Green Carnation*; Mona Caird, *The Daughters of Danaus*; death of Pater.

Dreyfus Affair; Nicholas II comes to the throne in Russia.

1894–95   Sino-Japanese War.

1895   Wilde visits Algeria with Douglas; his *An Ideal Husband* and *The Importance of Being Earnest* produced. Marquess of Queensberry accuses Wilde of being a "posing somdomite [*sic*]," and Wilde brings him to trial on libel charges. Queensberry wins the case, and Wilde is arrested on charges of "gross indecency." He and his gay associate Alfred Taylor are tried twice: the first trial ends in a hung jury; the second, with their conviction and sentencing to two years of hard labor. Several of the young men with whom Wilde had had sexual relations testify against him at these trials. Newspaper coverage is widespread and the sentence is applauded. Wilde goes to Pentonville, Wandsworth, and Reading prisons to serve his sentence in solitary confinement; conditions are miserable. Wilde's wife moves to Switzerland and changes her last name and that of Wilde's sons to Holland. Wilde declared bankrupt.

H. G. Wells, *The Time Machine*; George Bernard Shaw, *Candida*.

William Roentgen discovers the X ray.

1896   Wilde's mother dies; he sees Constance for the last time. *Salome* produced in Paris.

Hardy, *Jude the Obscure*; A. E. Housman, *A Shropshire Lad*; Giacomo Puccini, *La Bohème*.

1897   Wilde writes *De Profundis* in prison. Financial arrangement is made with Constance whereby he receives an allowance upon the condition that he not live with other men. Upon release, after his request for a six-month retreat at the Jesuit church in Farm Street is refused, he leaves England for France under the name "Sebastian Melmoth" and never returns to England. For a short time, he resumes relationship with Douglas, despite Constance's disapproval; Wilde and Douglas eventually break up.

Sarah Grand, *The Beth Book*; Havelock Ellis begins publishing *Studies in the Psychology of Sex*.

Queen Victoria's Diamond Jubilee.

1898   Wilde, lonely and destitute, lives in France. *The Ballad of Reading Gaol* published under pseudonym "C. 3. 3.," the number of Wilde's jail cell; Constance dies of spinal paralysis.

Shaw, *Plays Pleasant and Unpleasant*; death of Beardsley.

Outbreak of the Spanish-American War.

1899–1902 Boer War.

1899   Wilde is forced out of a hotel in Nice when English tourists learn he is staying there. Wilde's brother dies of alcoholism. Wilde travels in Europe.

Joseph Conrad, *Heart of Darkness*; Kate Chopin, *The Awakening*.

1900   Marquess of Queensberry dies. Wilde's health deteriorates rapidly; the exact causes are still debated. He visits Italy, then returns to Paris. Dies November 30, aged 46, after having been baptized a Roman Catholic, and is buried in Paris.

Conrad, *Lord Jim*; Freud, *The Interpretation of Dreams*.

1901	Death of Queen Victoria; succeeded by Edward VII.
1908	Robert Ross publishes Wilde's *Collected Works*.
1909	Ross has Wilde's remains transferred to Paris's Père Lachaise cemetery.
1912	By this year, *The Picture of Dorian Gray* has been translated into Czech, Danish, Dutch, Finnish, French, German, Greek, Hungarian, Italian, Polish, Russian, Swedish, and Yiddish.
1913	*The Picture of Dorian Gray* produced as a silent film.
1915	Cyril (Wilde) Holland killed in World War I.
1918	Death of Ross; he asks for his ashes to be placed in Wilde's tomb.
1945	Death of Douglas; MGM film of *The Picture of Dorian Gray*, with Hurd Hatfield and Angela Lansbury.
1967	Death of Vyvyan (Wilde) Holland.
1987	Publication of Richard Ellman's *Oscar Wilde*, a turning point in scholarship on Wilde.
1995	A memorial stained-glass window in Wilde's honor is unveiled in Poets' Corner, Westminster Abbey.

The Picture of Dorian Gray

by Oscar Wilde

Sir William Rothenstein, *The Painter Charles Conder* (1892). (Courtesy of the Toledo Museum of Art.)

The Preface[1]

THE *artist is the creator of beautiful things.*

To reveal art and conceal the artist is art's aim.

The critic is he who can translate into another manner or a new material his impression of beautiful things.

> *The highest as the lowest form of criticism is a mode of autobiography.*

Those who find ugly meanings in beautiful things are corrupt without being charming.

This is a fault.

> *Those who find beautiful meanings in beautiful things are the cultivated.*

> *For these there is hope.*

They are the elect to whom beautiful things mean only Beauty.

> *There is no such thing as a moral or an immoral book. Books are well written, or badly written. That is all.*

The nineteenth century dislike of Realism is the rage of Caliban[2] seeing his own face in a glass.

> *The nineteenth century dislike of Romanticism[3] is the rage of Caliban not seeing his own face in a glass.*

> *The moral life of man forms part of the subject-matter of the artist, but the morality of art consists in the perfect use of an imperfect medium.*

No artist desires to prove anything. Even things that are true can be proved.

No artist has ethical sympathies. An ethical sympathy in an artist is an unpardonable mannerism of style.

> *No artist is ever morbid. The artist can express everything.*

---

[1]Not in the first version of the novel (*Lippincott's Magazine*, 1890). First published in the *Fortnightly Review* in reaction to scandalized reviews, the "Preface" was revised slightly and added to the second, longer edition of *Dorian Gray* in 1891.

[2]The savage in Shakespeare's *The Tempest*.

[3]The aesthetic movement of the early 19th c. and, more generally, refusal of realism.

Thought and language are to the artist instruments of an art.

Vice and virtue are to the artist materials for an art.

From the point of view of form, the type of all the arts is the art of the musician.

From the point of view of feeling, the actor's craft is the type.

All art is at once surface and symbol.

Those who go beneath the surface do so at their peril.

Those who read the symbol do so at their peril.

It is the spectator, and not life, that art really mirrors.

Diversity of opinion about a work of art shows that the work is new, complex, and vital.

When critics disagree the artist is in accord with himself.

We can forgive a man for making a useful thing as long as he does not admire it.

The only excuse for making a useless thing is that one admires it intensely.

All art is quite useless.

OSCAR WILDE.

Chapter 1

The studio was filled with the rich odour of roses, and when the light summer wind stirred amidst the trees of the garden there came through the open door the heavy scent of the lilac, or the more delicate perfume of the pink-flowering thorn.[1]

From the corner of the divan of Persian saddle-bags[2] on which he was lying, smoking, as was his custom, innumerable cigarettes, Lord Henry Wotton[3] could just catch the gleam of the honey-sweet and honey-coloured blossoms of a laburnum,[4] whose tremulous branches seemed hardly able to bear the burden of a beauty so flame-like as theirs; and now and then the fantastic shadows of birds in flight flitted across the long tussore-silk[5] curtains that were stretched in front of the huge window, producing a kind of momentary Japanese effect, and making him think of those pallid jade-faced painters of Tokio who, through the medium of an art that is necessarily immobile, seek to convey the sense of swiftness and motion.[6] The sullen murmur of the bees shouldering their way through the long unmown grass, or circling with monotonous insistence round the dusty gilt horns of the straggling woodbine,[7] seemed to make the stillness more oppressive. The dim roar of London was like the bourdon[8] note of a distant organ.

In the centre of the room, clamped to an upright easel, stood the full-length portrait of a young man of extraordinary personal beauty, and in front of it, some little distance away, was sitting the artist himself, Basil Hallward, whose sudden disappearance some years ago caused, at the time, such public excitement, and gave rise to so many strange conjectures.

[1]Hawthorn tree.

[2]A sofa with upholstery patterned after camel saddlebags.

[3]This name may have been suggested by the Renaissance poet and diplomat Sir Henry Wotton (1568–1639), who proclaimed in his most famous poem, "The Character of a Happy Life," the value of personal independence: "How happy is he born and taught / That serveth not another's will" (1–2).

[4]A small ornamental tree.

[5]A coarse brown silk made in India.

[6]Japanese art provided an exotic counter-tradition to the conventions of Victorian artistic realism.

[7]Honeysuckle.

[8]Sustained low tones.

As the painter looked at the gracious and comely form he had so skilfully mirrored in his art, a smile of pleasure passed across his face, and seemed about to linger there. But he suddenly started up, and, closing his eyes, placed his fingers upon the lids, as though he sought to imprison within his brain some curious dream from which he feared he might awake.

"It is your best work, Basil, the best thing you have ever done," said Lord Henry, languidly. "You must certainly send it next year to the Grosvenor. The Academy is too large and too vulgar.[9] Whenever I have gone there, there have been either so many people that I have not been able to see the pictures, which was dreadful, or so many pictures that I have not been able to see the people, which was worse. The Grosvenor is really the only place."

"I don't think I shall send it anywhere," he answered, tossing his head back in that odd way that used to make his friends laugh at him at Oxford.[10] "No: I won't send it anywhere."

Lord Henry elevated his eyebrows, and looked at him in amazement through the thin blue wreaths of smoke that curled up in such fanciful whorls from his heavy opium-tainted cigarette.[11] "Not send it anywhere? My dear fellow, why? Have you any reason? What odd chaps you painters are! You do anything in the world to gain a reputation. As soon as you have one, you seem to want to throw it away. It is silly of you, for there is only one thing in the world worse than being talked about, and that is not being talked about. A portrait like this would set you far above all the young men in England, and make the old men quite jealous, if old men are ever capable of any emotion."

"I know you will laugh at me," he replied, "but I really can't exhibit it. I have put too much of myself into it."

Lord Henry stretched himself out on the divan and laughed.

"Yes, I knew you would; but it is quite true, all the same."

---

[9]Founded in 1877, the Grosvenor Gallery was known for displaying daring, unusual work. The Royal Academy of Arts (1768) represented the conservative establishment.

[10]Wilde's university, a center for both the Aesthetic movement and homoerotic subculture of classical studies.

[11]Cigarettes began to be manufactured in England after soldiers acquired a taste for them from Turkish soldiers during the Crimean War (1853–56); opium cigarettes were imported from Egypt.

"Too much of yourself in it! Upon my word, Basil, I didn't know you were so vain; and I really can't see any resemblance between you, with your rugged strong face and your coal-black hair, and this young Adonis,[12] who looks as if he was made out of ivory and rose-leaves. Why, my dear Basil, he is a Narcissus,[13] and you—well, of course you have an intellectual expression, and all that. But beauty, real beauty, ends where an intellectual expression begins. Intellect is in itself a mode of exaggeration, and destroys the harmony of any face. The moment one sits down to think, one becomes all nose, or all forehead, or something horrid. Look at the successful men in any of the learned professions. How perfectly hideous they are! Except, of course, in the Church. But then in the Church they don't think. A bishop keeps on saying at the age of eighty what he was told to say when he was a boy of eighteen, and as a natural consequence he always looks absolutely delightful. Your mysterious young friend, whose name you have never told me, but whose picture really fascinates me, never thinks. I feel quite sure of that. He is some brainless, beautiful creature, who should be always here in winter when we have no flowers to look at, and always here in summer when we want something to chill our intelligence. Don't flatter yourself, Basil: you are not in the least like him."

"You don't understand me, Harry," answered the artist. "Of course I am not like him. I know that perfectly well. Indeed, I should be sorry to look like him. You shrug your shoulders? I am telling you the truth. There is a fatality about all physical and intellectual distinction, the sort of fatality that seems to dog through history the faltering steps of kings. It is better not to be different from one's fellows. The ugly and the stupid have the best of it in this world. They can sit at their ease and gape at the play. If they know nothing of victory, they are at least spared the knowledge of defeat. They live as we all should live, undisturbed, indifferent, and without disquiet. They neither bring ruin upon others, nor ever receive it from alien hands. Your rank and wealth, Harry; my brains, such as they are—my art, whatever it

---

[12]The beautiful youth of Greek mythology, killed by a boar during a hunt, was a durable fascination in homoerotic culture.

[13]After spurning the love of the nymph Echo, this young man was condemned to pine away in love with his own image in a pool. The narcissus plant grew at the site.

may be worth; Dorian Gray's[14] good looks—we shall all suffer for what the gods have given us, suffer terribly."

"Dorian Gray? Is that his name?" asked Lord Henry, walking across the studio towards Basil Hallward.

"Yes, that is his name. I didn't intend to tell it to you."

"But why not?"

"Oh, I can't explain. When I like people immensely I never tell their names to any one. It is like surrendering a part of them. I have grown to love secrecy. It seems to be the one thing that can make modern life mysterious or marvellous to us. The commonest thing is delightful if one only hides it. When I leave town now I never tell my people where I am going. If I did, I would lose all my pleasure. It is a silly habit, I dare say, but somehow it seems to bring a great deal of romance into one's life. I suppose you think me awfully foolish about it?"

"Not at all," answered Lord Henry, "not at all, my dear Basil. You seem to forget that I am married, and the one charm of marriage is that it makes a life of deception absolutely necessary for both parties. I never know where my wife is, and my wife never knows what I am doing. When we meet—we do meet occasionally, when we dine out together, or go down to the Duke's—we tell each other the most absurd stories with the most serious faces. My wife is very good at it—much better, in fact, than I am. She never gets confused over her dates, and I always do. But when she does find me out, she makes no row at all. I sometimes wish she would; but she merely laughs at me."

"I hate the way you talk about your married life, Harry," said Basil Hallward, strolling towards the door that led into the garden. "I believe that you are really a very good husband, but that you are thoroughly ashamed of your own virtues. You are an extraordinary fellow. You never say a moral thing, and you never do a wrong thing. Your cynicism is simply a pose."

"Being natural is simply a pose, and the most irritating pose I know," cried Lord Henry, laughing; and the two young men went out into the garden together, and ensconced themselves on a long

---

[14]"Dorian Gray" combines a familiar English surname with a Greek-toned first name that was synonymous with classical Greek military culture. Since this culture also had homosexual elements, "Dorian" manliness was adopted by late-Victorian homosexual apologists to refute stereotypes of effeminacy.

bamboo seat that stood in the shade of a tall laurel bush. The sunlight slipped over the polished leaves. In the grass, white daisies were tremulous.

After a pause, Lord Henry pulled out his watch. "I am afraid I must be going, Basil," he murmured, "and before I go, I insist on your answering a question I put to you some time ago."

"What is that?" said the painter, keeping his eyes fixed on the ground.

"You know quite well."

"I do not, Harry."

"Well, I will tell you what it is. I want you to explain to me why you won't exhibit Dorian Gray's picture. I want the real reason."[15]

"I told you the real reason."

"No, you did not. You said it was because there was too much of yourself in it. Now, that is childish."

"Harry," said Basil Hallward, looking him straight in the face, "every portrait that is painted with feeling is a portrait of the artist, not of the sitter. The sitter is merely the accident, the occasion. It is not he who is revealed by the painter; it is rather the painter who, on the coloured canvas, reveals himself. The reason I will not exhibit this picture is that I am afraid that I have shown in it the secret of my own soul."

Lord Henry laughed. "And what is that?" he asked.

"I will tell you," said Hallward; but an expression of perplexity came over his face.

"I am all expectation, Basil," continued his companion, glancing at him.

"Oh, there is really very little to tell, Harry," answered the painter; "and I am afraid you will hardly understand it. Perhaps you will hardly believe it."

Lord Henry smiled, and leaning down, plucked a pink-petalled daisy from the grass and examined it. "I am quite sure I shall understand it," he replied, gazing intently at the little golden whitefeathered disk, "and as for believing things, I can believe anything, provided that it is quite incredible."

---

[15]The passage from this sentence to Basil's "I take no credit to myself for trying to escape" was quoted by the prosecution during the Wilde trials in 1895.

The wind shook some blossoms from the trees, and the heavy lilac-blooms, with their clustering stars, moved to and fro in the languid air.[16] A grasshopper began to chirrup by the wall, and like a blue thread a long thin dragon-fly floated past on its brown gauze wings. Lord Henry felt as if he could hear Basil Hallward's heart beating, and wondered what was coming.

"The story is simply this," said the painter after some time. "Two months ago I went to a crush[17] at Lady Brandon's. You know we poor artists have to show ourselves in society from time to time, just to remind the public that we are not savages. With an evening coat and a white tie, as you told me once, anybody, even a stock-broker, can gain a reputation for being civilized. Well, after I had been in the room about ten minutes, talking to huge over-dressed dowagers and tedious Academicians,[18] I suddenly became conscious that some one was looking at me. I turned half-way round, and saw Dorian Gray for the first time. When our eyes met, I felt that I was growing pale. A curious sensation of terror came over me. I knew that I had come face to face with some one whose mere personality[19] was so fascinating that, if I allowed it to do so, it would absorb my whole nature, my whole soul, my very art itself. I did not want any external influence in my life. You know yourself, Harry, how independent I am by nature. I have always been my own master; had at least always been so, till I met Dorian Gray. Then—but I don't know how to explain it to you. Something seemed to tell me that I was on the verge of a terrible crisis in my life. I had a strange feeling that Fate had in store for me exquisite joys and exquisite sorrows. I grew afraid, and turned to quit the room. It was not conscience that made me do so: it was a sort of cowardice.[20] I take no credit to myself for trying to escape."

"Conscience and cowardice are really the same things, Basil. Conscience is the trade-name of the firm. That is all."

---

[16]All the plants are simultaneously (fantastically) in full bloom (Sutherland 197–98).

[17]Slang: an upper-class party.

[18]Professional artists and members of the Royal Academy of Arts.

[19]A technical term in Victorian psychology describing the biological basis of behavior. According to psychologist Henry Maudsley (1835–1918), "personality" is based on a "physiological unity of organic functions" (Oxford English Dictionary: "personality").

[20]"Thus conscience does make cowards of us all," comments Hamlet, of his hesitation in avenging his father's murder (Hamlet 3.1.82).

"I don't believe that, Harry, and I don't believe you do either. However, whatever was my motive—and it may have been pride, for I used to be very proud—I certainly struggled to the door. There, of course, I stumbled against Lady Brandon. 'You are not going to run away so soon, Mr. Hallward?' she screamed out. You know her curiously shrill voice?"

"Yes; she is a peacock in everything but beauty," said Lord Henry, pulling the daisy to bits with his long, nervous fingers.

"I could not get rid of her. She brought me up to Royalties, and people with Stars and Garters,[21] and elderly ladies with gigantic tiaras and parrot noses. She spoke of me as her dearest friend. I had only met her once before, but she took it into her head to lionize[22] me. I believe some picture of mine had made a great success at the time, at least had been chattered about in the penny newspapers,[23] which is the nineteenth-century standard of immortality. Suddenly I found myself face to face with the young man whose personality had so strangely stirred me. We were quite close, almost touching. Our eyes met again. It was reckless of me, but I asked Lady Brandon to introduce me to him. Perhaps it was not so reckless, after all. It was simply inevitable. We would have spoken to each other without any introduction. I am sure of that. Dorian told me so afterwards. He, too, felt that we were destined to know each other."

"And how did Lady Brandon describe this wonderful young man?" asked his companion. "I know she goes in for giving a rapid *précis* of all her guests. I remember her bringing me up to a truculent and red-faced old gentleman covered all over with orders and ribbons, and hissing into my ear, in a tragic whisper which must have been perfectly audible to everybody in the room, the most astounding details. I simply fled. I like to find out people for myself. But Lady Brandon treats her guests exactly as an auctioneer treats his goods. She either explains them entirely away, or tells one everything about them except what one wants to know."

---

[21]The Order of the Garter, the oldest British Order of Chivalry, established in 1348, is a prestigious reward for loyalty to the Crown. Its various insignia include a ceremonial garter and a star-shaped badge. Norman Page suggests a coterie reference to the "Start and Garter," a pub in Richmond that was a gathering place for male homosexuals (49).

[22]Treat as a celebrity.

[23]Notorious for sensational news.

"Poor Lady Brandon! You are hard on her, Harry!" said Hallward, listlessly.

"My dear fellow, she tried to found a *salon*, and only succeeded in opening a restaurant. How could I admire her? But tell me, what did she say about Mr. Dorian Gray?"

"Oh, something like, 'Charming boy—poor dear mother and I absolutely inseparable. Quite forget what he does—afraid he—doesn't do anything—oh, yes, plays the piano—or is it the violin, dear Mr. Gray?' Neither of us could help laughing, and we became friends at once."

"Laughter is not at all a bad beginning for a friendship, and it is far the best ending for one," said the young lord, plucking another daisy.

Hallward shook his head. "You don't understand what friendship is, Harry," he murmured—"or what enmity is, for that matter. You like every one; that is to say, you are indifferent to every one."

"How horribly unjust of you!" cried Lord Henry, tilting his hat back, and looking up at the little clouds that, like ravelled skeins of glossy white silk, were drifting across the hollowed turquoise of the summer sky. "Yes; horribly unjust of you. I make a great difference between people. I choose my friends for their good looks, my acquaintances for their good characters, and my enemies for their good intellects. A man cannot be too careful in the choice of his enemies. I have not got one who is a fool. They are all men of some intellectual power, and consequently they all appreciate me. Is that very vain of me? I think it is rather vain."

"I should think it was, Harry. But according to your category I must be merely an acquaintance."

"My dear old Basil, you are much more than an acquaintance."

"And much less than a friend. A sort of brother, I suppose?"

"Oh, brothers! I don't care for brothers. My elder brother won't die,[24] and my younger brothers seem never to do anything else."

"Harry!" exclaimed Hallward, frowning.

"My dear fellow, I am not quite serious. But I can't help detesting my relations. I suppose it comes from the fact that none of us can stand other people having the same faults as ourselves. I

[24]In the system of primogeniture, only the eldest son was the heir of property.

quite sympathize with the rage of the English democracy[25] against what they call the vices of the upper orders. The masses feel that drunkenness, stupidity, and immorality should be their own special property, and that if any one of us makes an ass of himself he is poaching on their preserves. When poor Southwark got into the Divorce Court, their indignation was quite magnificent.[26] And yet I don't suppose that ten per cent of the proletariat live correctly."

"I don't agree with a single word that you have said, and, what is more, Harry, I feel sure you don't either."

Lord Henry stroked his pointed brown beard and tapped the toe of his patent-leather boot with a tasselled ebony cane. "How English you are Basil! That is the second time you have made that observation. If one puts forward an idea to a true Englishman—always a rash thing to do—he never dreams of considering whether the idea is right or wrong. The only thing he considers of any importance is whether one believes it oneself. Now, the value of an idea has nothing whatsoever to do with the sincerity of the man who expresses it. Indeed, the probabilities are that the more insincere the man is, the more purely intellectual will the idea be, as in that case it will not be coloured by either his wants, his desires, or his prejudices. However, I don't propose to discuss politics, sociology, or metaphysics with you. I like persons better than principles, and I like persons with no principles better than anything else in the world. Tell me more about Mr. Dorian Gray. How often do you see him?"

"Every day. I couldn't be happy if I didn't see him every day. He is absolutely necessary to me."

"How extraordinary! I thought you would never care for anything but your art."

"He is all my art to me now," said the painter, gravely. "I sometimes think, Harry, that there are only two eras of any importance in the world's history. The first is the appearance of a new medium for art, and the second is the appearance of a new personality for art also. What the invention of oil-painting was to the Venetians, the face of Antinoüs was to late Greek sculpture, and the face of Dorian Gray

---

[25]I.e., the common people.
[26]In conventional morality, divorce was a scandal.

will some day be to me.[27] It is not merely that I paint from him, draw from him, sketch from him. Of course I have done all that. But he is much more to me than a model or a sitter. I won't tell you that I am dissatisfied with what I have done of him, or that his beauty is such that Art cannot express it. There is nothing that Art cannot express, and I know that the work I have done, since I met Dorian Gray, is good work, is the best work of my life. But in some curious way—I wonder will you understand me?—his personality has suggested to me an entirely new manner in art, an entirely new mode of style. I see things differently, I think of them differently. I can now recreate life in a way that was hidden from me before. 'A dream of form in days of thought:'[28]—who is it who says that? I forget; but it is what Dorian Gray has been to me. The merely visible presence of this lad—for he seems to me little more than a lad, though he is really over twenty—his merely visible presence—ah! I wonder can you realize all that that means? Unconsciously he defines for me the lines of a fresh school, a school that is to have in it all the passion of the romantic spirit, all the perfection of the spirit that is Greek. The harmony of soul and body—how much that is! We in our madness have separated the two, and have invented a realism that is vulgar, an ideality that is void. Harry! if you only knew what Dorian Gray is to me! You remember that landscape of mine, for which Agnew[29] offered me such a huge price, but which I would not part with? It is one of the best things I have ever done. And why is it so? Because, while I was painting it, Dorian Gray sat beside me. Some subtle influence passed from him to me, and for the first time in my life I saw in the plain woodland the wonder I had always looked for, and always missed."

"Basil, this is extraordinary! I must see Dorian Gray."

Hallward got up from the seat, and walked up and down the garden. After some time he came back. "Harry," he said, "Dorian

---

[27]Wilde was much influenced by poet, art critic, and homosexual apologist John Addington Symonds (1840–93), who declared that "The Venetians perfected oil-painting, and set forth the glory of the world as it appeals to the imagination and the senses" (*The Renaissance in Italy* 3.182). "We have before us," he wrote of Antinous, a favorite of the Roman emperor Hadrian, "a real youth of incomparable beauty, just as nature made him, with all the inscrutableness of undeveloped character, with all the pathos of a most untimely doom" (*Sketches and Studies in Italy and Greece* 187).

[28]From "A Greek Girl" by Austin Dobson (1841–1920), describing her.

[29]Well-known late Victorian art dealer.

Gray is to me simply a motive in art. You might see nothing in him. I see everything in him. He is never more present in my work than when no image of him is there. He is a suggestion, as I have said, of a new manner. I find him in the curves of certain lines, in the loveliness and subtleties of certain colours. That is all."

"Then why won't you exhibit his portrait?" asked Lord Henry.

"Because, without intending it, I have put into it some expression of all this curious artistic idolatry, of which, of course, I have never cared to speak to him. He knows nothing about it. He shall never know anything about it. But the world might guess it; and I will not bare my soul to their shallow, prying eyes. My heart shall never be put under their microscope.[30] There is too much of myself in the thing, Harry—too much of myself!"

"Poets are not so scrupulous as you are. They know how useful passion is for publication. Nowadays a broken heart will run to many editions."[31]

"I hate them for it," cried Hallward. "An artist should create beautiful things, but should put nothing of his own life into them. We live in an age when men treat art as if it were meant to be a form of autobiography. We have lost the abstract sense of beauty. Some day I will show the world what it is; and for that reason the world shall never see my portrait of Dorian Gray."

"I think you are wrong, Basil, but I won't argue with you. It is only the intellectually lost who ever argue. Tell me, is Dorian Gray very fond of you?"

The painter considered for a few moments. "He likes me," he answered after a pause; "I know he likes me. Of course I flatter him dreadfully. I find a strange pleasure in saying things to him that I know I shall be sorry for having said. As a rule, he is charming to me, and we sit in the studio and talk of a thousand things. Now and then, however, he is horribly thoughtless, and seems to take a real delight in giving me pain. Then I feel, Harry, that I have given away my whole soul to some one who treats it as if it were a flower to put in his coat, a bit of decoration to charm his vanity, an ornament for a summer's day."

[30]"Under the Microscope" (1872) was the title of a defense of Pre-Raphaelite aesthetics by Algernon Charles Swinburne (1837–1909).

[31]Most famously Tennyson's *In Memoriam A. H. H.* (1850), his elegy for his ultimate friend, Arthur Henry Hallam.

"Days in summer, Basil, are apt to linger," murmured Lord Henry. "Perhaps you will tire sooner than he will. It is a sad thing to think of, but there is no doubt that Genius lasts longer than Beauty. That accounts for the fact that we all take such pains to over-educate ourselves. In the wild struggle for existence,[32] we want to have something that endures, and so we fill our minds with rubbish and facts, in the silly hope of keeping our place. The thoroughly well-informed man—that is the modern ideal. And the mind of the thoroughly well-informed man is a dreadful thing. It is like a bric-à-brac shop, all monsters and dust, with everything priced above its proper value. I think you will tire first, all the same. Some day you will look at your friend, and he will seem to you to be a little out of drawing,[33] or you won't like his tone of colour, or something. You will bitterly reproach him in your own heart, and seriously think that he has behaved very badly to you. The next time he calls, you will be perfectly cold and indifferent. It will be a great pity, for it will alter you. What you have told me is quite a romance, a romance of art one might call it, and the worst of having a romance of any kind is that it leaves one so unromantic."

"Harry, don't talk like that. As long as I live, the personality of Dorian Gray will dominate me. You can't feel what I feel. You change too often."

"Ah, my dear Basil, that is exactly why I can feel it. Those who are faithful know only the trivial side of love: it is the faithless who know love's tragedies." And Lord Henry struck a light on a dainty silver case and began to smoke a cigarette with a self-conscious and satisfied air, as if he had summed up the world in a phrase. There was a rustle of chirruping sparrows in the green lacquer leaves of the ivy, and the blue cloud-shadows chased themselves across the grass like swallows. How pleasant it was in the garden! And how delightful other people's emotions were!—much more delightful than their ideas, it seemed to him. One's own soul, and the passions of one's friends—those were the fascinating things in life. He pictured to himself with silent amusement the tedious luncheon that he had missed by staying so long with Basil Hallward. Had he gone to his aunt's, he would have been sure to have met

[32]Chapter 3 of Charles Darwin's *The Origin of Species* (1859) describes nature thus, in which the fittest survive.

[33]As if he were badly drawn.

Lord Goodbody there, and the whole conversation would have been about the feeding of the poor, and the necessity for model lodging-houses.[34] Each class would have preached the importance of those virtues, for whose exercise there was no necessity in their own lives. The rich would have spoken on the value of thrift, and the idle grown eloquent over the dignity of labour. It was charming to have escaped all that! As he thought of his aunt, an idea seemed to strike him. He turned to Hallward and said, "My dear fellow, I have just remembered."

"Remembered what, Harry?"

"Where I heard the name of Dorian Gray."

"Where was it?" asked Hallward, with a slight frown.

"Don't look so angry, Basil. It was at my aunt, Lady Agatha's. She told me she had discovered a wonderful young man who was going to help her in the East End,[35] and that his name was Dorian Gray. I am bound to state that she never told me he was good-looking. Women have no appreciation of good looks; at least, good women have not. She said that he was very earnest, and had a beautiful nature. I at once pictured to myself a creature with spectacles and lank hair, horribly freckled, and tramping about on huge feet. I wish I had known it was your friend."

"I am very glad you didn't, Harry."

"Why?"

"I don't want you to meet him."

"You don't want me to meet him?"

"No."

"Mr. Dorian Gray is in the studio, sir," said the butler, coming into the garden.

"You must introduce me now," cried Lord Henry, laughing.

The painter turned to his servant, who stood blinking in the sunlight. "Ask Mr. Gray to wait, Parker: I shall be in in a few moments." The man bowed, and went up the walk.

Then he looked at Lord Henry. "Dorian Gray is my dearest friend," he said. "He has a simple and a beautiful nature. Your aunt was quite right in what she said of him. Don't spoil him. Don't try to influence him. Your influence would be bad. The world is

---

[34]Built by social reformers.

[35]District of notorious slums.

wide, and has many marvellous people in it. Don't take away from me the one person who gives to my art whatever charm it possesses: my life as an artist depends on him. Mind, Harry, I trust you." He spoke very slowly, and the words seemed wrung out of him almost against his will.

"What nonsense you talk!" said Lord Henry, smiling, and, taking Hallward by the arm, he almost led him into the house.

Chapter 2

As they entered they saw Dorian Gray. He was seated at the piano, with his back to them, turning over the pages of a volume of Schumann's "Forest Scenes."[1] "You must lend me these, Basil," he cried. "I want to learn them. They are perfectly charming."

"That entirely depends on how you sit to-day, Dorian."

"Oh, I am tired of sitting, and I don't want a life-sized portrait of myself," answered the lad, swinging round on the music-stool, in a wilful, petulant manner. When he caught sight of Lord Henry, a faint blush coloured his cheeks for a moment, and he started up. "I beg your pardon, Basil, but I didn't know you had any one with you."

"This is Lord Henry Wotton, Dorian, an old Oxford friend of mine. I have just been telling him what a capital sitter you were, and now you have spoiled everything."

"You have not spoiled my pleasure in meeting you, Mr. Gray," said Lord Henry, stepping forward and extending his hand. "My aunt has often spoken to me about you. You are one of her favourites, and, I am afraid, one of her victims also."

"I am in Lady Agatha's black books at present," answered Dorian, with a funny look of penitence. "I promised to go to a club in Whitechapel[2] with her last Tuesday, and I really forgot all about it. We were to have played a duet together—three duets, I believe. I don't know what she will say to me. I am far too frightened to call."

"Oh, I will make your peace with my aunt. She is quite devoted to you. And I don't think it really matters about your not being there. The audience probably thought it was a duet. When Aunt Agatha sits down to the piano she makes quite enough noise for two people."

"That is very horrid to her, and not very nice to me," answered Dorian, laughing.

---

[1] *Waldscenen* (1848–49) by Robert Schumann, whose music was loved in the poignant knowledge of his descent into madness at the end of his life.

[2] "One of the very worst localities in London; a region of narrow and filthy streets, yards and alleys, many of them wholly occupied by thieves' dens, the receptacles of stolen property, gin-spinning dog-holes, low brothels, and putrescent lodging-houses" (Wheatley 3.500).

Lord Henry looked at him. Yes, he was certainly wonderfully handsome, with his finely-curved scarlet lips, his frank blue eyes, his crisp gold hair. There was something in his face that made one trust him at once. All the candour of youth was there, as well as all youth's passionate purity. One felt that he had kept himself unspotted from the world.[3] No wonder Basil Hallward worshipped him.

"You are too charming to go in for philanthropy, Mr. Gray— far too charming." And Lord Henry flung himself down on the divan, and opened his cigarette-case.

The painter had been busy mixing his colours and getting his brushes ready. He was looking worried, and when he heard Lord Henry's last remark he glanced at him, hesitated for a moment, and then said, "Harry, I want to finish this picture to-day. Would you think it awfully rude of me if I asked you to go away?"

Lord Henry smiled, and looked at Dorian Gray. "Am I to go, Mr. Gray?" he asked.

"Oh, please don't, Lord Henry. I see that Basil is in one of his sulky moods; and I can't bear him when he sulks. Besides, I want you to tell me why I should not go in for philanthropy."

"I don't know that I shall tell you that, Mr. Gray. It is so tedious a subject that one would have to talk seriously about it. But I certainly shall not run away, now that you have asked me to stop. You don't really mind, Basil, do you? You have often told me that you liked your sitters to have some one to chat to."

Hallward bit his lip. "If Dorian wishes it, of course you must stay. Dorian's whims are laws to everybody, except himself."

Lord Henry took up his hat and gloves. "You are very pressing, Basil, but I am afraid I must go. I have promised to meet a man at the Orleans.[4] Good-bye, Mr. Gray. Come and see me some afternoon in Curzon Street.[5] I am nearly always at home at five o'clock. Write to me when you are coming. I should be sorry to miss you."

"Basil," cried Dorian Gray, "if Lord Henry Wotton goes I shall go too. You never open your lips while you are painting, and it is

---

[3]"Pure religion and undefiled before God and the Father is this, To visit the fatherless and widows in their affliction, and to keep himself unspotted from the world" (James 1.27).

[4]A London club favored by sportsmen, including the Marquess of Queensberry, who provoked Wilde's trial for gross indecency.

[5]Fashionable street in Mayfair, noted for containing numerous residences for bachelors.

horribly dull standing on a platform and trying to look pleasant. Ask him to stay. I insist upon it."

"Stay, Harry, to oblige Dorian, and to oblige me," said Hallward, gazing intently at his picture. "It is quite true, I never talk when I am working, and never listen either, and it must be dreadfully tedious for my unfortunate sitters. I beg you to stay."

"But what about my man at the Orleans?"

The painter laughed. "I don't think there will be any difficulty about that. Sit down again, Harry. And now, Dorian, get up on the platform, and don't move about too much, or pay any attention to what Lord Henry says. He has a very bad influence over all his friends, with the single exception of myself."

Dorian Gray stepped up on the dais, with the air of a young Greek martyr, and made a little *moue*[6] of discontent to Lord Henry, to whom he had rather taken a fancy. He was so unlike Basil. They made a delightful contrast. And he had such a beautiful voice. After a few moments he said to him, "Have you really a very bad influence, Lord Henry? As bad as Basil says?"

"There is no such thing as a good influence, Mr. Gray. All influence is immoral—immoral from the scientific point of view."

"Why?"

"Because to influence a person is to give him one's own soul. He does not think his natural thoughts, or burn with his natural passions. His virtues are not real to him. His sins, if there are such things as sins, are borrowed. He becomes an echo of some one else's music, an actor of a part that has not been written for him. The aim of life is self-development. To realize one's nature perfectly—that is what each of us is here for. People are afraid of themselves, nowadays. They have forgotten the highest of all duties, the duty that one owes to one's self. Of course they are charitable. They feed the hungry, and clothe the beggar. But their own souls starve, and are naked. Courage has gone out of our race. Perhaps we never really had it. The terror of society, which is the basis of morals, the terror of God, which is the secret of religion—these are the two things that govern us. And yet—"

"Just turn your head a little more to the right, Dorian, like a good boy," said the painter, deep in his work and conscious only

[6]Pout (French).

that a look had come into the lad's face that he had never seen there before.

"And yet," continued Lord Henry, in his low, musical voice, and with that graceful wave of the hand that was always so characteristic of him, and that he had even in his Eton[7] days, "I believe that if one man were to live out his life fully and completely, were to give form to every feeling, expression to every thought, reality to every dream—I believe that the world would gain such a fresh impulse of joy that we would forget all the maladies of mediævalism, and return to the Hellenic ideal—to something finer, richer, than the Hellenic ideal, it may be.[8] But the bravest man amongst us is afraid of himself. The mutilation of the savage has its tragic survival in the self-denial that mars our lives. We are punished for our refusals. Every impulse that we strive to strangle broods in the mind, and poisons us. The body sins once, and has done with its sin, for action is a mode of purification. Nothing remains then but the recollection of a pleasure, or the luxury of a regret. The only way to get rid of a temptation is to yield to it. Resist it, and your soul grows sick with longing for the things it has forbidden to itself, with desire for what its monstrous laws have made monstrous and unlawful. It has been said that the great events of the world take place in the brain. It is in the brain, and the brain only, that the great sins of the world take place also. You, Mr. Gray, you yourself, with your rose-red youth and your rose-white boyhood, you have had passions that have made you afraid, thoughts that have filled you with terror, day-dreams and sleeping dreams whose mere memory might stain your cheek with shame—"

"Stop!" faltered Dorian Gray, "stop! you bewilder me. I don't know what to say. There is some answer to you, but I cannot find it. Don't speak. Let me think. Or, rather, let me try not to think."

For nearly ten minutes he stood there, motionless, with parted lips, and eyes strangely bright. He was dimly conscious that en-

---

[7]The most prestigious boys' school in England; the homosocial culture at such schools could sometimes become sexual. This and the following paragraphs to "How fascinating the lad was!" were quoted by the prosecution at Wilde's trials for gross indecency (Holland 259–60).

[8]In his essay "Winckelmann," Wilde's mentor at Oxford Walter Pater contrasted the "medievalism" of "Christian asceticism" to the "Hellenic ideal" in which "man is at unity with himself, with his physical nature, with the outward world."

tirely fresh influences were at work within him. Yet they seemed to him to have come really from himself. The few words that Basil's friend had said to him—words spoken by chance, no doubt, and with wilful paradox in them—had touched some secret chord that had never been touched before, but that he felt was now vibrating and throbbing to curious pulses.

Music had stirred him like that. Music had troubled him many times. But music was not articulate. It was not a new world, but rather another chaos, that it created in us. Words! Mere words! How terrible they were! How clear, and vivid, and cruel! One could not escape from them. And yet what a subtle magic there was in them! They seemed to be able to give a plastic form to formless things, and to have a music of their own as sweet as that of viol or of lute. Mere words! Was there anything so real as words?

Yes; there had been things in his boyhood that he had not understood. He understood them now. Life suddenly became fiery-coloured to him. It seemed to him that he had been walking in fire. Why had he not known it?

With his subtle smile, Lord Henry watched him. He knew the precise psychological moment when to say nothing. He felt intensely interested. He was amazed at the sudden impression that his words had produced, and, remembering a book that he had read when he was sixteen, a book which had revealed to him much that he had not known before, he wondered whether Dorian Gray was passing through a similar experience. He had merely shot an arrow into the air. Had it hit the mark? How fascinating the lad was!

Hallward painted away with that marvellous bold touch of his, that had the true refinement and perfect delicacy that in art, at any rate comes only from strength. He was unconscious of the silence.

"Basil, I am tired of standing," cried Dorian Gray, suddenly. "I must go out and sit in the garden. The air is stifling here."

"My dear fellow, I am so sorry. When I am painting, I can't think of anything else. But you never sat better. You were perfectly still. And I have caught the effect I wanted—the half-parted lips, and the bright look in the eyes. I don't know what Harry has been saying to you, but he has certainly made you have the most wonderful expression. I suppose he has been paying you compliments. You mustn't believe a word that he says."

"He has certainly not been paying me compliments. Perhaps that is the reason that I don't believe anything he has told me."

"You know you believe it all," said Lord Henry, looking at him with his dreamy, languorous eyes. "I will go out to the garden with you. It is horribly hot in the studio. Basil, let us have something iced to drink, something with strawberries in it."

"Certainly, Harry. Just touch the bell, and when Parker comes I will tell him what you want. I have got to work up this background, so I will join you later on. Don't keep Dorian too long. I have never been in better form for painting than I am to-day. This is going to be my masterpiece. It is my masterpiece as it stands."

Lord Henry went out to the garden, and found Dorian Gray burying his face in the great cool lilac-blossoms, feverishly drinking in their perfume as if it had been wine. He came close to him, and put his hand upon his shoulder. "You are quite right to do that," he murmured. "Nothing can cure the soul but the senses, just as nothing can cure the senses but the soul."

The lad started and drew back. He was bare-headed, and the leaves had tossed his rebellious curls and tangled all their gilded threads. There was a look of fear in his eyes, such as people have when they are suddenly awakened. His finely-chiselled nostrils quivered, and some hidden nerve shook the scarlet of his lips and left them trembling.

"Yes," continued Lord Henry, "that is one of the great secrets of life—to cure the soul by means of the senses, and the senses by means of the soul. You are a wonderful creation. You know more than you think you know, just as you know less than you want to know."

Dorian Gray frowned and turned his head away. He could not help liking the tall, graceful young man who was standing by him. His romantic olive-coloured face and worn expression interested him. There was something in his low, languid voice that was absolutely fascinating. His cool, white, flower-like hands, even, had a curious charm. They moved, as he spoke, like music, and seemed to have a language of their own. But he felt afraid of him, and ashamed of being afraid. Why had it been left for a stranger to reveal him to himself? He had known Basil Hallward for months, but the friendship between them had never altered him. Suddenly there had come some one across his life who seemed to have disclosed to him life's mystery. And, yet, what was there to be afraid of? He was not a schoolboy or a girl. It was absurd to be frightened.

"Let us go and sit in the shade," said Lord Henry. "Parker has brought out the drinks, and if you stay any longer in this glare, you will be quite spoiled, and Basil will never paint you again. You really must not allow yourself to become sunburnt.[9] It would be unbecoming."

"What can it matter?" cried Dorian Gray, laughing, as he sat down on the seat at the end of the garden.

"It should matter everything to you, Mr. Gray."

"Why?"

"Because you have the most marvellous youth, and youth is the one thing worth having."

"I don't feel that, Lord Henry."

"No, you don't feel it now. Some day, when you are old and wrinkled and ugly, when thought has seared your forehead with its lines, and passion branded your lips with its hideous fires, you will feel it, you will feel it terribly. Now, wherever you go, you charm the world. Will it always be so? . . . You have a wonderfully beautiful face, Mr. Gray. Don't frown. You have. And Beauty is a form of Genius—is higher, indeed, than Genius as it needs no explanation. It is of the great facts of the world, like sunlight, or spring-time, or the reflection in dark waters of that silver shell we call the moon. It cannot be questioned. It has its divine right of sovereignty. It makes princes of those who have it. You smile? Ah! when you have lost it you won't smile. . . . People say sometimes that beauty is only superficial. That may be so. But at least it is not so superficial as Thought is. To me, Beauty is the wonder of wonders. It is only shallow people who do not judge by appearances. The true mystery of the world is the visible, not the invisible. . . . Yes, Mr. Gray, the gods have been good to you. But what the gods give they quickly take away. You have only a few years in which to live really, perfectly, and fully. When your youth goes, your beauty will go with it, and then you will suddenly discover that there are no triumphs left for you, or have to content yourself with those mean triumphs that the memory of your past will make more bitter than defeats. Every month as it wanes brings you nearer to something dreadful. Time is jealous of you, and wars

[9]A sign of a manual laborer, thus ungentlemanly.

against your lilies and your roses. You will become sallow, and hollow-cheeked, and dull-eyed. You will suffer horribly. . . . Ah! realize your youth while you have it. Don't squander the gold of your days, listening to the tedious, trying to improve the hopeless failure, or giving away your life to the ignorant, the common, and the vulgar. These are the sickly aims, the false ideals, of our age. Live! Live the wonderful life that is in you! Let nothing be lost upon you. Be always searching for new sensations. Be afraid of nothing. . . . A new Hedonism—that is what our century wants. You might be its visible symbol. With your personality there is nothing you could not do. The world belongs to you for a season. . . . The moment I met you I saw that you were quite unconscious of what you really are, of what you really might be. There was so much in you that charmed me that I felt I must tell you something about yourself. I thought how tragic it would be if you were wasted. For there is such a little time that your youth will last—such a little time. The common hill-flowers wither, but they blossom again. The laburnum will be as yellow next June as it is now. In a month there will be purple stars on the clematis, and year after year the green night of its leaves will hold its purple stars. But we never get back our youth. The pulse of joy that beats in us at twenty, becomes sluggish. Our limbs fail, our senses rot. We degenerate into hideous puppets, haunted by the memory of the passions of which we were too much afraid, and the exquisite temptations that we had not the courage to yield to. Youth! Youth! There is absolutely nothing in the world but youth!"

Dorian Gray listened, open-eyed and wondering. The spray of lilac fell from his hand upon the gravel. A furry bee came and buzzed round it for a moment. Then it began to scramble all over the oval stellated[10] globe of the tiny blossoms. He watched it with that strange interest in trivial things that we try to develop when things of high import make us afraid, or when we are stirred by some new emotion for which we cannot find expression, or when some thought that terrifies us lays sudden siege to the brain and calls on us to yield. After a time the bee flew away. He saw it creeping into the stained trumpet of a Tyrian convolvulus.[11] The flower seemed to quiver, and then swayed gently to and fro.

[10]Star-shaped.

[11]Slender-stemmed plant with trumpet-shaped flowers; Tyrian is a deep purple (originally from Tyre).

Suddenly the painter appeared at the door of the studio, and made staccato[12] signs for them to come in. They turned to each other, and smiled.

"I am waiting," he cried. "Do come in. The light is quite perfect, and you can bring your drinks."

They rose up, and sauntered down the walk together. Two green-and-white butterflies fluttered past them, and in the pear-tree at the corner of the garden a thrush began to sing.

"You are glad you have met me, Mr. Gray," said Lord Henry, looking at him.

"Yes, I am glad now. I wonder shall I always be glad?"

"Always! That is a dreadful word. It makes me shudder when I hear it. Women are so fond of using it. They spoil every romance by trying to make it last for ever. It is a meaningless word, too. The only difference between a caprice and a life-long passion is that the caprice lasts a little longer."

As they entered the studio, Dorian Gray put his hand upon Lord Henry's arm. "In that case, let our friendship be a caprice," he murmured, flushing at his own boldness, then stepped up on the platform and resumed his pose.

Lord Henry flung himself into a large wicker arm-chair, and watched him. The sweep and dash of the brush on the canvas made the only sound that broke the stillness, except when, now and then, Hallward stepped back to look at his work from a distance. In the slanting beams that streamed through the open doorway the dust danced and was golden. The heavy scent of the roses seemed to brood over everything.

After about a quarter of an hour Hallward stopped painting, looked for a long time at Dorian Gray, and then for a long time at the picture, biting the end of one of his huge brushes, and frowning. "It is quite finished," he cried at last, and stooping down he wrote his name in long vermilion letters on the left-hand corner of the canvas.

Lord Henry came over and examined the picture. It was certainly a wonderful work of art, and a wonderful likeness as well.

"My dear fellow, I congratulate you most warmly," he said. "It is the finest portrait of modern times. Mr. Gray, come over and look at yourself."

[12]Abrupt, disjointed (Italian musical term).

The lad started, as if awakened from some dream. "Is it really finished?" he murmured, stepping down from the platform.

"Quite finished," said the painter. "And you have sat splendidly to-day. I am awfully obliged to you."

"That is entirely due to me," broke in Lord Henry. "Isn't it, Mr. Gray?"

Dorian made no answer, but passed listlessly in front of his picture and turned towards it. When he saw it he drew back, and his cheeks flushed for a moment with pleasure. A look of joy came into his eyes, as if he had recognized himself for the first time. He stood there motionless and in wonder, dimly conscious that Hallward was speaking to him, but not catching the meaning of his words. The sense of his own beauty came on him like a revelation. He had never felt it before. Basil Hallward's compliments had seemed to him to be merely the charming exaggeration of friendship. He had listened to them, laughed at them, forgotten them. They had not influenced his nature. Then had come Lord Henry Wotton with his strange panegyric on youth, his terrible warning of its brevity. That had stirred him at the time, and now, as he stood gazing at the shadow of his own loveliness, the full reality of the description flashed across him. Yes, there would be a day when his face would be wrinkled and wizen, his eyes dim and colourless, the grace of his figure broken and deformed. The scarlet would pass away from his lips, and the gold steal from his hair. The life that was to make his soul would mar his body. He would become dreadful, hideous, and uncouth.

As he thought of it, a sharp pang of pain struck through him like a knife, and made each delicate fibre of his nature quiver. His eyes deepened into amethyst, and across them came a mist of tears. He felt as if a hand of ice had been laid upon his heart.

"Don't you like it?" cried Hallward at last, stung a little by the lad's silence, not understanding what it meant.

"Of course he likes it," said Lord Henry. "Who wouldn't like it? It is one of the greatest things in modern art. I will give you anything you like to ask for it. I must have it."

"It is not my property, Harry."

"Whose property is it?"

"Dorian's, of course," answered the painter.

"He is a very lucky fellow."

"How sad it is!" murmured Dorian Gray, with his eyes still fixed upon his own portrait. "How sad it is! I shall grow old, and horrible, and dreadful. But this picture will remain always young. It will never be older than this particular day of June. . . . If it were only the other way! If it were I who was to be always young, and the picture that was to grow old! For that—for that—I would give everything! Yes, there is nothing in the whole world I would not give! I would give my soul for that!"[13]

"You would hardly care for such an arrangement, Basil," cried Lord Henry, laughing. "It would be rather hard lines[14] on your work."

"I should object very strongly, Harry," said Hallward.

Dorian Gray turned and looked at him. "I believe you would, Basil. You like your art better than your friends. I am no more to you than a green bronze figure. Hardly as much, I dare say."

The painter stared in amazement. It was so unlike Dorian to speak like that. What had happened? He seemed quite angry. His face was flushed and his cheeks burning.

"Yes," he continued, "I am less to you than your ivory Hermes or your silver Faun.[15] You will like them always. How long will you like me? Till I have my first wrinkle, I suppose. I know, now, that when one loses one's good looks, whatever they may be, one loses everything. Your picture has taught me that. Lord Henry Wotton is perfectly right. Youth is the only thing worth having. When I find that I am growing old, I shall kill myself."

Hallward turned pale, and caught his hand. "Dorian! Dorian!" he cried, "don't talk like that. I have never had such a friend as you, and I shall never have such another. You are not jealous of material things, are you?—you who are finer than any of them!"

"I am jealous of everything whose beauty does not die. I am jealous of the portrait you have painted of me. Why should it keep what I must lose? Every moment that passes takes something from me, and gives something to it. Oh, if it were only the other way! If

---

[13]Reference to the Faust legend, in which the Devil gets Faust's soul in exchange for granting his wish.

[14]Slang: rough treatment.

[15]Hermes, the messenger of the gods in Greek myth, is often sculpted as a beautiful nude youth. A faun has a man's face, with goat's horns, legs, and tail; these mythological creatures were associated with sensual lust.

the picture could change, and I could be always what I am now! Why did you paint it? It will mock me some day—mock me horribly!" The hot tears welled into his eyes; he tore his hand away, and, flinging himself on the divan, he buried his face in the cushions, as though he was praying.

"This is your doing, Harry," said the painter, bitterly.

Lord Henry shrugged his shoulders. "It is the real Dorian Gray—that is all."

"It is not."

"If it is not, what have I to do with it?"

"You should have gone away when I asked you," he muttered.

"I stayed when you asked me," was Lord Henry's answer.

"Harry, I can't quarrel with my two best friends at once, but between you both you have made me hate the finest piece of work I have ever done, and I will destroy it. What is it but canvas and colour? I will not let it come across our three lives and mar them."

Dorian Gray lifted his golden head from the pillow, and with pallid face and tear-stained eyes looked at him as he walked over to the deal painting-table that was set beneath the high curtained window. What was he doing there? His fingers were straying about among the litter of tin tubes and dry brushes, seeking for something. Yes, it was for the long palette-knife, with its thin blade of lithe steel.[16] He had found it at last. He was going to rip up the canvas.

With a stifled sob the lad leaped from the couch, and, rushing over to Hallward, tore the knife out of his hand, and flung it to the end of the studio. "Don't, Basil, don't!" he cried. "It would be murder!"

"I am glad you appreciate my work at last, Dorian," said the painter, coldly, when he had recovered from his surprise. "I never thought you would."

"Appreciate it? I am in love with it, Basil. It is part of myself. I feel that."

"Well, as soon as you are dry, you shall be varnished, and framed, and sent home. Then you can do what you like with yourself." And he walked across the room and rang the bell for tea. "You will have tea, of course, Dorian? And so will you, Harry? Or do you object to such simple pleasures?"

---

[16]Used for mixing oil-paint colors and applying them to a canvas.

"I adore simple pleasures," said Lord Henry. "They are the last refuge of the complex. But I don't like scenes, except on the stage. What absurd fellows you are, both of you! I wonder who it was defined man as a rational animal. It was the most premature definition ever given. Man is many things, but he is not rational. I am glad he is not, after all: though I wish you chaps would not squabble over the picture. You had much better let me have it, Basil. This silly boy doesn't really want it, and I really do."

"If you let any one have it but me, Basil, I shall never forgive you!" cried Dorian Gray; "and I don't allow people to call me a silly boy."

"You know the picture is yours, Dorian. I gave it to you before it existed."

"And you know you have been a little silly, Mr. Gray, and that you don't really object to being reminded that you are extremely young."

"I should have objected very strongly this morning, Lord Henry."

"Ah! this morning! You have lived since then."

There came a knock at the door, and the butler entered with a laden tea-tray and set it down upon a small Japanese table. There was a rattle of cups and saucers and the hissing of a fluted Georgian[17] urn. Two globe-shaped china dishes were brought in by a page. Dorian Gray went over and poured out the tea. The two men sauntered languidly to the table, and examined what was under the covers.

"Let us go to the theatre to-night," said Lord Henry. "There is sure to be something on, somewhere. I have promised to dine at White's,[18] but it is only with an old friend, so I can send him a wire to say that I am ill, or that I am prevented from coming in consequence of a subsequent engagement. I think that would be a rather nice excuse: it would have all the surprise of candour."

"It is such a bore putting on one's dress-clothes," muttered Hallward. "And, when one has them on, they are so horrid."

"Yes," answered Lord Henry, dreamily, "the costume of the nineteenth century is detestable. It is so sombre, so depressing.[19] Sin is the only real colour-element left in modern life."

[17]From the era of the four Kings George (1714–1830), ornate and neoclassical.

[18]Well-known Tory club, founded in the late 17th c.; had a reputation for heavy gambling. In Wilde's day, the Prince of Wales (later Edward VII) was a member.

[19]Men wore black for formal occasions.

"You really must not say things like that before Dorian, Harry."

"Before which Dorian? The one who is pouring out tea for us, or the one in the picture?"

"Before either."

"I should like to come to the theatre with you, Lord Henry," said the lad.

"Then you shall come; and you will come, too, Basil, won't you?"

"I can't, really. I would sooner not. I have a lot of work to do."

"Well, then, you and I will go alone, Mr. Gray."

"I should like that awfully."

The painter bit his lip and walked over, cup in hand, to the picture. "I shall stay with the real Dorian," he said, sadly.

"Is it the real Dorian?" cried the original of the portrait, strolling across to him. "Am I really like that?"

"Yes; you are just like that."

"How wonderful, Basil!"

"At least you are like it in appearance. But it will never alter," sighed Hallward. "That is something."

"What a fuss people make about fidelity!" exclaimed Lord Henry. "Why, even in love it is purely a question for physiology. It has nothing to do with our own will. Young men want to be faithful, and are not; old men want to be faithless, and cannot: that is all one can say."

"Don't go to the theatre to-night, Dorian," said Hallward. "Stop and dine with me."

"I can't, Basil."

"Why?"

"Because I have promised Lord Henry Wotton to go with him."

"He won't like you the better for keeping your promises. He always breaks his own. I beg you not to go."

Dorian Gray laughed and shook his head.

"I entreat you."

The lad hesitated, and looked over at Lord Henry, who was watching them from the tea-table with an amused smile.

"I must go, Basil," he answered.

"Very well," said Hallward; and he went over and laid down his cup on the tray. "It is rather late, and, as you have to dress, you had better lose no time. Good-bye, Harry. Good-bye, Dorian. Come and see me soon. Come to-morrow."

"Certainly."

"You won't forget?"

"No, of course not," cried Dorian.

"And . . . Harry!"

"Yes, Basil?"

"Remember what I asked you, when we were in the garden this morning."

"I have forgotten it."

"I trust you."

"I wish I could trust myself," said Lord Henry, laughing. "Come, Mr. Gray, my hansom[20] is outside, and I can drop you at your own place. Good-bye, Basil. It has been a most interesting afternoon."

As the door closed behind them, the painter flung himself down on a sofa, and a look of pain came into his face.

[20]A two-person carriage for hire, prized for its speed and better class of drivers.

Chapter 3

At half-past twelve next day Lord Henry Wotton strolled from Curzon Street over to the Albany[1] to call on his uncle, Lord Fermor, a genial if somewhat rough-mannered old bachelor, whom the outside world called selfish because it derived no particular benefit from him, but who was considered generous by Society as he fed the people who amused him. His father had been our ambassador at Madrid when Isabella was young, and Prim unthought of,[2] but had retired from the Diplomatic Service in a capricious moment of annoyance on not being offered the Embassy at Paris, a post to which he considered that he was fully entitled by reason of his birth, his indolence, the good English of his despatches, and his inordinate passion for pleasure. The son, who had been his father's secretary, had resigned along with his chief, somewhat foolishly as was thought at the time, and on succeeding some months later to the title, had set himself to the serious study of the great aristocratic art of doing absolutely nothing. He had two large town houses, but preferred to live in chambers as it was less trouble, and took most of his meals at his club. He paid some attention to the management of his collieries in the Midland counties, excusing himself for this taint of industry on the ground that the one advantage of having coal was that it enabled a gentleman to afford the decency of burning wood on his own hearth. In politics he was a Tory, except when the Tories were in office, during which period he roundly abused them for being a pack of Radicals.[3] He was a hero to his valet,[4] who bullied him, and a terror to most of his re-

---

[1]"The Albany is a collection of queer houses, let as chambers. At present it has but little significance, but when George IV was old, and when Queen Victoria was young, the 'Bachelor of the Albany' was a recognised variety of the 'man about town'" (Dickens 7). Earlier in the century, Lord Byron and "Monk" Lewis had had apartments there, and Jack Worthing of Wilde's *The Importance of Being Earnest* also lives there.

[2]Isabella II of Spain (1830–1904), whose tumultuous and scandalous reign began at age 13; her husband was reputed to be a homosexual. She was deposed in 1868 by Juan Prim, a military leader assassinated in 1870.

[3]The Tories were in office when Wilde was writing, under the leadership of Robert Cecil, Third Marquess of Salisbury (1830–1903). Though no radical, Salisbury maintained a long-term political association with leading radical Joseph Chamberlain (1836–1914).

[4]A play on the old epigram, "No man is a hero to his valet."

lations, whom he bullied in turn. Only England could have produced him, and he always said that the country was going to the dogs. His principles were out of date, but there was a good deal to be said for his prejudices.[5]

When Lord Henry entered the room, he found his uncle sitting in a rough shooting-coat, smoking a cheroot[6] and grumbling over *The Times*.[7] "Well, Harry," said the old gentleman, "what brings you out so early? I thought you dandies never got up till two, and were not visible till five."

"Pure family affection, I assure you, Uncle George. I want to get something out of you."

"Money, I suppose," said Lord Fermor, making a wry face. "Well, sit down and tell me all about it. Young people, nowadays, imagine that money is everything."

"Yes," murmured Lord Henry, settling his button-hole in his coat; "and when they grow older they know it. But I don't want money. It is only people who pay their bills who want that, Uncle George, and I never pay mine. Credit is the capital of a younger son, and one lives charmingly upon it. Besides, I always deal with Dartmoor's[8] tradesmen, and consequently they never bother me. What I want is information: not useful information, of course; useless information."

"Well, I can tell you anything that is in an English Blue-book,[9] Harry, although those fellows nowadays write a lot of nonsense. When I was in the Diplomatic, things were much better. But I hear they let them in now by examination.[10] What can you expect? Examinations, sir, are pure humbug from beginning to end. If a man is a gentleman, he knows quite enough, and if he is not a gentleman, whatever he knows is bad for him."

[5]Literally, innate attitudes (pre-judgment), a key term in the British conservative tradition, praised by Edmund Burke (1729–97): "Prejudice renders a man's virtue his habit; and not a series of unconnected acts. Through just prejudice, his duty becomes a part of his nature" (183).

[6]A cigar with both ends cut off square, and a sign of Lord Fermor's age (the younger generation smokes cigarettes).

[7]This "paper of choice for the governing class" cost threepence (Curtis 63).

[8]Dartmoor seems to be Lord Henry's elder brother.

[9]One of the official reports of Parliament and the Privy Council, issued in a dark blue paper cover.

[10]Examinations for the Foreign Office had been introduced back in 1856.

"Mr. Dorian Gray does not belong to Blue-books, Uncle George," said Lord Henry, languidly.

"Mr. Dorian Gray? Who is he?" asked Lord Fermor, knitting his bushy white eyebrows.

"That is what I have come to learn, Uncle George. Or rather, I know who he is. He is the last Lord Kelso's grandson. His mother was a Devereux, Lady Margaret Devereux.[11] I want you to tell me about his mother. What was she like? Whom did she marry? You have known nearly everybody in your time, so you might have known her. I am very much interested in Mr. Gray at present. I have only just met him."

"Kelso's grandson!" echoed the old gentleman—"Kelso's grandson! . . . Of course . . . I knew his mother intimately. I believe I was at her christening. She was an extraordinarily beautiful girl, Margaret Devereux, and made all the men frantic by running away with a penniless young fellow, a mere nobody, sir, a subaltern in a foot regiment,[12] or something of that kind. Certainly. I remember the whole thing as if it happened yesterday. The poor chap was killed in a duel at Spa[13] a few months after the marriage. There was an ugly story about it. They said Kelso got some rascally adventurer, some Belgian brute, to insult his son-in-law in public, paid him, sir, to do it, paid him, and that the fellow spitted his man as if he had been a pigeon. The thing was hushed up, but, egad, Kelso ate his chop alone at the club for some time afterwards. He brought his daughter back with him, I was told, and she never spoke to him again. Oh, yes; it was a bad business. The girl died too, died within a year. So she left a son, did she? I had forgotten that. What sort of boy is he? If he is like his mother he must be a good-looking chap."

"He is very good-looking," assented Lord Henry.

"I hope he will fall into proper hands," continued the old man. "He should have a pot of money waiting for him if Kelso did the right thing by him. His mother had money too. All the Selby property came to her, through her grandfather. Her grandfather hated

---

[11]Named after Robert Devereux, second Earl of Essex (1565–1601), was executed after a failed rebellion against Elizabeth I; a legend developed that the queen secretly loved him. Devereux was a close associate and biographical subject of the historical Lord Henry Wotton.

[12]A very low military post.

[13]Fashionable Belgian health resort.

Kelso, thought him a mean dog. He was, too. Came to Madrid once when I was there. Egad, I was ashamed of him. The Queen used to ask me about the English noble who was always quarrelling with the cabmen about their fares. They made quite a story of it. I didn't dare show my face at Court for a month. I hope he treated his grandson better than he did the jarvies."[14]

"I don't know," answered Lord Henry. "I fancy that the boy will be well off. He is not of age yet. He has Selby, I know. He told me so. And . . . his mother was very beautiful?"

"Margaret Devereux was one of the loveliest creatures I ever saw, Harry. What on earth induced her to behave as she did, I never could understand. She could have married anybody she chose. Carlington was mad after her. She was romantic, though. All the women of that family were. The men were a poor lot, but, egad! the women were wonderful. Carlington went on his knees to her. Told me so himself. She laughed at him, and there wasn't a girl in London at the time who wasn't after him. And by the way, Harry, talking about silly marriages, what is this humbug your father tells me about Dartmoor wanting to marry an American? Ain't English girls good enough for him?"

"It is rather fashionable to marry Americans just now, Uncle George."[15]

"I'll back English women against the world, Harry," said Lord Fermor, striking the table with his fist.

"The betting is on the Americans."

"They don't last, I am told," muttered his uncle.

"A long engagement exhausts them, but they are capital at a steeplechase. They take things flying. I don't think Dartmoor has a chance."

"Who are her people?" grumbled the old gentleman. "Has she got any?"

Lord Henry shook his head. "American girls are as clever at concealing their parents, as English women are at concealing their past," he said, rising to go.

[14] A driver of a hackney-coach, a commodious four-wheeler drawn by two horses.

[15] These many jabs at Americans did not appear in the first version of the novel, published in an American magazine, *Lippincott's*. Wilde introduced them in the expanded second version, produced by a British publisher. Examples of British men who had recently married American women (often for their money) include Lord Randolph Churchill (father of Winston Churchill), Robert Browning's son Pen, and radical leader Joseph Chamberlain.

"They are pork-packers, I suppose?"

"I hope so, Uncle George, for Dartmoor's sake. I am told that pork-packing is the most lucrative profession in America, after politics."

"Is she pretty?"

"She behaves as if she was beautiful. Most American women do. It is the secret of their charm."

"Why can't these American women stay in their own country? They are always telling us that it is the Paradise for women."[16]

"It is. That is the reason why, like Eve, they are so excessively anxious to get out of it," said Lord Henry. "Good-bye, Uncle George. I shall be late for lunch, if I stop any longer. Thanks for giving me the information I wanted. I always like to know everything about my new friends, and nothing about my old ones."

"Where are you lunching, Harry?"

"At Aunt Agatha's. I have asked myself and Mr. Gray. He is her latest *protégé*."

"Humph! tell your Aunt Agatha, Harry, not to bother me any more with her charity appeals. I am sick of them. Why, the good woman thinks that I have nothing to do but to write cheques for her silly fads."

"All right, Uncle George, I'll tell her, but it won't have any effect. Philanthropic people lose all sense of humanity. It is their distinguishing characteristic."

The old gentleman growled approvingly, and rang the bell for his servant. Lord Henry passed up the low arcade into Burlington Street and turned his steps in the direction of Berkeley Square.[17]

So that was the story of Dorian Gray's parentage. Crudely as it had been told to him, it had yet stirred him by its suggestion of a strange, almost modern romance. A beautiful woman risking everything for a mad passion. A few wild weeks of happiness cut short by a hideous, treacherous crime. Months of voiceless agony, and then a child born in pain. The mother snatched away by death, the boy left to solitude and the tyranny of an old and loveless man.

---

[16]Wilde may have found this description of America in a recent essay by Herbert Spencer: "Now that [women] are better treated than ever before, the proclaiming of their grievances daily strengthens: the loudest outcries coming from 'the paradise of women,' America" (Spencer 2).

[17]One of the wealthiest addresses in London.

Yes; it was an interesting background. It posed the lad, made him more perfect, as it were. Behind every exquisite thing that existed, there was something tragic. Worlds had to be in travail, that the meanest flower might blow.[18] . . . And how charming he had been at dinner the night before, as with startled eyes and lips parted in frightened pleasure he had sat opposite to him at the club, the red candleshades staining to a richer rose the wakening wonder of his face. Talking to him was like playing upon an exquisite violin. He answered to every touch and thrill of the bow. . . . There was something terribly enthralling in the exercise of influence. No other activity was like it. To project one's soul into some gracious form, and let it tarry there for a moment; to hear one's own intellectual views echoed back to one with all the added music of passion and youth; to convey one's temperament into another as though it were a subtle fluid or a strange perfume: there was a real joy in that—perhaps the most satisfying joy left to us in an age so limited and vulgar as our own, an age grossly carnal in its pleasures, and grossly common in its aims. . . . He was a marvellous type, too, this lad, whom by so curious a chance he had met in Basil's studio, or could be fashioned into a marvellous type, at any rate. Grace was his, and the white purity of boyhood, and beauty such as old Greek marbles kept for us. There was nothing that one could not do with him. He could be made a Titan[19] or a toy. What a pity it was that such beauty was destined to fade! . . . And Basil? From a psychological point of view, how interesting he was! The new manner in art, the fresh mode of looking at life, suggested so strangely by the merely visible presence of one who was unconscious of it all; the silent spirit that dwelt in dim woodland, and walked unseen in open field, suddenly showing herself, Dryad[20]-like and not afraid, because in his soul who sought for her there had been wakened that wonderful vision to which alone are wonderful things revealed; the mere shapes and patterns of things becoming, as it were, refined, and gaining a kind of symbolical value, as though they were themselves patterns of some other and more perfect form whose shadow they

---

[18]Reference to the conclusion of William Wordsworth's "Ode: Intimations of Immortality from Recollections of Early Childhood": "To me the meanest flower that blows can give / Thoughts that do often lie too deep for tears" (blows: blooms).

[19]Giants of Greek mythology, overthrown by the Olympian gods.

[20]Tree nymph of classical mythology.

made real: how strange it all was! He remembered something like it in history. Was it not Plato, that artist in thought, who had first analyzed it? Was it not Buonarotti who had carved it in the coloured marbles of a sonnet-sequence?[21] But in our own century it was strange. . . . Yes; he would try to be to Dorian Gray what, without knowing it, the lad was to the painter who had fashioned the wonderful portrait. He would seek to dominate him—had already, indeed, half done so. He would make that wonderful spirit his own. There was something fascinating in this son of Love and Death.

Suddenly he stopped and glanced up at the houses. He found that he had passed his aunt's some distance, and, smiling to himself, turned back. When he entered the somewhat sombre hall, the butler told him that they had gone in to lunch. He gave one of the footmen his hat and stick, and passed into the dining-room.

"Late as usual, Harry," cried his aunt, shaking her head at him.

He invented a facile excuse, and having taken the vacant seat next to her, looked round to see who was there. Dorian bowed to him shyly from the end of the table, a flush of pleasure stealing into his cheek. Opposite was the Duchess of Harley, a lady of admirable good-nature and good temper, much liked by every one who knew her, and of those ample architectural proportions that in women who are not Duchesses are described by contemporary historians as stoutness. Next to her sat, on her right, Sir Thomas Burdon, a Radical member of Parliament, who followed his leader in public life, and in private life followed the best cooks, dining with the Tories, and thinking with the Liberals, in accordance with a wise and well-known rule.[22] The post on her left was occupied by Mr. Erskine of Treadley, an old gentleman of considerable charm and culture, who had fallen, however, into bad habits of silence, having, as he explained once to Lady Agatha, said everything that he had to say before he was thirty. His own neighbour was Mrs. Vandeleur, one of

---

[21]Michelangelo Buonarotti (1475–1564), Renaissance painter, sculptor, and poet. Both he and Plato had celebrated homoerotic love in their work. J. A. Symonds translated Michelangelo's sonnets (1878), and, in his preface, summoned Plato to deflect their physical/erotic suggestions: "Nothing is more clear than that Michael Angelo worshipped beauty in the Platonic spirit, passing beyond its personal and specific manifestations to the universal and impersonal" ("Preface").

[22]*Dorian Gray* appeared during a weak time for the Liberals, headed by William Ewart Gladstone (1809–98), then in his 80s, whose obsession with Irish Home Rule had splintered his party.

his aunt's oldest friends, a perfect saint amongst women, but so dreadfully dowdy that she reminded one of a badly bound hymn-book. Fortunately for him she had on the other side Lord Faudel, a most intelligent middle-aged mediocrity, as bald as a Ministerial statement in the House of Commons, with whom she was conversing in that intensely earnest manner which is the one unpardonable error, as he remarked once himself, that all really good people fall into, and from which none of them ever quite escape.

"We are talking about poor Dartmoor, Lord Henry," cried the Duchess, nodding pleasantly to him across the table. "Do you think he will really marry this fascinating young person?"

"I believe she has made up her mind to propose to him, Duchess."

"How dreadful!" exclaimed Lady Agatha. "Really, some one should interfere."

"I am told, on excellent authority, that her father keeps an American dry-goods[23] store," said Sir Thomas Burdon, looking supercilious.

"My uncle has already suggested pork-packing, Sir Thomas."

"Dry-goods! What are American dry-goods?" asked the Duchess, raising her large hands in wonder, and accentuating the verb.

"American novels," answered Lord Henry, helping himself to some quail.

The Duchess looked puzzled.

"Don't mind him, my dear," whispered Lady Agatha. "He never means anything that he says."

"When America was discovered," said the Radical member, and he began to give some wearisome facts. Like all people who try to exhaust a subject, he exhausted his listeners. The Duchess sighed, and exercised her privilege of interruption. "I wish to goodness it never had been discovered at all!" she exclaimed. "Really, our girls have no chance nowadays. It is most unfair."

"Perhaps, after all, America never has been discovered," said Mr. Erskine; "I myself would say that it had merely been detected."

"Oh! but I have seen specimens of the inhabitants," answered the Duchess, vaguely. "I must confess that most of them are extremely pretty. And they dress well, too. They get all their dresses in Paris. I wish I could afford to do the same."

[23]Cloths and drapery, as opposed to food.

"They say that when good Americans die they go to Paris," chuckled Sir Thomas, who had a large wardrobe of Humour's cast-off clothes.

"Really! And where do bad Americans go to when they die?" inquired the Duchess.

"They go to America," murmured Lord Henry.

Sir Thomas frowned. "I am afraid that your nephew is prejudiced against that great country," he said to Lady Agatha. "I have travelled all over it, in cars provided by the directors, who, in such matters, are extremely civil. I assure you that it is an education to visit it."

"But must we really see Chicago in order to be educated?" asked Mr. Erskine plaintively. "I don't feel up to the journey."

Sir Thomas waved his hand. "Mr. Erskine of Treadley has the world on his shelves. We practical men like to see things, not to read about them. The Americans are an extremely interesting people. They are absolutely reasonable. I think that is their distinguishing characteristic. Yes, Mr. Erskine, an absolutely reasonable people. I assure you there is no nonsense about the Americans."

"How dreadful!" cried Lord Henry. "I can stand brute force, but brute reason is quite unbearable. There is something unfair about its use. It is hitting below the intellect."

"I do not understand you," said Sir Thomas, growing rather red.

"I do, Lord Henry," murmured Mr. Erskine, with a smile.

"Paradoxes are all very well in their way. . . ." rejoined the Baronet.

"Was that a paradox?" asked Mr. Erskine. "I did not think so. Perhaps it was. Well, the way of paradoxes is the way of truth. To test Reality we must see it on the tight-rope. When the Verities become acrobats we can judge them."

"Dear me!" said Lady Agatha, "how you men argue! I am sure I never can make out what you are talking about. Oh! Harry, I am quite vexed with you. Why do you try to persuade our nice Mr. Dorian Gray to give up the East End? I assure you he would be quite invaluable. They would love his playing."

"I want him to play to me," cried Lord Henry, smiling, and he looked down the table and caught a bright answering glance.

"But they are so unhappy in Whitechapel," continued Lady Agatha.

"I can sympathize with everything except suffering," said Lord Henry, shrugging his shoulders. "I cannot sympathize with that. It is too ugly, too horrible, too distressing. There is something terribly morbid in the modern sympathy with pain. One should sympathize with the colour, the beauty, the joy of life. The less said about life's sores the better."

"Still, the East End is a very important problem," remarked Sir Thomas, with a grave shake of the head.

"Quite so," answered the young lord. "It is the problem of slavery, and we try to solve it by amusing the slaves."

The politician looked at him keenly. "What change do you propose, then?" he asked.

Lord Henry laughed. "I don't desire to change anything in England except the weather," he answered. "I am quite content with philosophic contemplation. But, as the nineteenth century has gone bankrupt through an over-expenditure of sympathy, I would suggest that we should appeal to Science to put us straight. The advantage of the emotions is that they lead us astray, and the advantage of Science is that it is not emotional."

"But we have such grave responsibilities," ventured Mrs. Vandeleur timidly.

"Terribly grave," echoed Lady Agatha.

Lord Henry looked over at Mr. Erskine. "Humanity takes itself too seriously. It is the world's original sin. If the caveman had known how to laugh, History would have been different."

"You are really very comforting," warbled the Duchess. "I have always felt rather guilty when I came to see your dear aunt, for I take no interest at all in the East End. For the future I shall be able to look her in the face without a blush."

"A blush is very becoming, Duchess," remarked Lord Henry.

"Only when one is young," she answered. "When an old woman like myself blushes, it is a very bad sign. Ah! Lord Henry, I wish you would tell me how to become young again."

He thought for a moment. "Can you remember any great error that you committed in your early days, Duchess?" he asked, looking at her across the table.

"A great many, I fear," she cried.

"Then commit them over again," he said, gravely. "To get back one's youth, one has merely to repeat one's follies."

"A delightful theory!" she exclaimed. "I must put it into practice."
"A dangerous theory!" came from Sir Thomas's tight lips. Lady
Agatha shook her head, but could not help being amused. Mr.
Erskine listened. "Yes," he continued, "that is one of the great secrets of life.
Nowadays most people die of a sort of creeping common sense,
and discover when it is too late that the only things one never re-
grets are one's mistakes."

A laugh ran round the table.

He played with the idea and grew wilful; tossed it into the air
and transformed it; let it escape and recaptured it; made it iridescent with fancy, and winged it with paradox. The praise of folly,[24]
as he went on, soared into a philosophy, and Philosophy herself became young, and catching the mad music of Pleasure, wearing, one
might fancy, her wine-stained robe and wreath of ivy, danced like a
Bacchante[25] over the hills of life, and mocked the slow Silenus[26] for
being sober. Facts fled before her like frightened forest things. Her
white feet trod the huge press at which wise Omar sits, till the
seething grape-juice rose round her bare limbs in waves of purple
bubbles, or crawled in red foam over the vat's black, dripping,
sloping sides.[27] It was an extraordinary improvisation. He felt that
the eyes of Dorian Gray were fixed on him, and the consciousness
that amongst his audience there was one whose temperament he
wished to fascinate, seemed to give his wit keenness and to lend
colour to his imagination. He was brilliant, fantastic, irresponsible.
He charmed his listeners out of themselves, and they followed his
pipe laughing.[28] Dorian Gray never took his gaze off him, but sat
like one under a spell, smiles chasing each other over his lips, and
wonder growing grave in his darkening eyes.

---

[24]The title of a famous satire by Erasmus is *The Praise of Folly* (1509).

[25]A priestess of Bacchus, the Greek god of wine, noted for frenzied intoxication.

[26]An old satyr.

[27]Reference to Omar Khayyám, a medieval Persian poet whose *Rubáiyát* had been
freely translated by Edward Fitzgerald (1809–83) in 1859. It was a celebrated work
of hedonism: "Come, fill the Cup, and in the fire of Spring / Your Winter-garment of
Repentance fling" (vii).

[28]In *The Pied Piper of Hamelin* (1842) by Robert Browning, the title figure charms
the children of Hamelin, who "run merrily after / The wonderful music with shouting and laughter" (206–7).

At last, liveried in the costume of the age, Reality entered the room in the shape of a servant to tell the Duchess that her carriage was waiting. She wrung her hands in mock despair. "How annoying!" she cried. "I must go. I have to call for my husband at the club, to take him to some absurd meeting at Willis's Rooms,[29] where he is going to be in the chair. If I am late he is sure to be furious, and I couldn't have a scene in this bonnet. It is far too fragile. A harsh word would ruin it. No, I must go, dear Agatha. Goodbye, Lord Henry, you are quite delightful and dreadfully demoralizing. I am sure I don't know what to say about your views. You must come and dine with us some night. Tuesday? Are you disengaged Tuesday?"

"For you I would throw over anybody, Duchess," said Lord Henry, with a bow.

"Ah! that is very nice, and very wrong of you," she cried; "so mind you come"; and she swept out of the room, followed by Lady Agatha and the other ladies.

When Lord Henry had sat down again, Mr. Erskine moved round, and taking a chair close to him, placed his hand upon his arm.

"You talk books away," he said; "why don't you write one?"

"I am too fond of reading books to care to write them, Mr. Erskine. I should like to write a novel certainly, a novel that would be as lovely as a Persian carpet and as unreal. But there is no literary public in England for anything except newspapers, primers, and encyclopædias. Of all people in the world the English have the least sense of the beauty of literature."

"I fear you are right," answered Mr. Erskine. "I myself used to have literary ambitions, but I gave them up long ago. And now, my dear young friend, if you will allow me to call you so, may I ask if you really meant all that you said to us at lunch?"

"I quite forget what I said," smiled Lord Henry. "Was it all very bad?"

"Very bad indeed. In fact I consider you extremely dangerous, and if anything happens to our good Duchess we shall all look on you as being primarily responsible. But I should like to talk to you about life. The generation into which I was born was tedious. Some day, when you are tired of London, come down to Treadley, and

[29] A large suite of apartments known for its ballroom, cardrooms, and dining rooms.

expound to me your philosophy of pleasure over some admirable Burgundy I am fortunate enough to possess."

"I shall be charmed. A visit to Treadley would be a great privilege. It has a perfect host, and a perfect library."

"You will complete it," answered the old gentleman, with a courteous bow. "And now I must bid good-bye to your excellent aunt. I am due at the Athenæum.[30] It is the hour when we sleep there."

"All of you, Mr. Erskine?"

"Forty of us, in forty arm-chairs. We are practising for an English Academy of Letters."[31]

Lord Henry laughed, and rose. "I am going to the Park,"[32] he cried.

As he was passing out of the door Dorian Gray touched him on the arm. "Let me come with you," he murmured.

"But I thought you had promised Basil Hallward to go and see him," answered Lord Henry.

"I would sooner come with you; yes, I feel I must come with you. Do let me. And you will promise to talk to me all the time? No one talks so wonderfully as you do."

"Ah! I have talked quite enough for to-day," said Lord Henry, smiling. "All I want now is to look at life. You may come and look at it with me, if you care to."

---

[30]"Eminence in, or patronage of, science, literature, or any branch of the fine arts, are the qualifications for membership of this club. The Athenæum possesses one of the best club houses, and certainly the best club library in England" (Dickens 11).

[31]A much-discussed project among Victorian men of letters was the founding of an Academy of Letters modeled along French lines; the British Academy was established in 1902.

[32]Hyde Park, "the great fashionable promenade and public lounge of London" (Dickens 121).

William M'Connell, "Four O'Clock P.M.: The Park" (1858–59). From George Augustus Sala, *Twice Round the Clock; Or, the Hours of the Day and Night in London*, illus. William M'Connell (1859) (London: John and Robert Maxwell, 1878), p. 196. (Courtesy of Wilson Library, University of Minnesota.)

Chapter 4

One afternoon, a month later, Dorian Gray was reclining in a luxurious arm-chair, in the little library of Lord Henry's house in Mayfair.[1] It was, in its way, a very charming room, with its high panelled wainscoting of olive-stained oak, its cream-coloured frieze and ceiling of raised plaster-work, and its brickdust felt carpet strewn with silk long-fringed Persian rugs. On a tiny satin-wood table stood a statuette by Clodion, and beside it lay a copy of "Les Cent Nouvelles," bound for Margaret of Valois by Clovis Eve, and powdered with the gilt daisies that Queen had selected for her device.[2] Some large blue china jars and parrot-tulips were ranged on the mantelshelf,[3] and through the small leaded panes of the window streamed the apricot-coloured light of a summer day in London.

Lord Henry had not yet come in. He was always late on principle, his principle being that punctuality is the thief of time.[4] So the lad was looking rather sulky, as with listless fingers he turned over the pages of an elaborately-illustrated edition of "Manon Lescaut"[5] that he had found in one of the bookcases. The formal monotonous ticking of the Louis Quatorze[6] clock annoyed him. Once or twice he thought of going away.

At last he heard a step outside, and the door opened. "How late you are, Harry!" he murmured.

"I am afraid it is not Harry, Mr. Gray," answered a shrill voice.

[1]A wealthy West End district, with elite men's clubs, exclusive shops, and fashionable residential areas; "the *crème de la crème* of residential London" (Dickens 141).

[2]Claude Michael Clodion (1738–1814), Rococo French sculptor; "Les Cents Nouvelles," collection of bawdy prose tales (1462); Margaret of Valois (1553–1615), wife of Henry IV of France, reputed for beauty, wit, and sexual licentiousness; Clovis Eve (1584–1635), French bookbinder and illustrator for the court. Margaret's name means "pearl" in French, and the white daisies of her device were meant to mirror the whiteness of pearls. In 1883 and 1884, there had been a spectacular sale in England of books that had purportedly belonged to Margaret, with prices reaching over £100 (Lang 636).

[3]At Oxford, Wilde had become notorious for claiming, "I find it harder and harder every day to live up to my blue china," a remark later parodied in *Punch*; parrot-tulips sport large, colorful blossoms.

[4]Riffing on the old adage, "Procrastination is the thief of time."

[5]Short novel (1731) by Abbé de Prévost (1697–1763), in which Chevalier des Grieux sacrifices all for the beautiful, faithless Manon Lescaut.

[6]In the baroque style, or from the era of Louis XIV of France (1638–1714), the "Sun King" and builder of the palace at Versailles.

He glanced quickly round, and rose to his feet. "I beg your pardon. I thought—"

"You thought it was my husband. It is only his wife. You must let me introduce myself. I know you quite well by your photographs. I think my husband has got seventeen of them."

"Not seventeen, Lady Henry?"

"Well, eighteen, then. And I saw you with him the other night at the Opera."[7] She laughed nervously as she spoke, and watched him with her vague forget-me-not eyes. She was a curious woman, whose dresses always looked as if they had been designed in a rage and put on in a tempest. She was usually in love with somebody, and, as her passion was never returned, she had kept all her illusions. She tried to look picturesque, but only succeeded in being untidy. Her name was Victoria, and she had a perfect mania for going to church.

"That was at 'Lohengrin,' Lady Henry, I think?"[8]

"Yes; it was at dear 'Lohengrin.' I like Wagner's music better than anybody's. It is so loud that one can talk the whole time without other people hearing what one says.[9] That is a great advantage: don't you think so, Mr. Gray?"

The same nervous staccato laugh broke from her thin lips, and her fingers began to play with a long tortoise-shell paper-knife.[10]

Dorian smiled and shook his head: "I am afraid I don't think so, Lady Henry. I never talk during music—at least, during good music. If one hears bad music, it is one's duty to drown it in conversation."

"Ah! that is one of Harry's views, isn't it, Mr. Gray? I always hear Harry's views from his friends. It is the only way I get to know of them. But you must not think I don't like good music. I adore it, but I am afraid of it. It makes me too romantic. I have simply worshipped pianists—two at a time, sometimes, Harry tells me. I don't know what it is about them. Perhaps it is that they are foreigners. They all are, ain't they? Even those that are born in England

[7]Covent Garden Theatre (now the Royal Opera House).

[8]Opera by Richard Wagner (1813–83), first performed in 1850; it debuted in London in 1875. Wagner was a cult composer for the Victorian Aesthetic movement because of his experimental approach to drama and his use of subjects from medieval romance.

[9]Wagner dramatically increased the size of the opera orchestra, and consequently required singers with louder voices.

[10]For opening envelopes or cutting apart the folded pages of books.

become foreigners after a time, don't they? It is so clever of them, and such a compliment to art. Makes it quite cosmopolitan, doesn't it? You have never been to any of my parties, have you, Mr. Gray? You must come. I can't afford orchids, but I spare no expense in foreigners. They make one's rooms look so picturesque. But here is Harry!—Harry, I came in to look for you, to ask you something—I forget what it was—and I found Mr. Gray here. We have had such a pleasant chat about music. We have quite the same ideas. No; I think our ideas are quite different. But he has been most pleasant. I am so glad I've seen him."

"I am charmed, my love, quite charmed," said Lord Henry, elevating his dark crescent-shaped eyebrows and looking at them both with an amused smile. "So sorry I am late, Dorian. I went to look after a piece of old brocade in Wardour Street[11] and had to bargain for hours for it. Nowadays people know the price of everything, and the value of nothing."

"I am afraid I must be going," exclaimed Lady Henry, breaking an awkward silence with her silly sudden laugh. "I have promised to drive with the Duchess. Good-bye, Mr. Gray. Good-bye Harry. You are dining out, I suppose? So am I. Perhaps I shall see you at Lady Thornbury's."

"I dare say, my dear," said Lord Henry, shutting the door behind her as, looking like a bird of paradise that had been out all night in the rain, she flitted out of the room, leaving a faint odour of frangipanni.[12] Then he lit a cigarette, and flung himself down on the sofa.

"Never marry a woman with straw-coloured hair, Dorian," he said after a few puffs.

"Why, Harry?"

"Because they are so sentimental."

"But I like sentimental people."

"Never marry at all, Dorian. Men marry because they are tired; women, because they are curious: both are disappointed."

"I don't think I am likely to marry, Harry. I am too much in love. That is one of your aphorisms. I am putting it into practice, as I do everything that you say."

[11]"Here are many shops exclusively devoted to the sale of old furniture, pictures, china, and other articles" (Wheatley 3.448).

[12]Perfume of red jasmine.

"Who are you in love with?" asked Lord Henry, after a pause.

"With an actress," said Dorian Gray, blushing.

Lord Henry shrugged his shoulders. "That is a rather commonplace *début*."

"You would not say so if you saw her, Harry."

"Who is she?"

"Her name is Sibyl[13] Vane."

"Never heard of her."

"No one has. People will some day, however. She is a genius."

"My dear boy, no woman is a genius. Women are a decorative sex. They never have anything to say, but they say it charmingly. Women represent the triumph of matter over mind, just as men represent the triumph of mind over morals."

"Harry, how can you?"

"My dear Dorian, it is quite true. I am analysing women at present, so I ought to know. The subject is not so abstruse as I thought it was. I find that, ultimately, there are only two kinds of women, the plain and the coloured. The plain women are very useful. If you want to gain a reputation for respectability, you have merely to take them down to supper. The other women are very charming. They commit one mistake, however. They paint in order to try and look young. Our grandmothers painted in order to try and talk brilliantly. *Rouge* and *esprit*[14] used to go together. That is all over now. As long as a woman can look ten years younger than her own daughter, she is perfectly satisfied. As for conversation, there are only five women in London worth talking to, and two of these can't be admitted into decent society. However, tell me about your genius. How long have you known her?"

"Ah! Harry, your views terrify me."

"Never mind that. How long have you known her?"

"About three weeks."

"And where did you come across her?"

"I will tell you, Harry; but you mustn't be unsympathetic about it. After all, it never would have happened if I had not met you. You filled me with a wild desire to know everything about life. For days

---

[13]Female oracle, noted for mysteriousness of her prophecies. Benjamin Disraeli (1804–81) had used the name for the virtuous heroine of his industrial novel *Sybil* (1845).

[14]Wit, liveliness (French).

after I met you, something seemed to throb in my veins. As I lounged in the Park, or strolled down Piccadilly,[15] I used to look at every one who passed me, and wonder, with a mad curiosity, what sort of lives they led. Some of them fascinated me. Others filled me with terror. There was an exquisite poison in the air. I had a passion for sensations. . . . Well, one evening about seven o'clock, I determined to go out in search of some adventure. I felt that this grey, monstrous London of ours, with its myriads of people, its sordid sinners, and its splendid sins, as you once phrased it, must have something in store for me. I fancied a thousand things. The mere danger gave me a sense of delight. I remembered what you had said to me on that wonderful evening when we first dined together, about the search for beauty being the real secret of life. I don't know what I expected, but I went out and wandered eastward, soon losing my way in a labyrinth of grimy streets and black, grassless squares. About half-past eight I passed by an absurd little theatre, with great flaring gas-jets and gaudy play-bills. A hideous Jew,[16] in the most amazing waistcoat I ever beheld in my life, was standing at the entrance, smoking a vile cigar. He had greasy ringlets, and an enormous diamond blazed in the centre of a soiled shirt. 'Have a box,[17] my Lord?' he said, when he saw me, and he took off his hat with an air of gorgeous servility. There was something about him, Harry, that amused me. He was such a monster. You will laugh at me, I know, but I really went in and paid a whole guinea[18] for the stage-box. To the present day I can't make out why I did so; and yet if I hadn't—my dear Harry, if I hadn't—I should have missed the greatest romance of my life. I see you are laughing. It is horrid of you!"

"I am not laughing, Dorian; at least I am not laughing at you. But you should not say the greatest romance of your life. You

[15]"The high road to the most fashionable quarters in the west and south-west of London" (Dickens 200).

[16]Wilde's work shares the anti-Semitism that is pervasive in Victorian literature. It may also be a reaction to the increasing prominence of Jews in London life; London had Jewish lord mayors in 1889 and 1896, and Jews had long played a substantial role in London theaters as actors and managers (Cowen and Cowen 83, 84, 95).

[17]Most expensive seat in the theater, a private compartment near the stage raised so as to be a kind of stage itself, visible to, and often observed by, those in the orchestra seats below.

[18]21 shillings; no longer an actual coin, but associated with the cost of luxury goods because it represented one shilling more than a pound (Pool 19). The 1891 deluxe version of *Dorian Gray* cost one guinea (Guy and Small 57).

should say the first romance of your life. You will always be loved, and you will always be in love with love. A *grande passion* is the privilege of people who have nothing to do. That is the one use of the idle classes of a country. Don't be afraid. There are exquisite things in store for you. This is merely the beginning."

"Do you think my nature so shallow?" cried Dorian Gray, angrily.

"No; I think your nature so deep."

"How do you mean?"

"My dear boy, the people who love only once in their lives are really the shallow people. What they call their loyalty, and their fidelity, I call either the lethargy of custom or their lack of imagination. Faithfulness is to the emotional life what consistency is to the life of the intellect—simply a confession of failure. Faithfulness! I must analyse it some day. The passion for property is in it. There are many things that we would throw away if we were not afraid that others might pick them up. But I don't want to interrupt you. Go on with your story."

"Well, I found myself seated in a horrid little private box, with a vulgar drop-scene staring me in the face. I looked out from behind the curtain, and surveyed the house. It was a tawdry affair, all Cupids and cornucopias, like a third-rate wedding-cake. The gallery and pit were fairly full, but the two rows of dingy stalls were quite empty,[19] and there was hardly a person in what I suppose they called the dress-circle. Women went about with oranges and ginger-beer,[20] and there was a terrible consumption of nuts going on."

"It must have been just like the palmy days of the British Drama."[21]

"Just like, I should fancy, and very depressing. I began to wonder what on earth I should do, when I caught sight of the play-bill. What do you think the play was, Harry?"

"I should think 'The Idiot Boy, or Dumb but Innocent'.[22] Our fathers used to like that sort of piece, I believe. The longer I live,

---

[19]The stalls and dress-circle are the expensive seats, between the pit and the gallery.

[20]Non-alcoholic soda water; the *Oxford English Dictionary* also notes 20th-c. instances of slang for homosexual (from its rhyme with "queer").

[21]Like Shakespeare's audiences at The Globe.

[22]A title that parodies the sentimental conventions of Victorian melodrama; it recalls William Wordsworth's much-parodied poem, "The Idiot Boy" (1798) and Mary Martha Sherwood's *The Idiot Boy* (1829), a children's tale (Bristow 383).

Dorian, the more keenly I feel that whatever was good enough for our fathers is not good enough for us. In art, as in politics, *les grandpères ont toujours tort.*"[23]

"This play was good enough for us, Harry. It was 'Romeo and Juliet.' I must admit that I was rather annoyed at the idea of seeing Shakespeare done in such a wretched hole of a place. Still, I felt interested, in a sort of way. At any rate, I determined to wait for the first act. There was a dreadful orchestra, presided over by a young Hebrew who sat at a cracked piano, that nearly drove me away, but at last the drop-scene was drawn up and the play began. Romeo was a stout elderly gentleman, with corked eyebrows, a husky tragedy voice, and a figure like a beer-barrel. Mercutio was almost as bad.[24] He was played by the low-comedian, who had introduced gags of his own and was on most friendly terms with the pit. They were both as grotesque as the scenery, and that looked as if it had come out of a country-booth. But Juliet! Harry, imagine a girl, hardly seventeen years of age, with a little, flower-like face, a small Greek head with plaited coils of dark-brown hair, eyes that were violet wells of passion, lips that were like the petals of a rose. She was the loveliest thing I had ever seen in my life. You said to me once that pathos left you unmoved, but that beauty, mere beauty, could fill your eyes with tears. I tell you, Harry, I could hardly see this girl for the mist of tears that came across me. And her voice—I never heard such a voice. It was very low at first, with deep mellow notes, that seemed to fall singly upon one's ear. Then it became a little louder, and sounded like a flute or a distant hautbois.[25] In the garden-scene it had all the tremulous ecstasy that one hears just before dawn when nightingales are singing. There were moments, later on, when it had the wild passion of violins. You know how a voice can stir one. Your voice and the voice of Sibyl Vane are two things that I shall never forget. When I close my eyes, I hear them, and each of them says something different. I don't know which to follow. Why should I not love her? Harry, I do love her. She is everything to me in life. Night after night I go to see her play. One evening she is Rosalind, and the next evening she is Imogen. I have seen her die in

---

[23]Grandparents are always wrong (French).

[24]Mercutio is Romeo's witty, manic friend, killed in a street brawl.

[25]Oboe (archaic).

the gloom of an Italian tomb, sucking the poison from her lover's lips. I have watched her wandering through the forest of Arden, disguised as a pretty boy in hose and doublet and dainty cap. She has been mad, and has come into the presence of a guilty king, and given him rue to wear, and bitter herbs to taste of. She has been innocent, and the black hands of jealousy have crushed her reed-like throat.[26] I have seen her in every age and in every costume. Ordinary women never appeal to one's imagination. They are limited to their century. No glamour ever transfigures them. One knows their minds as easily as one knows their bonnets. One can always find them. There is no mystery in any of them. They ride in the Park in the morning, and chatter at tea-parties in the afternoon. They have their stereotyped smile, and their fashionable manner. They are quite obvious. But an actress! How different an actress is! Harry! why didn't you tell me that the only thing worth loving is an actress?"

"Because I have loved so many of them, Dorian."

"Oh, yes, horrid people with dyed hair and painted faces."

"Don't run down dyed hair and painted faces. There is an extraordinary charm in them, sometimes," said Lord Henry.

"I wish now I had not told you about Sibyl Vane."

"You could not have helped telling me, Dorian. All through your life you will tell me everything you do."

"Yes, Harry, I believe that is true. I cannot help telling you things. You have a curious influence over me. If I ever did a crime, I would come and confess it to you. You would understand me."

"People like you—the wilful sunbeams of life—don't commit crimes, Dorian. But I am much obliged for the compliment, all the same. And now tell me—reach me the matches, like a good boy: thanks:—what are your actual relations with Sibyl Vane?"

Dorian Gray leaped to his feet, with flushed cheeks and burning eyes. "Harry! Sibyl Vane is sacred!"

"It is only the sacred things that are worth touching, Dorian," said Lord Henry, with a strange touch of pathos in his voice. "But why should you be annoyed? I suppose she will belong to you some

---

[26]Rosalind, the cross-dressing heroine of *As You Like It*, who takes refuge in the forest of Arden; Imogen, the faithful lover in *Cymbeline*; Juliet; Ophelia's famous mad scene in *Hamlet*; and Desdemona, murdered by her jealous husband Othello, the Moor.

day. When one is in love, one always begins by deceiving one's self, and one always ends by deceiving others. That is what the world calls a romance. You know her, at any rate, I suppose?"

"Of course I know her. On the first night I was at the theatre, the horrid old Jew came round to the box after the performance was over, and offered to take me behind the scenes and introduce me to her.[27] I was furious with him, and told him that Juliet had been dead for hundreds of years, and that her body was lying in a marble tomb in Verona. I think, from his blank look of amazement, that he was under the impression that I had taken too much champagne, or something."

"I am not surprised."

"Then he asked me if I wrote for any of the newspapers. I told him I never even read them. He seemed terribly disappointed at that, and confided to me that all the dramatic critics were in a conspiracy against him, and that they were every one of them to be bought."

"I should not wonder if he was quite right there. But, on the other hand, judging from their appearance, most of them cannot be at all expensive."

"Well, he seemed to think they were beyond his means," laughed Dorian. "By this time, however, the lights were being put out in the theatre, and I had to go. He wanted me to try some cigars that he strongly recommended. I declined. The next night, of course, I arrived at the place again. When he saw me, he made me a low bow, and assured me that I was a munificent patron of art. He was a most offensive brute, though he had an extraordinary passion for Shakespeare. He told me once, with an air of pride, that his five bankruptcies were entirely due to 'The Bard,' as he insisted on calling him. He seemed to think it a distinction."

"It was a distinction, my dear Dorian—a great distinction. Most people become bankrupt through having invested too heavily in the prose of life. To have ruined one's self over poetry is an honour. But when did you first speak to Miss Sibyl Vane?"

"The third night. She had been playing Rosalind. I could not help going round. I had thrown her some flowers, and she had looked at me—at least I fancied that she had. The old Jew was per-

---

[27]I.e., the manager is serving as Sibyl Vane's pimp.

sistent. He seemed determined to take me behind, so I consented. It was curious my not wanting to know her, wasn't it?"

"No; I don't think so."

"My dear Harry, why?"

"I will tell you some other time. Now I want to know about the girl."

"Sibyl? Oh, she was so shy, and so gentle. There is something of a child about her. Her eyes opened wide in exquisite wonder when I told her what I thought of her performance, and she seemed quite unconscious of her power. I think we were both rather nervous. The old Jew stood grinning at the doorway of the dusty greenroom, making elaborate speeches about us both, while we stood looking at each other like children. He would insist on calling me 'My Lord,' so I had to assure Sibyl that I was not anything of the kind. She said quite simply to me, 'You look more like a prince. I must call you Prince Charming.'"[28]

"Upon my word, Dorian, Miss Sibyl knows how to pay compliments."

"You don't understand her, Harry. She regarded me merely as a person in a play. She knows nothing of life. She lives with her mother, a faded tired woman who played Lady Capulet[29] in a sort of magenta dressing-wrapper on the first night, and looks as if she had seen better days."

"I know that look. It depresses me," murmured Lord Henry, examining his rings.

"The Jew wanted to tell me her history, but I said it did not interest me."

"You were quite right. There is always something infinitely mean about other people's tragedies."

"Sibyl is the only thing I care about. What is it to me where she came from? From her little head to her little feet, she is absolutely and entirely divine. Every night of my life I go to see her act, and every night she is more marvellous."

"That is the reason, I suppose, that you never dine with me now. I thought you must have some curious romance on hand. You have; but it is not quite what I expected."

---

[28]Wilde may have gotten the name from "The Story of Pretty Goldilocks," by Madame d'Aulnoy, translated by Andrew Lang in his *Blue Fairy Book* (1889).

[29]Juliet's mother.

"My dear Harry, we either lunch or sup together every day, and I have been to the Opera with you several times," said Dorian, opening his blue eyes in wonder.

"You always come dreadfully late."

"Well, I can't help going to see Sibyl play," he cried, "even if it is only for a single act. I get hungry for her presence; and when I think of the wonderful soul that is hidden away in that little ivory body, I am filled with awe."

"You can dine with me to-night, Dorian, can't you?"

He shook his head. "To-night she is Imogen," he answered, "and to-morrow night she will be Juliet."

"When is she Sibyl Vane?"

"Never."

"I congratulate you."

"How horrid you are! She is all the great heroines of the world in one. She is more than an individual. You laugh, but I tell you she has genius. I love her, and I must make her love me. You, who know all the secrets of life, tell me how to charm Sibyl Vane to love me! I want to make Romeo jealous. I want the dead lovers of the world to hear our laughter, and grow sad. I want a breath of our passion to stir their dust into consciousness, to wake their ashes into pain. My God, Harry, how I worship her!" He was walking up and down the room as he spoke. Hectic spots of red burned on his cheeks. He was terribly excited.

Lord Henry watched him with a subtle sense of pleasure. How different he was now from the shy, frightened boy he had met in Basil Hallward's studio! His nature had developed like a flower, had borne blossoms of scarlet flame. Out of its secret hiding-place had crept his Soul, and Desire had come to meet it on the way.

"And what do you propose to do?" said Lord Henry, at last.

"I want you and Basil to come with me some night and see her act. I have not the slightest fear of the result. You are certain to acknowledge her genius. Then we must get her out of the Jew's hands. She is bound[30] to him for three years—at least for two years and eight months—from the present time. I shall have to pay him something, of course. When all that is settled, I shall take a West

---

[30]Contracted.

End theatre and bring her out properly. She will make the world as mad as she has made me."

"That would be impossible, my dear boy."

"Yes she will. She has not merely art, consummate art-instinct, in her, but she has personality also; and you have often told me that it is personalities, not principles, that move the age."

"Well, what night shall we go?"

"Let me see. To-day is Tuesday. Let us fix to-morrow. She plays Juliet to-morrow."

"All right. The Bristol[31] at eight o'clock; and I will get Basil."

"Not eight, Harry, please. Half-past six. We must be there before the curtain rises. You must see her in the first act, where she meets Romeo."

"Half-past six! What an hour! It will be like having a meat-tea,[32] or reading an English novel. It must be seven. No gentleman dines before seven. Shall you see Basil between this and then? Or shall I write to him?"

"Dear Basil! I have not laid eyes on him for a week. It is rather horrid of me, as he has sent me my portrait in the most wonderful frame, specially designed by himself, and, though I am a little jealous of the picture for being a whole month younger than I am, I must admit that I delight in it. Perhaps you had better write to him. I don't want to see him alone. He says things that annoy me. He gives me good advice."

Lord Henry smiled. "People are very fond of giving away what they need most themselves. It is what I call the depth of generosity."

"Oh, Basil is the best of fellows, but he seems to me to be just a bit of a Philistine.[33] Since I have known you, Harry, I have discovered that."

"Basil, my dear boy, puts everything that is charming in him into his work. The consequence is that he has nothing left for life but his prejudices, his principles, and his common sense. The only artists I have ever known who are personally delightful, are bad artists. Good artists exist simply in what they make, and consequently are perfectly uninteresting in what they are. A great poet, a

---

[31]Fine London restaurant (Yates 99).

[32]A light meal that includes meat.

[33]Matthew Arnold's term in *Culture and Anarchy* (1882) to describe the complacent materialism and self-satisfaction of the British middle class.

really great poet, is the most unpoetical of all creatures.[34] But inferior poets are absolutely fascinating. The worse their rhymes are, the more picturesque they look. The mere fact of having published a book of second-rate sonnets makes a man quite irresistible. He lives the poetry that he cannot write. The others write the poetry that they dare not realize."

"I wonder is that really so, Harry?" said Dorian Gray, putting some perfume on his handkerchief out of a large gold-topped bottle that stood on the table. "It must be, if you say it. And now I am off. Imogen is waiting for me. Don't forget about to-morrow. Good-bye."

As he left the room, Lord Henry's heavy eyelids drooped, and he began to think. Certainly few people had ever interested him so much as Dorian Gray, and yet the lad's mad adoration of some one else caused him not the slightest pang of annoyance or jealousy. He was pleased by it. It made him a more interesting study. He had been always enthralled by the methods of natural science, but the ordinary subject-matter of that science had seemed to him trivial and of no import. And so he had begun by vivisecting[35] himself, as he had ended by vivisecting others. Human life—that appeared to him the one thing worth investigating. Compared to it there was nothing else of any value. It was true that as one watched life in its curious crucible of pain and pleasure, one could not wear over one's face a mask of glass, nor keep the sulphurous fumes from troubling the brain and making the imagination turbid with monstrous fancies and misshapen dreams. There were poisons so subtle that to know their properties one had to sicken of them. There were maladies so strange that one had to pass through them if one sought to understand their nature. And, yet, what a great reward one received! How wonderful the whole world became to one! To note the curious hard logic of passion, and the emotional coloured life of the intellect—to observe where they met, and where they separated, at what point they were in unison, and at what point they were at discord—there was a delight in that! What matter what the cost was? One could never pay too high a price for any sensation.

---

[34]A reference to a famous self-definition by John Keats: "A Poet is the most unpoetical of any thing in existence; because he has no Identity—he is continually in for—and filling some other Body" (letter, Oct. 1818).

[35]Dissecting a live animal, a subject of considerable ethical debate.

He was conscious—and the thought brought a gleam of pleasure into his brown agate eyes—that it was through certain words of his, musical words said with musical utterance, that Dorian Gray's soul had turned to this white girl and bowed in worship before her. To a large extent the lad was his own creation. He had made him premature. That was something. Ordinary people waited till life disclosed to them its secrets, but to the few, to the elect, the mysteries of life were revealed before the veil was drawn away. Sometimes this was the effect of art, and chiefly of the art of literature, which dealt immediately with the passions and the intellect. But now and then a complex personality took the place and assumed the office of art, was indeed, in its way, a real work of art, Life having its elaborate masterpieces, just as poetry has, or sculpture, or painting.

Yes, the lad was premature. He was gathering his harvest while it was yet spring. The pulse and passion of youth were in him, but he was becoming self-conscious. It was delightful to watch him. With his beautiful face, and his beautiful soul, he was a thing to wonder at. It was no matter how it all ended, or was destined to end. He was like one of those gracious figures in a pageant or a play, whose joys seem to be remote from one, but whose sorrows stir one's sense of beauty, and whose wounds are like red roses.

Soul and body, body and soul—how mysterious they were! There was animalism in the soul, and the body had its moments of spirituality. The senses could refine, and the intellect could degrade. Who could say where the fleshly impulse ceased, or the psychical impulse began? How shallow were the arbitrary definitions of ordinary psychologists! And yet how difficult to decide between the claims of the various schools! Was the soul a shadow seated in the house of sin? Or was the body really in the soul, as Giordano Bruno thought?[36] The separation of spirit from matter was a mystery, and the union of spirit with matter was a mystery also.

He began to wonder whether we could ever make psychology so absolute a science that each little spring of life would be revealed

---

[36]Giordano Bruno (1548–1600), Italian philosopher and martyr, condemned and burned at the stake by the Inquisition. Commenting on Bruno's philosophy, Walter Pater wrote: "If God the Spirit had made, nay! was, all things indifferently, then, matter and spirit, the spirit and the flesh, heaven and earth, freedom and necessity, the first and the last, good and evil, would be superficial rather than substantial differences" (237).

to us. As it was, we always misunderstood ourselves, and rarely understood others. Experience was of no ethical value. It was merely the name men gave to their mistakes. Moralists had, as a rule, regarded it as a mode of warning, had claimed for it a certain ethical efficacy in the formation of character, had praised it as something that taught us what to follow and showed us what to avoid. But there was no motive power in experience. It was as little of an active cause as conscience itself. All that it really demonstrated was that our future would be the same as our past, and that the sin we had done once, and with loathing, we would do many times, and with joy.

It was clear to him that the experimental method was the only method by which one could arrive at any scientific analysis of the passions; and certainly Dorian Gray was a subject made to his hand, and seemed to promise rich and fruitful results. His sudden mad love for Sibyl Vane was a psychological phenomenon of no small interest. There was no doubt that curiosity had much to do with it, curiosity and the desire for new experiences; yet it was not a simple, but rather a very complex passion. What there was in it of the purely sensuous instinct of boyhood had been transformed by the workings of the imagination, changed into something that seemed to the lad himself to be remote from sense, and was for that very reason all the more dangerous. It was the passions about whose origin we deceived ourselves that tyrannized most strongly over us. Our weakest motives were those of whose nature we were conscious. It often happened that when we thought we were experimenting on others we were really experimenting on ourselves.

While Lord Henry sat dreaming on these things, a knock came to the door, and his valet entered, and reminded him it was time to dress for dinner. He got up and looked out into the street. The sunset had smitten into scarlet gold the upper windows of the houses opposite. The panes glowed like plates of heated metal. The sky above was like a faded rose. He thought of his friend's young fiery-coloured life, and wondered how it was all going to end.

When he arrived home, about half-past twelve o'clock, he saw a telegram lying on the hall table. He opened it, and found it was from Dorian Gray. It was to tell him that he was engaged to be married to Sibyl Vane.

Chapter 5

"Mother, mother, I am so happy!" whispered the girl, burying her face in the lap of the faded, tired-looking woman who, with back turned to the shrill intrusive light, was sitting in the one arm-chair that their dingy sitting-room contained. "I am so happy!" she repeated, "and you must be happy too!"

Mrs. Vane winced and put her thin bismuth-whitened[1] hands on her daughter's head. "Happy!" she echoed, "I am only happy, Sibyl, when I see you act. You must not think of anything but your acting. Mr. Isaacs has been very good to us, and we owe him money."

The girl looked up and pouted. "Money, mother?" she cried, "what does money matter? Love is more than money."

"Mr. Isaacs has advanced us fifty pounds[2] to pay off our debts, and to get a proper outfit for James. You must not forget that, Sibyl. Fifty pounds is a very large sum. Mr. Isaacs has been most considerate."

"He is not a gentleman, mother, and I hate the way he talks to me," said the girl, rising to her feet, and going over to the window.

"I don't know how we could manage without him," answered the elder woman, querulously.

Sibyl Vane tossed her head and laughed. "We don't want him any more, mother. Prince Charming rules life for us now." Then she paused. A rose shook in her blood, and shadowed her cheeks. Quick breath parted the petals of her lips. They trembled. Some southern wind of passion swept over her, and stirred the dainty folds of her dress. "I love him," she said, simply.

"Foolish child! foolish child!" was the parrot-phrase flung in answer. The waving of crooked, false-jewelled fingers gave grotesqueness to the words.

The girl laughed again. The joy of a caged bird was in her voice. Her eyes caught the melody, and echoed it in radiance: then closed for a moment, as though to hide their secret. When they opened, the mist of a dream had passed across them.

[1]Bismuth was used as makeup to whiten the skin.

[2]It is difficult to give a present-day sense of the value of Victorian money, but Wilde himself received £200 from *Lippincott's* as his payment for the 1890 version of *The Picture of Dorian Gray* (Guy and Small 57).

Thin-lipped wisdom spoke at her from the worn chair, hinted at prudence, quoted from that book of cowardice whose author apes the name of common sense. She did not listen. She was free in her prison of passion. Her prince, Prince Charming, was with her. She had called on Memory to remake him. She had sent her soul to search for him, and it had brought him back. His kiss burned again upon her mouth. Her eyelids were warm with his breath.

Then Wisdom altered its method and spoke of espial and discovery. This young man might be rich. If so, marriage should be thought of. Against the shell of her ear broke the waves of worldly cunning. The arrows of craft shot by her. She saw the thin lips moving, and smiled.

Suddenly she felt the need to speak. The wordy silence troubled her. "Mother, mother," she cried, "why does he love me so much? I know why I love him. I love him because he is like what Love himself should be. But what does he see in me? I am not worthy of him. And yet—why, I cannot tell—though I feel so much beneath him, I don't feel humble. I feel proud, terribly proud. Mother, did you love my father as I love Prince Charming?"

The elder woman grew pale beneath the coarse powder that daubed her cheeks, and her dry lips twitched with a spasm of pain. Sybil rushed to her, flung her arms round her neck, and kissed her. "Forgive me, mother. I know it pains you to talk about our father. But it only pains you because you loved him so much. Don't look so sad. I am as happy to-day as you were twenty years ago. Ah! let me be happy for ever!"

"My child, you are far too young to think of falling in love. Besides, what do you know of this young man? You don't even know his name. The whole thing is most inconvenient, and really, when James is going away to Australia,[3] and I have so much to think of, I must say that you should have shown more consideration. However, as I said before, if he is rich . . ."

"Ah! mother, mother, let me be happy!"

---

[3] A penal colony until 1868, Australia became a destination for those who were unable to make a living in England. Like the American West, it was a challenging frontier existence, where the chief opportunities were herding, farming, and mining. But fortunes could be made, as Dickens's Abel Magwitch in *Great Expectations* (1860–61) does.

Mrs. Vane glanced at her, and with one of those false theatrical gestures that so often become a mode of second nature to a stage-player, clasped her in her arms. At this moment, the door opened, and a young lad with rough brown hair came into the room. He was thick-set of figure, and his hands and feet were large, and somewhat clumsy in movement. He was not so finely bred as his sister. One would hardly have guessed the close relationship that existed between them. Mrs. Vane fixed her eyes on him, and intensified her smile. She mentally elevated her son to the dignity of an audience. She felt sure that the *tableau*[4] was interesting.

"You might keep some of your kisses for me, Sibyl, I think," said the lad, with a good-natured grumble.

"Ah! but you don't like being kissed, Jim," she cried. "You are a dreadful old bear." And she ran across the room and hugged him.

James Vane looked into his sister's face with tenderness. "I want you to come out with me for a walk, Sibyl. I don't suppose I shall ever see this horrid London again. I am sure I don't want to."

"My son, don't say such dreadful things," murmured Mrs. Vane, taking up a tawdry theatrical dress, with a sigh, and beginning to patch it. She felt a little disappointed that he had not joined the group. It would have increased the theatrical picturesqueness of the situation.

"Why not, mother? I mean it."

"You pain me, my son. I trust you will return from Australia in a position of affluence. I believe there is no society of any kind in the Colonies, nothing that I would call society; so when you have made your fortune, you must come back and assert yourself in London."

"Society!" muttered the lad. "I don't want to know anything about that. I should like to make some money to take you and Sibyl off the stage. I hate it."

"Oh, Jim!" said Sibyl, laughing, "how unkind of you! But are you really going for a walk with me? That will be nice! I was afraid you were going to say good-bye to some of your friends—to Tom Hardy, who gave you that hideous pipe, or Ned Langton, who makes fun of you for smoking it. It is very sweet of you to let me have your last afternoon. Where shall we go? Let us go to the Park."

[4]Carefully arranged scene, usually at climaxes.

"I am too shabby," he answered, frowning. "Only swell people go to the Park."

"Nonsense, Jim," she whispered, stroking the sleeve of his coat. He hesitated for a moment. "Very well," he said at last, "but don't be too long dressing." She danced out of the door. One could hear her singing as she ran upstairs. Her little feet pattered overhead.

He walked up and down the room two or three times. Then he turned to the still figure in the chair. "Mother, are my things ready?" he asked.

"Quite ready, James," she answered, keeping her eyes on her work. For some months past she had felt ill at ease when she was alone with this rough, stern son of hers. Her shallow secret nature was troubled when their eyes met. She used to wonder if he suspected anything. The silence, for he made no other observation, became intolerable to her. She began to complain. Women defend themselves by attacking, just as they attack by sudden and strange surrenders. "I hope you will be contented, James, with your sea-faring life," she said. "You must remember that it is your own choice. You might have entered a solicitor's[5] office. Solicitors are a very respectable class, and in the country often dine with the best families."

"I hate offices, and I hate clerks," he replied. "But you are quite right. I have chosen my own life. All I say is, watch over Sibyl. Don't let her come to any harm. Mother, you must watch over her."

"James, you really talk very strangely. Of course I watch over Sibyl."

"I hear a gentleman comes every night to the theatre, and goes behind to talk to her. Is that right? What about that?"

"You are speaking about things you don't understand, James. In the profession we are accustomed to receive a great deal of most gratifying attention. I myself used to receive many bouquets at one time. That was when acting was really understood. As for Sibyl, I do not know at present whether her attachment is serious or not. But there is no doubt that the young man in question is a perfect gentleman. He is always most polite to me. Besides, he has the appearance of being rich, and the flowers he sends are lovely."

"You don't know his name, though," said the lad harshly.

[5]Lawyer's.

"No," answered his mother, with a placid expression in her face. "He has not yet revealed his real name. I think it is quite romantic of him. He is probably a member of the aristocracy."

James Vane bit his lip. "Watch over Sibyl, mother," he cried, "watch over her."

"My son, you distress me very much. Sibyl is always under my special care. Of course, if this gentleman is wealthy, there is no reason why she should not contract an alliance with him. I trust he is one of the aristocracy. He has all the appearance of it, I must say. It might be a most brilliant marriage for Sibyl. They would make a charming couple. His good looks are really quite remarkable; everybody notices them."

The lad muttered something to himself, and drummed on the window-pane with his coarse fingers. He had just turned round to say something, when the door opened, and Sibyl ran in.

"How serious you both are!" she cried. "What is the matter?"

"Nothing," he answered. "I suppose one must be serious sometimes. Good-bye, mother; I will have my dinner at five o'clock. Everything is packed, except my shirts, so you need not trouble."

"Good-bye, my son," she answered, with a bow of strained stateliness.

She was extremely annoyed at the tone he had adopted with her, and there was something in his look that had made her feel afraid.

"Kiss me, mother," said the girl. Her flower-like lips touched the withered cheek, and warmed its frost.

"My child! my child!" cried Mrs. Vane, looking up to the ceiling in search of an imaginary gallery.

"Come, Sibyl," said her brother, impatiently. He hated his mother's affectations.

They went out into the flickering wind-blown sunlight, and strolled down the dreary Euston Road.[6] The passers-by glanced in wonder at the sullen, heavy youth, who, in coarse, ill-fitting clothes, was in the company of such a graceful, refined-looking girl. He was like a common gardener walking with a rose.

---

[6]A haunt for the sex trade: "Look at the state of this Euston Road. Count them up:—three hundred street walkers, from grey haired decrepitude, to the slender girl of twelve or thirteen . . . all now the blighted, wretched inmates of the brothels which abound at the rear of their present public promenade" (Vigar-Harris 18).

Jim frowned from time to time when he caught the inquisitive glance of some stranger. He had that dislike of being stared at which comes on geniuses late in life, and never leaves the commonplace. Sibyl, however, was quite unconscious of the effect she was producing. Her love was trembling in laughter on her lips. She was thinking of Prince Charming, and, that she might think of him all the more, she did not talk of him, but prattled on about the ship in which Jim was going to sail, about the gold he was certain to find, about the wonderful heiress whose life he was to save from the wicked, red-shirted bushrangers.[7] For he was not to remain a sailor, or a super-cargo,[8] or whatever he was going to be. Oh, no! A sailor's existence was dreadful. Fancy being cooped up in a horrid ship, with the hoarse, hump-backed waves trying to get in, and a black wind blowing the masts down, and tearing the sails into long screaming ribands! He was to leave the vessel at Melbourne, bid a polite good-bye to the captain, and go off at once to the gold-fields. Before a week was over he was to come across a large nugget of pure gold, the largest nugget that had ever been discovered, and bring it down to the coast in a waggon guarded by six mounted policemen. The bushrangers were to attack them three times, and be defeated with immense slaughter. Or, no. He was not to go to the gold-fields at all. They were horrid places, where men got intoxicated, and shot each other in bar-rooms, and used bad language. He was to be a nice sheep-farmer, and one evening, as he was riding home, he was to see the beautiful heiress being carried off by a robber on a black horse, and give chase, and rescue her. Of course she would fall in love with him, and he with her, and they would get married, and come home, and live in an immense house in London. Yes, there were delightful things in store for him. But he must be very good, and not lose his temper, or spend his money foolishly. She was only a year older than he was, but she knew so much more of life. He must be sure, also, to write to her by every mail, and to say his prayers each night before he went to sleep. God was very good, and would watch over him. She would pray for him too, and in a few years he would come back quite rich and happy.

[7]Escaped convicts living in the Australian bush.

[8]An officer on a ship who supervises the cargo and commercial transactions.

The lad listened sulkily to her, and made no answer. He was heart-sick at leaving home.

Yet it was not this alone that made him gloomy and morose. Inexperienced though he was, he had still a strong sense of the danger of Sibyl's position. This young dandy who was making love to her could mean her no good. He was a gentleman, and he hated him for that, hated him through some curious race-instinct for which he could not account, and which for that reason was all the more dominant within him. He was conscious also of the shallowness and vanity of his mother's nature, and in that saw infinite peril for Sibyl and Sibyl's happiness. Children begin by loving their parents; as they grow older they judge them; sometimes they forgive them.

His mother! He had something on his mind to ask of her, something that he had brooded on for many months of silence. A chance phrase that he had heard at the theatre, a whispered sneer that had reached his ears one night as he waited at the stage-door, had set loose a train of horrible thoughts. He remembered it as if it had been the lash of a hunting-crop across his face. His brows knit together into a wedge-like furrow, and with a twitch of pain he bit his under-lip.

"You are not listening to a word I am saying, Jim," cried Sibyl, "and I am making the most delightful plans for your future. Do say something."

"What do you want me to say?"

"Oh! that you will be a good boy, and not forget us," she answered, smiling at him.

He shrugged his shoulders. "You are more likely to forget me than I am to forget you, Sibyl."

She flushed. "What do you mean, Jim?" she asked.

"You have a new friend, I hear. Who is he? Why have you not told me about him? He means you no good."

"Stop, Jim!" she exclaimed. "You must not say anything against him. I love him."

"Why, you don't even know his name," answered the lad. "Who is he? I have a right to know."

"He is called Prince Charming. Don't you like the name? Oh! you silly boy! you should never forget it. If you only saw him, you would think him the most wonderful person in the world. Some day you will meet him: when you come back from Australia. You will like him so much. Everybody likes him, and I . . . love him. I wish you could come to the theatre to-night. He is going to be there, and I am to play Juliet. Oh! how I shall play it! Fancy, Jim, to be in love and play Juliet! To have him sitting there! To play for his delight! I am afraid I may frighten the company, frighten or enthrall them. To be in love is to surpass one's self. Poor dreadful Mr. Isaacs will be shouting 'genius' to his loafers at the bar. He has preached me as a dogma; to-night he will announce me as a revelation. I feel it. And it is all his, his only, Prince Charming, my wonderful lover, my god of graces. But I am poor beside him. Poor? What does that matter? When poverty creeps in at the door, love flies in through the window. Our proverbs want re-writing. They were made in winter, and it is summer now; spring-time for me, I think, a very dance of blossoms in blue skies."

"He is a gentleman," said the lad, sullenly.

"A Prince!" she cried, musically. "What more do you want?"

"He wants to enslave you."

"I shudder at the thought of being free."

"I want you to beware of him."

"To see him is to worship him, to know him is to trust him."

"Sibyl, you are mad about him."

She laughed, and took his arm. "You dear old Jim, you talk as if you were a hundred. Some day you will be in love yourself. Then you will know what it is. Don't look so sulky. Surely you should be glad to think that, though you are going away, you leave me happier than I have ever been before. Life has been hard for us both, terribly hard and difficult. But it will be different now. You are going to a new world, and I have found one. Here are two chairs; let us sit down and see the smart people go by."

They took their seats amidst a crowd of watchers. The tulip-beds across the road flamed like throbbing rings of fire. A white dust, tremulous cloud of orris-root[9] it seemed, hung in the panting air. The brightly-coloured parasols danced and dipped like monstrous butterflies.

She made her brother talk of himself, his hopes, his prospects. He spoke slowly and with effort. They passed words to each other as players at a game pass counters. Sibyl felt oppressed. She

[9]A powder made from irises, used in perfumes.

could not communicate her joy. A faint smile curving that sullen mouth was all the echo she could win. After some time she became silent. Suddenly she caught a glimpse of golden hair and laughing lips, and in an open carriage with two ladies Dorian Gray drove past.

She started to her feet. "There he is!" she cried.

"Who?" said Jim Vane.

"Prince Charming," she answered, looking after the victoria.[10]

He jumped up, and seized her roughly by the arm. "Show him to me. Which is he? Point him out. I must see him!" he exclaimed; but at that moment the Duke of Berwick's four-in-hand[11] came between, and when it had left the space clear, the carriage had swept out of the Park.

"He is gone," murmured Sibyl, sadly. "I wish you had seen him."

"I wish I had, for as sure as there is a God in heaven, if he ever does you any wrong, I shall kill him."

She looked at him in horror. He repeated his words. They cut the air like a dagger. The people round began to gape. A lady standing close to her tittered.

"Come away, Jim; come away," she whispered. He followed her doggedly as she passed through the crowd. He felt glad at what he had said.

When they reached the Achilles Statue[12] she turned round. There was pity in her eyes that became laughter on her lips. She shook her head at him. "You are foolish, Jim, utterly foolish; a bad-tempered boy, that is all. How can you say such horrible things? You don't know what you are talking about. You are simply jealous and unkind. Ah! I wish you would fall in love. Love makes people good, and what you said was wicked."

"I am sixteen," he answered, "and I know what I am about. Mother is no help to you. She doesn't understand how to look after you. I wish now that I was not going to Australia at all. I have a great mind to chuck the whole thing up. I would, if my articles[13] hadn't been signed."

[10]A four-wheeled carriage with a collapsible hood, named after the Queen.

[11]A four-horse luxury carriage.

[12]Large nude statue of Achilles, erected in honor of the Duke of Wellington in 1822, victor over Napoleon at Waterloo, and made from melted-down French guns.

[13]An apprentice's contract.

"Oh, don't be so serious, Jim. You are like one of the heroes of those silly melodramas Mother used to be so fond of acting in. I am not going to quarrel with you. I have seen him, and oh! to see him is perfect happiness. We won't quarrel. I know you would never harm any one I love, would you?"

"Not as long as you love him, I suppose," was the sullen answer.

"I shall love him for ever!" she cried.

"And he?"

"For ever, too!"

"He had better."

She shrank from him. Then she laughed and put her hand on his arm. He was merely a boy.

At the Marble Arch[14] they hailed an omnibus, which left them close to their shabby home in the Euston Road. It was after five o'clock, and Sibyl had to lie down for a couple of hours before acting. Jim insisted that she should do so. He said that he would sooner part with her when their mother was not present. She would be sure to make a scene, and he detested scenes of every kind.

In Sybil's own room they parted. There was jealousy in the lad's heart, and a fierce murderous hatred of the stranger who, as it seemed to him, had come between them. Yet, when her arms were flung round his neck, and her fingers strayed through his hair, he softened and kissed her with real affection. There were tears in his eyes as he went downstairs.

His mother was waiting for him below. She grumbled at his unpunctuality, as he entered. He made no answer, but sat down to his meagre meal. The flies buzzed round the table, and crawled over the stained cloth. Through the rumble of omnibuses, and the clatter of street-cabs, he could hear the droning voice devouring each minute that was left to him.

After some time, he thrust away his plate, and put his head in his hands. He felt that he had a right to know. It should have been told to him before, if it was as he suspected. Leaden with fear, his mother watched him. Words dropped mechanically from her lips. A tattered lace handkerchief twitched in her fingers. When the clock struck six, he got up, and went to the door. Then he turned

[14]London landmark in classical style, originally built for Buckingham Palace and moved in 1851 to the northeast entrance to Hyde Park.

back, and looked at her. Their eyes met. In hers he saw a wild appeal for mercy. It enraged him.

"Mother, I have something to ask you," he said. Her eyes wandered vaguely about the room. She made no answer. "Tell me the truth. I have a right to know. Were you married to my father?" She heaved a deep sigh. It was a sigh of relief. The terrible moment, the moment that night and day, for weeks and months, she had dreaded, had come at last, and yet she felt no terror. Indeed, in some measure it was a disappointment to her. The vulgar directness of the question called for a direct answer. The situation had not been gradually led up to. It was crude. It reminded her of a bad rehearsal.

"No," she answered, wondering at the harsh simplicity of life.

"My father was a scoundrel then!" cried the lad, clenching his fists.

She shook her head. "I knew he was not free. We loved each other very much. If he had lived, he would have made provision for us. Don't speak against him, my son. He was your father, and a gentleman. Indeed, he was highly connected."[15]

An oath broke from his lips. "I don't care for myself," he exclaimed, "but don't let Sibyl. . . . It is a gentleman, isn't it, who is in love with her, or says he is? Highly connected, too, I suppose."

For a moment a hideous sense of humiliation came over the woman. Her head drooped. She wiped her eyes with shaking hands. "Sibyl has a mother," she murmured; "I had none."

The lad was touched. He went towards her, and stooping down he kissed her. "I am sorry if I have pained you by asking about my father," he said, "but I could not help it. I must go now. Good-bye. Don't forget that you will have only one child now to look after, and believe me that if this man wrongs my sister, I will find out who he is, track him down, and kill him like a dog. I swear it."

The exaggerated folly of the threat, the passionate gesture that accompanied it, the mad melodramatic words, made life seem more vivid to her. She was familiar with the atmosphere. She breathed more freely, and for the first time for many months she really admired her son. She would have liked to have continued the scene on the same emotional scale, but he cut her short. Trunks

[15]Had aristocratic friends or relatives.

had to be carried down, and mufflers looked for. The lodging-house drudge bustled in and out. There was the bargaining with the cab-man. The moment was lost in vulgar details. It was with a renewed feeling of disappointment that she waved the tattered lace handkerchief from the window, as her son drove away. She was conscious that a great opportunity had been wasted. She consoled herself by telling Sibyl how desolate she felt her life would be, now that she had only one child to look after. She remembered the phrase. It had pleased her. Of the threat she said nothing. It was vividly and dramatically expressed. She felt that they would all laugh at it some day.

Chapter 6

"I suppose you have heard the news, Basil?" said Lord Henry that evening, as Hallward was shown into a little private room at the Bristol where dinner had been laid for three.

"No, Harry," answered the artist, giving his hat and coat to the bowing waiter. "What is it? Nothing about politics, I hope? They don't interest me. There is hardly a single person in the House of Commons worth painting; though many of them would be the better for a little whitewashing."

"Dorian Gray is engaged to be married," said Lord Henry, watching him as he spoke.

Hallward started, and then frowned. "Dorian engaged to be married!" he cried. "Impossible!"

"It is perfectly true."

"To whom?"

"To some little actress or other."

"I can't believe it. Dorian is far too sensible."

"Dorian is far too wise not to do foolish things now and then, my dear Basil."

"Marriage is hardly a thing that one can do now and then, Harry."

"Except in America," rejoined Lord Henry, languidly. "But I didn't say he was married. I said he was engaged to be married. There is a great difference. I have a distinct remembrance of being married, but I have no recollection at all of being engaged. I am inclined to think that I never was engaged."

"But think of Dorian's birth, and position, and wealth. It would be absurd for him to marry so much beneath him."

"If you want to make him marry this girl tell him that, Basil. He is sure to do it, then. Whenever a man does a thoroughly stupid thing, it is always from the noblest motives."

"I hope the girl is good, Harry. I don't want to see Dorian tied to some vile creature, who might degrade his nature and ruin his intellect."

"Oh, she is better than good—she is beautiful," murmured Lord Henry, sipping a glass of vermouth and orange-bitters. "Dorian says she is beautiful; and he is not often wrong about things of that kind. Your portrait of him has quickened his appreciation of the personal appearance of other people. It has had that excellent effect, amongst others. We are to see her to-night, if that boy doesn't forget his appointment."

"Are you serious?"

"Quite serious, Basil. I should be miserable if I thought I should ever be more serious than I am at the present moment."

"But do you approve of it, Harry?" asked the painter, walking up and down the room and biting his lip. "You can't approve of it, possibly. It is some silly infatuation."

"I never approve, or disapprove, of anything now. It is an absurd attitude to take towards life. We are not sent into the world to air our moral prejudices. I never take any notice of what common people say, and I never interfere with what charming people do. If a personality fascinates me, whatever mode of expression that personality selects is absolutely delightful to me. Dorian Gray falls in love with a beautiful girl who acts Juliet, and proposes to marry her. Why not? If he wedded Messalina[1] he would be none the less interesting. You know I am not a champion of marriage. The real drawback to marriage is that it makes one unselfish. And unselfish people are colourless. They lack individuality. Still, there are certain temperaments that marriage makes more complex. They retain their egotism, and add to it many other egos. They are forced to have more than one life. They become more highly organized, and to be highly organized is, I should fancy, the object of man's existence. Besides, every experience is of value, and, whatever one may say against marriage, it is certainly an experience. I hope that Dorian Gray will make this girl his wife, passionately adore her for six months, and then suddenly become fascinated by some one else. He would be a wonderful study."

"You don't mean a single word of all that, Harry; you know you don't. If Dorian Gray's life were spoiled, no one would be sorrier than yourself. You are much better than you pretend to be."

Lord Henry laughed. "The reason we all like to think so well of others is that we are all afraid for ourselves. The basis of optimism is sheer terror. We think that we are generous because we credit our neighbour with the possession of those virtues that are likely to be

---

[1]Third wife of Roman Emperor Claudius, notorious for sexual appetite, executed in 46 C.E. for treason.

a benefit to us. We praise the banker that we may overdraw our account, and find good qualities in the highwayman in the hope that he may spare our pockets. I mean everything that I have said. I have the greatest contempt for optimism. As for a spoiled life, no life is spoiled but one whose growth is arrested. If you want to mar a nature, you have merely to reform it. As for marriage, of course that would be silly, but there are other and more interesting bonds between men and women. I will certainly encourage them. They have the charm of being fashionable. But here is Dorian himself. He will tell you more than I can."

"My dear Harry, my dear Basil, you must both congratulate me!" said the lad, throwing off his evening cape with its satin-lined wings, and shaking each of his friends by the hand in turn. "I have never been so happy. Of course, it is sudden: all really delightful things are. And yet it seems to me to be the one thing I have been looking for all my life." He was flushed with excitement and pleasure, and looked extraordinarily handsome.

"I hope you will always be very happy, Dorian," said Hallward, "but I don't quite forgive you for not having let me know of your engagement. You let Harry know."

"And I don't forgive you for being late for dinner," broke in Lord Henry, putting his hand on the lad's shoulder, and smiling as he spoke. "Come, let us sit down and try what the new *chef* here is like, and then you will tell us how it all came about."

"There is really not much to tell," cried Dorian, as they took their seats at the small round table. "What happened was simply this. After I left you yesterday evening, Harry, I dressed, had some dinner at that little Italian restaurant in Rupert Street you introduced me to, and went down at eight o'clock to the theatre. Sibyl was playing Rosalind. Of course the scenery was dreadful, and the Orlando absurd. But Sibyl! You should have seen her! When she came on in her boy's clothes she was perfectly wonderful.[2] She wore a moss-coloured velvet jerkin with cinnamon sleeves, slim brown, cross-gartered hose, a dainty little green cap with a hawk's feather caught in a jewel, and a hooded cloak lined with dull red.

[2]In *As You Like It*, Rosalind (originally played by a boy in Shakespeare's day) cross-dresses as the young boy Ganymede, named after a Trojan youth who was so beautiful that Zeus took him to Olympus to be his cup-bearer. The comedy thus foregrounds homoerotic spectacle.

She had never seemed to me more exquisite. She had all the delicate grace of that Tanagra figurine[3] that you have in your studio, Basil. Her hair clustered round her face like dark leaves round a pale rose. As for her acting—well, you shall see her to-night. She is simply a born artist. I sat in the dingy box absolutely enthralled. I forgot that I was in London and in the nineteenth century. I was away with my love in a forest that no man had ever seen. After the performance was over I went behind, and spoke to her. As we were sitting together, suddenly there came into her eyes a look that I had never seen there before. My lips moved towards hers. We kissed each other. I can't describe to you what I felt at that moment. It seemed to me that all my life had been narrowed to one perfect point of rose-coloured joy. She trembled all over, and shook like a white narcissus. Then she flung herself on her knees and kissed my hands. I feel that I should not tell you all this, but I can't help it. Of course our engagement is a dead secret. She has not even told her own mother. I don't know what my guardians will say. Lord Radley is sure to be furious. I don't care. I shall be of age in less than a year, and then I can do what I like. I have been right, Basil, haven't I, to take my love out of poetry, and to find my wife in Shakespeare's plays? Lips that Shakespeare taught to speak have whispered their secret in my ear. I have had the arms of Rosalind around me, and kissed Juliet on the mouth."

"Yes, Dorian, I suppose you were right," said Hallward, slowly.

"Have you seen her to-day?" asked Lord Henry.

Dorian Gray shook his head. "I left her in the forest of Arden, I shall find her in an orchard in Verona."

Lord Henry sipped his champagne in a meditative manner. "At what particular point did you mention the word marriage, Dorian? And what did she say in answer? Perhaps you forgot all about it."

"My dear Harry, I did not treat it as a business transaction, and I did not make any formal proposal. I told her that I loved her, and she said she was not worthy to be my wife. Not worthy! Why, the whole world is nothing to me compared with her."

"Women are wonderfully practical," murmured Lord Henry,— "much more practical than we are. In situations of that kind we often forget to say anything about marriage, and they always remind us."

[3]Terracotta statuette, found in tombs from ancient Greece; Wilde owned one.

Hallward laid his hand upon his arm. "Don't, Harry. You have annoyed Dorian. He is not like other men. He would never bring misery upon any one. His nature is too fine for that."

Lord Henry looked across the table. "Dorian is never annoyed with me," he answered. "I asked the question for the best reason possible, for the only reason, indeed, that excuses one for asking any question—simple curiosity. I have a theory that it is always the women who propose to us, and not we who propose to the women. Except, of course, in middle-class life. But then the middle classes are not modern."

Dorian Gray laughed, and tossed his head. "You are quite incorrigible, Harry; but I don't mind. It is impossible to be angry with you. When you see Sibyl Vane you will feel that the man who could wrong her would be a beast, a beast without a heart. I cannot understand how any one can wish to shame the thing he loves. I love Sibyl Vane. I want to place her on a pedestal of gold, and to see the world worship the woman who is mine. What is marriage? An irrevocable vow. You mock at it for that. Ah! don't mock. It is an irrevocable vow that I want to take. Her trust makes me faithful, her belief makes me good. When I am with her, I regret all that you have taught me. I become different from what you have known me to be. I am changed, and the mere touch of Sibyl Vane's hand makes me forget you and all your wrong, fascinating, poisonous, delightful theories."

"And those are . . . ?" asked Lord Henry, helping himself to some salad.

"Oh, your theories about life, your theories about love, your theories about pleasure. All your theories, in fact, Harry."

"Pleasure is the only thing worth having a theory about," he answered, in his slow, melodious voice. "But I am afraid I cannot claim my theory as my own. It belongs to Nature, not to me. Pleasure is Nature's test, her sign of approval. When we are happy, we are always good, but when we are good, we are not always happy."

"Ah! but what do you mean by good?" cried Basil Hallward.

"Yes," echoed Dorian, leaning back in his chair, and looking at Lord Henry over the heavy clusters of purple-lipped irises that stood in the centre of the table, "what do you mean by good, Harry?"

"To be good is to be in harmony with one's self," he replied, touching the thin stem of his glass with his pale, fine-pointed fingers. "Discord is to be forced to be in harmony with others. One's own life—that is the important thing. As for the lives of one's neighbours, if one wishes to be a prig or a Puritan, one can flaunt one's moral views about them, but they are not one's concern. Besides, Individualism has really the higher aim. Modern morality consists in accepting the standard of one's age. I consider that for any man of culture to accept the standard of his age is a form of the grossest immorality."

"But, surely, if one lives merely for one's self, Harry, one pays a terrible price for doing so?" suggested the painter.

"Yes, we are overcharged for everything nowadays. I should fancy that the real tragedy of the poor is that they can afford nothing but self-denial. Beautiful sins, like beautiful things, are the privilege of the rich."

"One has to pay in other ways but money."

"What sort of ways, Basil?"

"Oh! I should fancy in remorse, in suffering, in . . . well, in the consciousness of degradation."

Lord Henry shrugged his shoulders. "My dear fellow, mediæval art is charming, but mediæval emotions are out of date. One can use them in fiction, of course. But then the only things that one can use in fiction are the things that one has ceased to use in fact. Believe me, no civilized man ever regrets a pleasure, and no uncivilized man ever knows what a pleasure is."

"I know what pleasure is," cried Dorian Gray. "It is to adore some one."

"That is certainly better than being adored," he answered, toying with some fruits. "Being adored is a nuisance. Women treat us just as Humanity treats its gods. They worship us, and are always bothering us to do something for them."

"I should have said that whatever they ask for they had first given to us," murmured the lad, gravely. "They create Love in our natures. They have a right to demand it back."

"That is quite true, Dorian," cried Hallward.

"Nothing is ever quite true," said Lord Henry.

"This is," interrupted Dorian. "You must admit, Harry, that women give to men the very gold of their lives."

"Possibly," he sighed, "but they invariably want it back in such very small change. That is the worry. Women, as some witty

Frenchman once put it, inspire us with the desire to do master-pieces, and always prevent us from carrying them out."

"Harry, you are dreadful! I don't know why I like you so much."

"You will always like me, Dorian," he replied. "Will you have some coffee, you fellows?—Waiter, bring coffee, and *fine-champagne*,[4] and some cigarettes. No: don't mind the cigarettes; I have some. Basil, I can't allow you to smoke cigars. You must have a cigarette. A cigarette is the perfect type of a perfect pleasure. It is exquisite, and it leaves one unsatisfied. What more can one want? Yes, Dorian, you will always be fond of me. I represent to you all the sins you have never had the courage to commit."

"What nonsense you talk, Harry!" cried the lad, taking a light from a fire-breathing silver dragon that the waiter had placed on the table. "Let us go down to the theatre. When Sibyl comes on the stage you will have a new ideal of life. She will represent something to you that you have never known."

"I have known everything," said Lord Henry, with a tired look in his eyes, "but I am always ready for a new emotion. I am afraid, however, that, for me at any rate, there is no such thing. Still, your wonderful girl may thrill me. I love acting. It is so much more real than life. Let us go. Dorian, you will come with me. I am so sorry, Basil, but there is only room for two in the brougham. You must follow us in a hansom."[5]

They got up and put on their coats, sipping their coffee standing. The painter was silent and preoccupied. There was a gloom over him. He could not bear this marriage, and yet it seemed to him to be better than many other things that might have happened. After a few minutes, they all passed downstairs. He drove off by himself, as had been arranged, and watched the flashing lights of the little brougham in front of him. A strange sense of loss came over him. He felt that Dorian Gray would never again be to him all that he had been in the past. Life had come between them. . . . His eyes darkened, and the crowded flaring streets became blurred to his eyes. When the cab drew up at the theatre, it seemed to him that he had grown years older.

---

[4] Old liqueur brandy.
[5] The brougham is a one-horse closed carriage; Basil must hire a cab.

Chapter 7

For some reason or other, the house was crowded that night, and the fat Jew manager who met them at the door was beaming from ear to ear with an oily, tremulous smile. He escorted them to their box with a sort of pompous humility, waving his fat jewelled hands, and talking at the top of his voice. Dorian Gray loathed him more than ever. He felt as if he had come to look for Miranda and had been met by Caliban.[1] Lord Henry, upon the other hand, rather liked him. At least he declared he did, and insisted on shaking him by the hand, and assuring him that he was proud to meet a man who had discovered a real genius and gone bankrupt over a poet. Hallward amused himself with watching the faces in the pit. The heat was terribly oppressive, and the huge sunlight[2] flamed like a monstrous dahlia with petals of yellow fire. The youths in the gallery had taken off their coats and waistcoats and hung them over the side. They talked to each other across the theatre, and shared their oranges with the tawdry girls who sat beside them. Some women were laughing in the pit. Their voices were horribly shrill and discordant. The sound of the popping of corks came from the bar.

"What a place to find one's divinity in!" said Lord Henry.

"Yes!" answered Dorian Gray. "It was here I found her, and she is divine beyond all living things. When she acts you will forget everything. These common, rough people, with their coarse faces and brutal gestures, become quite different when she is on the stage. They sit silently and watch her. They weep and laugh as she wills them to do. She makes them as responsive as a violin. She spiritualizes them, and one feels that they are of the same flesh and blood as one's self."

"The same flesh and blood as one's self! Oh, I hope not!" exclaimed Lord Henry, who was scanning the occupants of the gallery through his opera-glass.

"Don't pay any attention to him, Dorian," said the painter. "I understand what you mean, and I believe in this girl. Any one you love must be marvellous, and any girl who has the effect you de-

---

[1]Miranda is the young, virtuous heroine of Shakespeare's *Tempest*; Wilde cites Caliban in the "Preface."

[2]A group of gas-burners with reflectors, circularly arranged near the ceiling of a large room for lighting and (often) for ventilation through an opening above.

scribe must be fine and noble. To spiritualize one's age—that is something worth doing. If this girl can give a soul to those who have lived without one, if she can create the sense of beauty in people whose lives have been sordid and ugly, if she can strip them of their selfishness and lend them tears for sorrows that are not their own, she is worthy of all your adoration, worthy of the adoration of the world. This marriage is quite right. I did not think so at first, but I admit it now. The gods made Sibyl Vane for you. Without her you would have been incomplete."

"Thanks, Basil," answered Dorian Gray, pressing his hand. "I knew that you would understand me. Harry is so cynical, he terrifies me. But here is the orchestra. It is quite dreadful, but it only lasts for about five minutes. Then the curtain rises, and you will see the girl to whom I am going to give all my life, to whom I have given everything that is good in me."

A quarter of an hour afterwards, amidst an extraordinary turmoil of applause, Sibyl Vane stepped on to the stage. Yes, she was certainly lovely to look at—one of the loveliest creatures, Lord Henry thought, that he had ever seen. There was something of the fawn in her shy grace and startled eyes. A faint blush, like the shadow of a rose in a mirror of silver, came to her cheeks as she glanced at the crowded, enthusiastic house. She stepped back a few paces, and her lips seemed to tremble. Basil Hallward leaped to his feet and began to applaud. Motionless, and as one in a dream, sat Dorian Gray, gazing at her. Lord Henry peered through his glasses, murmuring, "Charming! charming!"

The scene was the hall of Capulet's house, and Romeo in his pilgrim's dress had entered with Mercutio and his other friends. The band, such as it was, struck up a few bars of music, and the dance began. Through the crowd of ungainly, shabbily-dressed actors, Sibyl Vane moved like a creature from a finer world. Her body swayed, while she danced, as a plant sways in the water. The curves of her throat were the curves of a white lily. Her hands seemed to be made of cool ivory.

Yet she was curiously listless. She showed no sign of joy when her eyes rested on Romeo. The few words she had to speak—

Good pilgrim, you do wrong your hand too much,
Which mannerly devotion shows in this;

> *For saints have hands that pilgrims' hands do touch,*
> *And palm to palm is holy palmers' kiss—*[3]

with the brief dialogue that follows, were spoken in a thoroughly artificial manner. The voice was exquisite, but from the point of view of tone it was absolutely false. It was wrong in colour. It took away all the life from the verse. It made the passion unreal.

Dorian Gray grew pale as he watched her. He was puzzled and anxious. Neither of his friends dared to say anything to him. She seemed to them to be absolutely incompetent. They were horribly disappointed.

Yet they felt that the true test of any Juliet is the balcony scene of the second act. They waited for that. If she failed there, there was nothing in her.

She looked charming as she came out in the moonlight. That could not be denied. But the staginess of her acting was unbearable, and grew worse as she went on. Her gestures became absurdly artificial. She overemphasized everything that she had to say. The beautiful passage—

> *Thou knowest the mask of night is on my face,*
> *Else would a maiden blush bepaint my cheek*
> *For that which thou hast heard me speak to-night—*[4]

was declaimed with the painful precision of a school-girl who has been taught to recite by some second-rate professor of elocution.[5] When she leaned over the balcony and came to those wonderful lines—

> *Although I joy in thee,*
> *I have no joy of this contract to-night:*
> *It is too rash, too unadvised, too sudden;*

---

[3]Romeo, having compared Juliet to a sacred shrine at their first meeting and touched her hand, lets her know that he would like to kiss her as well. She responds that, for true pilgrims, touching "palm to palm" counts as a kiss. Their dialogue (1.5) is set in the form of a sonnet.

[4]Juliet claims to be embarrassed that Romeo has overheard her confession of love for him (2.2.85–87).

[5]Speech teacher (not necessarily employed by a college or university).

Too like the lightning, which doth cease to be
Ere one can say, "It lightens." Sweet, good-night!
This bud of love by summer's ripening breath
May prove a beauteous flower when next we meet—[6]

she spoke the words as though they conveyed no meaning to her. It was not nervousness. Indeed, so far from being nervous, she was absolutely self-contained. It was simply bad art. She was a complete failure.

Even the common, uneducated audience of the pit and gallery lost their interest in the play. They got restless, and began to talk loudly and to whistle. The Jew manager, who was standing at the back of the dress-circle, stamped and swore with rage. The only person unmoved was the girl herself.

When the second act was over there came a storm of hisses, and Lord Henry got up from his chair and put on his coat. "She is quite beautiful, Dorian," he said, "but she can't act. Let us go."

"I am going to see the play through," answered the lad, in a hard, bitter voice. "I am awfully sorry that I have made you waste an evening, Harry. I apologize to you both."

"My dear Dorian, I should think Miss Vane was ill," interrupted Hallward. "We will come some other night."

"I wish she were ill," he rejoined. "But she seems to me to be simply callous and cold. She has entirely altered. Last night she was a great artist. This evening she is merely a commonplace, mediocre actress."

"Don't talk like that about any one you love, Dorian. Love is a more wonderful thing than Art."

"They are both simply forms of imitation," remarked Lord Henry. "But do let us go. Dorian, you must not stay here any longer. It is not good for one's morals to see bad acting. Besides, I don't suppose you will want your wife to act. So what does it matter if she plays Juliet like a wooden doll? She is very lovely, and if she knows as little about life as she does about acting, she will be a delightful experience. There are only two kinds of people who are really fascinating—people who know absolutely everything, and people who know absolutely nothing. Good heavens, my dear boy,

[6]Juliet laments how quickly she and Romeo have confessed their love for each other and longs that their love will have matured when they meet again (2.2.116–22).

don't look so tragic! The secret of remaining young is never to have an emotion that is unbecoming. Come to the club with Basil and myself. We will smoke cigarettes and drink to the beauty of Sibyl Vane. She is beautiful. What more can you want?"

"Go away, Harry," cried the lad. "I want to be alone. Basil, you must go. Ah! can't you see that my heart is breaking?" The hot tears came to his eyes. His lips trembled, and, rushing to the back of the box, he leaned up against the wall, hiding his face in his hands.

"Let us go, Basil," said Lord Henry with a strange tenderness in his voice; and the two young men passed out together.

A few moments afterwards the footlights flared up, and the curtain rose on the third act. Dorian Gray went back to his seat. He looked pale, and proud, and indifferent. The play dragged on, and seemed interminable. Half of the audience went out, tramping in heavy boots, and laughing. The whole thing was a *fiasco*. The last act was played to almost empty benches. The curtain went down on a titter, and some groans.

As soon as it was over, Dorian Gray rushed behind the scenes into the greenroom. The girl was standing there alone, with a look of triumph on her face. Her eyes were lit with an exquisite fire. There was a radiance about her. Her parted lips were smiling over some secret of their own.

When he entered, she looked at him, and an expression of infinite joy came over her. "How badly I acted to-night, Dorian!" she cried.

"Horribly!" he answered, gazing at her in amazement—"horribly! It was dreadful. Are you ill? You have no idea what it was. You have no idea what I suffered."

The girl smiled. "Dorian," she answered, lingering over his name with long-drawn music in her voice, as though it were sweeter than honey to the red petals of her mouth—"Dorian, you should have understood. But you understand now, don't you?"

"Understand what?" he asked, angrily.

"Why I was so bad to-night. Why I shall always be bad. Why I shall never act well again."

He shrugged his shoulders. "You are ill, I suppose. When you are ill you shouldn't act. You make yourself ridiculous. My friends were bored. I was bored."

She seemed not to listen to him. She was transfigured with joy. An ecstasy of happiness dominated her.

"Dorian, Dorian," she cried, "before I knew you, acting was the one reality of my life. It was only in the theatre that I lived. I thought that it was all true. I was Rosalind one night, and Portia the other. The joy of Beatrice was my joy, and the sorrows of Cordelia were mine also.[7] I believed in everything. The common people who acted with me seemed to me to be godlike. The painted scenes were my world. I knew nothing but shadows, and I thought them real. You came—oh, my beautiful love!—and you freed my soul from prison. You taught me what reality really is. To-night, for the first time in my life, I saw through the hollowness, the sham, the silliness of the empty pageant in which I had always played. To-night, for the first time, I became conscious that the Romeo was hideous, and old, and painted, that the moonlight in the orchard was false, that the scenery was vulgar, and that the words I had to speak were unreal, were not my words, were not what I wanted to say. You had brought me something higher, something of which all art is but a reflection. You had made me understand what love really is. My love! my love! Prince Charming! Prince of life! I have grown sick of shadows.[8] You are more to me than all art can ever be. What have I to do with the puppets of a play? When I came on to-night, I could not understand how it was that everything had gone from me. I thought that I was going to be wonderful. I found that I could do nothing. Suddenly it dawned on my soul what it all meant. The knowledge was exquisite to me. I heard them hissing, and I smiled. What could they know of love such as ours? Take me away, Dorian—take me away with you, where we can be quite alone. I hate the stage. I might mimic a passion that I do not feel, but I cannot mimic one that burns me like fire. Oh, Dorian, Dorian, you understand now what it signifies? Even if I could do it, it would be profanation for me to play at being in love. You have made me see that."

He flung himself down on the sofa, and turned away his face. "You have killed my love," he muttered.

She looked at him in wonder, and laughed. He made no answer. She came across to him, and with her little fingers stroked his hair.

---

[7]The heroines of *As You Like It*, *The Merchant of Venice*, *Much Ado About Nothing*, and *King Lear*.

[8]Tennyson's "The Lady of Shalott": "I am half sick of shadows" (79). The Lady, who sees the world only in a mirror, grows weary of its images and longs to enter reality to meet the knight she's loved from afar (Sir Lancelot)—a fatal adventure.

She knelt down and pressed his hands to her lips. He drew them away, and a shudder ran through him.

Then he leaped up, and went to the door. "Yes," he cried, "you have killed my love. You used to stir my imagination. Now you don't even stir my curiosity. You simply produce no effect. I loved you because you were marvellous, because you had genius and intellect, because you realized the dreams of great poets and gave shape and substance to the shadows of art. You have thrown it all away. You are shallow and stupid. My God! how mad I was to love you! What a fool I have been! You are nothing to me now. I will never see you again. I will never think of you. I will never mention your name. You don't know what you were to me, once. Why, once . . . Oh, I can't bear to think of it! I wish I had never laid eyes upon you! You have spoiled the romance of my life. How little you can know of love, if you say it mars your art! Without your art you are nothing. I would have made you famous, splendid, magnificent. The world would have worshipped you, and you would have borne my name. What are you now? A third-rate actress with a pretty face."

The girl grew white, and trembled. She clenched her hands together, and her voice seemed to catch in her throat. "You are not serious, Dorian?" she murmured. "You are acting."

"Acting! I leave that to you. You do it so well," he answered, bitterly.

She rose from her knees, and, with a piteous expression of pain in her face, came across the room to him. She put her hand upon his arm, and looked into his eyes. He thrust her back. "Don't touch me!" he cried.

A low moan broke from her, and she flung herself at his feet, and lay there like a trampled flower. "Dorian, Dorian, don't leave me!" she whispered. "I am so sorry I didn't act well. I was thinking of you all the time. But I will try—indeed, I will try. It came so suddenly across me, my love for you. I think I should never have known it if you had not kissed me—if we had not kissed each other. Kiss me again, my love. Don't go away from me. I couldn't bear it. Oh! don't go away from me. My brother . . . No; never mind. He didn't mean it. He was in jest. . . . But you, oh! can't you forgive me for to-night? I will work so hard, and try to improve. Don't be cruel to me because I love you better than anything in the world. After all, it is only once that I have not pleased you. But you are quite right, Dorian. I should have shown myself more of an artist. It was foolish of me; and yet I couldn't help it. Oh, don't leave me, don't leave me." A fit of passionate sobbing choked her. She crouched on the floor like a wounded thing, and Dorian Gray, with his beautiful eyes, looked down at her, and his chiselled lips curled in exquisite disdain. There is always something ridiculous about the emotions of people whom one has ceased to love. Sibyl Vane seemed to him to be absurdly melodramatic. Her tears and sobs annoyed him.

"I am going," he said at last, in his calm, clear voice. "I don't wish to be unkind, but I can't see you again. You have disappointed me."

She wept silently, and made no answer, but crept nearer. Her little hands stretched blindly out, and appeared to be seeking for him. He turned on his heel, and left the room. In a few moments he was out of the theatre.

Where he went to he hardly knew. He remembered wandering through dimly-lit streets, past gaunt black-shadowed archways and evil-looking houses. Women with hoarse voices and harsh laughter had called after him. Drunkards had reeled by, cursing and chattering to themselves like monstrous apes. He had seen grotesque children huddled upon door-steps, and heard shrieks and oaths from gloomy courts.

As the dawn was just breaking he found himself close to Covent Garden.[9] The darkness lifted, and, flushed with faint fires, the sky hollowed itself into a perfect pearl. Huge carts filled with nodding lilies rumbled slowly down the polished empty street. The air was heavy with the perfume of the flowers, and their beauty seemed to bring him an anodyne for his pain. He followed into the market, and watched the men unloading their waggons. A white-smocked carter offered him some cherries. He thanked him, wondered why he refused to accept any money for them, and began to eat them listlessly. They had been plucked at midnight, and the coldness of the moon had entered into them. A long line of boys carrying crates of striped tulips, and of yellow and red roses, defiled[10] in front of him, threading their way

[9]The main fruit, vegetable, and flower market; "the show of fruits and flowers is one of the finest in the world, presenting a gorgeous array of colours and diffusing a delicious fragrance" (Baedeker 180).

[10]Marched in a line.

through the huge, jade-green piles of vegetables. Under the portico, with its grey sun-bleached pillars, loitered a troop of draggled bare-headed girls, waiting for the auction to be over. Others crowded round the swinging doors of the coffee-house in the Piazza.[11] The heavy cart-horses slipped and stamped upon the rough stones, shaking their bells and trappings. Some of the drivers were lying asleep on a pile of sacks. Iris-necked and pink-footed, the pigeons ran about picking up seeds.

After a little while, he hailed a hansom, and drove home. For a few moments he loitered upon the doorstep, looking round at the silent Square,[12] with its blank close-shuttered windows, and its staring blinds. The sky was pure opal now, and the roofs of the houses glistened like silver against it. From some chimney opposite a thin wreath of smoke was rising. It curled, a violet riband, through the nacre[13]-coloured air.

In the huge gilt Venetian lantern, spoil of some Doge's[14] barge, that hung from the ceiling of the great oak-panelled hall of entrance, lights were still burning from three flickering jets: thin blue petals of flame they seemed, rimmed with white fire. He turned them out, and, having thrown his hat and cape on the table, passed through the library towards the door of his bed-room, a large octagonal chamber on the ground floor that, in his new-born feeling for luxury, he had just had decorated for him-self, and hung with some curious Renaissance tapestries that had been discovered stored in a disused attic at Selby Royal.[15] As he was turning the handle of the door, his eye fell upon the portrait Basil Hallward had painted of him. He started back as if in sur-prise. Then he went on into his own room, looking somewhat puzzled. After he had taken the buttonhole out of his coat, he seemed to hesitate. Finally he came back, went over to the pic-ture, and examined it. In the dim arrested light that struggled through the cream-coloured silk blinds, the face appeared to

[11] Arcade on the northeast side of Covent Garden.

[12] On which Dorian's residence abuts.

[13] Mother-of-pearl.

[14] Chief magistrate of Venice when it was the commercial center of Europe. By the 19th c., Venice was the iconic beautiful city in decay, with a long history of homo-erotic adventure.

[15] Country estate of Dorian's family.

him to be a little changed. The expression looked different. One would have said that there was a touch of cruelty in the mouth. It was certainly strange.

He turned round, and, walking to the window, drew up the blind. The bright dawn flooded the room, and swept the fantastic shadows into dusky corners, where they lay shuddering. But the strange expression that he had noticed in the face of the portrait seemed to linger there, to be more intensified even. The quivering, ardent sunlight showed him the lines of cruelty round the mouth as clearly as if he had been looking into a mirror after he had done some dreadful thing.

He winced, and, taking up from the table an oval glass framed in ivory Cupids, one of Lord Henry's many presents to him, glanced hurriedly into its polished depths. No line like that warped his red lips. What did it mean?

He rubbed his eyes, and came close to the picture, and examined it again. There were no signs of any change when he looked into the actual painting, and yet there was no doubt that the whole expression had altered. It was not a mere fancy of his own. The thing was horribly apparent.

He threw himself into a chair, and began to think. Suddenly there flashed across his mind what he had said in Basil Hallward's studio the day the picture had been finished. Yes, he remembered it perfectly. He had uttered a mad wish that he himself might remain young, and the portrait grow old; that his own beauty might be untarnished, and the face on the canvas bear the burden of his passions and his sins; that the painted image might be seared with the lines of suffering and thought, and that he might keep all the delicate bloom and loveliness of his then just conscious boyhood. Surely his wish had not been fulfilled? Such things were impossible. It seemed monstrous even to think of them. And, yet, there was the picture before him, with the touch of cruelty in the mouth.

Cruelty! Had he been cruel? It was the girl's fault, not his. He had dreamed of her as a great artist, had given his love to her because he had thought her great. Then she had disappointed him. She had been shallow and unworthy. And, yet, a feeling of infinite regret came over him, as he thought of her lying at his feet sobbing like a little child. He remembered with what callousness he had watched her. Why had he been made like that? Why had such a soul been given to him? But he had suffered also. During the three terrible hours that the play had lasted, he had lived centuries of pain, æon upon æon of torture. His life was well worth hers. She had marred him for a moment, if he had wounded her for an age. Besides, women were better suited to bear sorrow than men. They lived on their emotions. They only thought of their emotions. When they took lovers, it was merely to have some one with whom they could have scenes. Lord Henry had told him that, and Lord Henry knew what women were. Why should he trouble about Sibyl Vane? She was nothing to him now.

But the picture? What was he to say of that? It held the secret of his life, and told his story. It had taught him to love his own beauty. Would it teach him to loathe his own soul? Would he ever look at it again?

No; it was merely an illusion wrought on the troubled senses. The horrible night that he had passed had left phantoms behind it. Suddenly there had fallen upon his brain that tiny scarlet speck that makes men mad. The picture had not changed. It was folly to think so.

Yet it was watching him, with its beautiful marred face and its cruel smile. Its bright hair gleamed in the early sunlight. Its blue eyes met his own. A sense of infinite pity, not for himself, but for the painted image of himself, came over him. It had altered already, and would alter more. Its gold would wither into grey. Its red and white roses would die. For every sin that he committed, a stain would fleck and wreck its fairness. But he would not sin. The picture, changed or unchanged, would be to him the visible emblem of conscience. He would resist temptation. He would not see Lord Henry any more—would not, at any rate, listen to those subtle poisonous theories that in Basil Hallward's garden had first stirred within him the passion for impossible things. He would go back to Sibyl Vane, make her amends, marry her, try to love her again. Yes, it was his duty to do so. She must have suffered more than he had. Poor child! He had been selfish and cruel to her. The fascination that she had exercised over him would return. They would be happy together. His life with her would be beautiful and pure.

He got up from his chair, and drew a large screen right in front of the portrait, shuddering as he glanced at it. "How horrible!" he murmured to himself, and he walked across to the window and opened it. When he stepped out on to the grass, he drew a deep breath. The fresh morning air seemed to drive away all his sombre passions. He thought only of Sibyl. A faint echo of his love came back to him. He repeated her name over and over again. The birds that were singing in the dew-drenched garden seemed to be telling the flowers about her.

Chapter 8

It was long past noon when he awoke. His valet had crept several times on tiptoe into the room to see if he was stirring, and had wondered what made his young master sleep so late. Finally his bell sounded, and Victor came in softly with a cup of tea, and a pile of letters, on a small tray of old Sèvres[1] china, and drew back the olive-satin curtains, with their shimmering blue lining, that hung in front of the three tall windows.

"Monsieur has well slept this morning," he said, smiling.

"What o'clock is it, Victor?" asked Dorian Gray, drowsily.

"One hour and a quarter, Monsieur."

How late it was! He sat up, and having sipped some tea, turned over his letters. One of them was from Lord Henry, and had been brought by hand that morning. He hesitated for a moment, and then put it aside. The others he opened listlessly. They contained the usual collection of cards, invitations to dinner, tickets for private views, programmes of charity concerts, and the like, that are showered on fashionable young men every morning during the season.[2] There was a rather heavy bill, for a chased silver Louis-Quinze toilet-set,[3] that he had not yet had the courage to send on to his guardians, who were extremely old-fashioned people and did not realize that we live in an age when unnecessary things are our only necessities; and there were several very courteously worded communications from Jermyn Street money-lenders[4] offering to advance any sum of money at a moment's notice and at the most reasonable rates of interest.

After about ten minutes he got up, and, throwing on an elaborate dressing-gown of silk-embroidered cashmere wool, passed into the onyx-paved bathroom. The cool water refreshed him after his long sleep. He seemed to have forgotten all that he had gone

---

[1]Elegant French porcelain.

[2]The months from Easter to midsummer when fashionable society was in town, and busy with dinners, balls, and parties. Wilde sets Chapters 1–10 "during the season." In August, after Parliament ended, the rich decamped to their country estates.

[3]"Chased silver" has been engraved in relief; "Louis-Quinze" refers to Louis XV (1715–74) of France and the rococo style of his reign; a toilet-set is a dressing-table array of combs, brushes, and other articles for washing and grooming.

[4]Street with numerous hotels and lodging-houses, often occupied by young spendthrift bachelors, who found themselves seeking money-lenders.

through. A dim sense of having taken part in some strange tragedy came to him once or twice, but there was the unreality of a dream about it.

As soon as he was dressed, he went into the library and sat down to a light French breakfast,[5] that had been laid out for him on a small round table close to the open window. It was an exquisite day. The warm air seemed laden with spices. A bee flew in, and buzzed round the blue-dragon bowl that, filled with sulphur-yellow roses, stood before him. He felt perfectly happy.

Suddenly his eye fell on the screen that he had placed in front of the portrait, and he started.

"Too cold for Monsieur?" asked his valet, putting an omelette on the table. "I shut the window?"

Dorian shook his head. "I am not cold," he murmured.

Was it all true? Had the portrait really changed? Or had it been simply his own imagination that had made him see a look of evil where there had been a look of joy? Surely a painted canvas could not alter? The thing was absurd. It would serve as a tale to tell Basil some day. It would make him smile.

And, yet, how vivid was his recollection of the whole thing! First in the dim twilight, and then in the bright dawn, he had seen the touch of cruelty round the warped lips. He almost dreaded his valet leaving the room. He knew that when he was alone he would have to examine the portrait. He was afraid of certainty. When the coffee and cigarettes had been brought and the man turned to go, he felt a wild desire to tell him to remain. As the door was closing behind him he called him back. The man stood waiting for his orders. Dorian looked at him for a moment. "I am not at home to any one, Victor," he said, with a sigh. The man bowed and retired.

Then he rose from the table, lit a cigarette, and flung himself down on a luxuriously-cushioned couch that stood facing the screen. The screen was an old one, of gilt Spanish leather, stamped and wrought with a rather florid Louis-Quatorze pattern. He scanned it curiously, wondering if ever before it had concealed the secret of a man's life.

Should he move it aside, after all? Why not let it stay there? What was the use of knowing? If the thing was true, it was terrible.

[5]Rolls and coffee, as opposed to the much heavier and substantial English breakfast.

If it was not true, why trouble about it? But what if, by some fate or deadlier chance, eyes other than his spied behind, and saw the horrible change? What should he do if Basil Hallward came and asked to look at his own picture? Basil would be sure to do that. No; the thing had to be examined, and at once. Anything would be better than this dreadful state of doubt.

He got up, and locked both doors. At least he would be alone when he looked upon the mask of his shame. Then he drew the screen aside and saw himself face to face. It was perfectly true. The portrait had altered.

As he often remembered afterwards, and always with no small wonder, he found himself at first gazing at the portrait with a feeling of almost scientific interest. That such a change should have taken place was incredible to him. And yet it was a fact. Was there some subtle affinity between the chemical atoms, that shaped themselves into form and colour on the canvas, and the soul that was within him? Could it be that what that soul thought, they realized?—that what it dreamed, they made true? Or was there some other, more terrible reason? He shuddered, and felt afraid, and, going back to the couch, lay there, gazing at the picture in sickened horror.

One thing, however, he felt that it had done for him. It had made him conscious how unjust, how cruel, he had been to Sibyl Vane. It was not too late to make reparation for that. She could still be his wife. His unreal and selfish love would yield to some higher influence, would be transformed into some nobler passion, and the portrait that Basil Hallward had painted of him would be a guide to him through life, would be to him what holiness is to some, and conscience to others, and the fear of God to us all. There were opiates for remorse, drugs that could lull the moral sense to sleep. But here was a visible symbol of the degradation of sin. Here was an ever-present sign of the ruin men brought upon their souls.

Three o'clock struck, and four, and the half-hour rang its double chime, but Dorian Gray did not stir. He was trying to gather up the scarlet threads of life, and to weave them into a pattern; to find his way through the sanguine labyrinth of passion through which he was wandering. He did not know what to do, or what to think. Finally, he went over to the table, and wrote a passionate letter to the girl he had loved, imploring her forgiveness, and accusing himself of madness. He covered page after page with wild words of sorrow and wilder words of pain. There is a luxury in self-reproach. When we blame ourselves we feel that no one else has a right to blame us. It is the confession, not the priest, that gives us absolution. When Dorian had finished the letter, he felt that he had been forgiven.

Suddenly there came a knock to the door, and he heard Lord Henry's voice outside. "My dear boy, I must see you. Let me in at once. I can't bear your shutting yourself up like this."

He made no answer at first, but remained quite still. The knocking still continued, and grew louder. Yes, it was better to let Lord Henry in, and to explain to him the new life he was going to lead, to quarrel with him if it became necessary to quarrel, to part if parting was inevitable. He jumped up, drew the screen hastily across the picture, and unlocked the door.

"I am so sorry for it all, Dorian," said Lord Henry, as he entered. "But you must not think too much about it."

"Do you mean about Sibyl Vane?" asked the lad.

"Yes, of course," answered Lord Henry, sinking into a chair, and slowly pulling off his yellow gloves. "It is dreadful, from one point of view, but it was not your fault. Tell me, did you go behind and see her, after the play was over?"

"Yes."

"I felt sure you had. Did you make a scene with her?"

"I was brutal, Harry—perfectly brutal. But it is all right now. I am not sorry for anything that has happened. It has taught me to know myself better."

"Ah, Dorian, I am so glad you take it in that way! I was afraid I would find you plunged in remorse, and tearing that nice curly hair of yours."

"I have got through all that," said Dorian, shaking his head, and smiling. "I am perfectly happy now. I know what conscience is, to begin with. It is not what you told me it was. It is the divinest thing in us. Don't sneer at it, Harry, any more—at least not before me. I want to be good. I can't bear the idea of my soul being hideous."

"A very charming artistic basis for ethics, Dorian! I congratulate you on it. But how are you going to begin?"

"By marrying Sibyl Vane."

"Marrying Sibyl Vane!" cried Lord Henry, standing up, and looking at him in perplexed amazement. "But, my dear Dorian—" "Yes, Harry, I know what you are going to say. Something dreadful about marriage. Don't say it. Don't ever say things of that kind to me again. Two days ago I asked Sibyl to marry me. I am not going to break my word to her. She is to be my wife."

"Your wife! Dorian! . . . Didn't you get my letter? I wrote to you this morning, and sent the note down, by my own man."

"Your letter? Oh, yes, I remember. I have not read it yet, Harry. I was afraid there might be something in it that I wouldn't like. You cut life to pieces with your epigrams."

"You know nothing then?"

"What do you mean?"

Lord Henry walked across the room, and, sitting down by Dorian Gray, took both his hands in his own, and held them tightly. "Dorian," he said, "my letter—don't be frightened—was to tell you that Sibyl Vane is dead."

A cry of pain broke from the lad's lips, and he leaped to his feet, tearing his hands away from Lord Henry's grasp. "Dead! Sibyl dead! It is not true! It is a horrible lie! How dare you say it?"

"It is quite true, Dorian," said Lord Henry, gravely. "It is in all the morning papers. I wrote down to you to ask you not to see any one till I came. There will have to be an inquest, of course, and you must not be mixed up in it. Things like that make a man fashionable in Paris. But in London people are so prejudiced. Here, one should never make one's *début* with a scandal. One should reserve that to give an interest to one's old age. I suppose they don't know your name at the theatre? If they don't, it is all right. Did any one see you going round to her room? That is an important point."

Dorian did not answer for a few moments. He was dazed with horror. Finally he stammered, in a stifled voice, "Harry, did you say an inquest? What did you mean by that? Did Sibyl—? Oh, Harry, I can't bear it! But be quick. Tell me everything at once."

"I have no doubt it was not an accident, Dorian, though it must be put in that way to the public. It seems that as she was leaving the theatre with her mother, about half-past twelve or so, she said she had forgotten something upstairs. They waited some time for her, but she did not come down again. They ultimately found her lying dead on the floor of her dressing-room. She had swallowed something by mistake, some dreadful thing they use at theatres. I don't know what it was, but it had either prussic acid[6] or white lead[7] in it. I should fancy it was prussic acid, as she seems to have died instantaneously."

"Harry, Harry, it is terrible!" cried the lad.

"Yes; it is very tragic, of course, but you must not get yourself mixed up in it. I see by *The Standard*[8] that she was seventeen. I should have thought she was almost younger than that. She looked such a child, and seemed to know so little about acting. Dorian, you mustn't let this thing get on your nerves. You must come and dine with me, and afterwards we will look in at the Opera. It is a Patti[9] night, and everybody will be there. You can come to my sister's box. She has got some smart women with her."

"So I have murdered Sibyl Vane," said Dorian Gray, half to himself—"murdered her as surely as if I had cut her little throat with a knife. Yet the roses are not less lovely for all that. The birds sing just as happily in my garden. And to-night I am to dine with you, and then go on to the Opera, and sup somewhere, I suppose, afterwards. How extraordinarily dramatic life is! If I had read all this in a book, Harry, I think I would have wept over it. Somehow, now that it has happened actually, and to me, it seems far too wonderful for tears. Here is the first passionate love-letter I have ever written in my life. Strange, that my first passionate love-letter should have been addressed to a dead girl. Can they feel, I wonder, those white silent people we call the dead? Sibyl! Can she feel, or know, or listen? Oh, Harry, how I loved her once! It seems years ago to me now. She was everything to me. Then came that dreadful night—was it really only last night?—when she played so badly, and my heart almost broke. She explained it all to me. It was terribly pathetic. But I was not moved a bit. I thought her shallow.

[6]Extremely poisonous form of cyanide; a favorite for suicide in Victorian novels. Popular poet Letitia Elizabeth Landon (L. E. L.) died from it in 1838.

[7]Lead compound used in paint and makeup.

[8]One of the penny newspapers, *The Standard* was noted for its conservative viewpoint (Brown 183–85).

[9]Italian soprano, Adelina Patti (1843–1919), a favorite at the Covent Garden opera: "Certainly no operatic artist I ever saw or heard, and they were not a few, approached this Adelina, veritable nightingale from Olympus. The best blessings of the gods were hers—beauty in a high degree, voice incomparable, acting excellent, vivacity overflowing" (Bennett 331).

Suddenly something happened that made me afraid. I can't tell you what it was, but it was terrible. I said I would go back to her. I felt I had done wrong. And now she is dead. My God! my God! Harry, what shall I do? You don't know the danger I am in, and there is nothing to keep me straight. She would have done that for me. She had no right to kill herself. It was selfish of her."

"My dear Dorian," answered Lord Henry, taking a cigarette from his case, and producing a gold-latten[10] matchbox, "the only way a woman can ever reform a man is by boring him so completely that he loses all possible interest in life. If you had married this girl you would have been wretched. Of course you would have treated her kindly. One can always be kind to people about whom one cares nothing. But she would have soon found out that you were absolutely indifferent to her. And when a woman finds that out about her husband, she either becomes dreadfully dowdy, or wears very smart bonnets that some other woman's husband has to pay for. I say nothing about the social mistake, which would have been abject, which, of course, I would not have allowed, but I assure you that in any case the whole thing would have been an absolute failure."

"I suppose it would," muttered the lad, walking up and down the room, and looking horribly pale. "But I thought it was my duty. It is not my fault that this terrible tragedy has prevented my doing what was right. I remember your saying once that there is a fatality about good resolutions—that they are always made too late. Mine certainly were."

"Good resolutions are useless attempts to interfere with scientific laws. Their origin is pure vanity. Their result is absolutely *nil*. They give us, now and then, some of those luxurious sterile emotions that have a certain charm for the weak. That is all that can be said for them. They are simply cheques that men draw on a bank where they have no account."

"Harry," cried Dorian Gray, coming over and sitting down beside him, "why is it that I cannot feel this tragedy as much as I want to? I don't think I am heartless. Do you?"

"You have done too many foolish things during the last fortnight to be entitled to give yourself that name, Dorian," answered Lord Henry, with his sweet melancholy smile.

[10]Made of gold hammered into thin sheets.

The lad frowned. "I don't like that explanation, Harry," he rejoined, "but I am glad you don't think I am heartless. I am nothing of the kind. I know I am not. And yet I must admit that this thing that has happened does not affect me as it should. It seems to me to be simply like a wonderful ending to a wonderful play. It has all the terrible beauty of a Greek tragedy, a tragedy in which I took a great part, but by which I have not been wounded."

"It is an interesting question," said Lord Henry, who found an exquisite pleasure in playing on the lad's unconscious egotism—"an extremely interesting question. I fancy that the true explanation is this. It often happens that the real tragedies of life occur in such an inartistic manner that they hurt us by their crude violence, their absolute incoherence, their absurd want of meaning, their entire lack of style. They affect us just as vulgarity affects us. They give us an impression of sheer brute force, and we revolt against that. Sometimes, however, a tragedy that possesses artistic elements of beauty crosses our lives. If these elements of beauty are real, the whole thing simply appeals to our sense of dramatic effect. Suddenly we find that we are no longer the actors, but the spectators of the play. Or rather we are both. We watch ourselves, and the mere wonder of the spectacle enthralls us. In the present case, what is it that has really happened? Some one has killed herself for love of you. I wish that I had ever had such an experience. It would have made me in love with love for the rest of my life. The people who have adored me—there have not been very many, but there have been some—have always insisted on living on, long after I had ceased to care for them, or they to care for me. They have become stout and tedious, and when I meet them they go in at once for reminiscences. That awful memory of woman! What a fearful thing it is! And what an utter intellectual stagnation it reveals! One should absorb the colour of life, but one should never remember its details. Details are always vulgar."

"I must sow poppies in my garden," sighed Dorian.[11]

"There is no necessity," rejoined his companion. "Life has always poppies in her hands. Of course, now and then things linger. I once wore nothing but violets all through one season, as a form of artistic mourning for a romance that would not die. Ultimately,

[11]Poppy juice has narcotic properties, and the flower was a conventional image for sleep and forgetting.

however, it did die. I forget what killed it. I think it was her proposing to sacrifice the whole world for me. That is always a dreadful moment. It fills one with the terror of eternity. Well—would you believe it?—a week ago, at Lady Hampshire's, I found myself seated at dinner next the lady in question, and she insisted on going over the whole thing again, and digging up the past, and raking up the future. I had buried my romance in a bed of asphodel.[12] She dragged it out again, and assured me that I had spoiled her life. I am bound to state that she ate an enormous dinner, so I did not feel any anxiety. But what a lack of taste she showed! The one charm of the past is that it is the past. But women never know when the curtain has fallen. They always want a sixth act, and as soon as the interest of the play is entirely over they propose to continue it. If they were allowed their own way, every comedy would have a tragic ending, and every tragedy would culminate in a farce. They are charmingly artificial, but they have no sense of art. You are more fortunate than I am. I assure you, Dorian, that not one of the women I have known would have done for me what Sibyl Vane did for you. Ordinary women always console themselves. Some of them do it by going in for sentimental colours. Never trust a woman who wears mauve, whatever her age may be, or a woman over thirty-five who is fond of pink ribbons. It always means that they have a history. Others find a great consolation in suddenly discovering the good qualities of their husbands. They flaunt their conjugal felicity in one's face, as if it were the most fascinating of sins. Religion consoles some. Its mysteries have all the charm of a flirtation, a woman once told me; and I can quite understand it. Besides, nothing makes one so vain as being told that one is a sinner. Conscience makes egotists of us all.[13] Yes; there is really no end to the consolations that women find in modern life. Indeed, I have not mentioned the most important one."

"What is that, Harry?" said the lad, listlessly.

"Oh, the obvious consolation. Taking some one else's admirer when one loses one's own. In good society that always whitewashes

---

[12]A plant with white flowers; in Greek mythology, supposed to cover the fields of Elysium (the paradisal world of the afterlife). To enter Elysium, spirits had to drink from the river Lethe, which made them forget their earthly existence.

[13]Another echo of Hamlet's "Thus conscience does make cowards of us all" (see ch. 1, n. 20).

a woman. But really, Dorian, how different Sibyl Vane must have been from all the women one meets! There is something to me quite beautiful about her death. I am glad I am living in a century when such wonders happen. They make one believe in the reality of the things we all play with, such as romance, passion, and love."

"I was terribly cruel to her. You forget that."

"I am afraid that women appreciate cruelty, downright cruelty, more than anything else. They have wonderfully primitive instincts. We have emancipated them, but they remain slaves looking for their masters, all the same. They love being dominated. I am sure you were splendid. I have never seen you really and absolutely angry, but I can fancy how delightful you looked. And, after all, you said something to me the day before yesterday that seemed to me at the time to be merely fanciful, but that I see now was absolutely true, and it holds the key to everything."

"What was that, Harry?"

"You said to me that Sibyl Vane represented to you all the heroines of romance—that she was Desdemona one night, and Ophelia the other; that if she died as Juliet, she came to life as Imogen."

"She will never come to life again now," muttered the lad, burying his face in his hands.

"No, she will never come to life. She has played her last part. But you must think of that lonely death in the tawdry dressing-room simply as a strange lurid fragment from some Jacobean tragedy, as a wonderful scene from Webster, or Ford, or Cyril Tourneur.[14] The girl never really lived, and so she has never really died. To you at least she was always a dream, a phantom that flitted through Shakespeare's plays and left them lovelier for its presence, a reed through which Shakespeare's music sounded richer and more full of joy. The moment she touched actual life, she marred it, and it marred her, and so she passed away. Mourn for Ophelia, if you like. Put ashes on your head because Cordelia was strangled. Cry out against Heaven because the daughter of Brabantio[15] died.

[14]John Webster (1578?–1632?), John Ford (1586–post-1639), Cyril Tourneur (1575?–1626): playwrights during the reign of James I (1566–1625); the term "Jacobean" comes from "Jacobus," the Latin version of "James." Their plays, highly prized by the Aesthetic movement, were noted for their extravagant violence and passion.

[15]Desdemona.

But don't waste your tears over Sibyl Vane. She was less real than they are."

There was a silence. The evening darkened in the room. Noiselessly, and with silver feet, the shadows crept in from the garden. The colours faded wearily out of things.

After some time Dorian Gray looked up. "You have explained me to myself, Harry," he murmured, with something of a sigh of relief. "I felt all that you have said, but somehow I was afraid of it, and I could not express it to myself. How well you know me! But we will not talk again of what has happened. It has been a marvellous experience. That is all. I wonder if life has still in store for me anything as marvellous."

"Life has everything in store for you, Dorian. There is nothing that you, with your extraordinary good looks, will not be able to do."

"But suppose, Harry, I became haggard, and old, and wrinkled? What then?"

"Ah, then," said Lord Henry, rising to go—"then, my dear Dorian, you would have to fight for your victories. As it is, they are brought to you. No, you must keep your good looks. We live in an age that reads too much to be wise, and that thinks too much to be beautiful. We cannot spare you. And now you had better dress, and drive down to the club. We are rather late, as it is."

"I think I shall join you at the Opera, Harry. I feel too tired to eat anything. What is the number of your sister's box?"

"Twenty-seven, I believe. It is on the grand tier.[16] You will see her name on the door. But I am sorry you won't come and dine."

"I don't feel up to it," said Dorian listlessly. "But I am awfully obliged to you for all that you have said to me. You are certainly my best friend. No one has ever understood me as you have."

"We are only at the beginning of our friendship, Dorian," answered Lord Henry, shaking him by the hand. "Good-bye. I shall see you before nine-thirty, I hope.[17] Remember, Patti is singing."

As he closed the door behind him, Dorian Gray touched the bell, and in a few minutes Victor appeared with the lamps and drew the blinds down. He waited impatiently for him to go. The man seemed to take an interminable time over everything.

---

[16]The upper level, with expensive, private boxes.

[17]The performance would have started at 8 or 8:30 P.M. (Baedeker 40).

As soon as he had left, he rushed to the screen, and drew it back. No; there was no further change in the picture. It had received the news of Sibyl Vane's death before he had known of it himself. It was conscious of the events of life as they occurred. The vicious cruelty that marred the fine lines of the mouth had, no doubt, appeared at the very moment that the girl had drunk the poison, whatever it was. Or was it indifferent to results? Did it merely take cognizance of what passed within the soul? He wondered, and hoped that some day he would see the change taking place before his very eyes, shuddering as he hoped it.

Poor Sibyl! what a romance[18] it had all been! She had often mimicked death on the stage. Then Death himself had touched her, and taken her with him. How had she played that dreadful last scene? Had she cursed him, as she died? No; she had died for love of him, and love would always be a sacrament to him now. She had atoned for everything, by the sacrifice she had made of her life. He would not think any more of what she had made him go through, on that horrible night at the theatre. When he thought of her, it would be as a wonderful tragic figure sent on to the world's stage to show the supreme reality of Love. A wonderful tragic figure? Tears came to his eyes as he remembered her childlike look and winsome fanciful ways and shy tremulous grace. He brushed them away hastily, and looked again at the picture.

He felt that the time had really come for making his choice. Or had his choice already been made? Yes, life had decided that for him—life, and his own infinite curiosity about life. Eternal youth, infinite passion, pleasures subtle and secret, wild joys and wilder sins—he was to have all these things. The portrait was to bear the burden of his shame: that was all.

A feeling of pain crept over him as he thought of the desecration that was in store for the fair face on the canvas. Once, in boyish mockery of Narcissus,[19] he had kissed, or feigned to kiss, those painted lips that now smiled so cruelly at him. Morning after morning he had sat before the portrait wondering at its beauty, almost enamoured of it, as it seemed to him at times. Was it to alter now with every mood to which he yielded? Was it to become a monstrous and

[18]Not just a love affair, but a literary mode that Wilde, in the "Preface," opposed to realism.
[19]The fatally self-adoring youth of Greek myth.

loathsome thing, to be hidden away in a locked room, to be shut out from the sunlight that had so often touched to brighter gold the waving wonder of its hair? The pity of it! the pity of it![20]

For a moment, he thought of praying that the horrible sympathy[21] that existed between him and the picture might cease. It had changed in answer to a prayer; perhaps in answer to a prayer it might remain unchanged. And, yet, who, that knew anything about Life, would surrender the chance of remaining always young, however fantastic that chance might be, or with what fateful consequences it might be fraught? Besides, was it really under his control? Had it indeed been prayer that had produced the substitution? Might there not be some curious scientific reason for it all? If thought could exercise its influence upon a living organism, might not thought exercise an influence upon dead and inorganic things? Nay, without thought or conscious desire, might not things external to ourselves vibrate in unison with our moods and passions, atom calling to atom in secret love or strange affinity? But the reason was of no importance. He would never again tempt by a prayer any terrible power. If the picture was to alter, it was to alter. That was all. Why inquire too closely into it?

For there would be a real pleasure in watching it. He would be able to follow his mind into its secret places. This portrait would be to him the most magical of mirrors. As it had revealed to him his own body, so it would reveal to him his own soul. And when winter came upon it, he would still be standing where spring trembles on the verge of summer. When the blood crept from its face, and left behind a pallid mask of chalk with leaden eyes, he would keep the glamour of boyhood. Not one blossom of his loveliness would ever fade. Not one pulse of his life would ever weaken. Like the gods of the Greeks, he would be strong, and fleet, and joyous. What did it matter what happened to the coloured image on the canvas? He would be safe. That was everything.

He drew the screen back into its former place in front of the picture, smiling as he did so, and passed into his bedroom, where his valet was already waiting for him. An hour later he was at the Opera, and Lord Henry was leaning over his chair.

---

[20]Othello's sigh on his impending murder of Desdemona: "But yet the pity of it, Iago. O, Iago, the pity of it, Iago!" (*Othello* 4.1.196).

[21]In the literal sense of "feeling with," a secret connection that produces mutual influence.

Chapter 9

As he was sitting at breakfast next morning, Basil Hallward was shown into the room.

"I am so glad I have found you, Dorian," he said, gravely. "I called last night, and they told me you were at the Opera. Of course I knew that was impossible. But I wish you had left word where you had really gone to. I passed a dreadful evening, half afraid that one tragedy might be followed by another. I think you might have telegraphed for me when you heard of it first. I read of it quite by chance in a late edition of *The Globe*,[1] that I picked up at the club. I came here at once, and was miserable at not finding you. I can't tell you how heart-broken I am about the whole thing. I know what you must suffer. But where were you? Did you go down and see the girl's mother? For a moment I thought of following you there. They gave the address in the paper. Somewhere in the Euston Road, isn't it? But I was afraid of intruding upon a sorrow that I could not lighten. Poor woman! What a state she must be in! And her only child, too! What did she say about it all?"

"My dear Basil, how do I know?" murmured Dorian Gray, sipping some pale-yellow wine from a delicate gold-beaded bubble of Venetian glass, and looking dreadfully bored. "I was at the Opera. You should have come on there. I met Lady Gwendolen, Harry's sister, for the first time. We were in her box. She is perfectly charming; and Patti sang divinely. Don't talk about horrid subjects. If one doesn't talk about a thing, it has never happened. It is simply expression, as Harry says, that gives reality to things. I may mention that she was not the woman's only child. There is a son, a charming fellow, I believe. But he is not on the stage. He is a sailor, or something. And now, tell me about yourself and what you are painting."

"You went to the Opera?" said Hallward, speaking very slowly, and with a strained touch of pain in his voice. "You went to the Opera while Sibyl Vane was lying dead in some sordid lodging? You can talk to me of other women being charming, and of Patti singing divinely, before the girl you loved has even the quiet of a grave to sleep in? Why, man, there are horrors in store for that little white body of hers!"

---

[1] Conservative evening newspaper (Curtis 109), read by Sherlock Holmes.

"Stop, Basil! I won't hear it!" cried Dorian, leaping to his feet. "You must not tell me about things. What is done is done. What is past is past."

"You call yesterday the past?"

"What has the actual lapse of time got to do with it? It is only shallow people who require years to get rid of an emotion. A man who is master of himself can end a sorrow as easily as he can invent a pleasure. I don't want to be at the mercy of my emotions. I want to use them, to enjoy them, and to dominate them."

"Dorian, this is horrible! Something has changed you completely. You look exactly the same wonderful boy who, day after day, used to come down to my studio to sit for his picture. But you were simple, natural, and affectionate then. You were the most unspoiled creature in the whole world. Now, I don't know what has come over you. You talk as if you had no heart, no pity in you. It is all Harry's influence. I see that."

The lad flushed up, and, going to the window, looked out for a few moments on the green, flickering, sun-lashed garden. "I owe a great deal to Harry, Basil," he said at last,—"more than I owe to you. You only taught me to be vain."

"Well, I am punished for that, Dorian—or shall be some day."

"I don't know what you mean, Basil," he exclaimed, turning round. "I don't know what you want. What do you want?"

"I want the Dorian Gray I used to paint," said the artist, sadly.

"Basil," said the lad, going over to him and putting his hand on his shoulder, "you have come too late. Yesterday, when I heard that Sibyl Vane had killed herself—"

"Killed herself! Good heavens! is there no doubt about that?" cried Hallward, looking up at him with an expression of horror.

"My dear Basil! Surely you don't think it was a vulgar accident? Of course she killed herself."

The elder man buried his face in his hands. "How fearful," he muttered, and a shudder ran through him.

"No," said Dorian Gray, "there is nothing fearful about it. It is one of the great romantic tragedies of the age. As a rule, people who act lead the most commonplace lives. They are good husbands, or faithful wives, or something tedious. You know what I mean—middle-class virtue and all that kind of thing. How different Sibyl was! She lived her finest tragedy. She was always a heroine.

The last night she played—the night you saw her—she acted badly because she had known the reality of love. When she knew its unreality, she died, as Juliet might have died. She passed again into the sphere of art. There is something of the martyr about her. Her death has all the pathetic uselessness of martyrdom, all its wasted beauty. But, as I was saying, you must not think I have not suffered. If you had come in yesterday at a particular moment—about half-past five, perhaps, or a quarter to six—you would have found me in tears. Even Harry, who was here, who brought me the news, in fact, had no idea what I was going through. I suffered immensely. Then it passed away. I cannot repeat an emotion. No one can, except sentimentalists. And you are awfully unjust, Basil. You come down here to console me. That is charming of you. You find me consoled, and you are furious. How like a sympathetic person! You remind me of a story Harry told me about a certain philanthropist who spent twenty years of his life in trying to get some grievance redressed, or some unjust law altered—I forget exactly what it was. Finally he succeeded, and nothing could exceed his disappointment. He had absolutely nothing to do, almost died of *ennui*, and became a confirmed misanthrope. And besides, my dear old Basil, if you really want to console me, teach me rather to forget what has happened, or to see it from a proper artistic point of view. Was it not Gautier who used to write about *la consolation des arts*?[2] I remember picking up a little vellum-covered book in your studio one day and chancing on that delightful phrase. Well, I am not like that young man you told me of when we were down at Marlow[3] together, the young man who used to say that yellow satin could console one for all the miseries of life. I love beautiful things that one can touch and handle. Old brocades, green bronzes, lacquer-work, carved ivories, exquisite surroundings, luxury, pomp, there is much to be got from all these. But the artistic temperament that they create, or at any rate reveal, is still more to me. To become the specta-

---

[2]Théophile Gautier (1811–72), French poet and novelist, whose "art for art's sake" ethos was a major inspiration for the Victorian Aesthetic movement. Wilde may have adapted the French phrase from an essay "Théophile Gautier" (1859) by Charles Baudelaire (1821–67), French poet and essayist and another important inspiration for Aestheticism.

[3]Town on the Thames, west of London; a famous boat race, the Marlow Regatta, was held there annually.

tor of one's own life, as Harry says, is to escape the suffering of life. I know you are surprised at my talking to you like this. You have not realized how I have developed. I was a schoolboy when you knew me. I am a man now. I have new passions, new thoughts, new ideas. I am different, but you must not like me less. I am changed, but you must always be my friend. Of course I am very fond of Harry. But I know that you are better than he is. You are not stronger—you are too much afraid of life—but you are better. And how happy we used to be together! Don't leave me, Basil, and don't quarrel with me. I am what I am. There is nothing more to be said."

The painter felt strangely moved. The lad was infinitely dear to him, and his personality had been the great turning-point in his art. He could not bear the idea of reproaching him any more. After all, his indifference was probably merely a mood that would pass away. There was so much in him that was good, so much in him that was noble.

"Well, Dorian," he said, at length, with a sad smile, "I won't speak to you again about this horrible thing, after to-day. I only trust your name won't be mentioned in connection with it. The inquest is to take place this afternoon. Have they summoned you?"

Dorian shook his head, and a look of annoyance passed over his face at the mention of the word "inquest." There was something so crude and vulgar about everything of the kind. "They don't know my name," he answered.

"But surely she did?"

"Only my Christian name,[4] and that I am quite sure she never mentioned to any one. She told me once that they were all rather curious to learn who I was, and that she invariably told them my name was Prince Charming. It was pretty of her. You must do me a drawing of Sibyl, Basil. I should like to have something more of her than the memory of a few kisses and some broken pathetic words."

"I will try and do something, Dorian, if it would please you. But you must come and sit to me yourself again. I can't get on without you."

"I can never sit to you again, Basil. It is impossible!" he exclaimed, starting back.

The painter stared at him. "My dear boy, what nonsense!" he cried. "Do you mean to say you don't like what I did of you?

[4] His first name, given at christening.

Where is it? Why have you pulled the screen in front of it? Let me look at it. It is the best thing I have ever done. Do take the screen away, Dorian. It is simply disgraceful of your servant hiding my work like that. I felt the room looked different as I came in."

"My servant has nothing to do with it, Basil. You don't imagine I let him arrange my room for me? He settles my flowers for me sometimes—that is all. No; I did it myself. The light was too strong on the portrait."

"Too strong! Surely not, my dear fellow? It is an admirable place for it. Let me see it." And Hallward walked towards the corner of the room.

A cry of terror broke from Dorian Gray's lips, and he rushed between the painter and the screen. "Basil," he said, looking very pale, "you must not look at it. I don't wish you to."

"Not look at my own work! you are not serious. Why shouldn't I look at it?" exclaimed Hallward, laughing.

"If you try to look at it, Basil, on my word of honour I will never speak to you again as long as I live. I am quite serious. I don't offer any explanation, and you are not to ask for any. But, remember, if you touch this screen, everything is over between us."

Hallward was thunderstruck. He looked at Dorian Gray in absolute amazement. He had never seen him like this before. The lad was actually pallid with rage. His hands were clenched, and the pupils of his eyes were like disks of blue fire. He was trembling all over.

"Dorian!"

"Don't speak!"

"But what is the matter? Of course I won't look at it if you don't want me to," he said, rather coldly, turning on his heel and going over towards the window. "But, really, it seems rather absurd that I shouldn't see my own work, especially as I am going to exhibit it in Paris in the autumn. I shall probably have to give it another coat of varnish before that, so I must see it some day, and why not to-day?"

"To exhibit it! You want to exhibit it?" exclaimed Dorian Gray, a strange sense of terror creeping over him. Was the world going to be shown his secret? Were people to gape at the mystery of his life? That was impossible. Something—he did not know what—had to be done at once.

"Yes; I don't suppose you will object to that. Georges Petit is going to collect all my best pictures for a special exhibition in the Rue de Sèze,[5] which will open the first week in October. The portrait will only be away a month. I should think you could easily spare it for that time. In fact, you are sure to be out of town. And if you keep it always behind a screen, you can't care much about it."

Dorian Gray passed his hand over his forehead. There were beads of perspiration there. He felt that he was on the brink of a horrible danger. "You told me a month ago that you would never exhibit it," he cried. "Why have you changed your mind? You people who go in for being consistent have just as many moods as others have. The only difference is that your moods are rather meaningless. You can't have forgotten that you assured me most solemnly that nothing in the world would induce you to send it to any exhibition. You told Harry exactly the same thing." He stopped suddenly, and a gleam of light came into his eyes. He remembered that Lord Henry had said to him once, half seriously and half in jest, "If you want to have a strange quarter of an hour, get Basil to tell you why he won't exhibit your picture. He told me why he wouldn't, and it was a revelation to me." Yes, perhaps Basil, too, had his secret. He would ask him and try.

"Basil," he said, coming over quite close, and looking him straight in the face, "we have each of us a secret. Let me know yours, and I shall tell you mine. What was your reason for refusing to exhibit my picture?"

The painter shuddered in spite of himself. "Dorian, if I told you, you might like me less than you do, and you would certainly laugh at me. I could not bear your doing either of those two things. If you wish me never to look at your picture again, I am content. I have always you to look at. If you wish the best work I have ever done to be hidden from the world, I am satisfied. Your friendship is dearer to me than any fame or reputation."

"No, Basil, you must tell me," insisted Dorian Gray. "I think I have a right to know." His feeling of terror had passed away, and curiosity had taken its place. He was determined to find out Basil Hallward's mystery.

[5]A major Paris art gallery, opened by Petit in 1882, noted for new and experimental work, such as that by the Impressionists.

"Let us sit down, Dorian," said the painter, looking troubled. "Let us sit down. And just answer me one question. Have you noticed in the picture something curious?—something that probably at first did not strike you, but that revealed itself to you suddenly?"

"Basil!" cried the lad, clutching the arms of his chair with trembling hands and gazing at him with wild, startled eyes.

"I see you did. Don't speak. Wait till you hear what I have to say. Dorian, from the moment I met you, your personality had the most extraordinary influence over me. I was dominated, soul, brain, and power by you. You became to me the visible incarnation of that unseen ideal whose memory haunts us artists like an exquisite dream. I worshipped you. I grew jealous of every one to whom you spoke. I wanted to have you all to myself. I was only happy when I was with you. When you were away from me, you were still present in my art. . . . Of course, I never let you know anything about this. It would have been impossible. You would not have understood it. I hardly understood it myself. I only knew that I had seen perfection face to face, and that the world had become wonderful to my eyes—too wonderful, perhaps, for in such mad worships there is peril, the peril of losing them, no less than the peril of keeping them. . . . Weeks and weeks went on, and I grew more and more absorbed in you. Then came a new development. I had drawn you as Paris in dainty armour, and as Adonis with huntsman's cloak and polished boar-spear. Crowned with heavy lotus-blossoms you had sat on the prow of Adrian's barge, gazing across the green turbid Nile. You had leaned over the still pool of some Greek woodland, and seen in the water's silent silver the marvel of your own face.[6] And it had all been what art should be, unconscious, ideal, and remote. One day, a fatal day I sometimes think, I determined to paint a wonderful portrait of you as you actually are, not in the costume of dead ages, but in your own dress and in your own time. Whether it was the Realism of the method, or the mere wonder of your own personality, thus directly presented to me without mist or veil, I cannot tell. But I know that as I worked at it, every

[6]These images may be less flattering than Basil seems to think. Paris, the youth whose kidnapping of Helen begins the Trojan War, is consistently portrayed as a coward by Homer. Adonis, beloved by Venus, is killed in a boar hunt. The figure on the barge is Antinoüs, favorite of the Emperor Hadrian ("Adrian"), who later drowns in the Nile. The youth at the pool is Narcissus. All were noted homoerotic icons.

flake and film of colour seemed to me to reveal my secret. I grew afraid that others would know of my idolatry. I felt, Dorian, that I had told too much, that I had put too much of myself into it. Then it was that I resolved never to allow the picture to be exhibited. You were a little annoyed; but then you did not realize all that it meant to me. Harry, to whom I talked about it, laughed at me. But I did not mind that. When the picture was finished, and I sat alone with it, I felt that I was right. . . . Well, after a few days the thing left my studio, and as soon as I had got rid of the intolerable fascination of its presence, it seemed to me that I had been foolish in imagining that I had seen anything in it, more than that you were extremely good-looking and that I could paint. Even now I cannot help feeling that it is a mistake to think that the passion one feels in creation is ever really shown in the work one creates. Art is always more abstract than we fancy. Form and colour tell us of form and colour—that is all. It often seems to me that art conceals the artist far more completely than it ever reveals him. And so when I got this offer from Paris I determined to make your portrait the principal thing in my exhibition. It never occurred to me that you would refuse. I see now that you were right. The picture cannot be shown. You must not be angry with me, Dorian, for what I have told you. As I said to Harry, once, you are made to be worshipped."

Dorian Gray drew a long breath. The colour came back to his cheeks, and a smile played about his lips. The peril was over. He was safe for the time. Yet he could not help feeling infinite pity for the painter who had just made this strange confession to him, and wondered if he himself would ever be so dominated by the personality of a friend. Lord Henry had the charm of being very dangerous. But that was all. He was too clever and too cynical to be really fond of. Would there ever be some one who would fill him with a strange idolatry? Was that one of the things that life had in store?

"It is extraordinary to me, Dorian," said Hallward, "that you should have seen this in the portrait. Did you really see it?"

"I saw something in it," he answered, "something that seemed to me very curious."

"Well, you don't mind my looking at the thing now?"

Dorian shook his head. "You must not ask me that, Basil. I could not possibly let you stand in front of that picture."

"You will some day, surely?"

"Never."

"Well, perhaps you are right. And now good-bye, Dorian. You have been the one person in my life who has really influenced my art. Whatever I have done that is good, I owe to you. Ah! you don't know what it cost me to tell you all that I have told you."

"My dear Basil," said Dorian, "what have you told me? Simply that you felt that you admired me too much. That is not even a compliment."

"It was not intended as a compliment. It was a confession. Now that I have made it, something seems to have gone out of me. Perhaps one should never put one's worship into words."

"It was a very disappointing confession."

"Why, what did you expect, Dorian? You didn't see anything else in the picture, did you? There was nothing else to see?"

"No; there was nothing else to see. Why do you ask? But you mustn't talk about worship. It is foolish. You and I are friends, Basil, and we must always remain so."

"You have got Harry," said the painter sadly.

"Oh, Harry!" cried the lad, with a ripple of laughter. "Harry spends his days in saying what is incredible, and his evenings in doing what is improbable. Just the sort of life I would like to lead. But still I don't think I would go to Harry if I were in trouble. I would sooner go to you, Basil."

"You will sit to me again?"

"Impossible!"

"You spoil my life as an artist by refusing, Dorian. No man comes across two ideal things. Few come across one."

"I can't explain it to you, Basil, but I must never sit to you again. There is something fatal about a portrait. It has a life of its own. I will come and have tea with you. That will be just as pleasant."

"Pleasanter for you, I am afraid," murmured Hallward, regretfully. "And now good-bye. I am sorry you won't let me look at the picture once again. But that can't be helped. I quite understand what you feel about it."

As he left the room, Dorian Gray smiled to himself. Poor Basil! how little he knew of the true reason! And how strange it was that, instead of having been forced to reveal his own secret, he had succeeded, almost by chance, in wresting a secret from his friend! How much that strange confession explained to him! The painter's absurd fits of jealousy, his wild devotion, his extravagant panegyrics, his curious reticences—he understood them all now, and he felt sorry. There seemed to him to be something tragic in a friendship so coloured by romance.

He sighed, and touched the bell. The portrait must be hidden away at all costs. He could not run such a risk of discovery again. It had been mad of him to have allowed the thing to remain, even for an hour, in a room to which any of his friends had access.

Chapter 10

When his servant entered, he looked at him steadfastly, and wondered if he had thought of peering behind the screen. The man was quite impassive, and waited for his orders. Dorian lit a cigarette, and walked over to the glass and glanced into it. He could see the reflection of Victor's face perfectly. It was like a placid mask of servility. There was nothing to be afraid of, there. Yet he thought it best to be on his guard.

Speaking very slowly, he told him to tell the housekeeper that he wanted to see her, and then to go to the frame-maker and ask him to send two of his men round at once. It seemed to him that as the man left the room his eyes wandered in the direction of the screen. Or was that merely his own fancy?

After a few moments, in her black silk dress, with old-fashioned thread mittens on her wrinkled hands, Mrs. Leaf bustled into the library. He asked her for the key of the schoolroom.

"The old schoolroom, Mr. Dorian?" she exclaimed. "Why, it is full of dust. I must get it arranged, and put straight before you go into it. It is not fit for you to see, sir. It is not, indeed."

"I don't want it put straight, Leaf. I only want the key."

"Well, sir, you'll be covered with cobwebs if you go into it. Why, it hasn't been opened for nearly five years, not since his lordship died."

He winced at the mention of his grandfather. He had hateful memories of him. "That does not matter," he answered. "I simply want to see the place—that is all. Give me the key."

"And here is the key, sir," said the old lady, going over the contents of her bunch with tremulously uncertain hands. "Here is the key. I'll have it off the bunch in a moment. But you don't think of living up there, sir, and you so comfortable here?"

"No, no," he cried, petulantly. "Thank you, Leaf. That will do."

She lingered for a few moments, and was garrulous over some detail of the household. He sighed, and told her to manage things as she thought best. She left the room, wreathed in smiles.[1]

As the door closed, Dorian put the key in his pocket, and looked round the room. His eye fell on a large purple satin cover-

[1]Reference to "L'Allegro" by John Milton (1608–74): "Nods and Becks, and Wreathèd Smiles" (28)

let heavily embroidered with gold, a splendid piece of late seventeenth-century Venetian work that his grandfather had found in a convent near Bologna. Yes, that would serve to wrap the dreadful thing in. It had perhaps served often as a pall for the dead. Now it was to hide something that had a corruption of its own, worse than the corruption of death itself—something that would breed horrors and yet would never die. What the worm was to the corpse, his sins would be to the painted image on the canvas. They would mar its beauty, and eat away its grace. They would defile it, and make it shameful. And yet the thing would still live on. It would be always alive.

He shuddered, and for a moment he regretted that he had not told Basil the true reason why he had wished to hide the picture away. Basil would have helped him to resist Lord Henry's influence, and the still more poisonous influences that came from his own temperament. The love that he bore him—for it was really love—had nothing in it that was not noble and intellectual. It was not that mere physical admiration of beauty that is born of the senses, and that dies when the senses tire. It was such love as Michael Angelo had known, and Montaigne, and Winckelmann, and Shakespeare himself.[2] Yes, Basil could have saved him. But it was too late now. The past could always be annihilated. Regret, denial, or forgetfulness could do that. But the future was inevitable. There were passions in him that would find their terrible outlet, dreams that would make the shadow of their evil real.

He took up from the couch the great purple-and-gold texture that covered it, and, holding it in his hands, passed behind the screen. Was the face on the canvas viler than before? It seemed to him that it was unchanged; and yet his loathing of it was intensified. Gold hair, blue eyes, and rose-red lips—they all were there. It was simply the expression that had altered. That was horrible in

---

[2]Michelangelo Buonarotti (see ch. 3, n. 21); the essayist Michel Eyquem, seigneuer de Montaigne (1533–92); the Hellenist Johann Winckelmann (1717–68); and Shakespeare (1564–1616) all had become associated with homosexual desire by some 19th-c. writers. At his second trial, Wilde claimed, "'The love that dare not speak its name' in this century is such a great affection of an elder for a younger man as there was between David and Jonathan, such as Plato made the very basis of his philosophy, and such as you find in the sonnets of Michelangelo and Shakespeare." Max Beerbohm noted of this speech that it "was simply wonderful and carried the whole court right away, quite a tremendous burst of applause" (Wilde and Beerbohm q. in Ellman 463).

its cruelty. Compared to what he saw in it of censure or rebuke, how shallow Basil's reproaches about Sibyl Vane had been!—how shallow, and of what little account! His own soul was looking out at him from the canvas and calling him to judgement. A look of pain came across him, and he flung the rich pall over the picture. As he did so, a knock came to the door. He passed out as his servant entered.

"The persons are here, Monsieur."

He felt that the man must be got rid of at once. He must not be allowed to know where the picture was being taken to. There was something sly about him, and he had thoughtful, treacherous eyes. Sitting down at the writing-table, he scribbled a note to Lord Henry, asking him to send him round something to read, and reminding him that they were to meet at eight-fifteen that evening.

"Wait for an answer," he said, handing it to him, "and show the men in here."

In two or three minutes there was another knock, and Mr. Hubbard himself, the celebrated frame-maker of South Audley Street,[3] came in with a somewhat rough-looking young assistant. Mr. Hubbard was a florid, red-whiskered little man, whose admiration for art was considerably tempered by the inveterate impecuniosity of most of the artists who dealt with him. As a rule, he never left his shop. He waited for people to come to him. But he always made an exception in favour of Dorian Gray. There was something about Dorian that charmed everybody. It was a pleasure even to see him.

"What can I do for you, Mr. Gray?" he said, rubbing his fat freckled hands. "I thought I would do myself the honour of coming round in person. I have just got a beauty of a frame, sir. Picked it up at a sale. Old Florentine.[4] Came from Fonthill,[5] I believe. Admirably suited for a religious subject, Mr. Gray."

"I am so sorry you have given yourself the trouble of coming round, Mr. Hubbard. I shall certainly drop in and look at the

[3]Near Hyde Park; it runs into Curzon Street, where Lord Henry Wotton lives.

[4]A tondo, a circular frame often used for images of the Madonna and Child or the Holy Family in Renaissance paintings from Tuscany (Newbery et al. 27–28).

[5]Spectacular estate of William Beckford (1760–1844), who, after a homosexual scandal, built Fonthill and lived there in seclusion. His collections were the finest in England. When he sold his estate in 1822, Christie's in London managed the auction of its contents.

frame—though I don't go in much at present for religious art—but to-day I only want a picture carried to the top of the house for me. It is rather heavy, so I thought I would ask you to lend me a couple of your men."

"No trouble at all, Mr. Gray. I am delighted to be of any service to you. Which is the work of art, sir?"

"This," replied Dorian, moving the screen back. "Can you move it, covering and all, just as it is? I don't want it to get scratched going upstairs."

"There will be no difficulty, sir," said the genial frame-maker, beginning, with the aid of his assistant, to unhook the picture from the long brass chains by which it was suspended. "And, now, where shall we carry it to, Mr. Gray?"

"I will show you the way, Mr. Hubbard, if you will kindly follow me. Or perhaps you had better go in front. I am afraid it is right at the top of the house. We will go up by the front staircase, as it is wider."

He held the door open for them, and they passed out into the hall and began the ascent. The elaborate character of the frame had made the picture extremely bulky, and now and then, in spite of the obsequious protests of Mr. Hubbard, who had the true tradesman's spirited dislike of seeing a gentleman doing anything useful, Dorian put his hand to it so as to help them.

"Something of a load to carry, sir," gasped the little man, when they reached the top landing. And he wiped his shiny forehead.

"I am afraid it is rather heavy," murmured Dorian, as he unlocked the door that opened into the room that was to keep for him the curious secret of his life and hide his soul from the eyes of men.

He had not entered the place for more than four years—not, indeed, since he had used it first as a play-room when he was a child, and then as a study when he grew somewhat older. It was a large, well-proportioned room, which had been specially built by the last Lord Kelso for the use of the little grandson whom, for his strange likeness to his mother, and also for other reasons, he had always hated and desired to keep at a distance. It appeared to Dorian to have but little changed. There was the huge Italian *cassone*,[6] with its fantastically-painted panels and its tarnished gilt mouldings, in

---

[6]A large, elaborately wrought Italian chest, originally used for a bride's trousseau.

which he had so often hidden himself as a boy. There the satinwood bookcase filled with his dog-eared schoolbooks. On the wall behind it was hanging the same ragged Flemish tapestry where a faded king and queen were playing chess in a garden, while a company of hawkers rode by, carrying hooded birds on their gauntleted wrists. How well he remembered it all! Every moment of his lonely childhood came back to him as he looked round. He recalled the stainless purity of his boyish life, and it seemed horrible to him that it was here the fatal portrait was to be hidden away. How little he had thought, in those dead days, of all that was in store for him!

But there was no other place in the house so secure from prying eyes as this. He had the key, and no one else could enter it. Beneath its purple pall, the face painted on the canvas could grow bestial, sodden, and unclean. What did it matter? No one could see it. He himself would not see it. Why should he watch the hideous corruption of his soul? He kept his youth—that was enough. And, besides, might not his nature grow finer, after all? There was no reason that the future should be so full of shame. Some love might come across his life, and purify him, and shield him from those sins that seemed to be already stirring in spirit and in flesh—those curious unpictured sins whose very mystery lent them their subtlety and their charm. Perhaps, some day, the cruel look would have passed away from the scarlet sensitive mouth, and he might show to the world Basil Hallward's masterpiece.

No; that was impossible. Hour by hour, and week by week, the thing upon the canvas was growing old. It might escape the hideousness of sin, but the hideousness of age was in store for it. The cheeks would become hollow or flaccid. Yellow crow's feet would creep round the fading eyes and make them horrible. The hair would lose its brightness, the mouth would gape or droop, would be foolish or gross, as the mouths of old men are. There would be the wrinkled throat, the cold, blue-veined hands, the twisted body, that he remembered in the grandfather who had been so stern to him in his boyhood. The picture had to be concealed. There was no help for it.

"Bring it in, Mr. Hubbard, please," he said, wearily, turning round. "I am sorry I kept you so long. I was thinking of something else."

"Always glad to have a rest, Mr. Gray," answered the framemaker, who was still gasping for breath. "Where shall we put it, sir?"

"Oh, anywhere. Here: this will do. I don't want to have it hung up. Just lean it against the wall. Thanks."

"Might one look at the work of art, sir?"

Dorian started. "It would not interest you, Mr. Hubbard," he said, keeping his eye on the man. He felt ready to leap upon him and fling him to the ground if he dared to lift the gorgeous hanging that concealed the secret of his life. "I sha'n't trouble you any more now. I am much obliged for your kindness in coming round."

"Not at all, not at all, Mr. Gray. Ever ready to do anything for you, sir." And Mr. Hubbard tramped downstairs, followed by the assistant, who glanced back at Dorian with a look of shy wonder in his rough, uncomely face. He had never seen any one so marvellous.

When the sound of their footsteps had died away, Dorian locked the door, and put the key in his pocket. He felt safe now. No one would ever look upon the horrible thing. No eye but his would ever see his shame.

On reaching the library, he found that it was just after five o'-clock, and that the tea had been already brought up. On a little table of dark perfumed wood thickly incrusted with nacre, a pre-sent from Lady Radley, his guardian's wife, a pretty professional in-valid, who had spent the preceding winter in Cairo, was lying a note from Lord Henry, and beside it was a book bound in yellow paper, the cover slightly torn and the edges soiled. A copy of the third edition of *The St. James's Gazette*[7] had been placed on the tea-tray. It was evident that Victor had returned. He wondered if he had met the men in the hall as they were leaving the house, and had wormed out of them what they had been doing. He would be sure to miss the picture—had no doubt missed it already, while he had been laying the tea-things. The screen had not been set back, and a blank space was visible on the wall. Perhaps some night he might find him creeping upstairs and trying to force the door of the room. It was a horrible thing to have a spy in one's house. He had heard of rich men who had been blackmailed all their lives by some ser-vant who had read a letter, or overheard a conversation, or picked up a card with an address, or found beneath a pillow a withered flower or a shred of crumpled lace.

---

[7]Conservative evening newspaper that gave the 1890 version of *The Picture of Dorian Gray* an extremely harsh review, to which Wilde replied in its pages (see p. 240).

He sighed, and, having poured himself out some tea, opened Lord Henry's note. It was simply to say that he sent him round the evening paper, and a book that might interest him, and that he would be at the club at eight-fifteen. He opened *The St. James's* languidly, and looked through it. A red pencil-mark on the fifth page caught his eye. It drew attention to the following paragraph:

"INQUEST ON AN ACTRESS.—An inquest was held this morning at the Bell Tavern, Hoxton Road, by Mr. Danby, the District Coroner, on the body of Sibyl Vane, a young actress recently engaged at the Royal Theatre, Holborn.[8] A verdict of death by misadventure was returned. Considerable sympathy was expressed for the mother of the deceased, who was greatly affected during the giving of her own evidence, and that of Dr. Birrell, who had made the post-mortem examination of the deceased."

He frowned, and, tearing the paper in two went across the room and flung the pieces away. How ugly it all was! And how horribly real ugliness made things! He felt a little annoyed with Lord Henry for having sent him the report. And it was certainly stupid of him to have marked it with red pencil. Victor might have read it. The man knew more than enough English for that.

Perhaps he had read it, and had begun to suspect something. And, yet, what did it matter? What had Dorian Gray to do with Sibyl Vane's death? There was nothing to fear. Dorian Gray had not killed her.

His eye fell on the yellow book[9] that Lord Henry had sent him. What was it, he wondered. He went towards the little pearl-coloured octagonal stand, that had always looked to him like the work of some strange Egyptian bees that wrought in silver,[10] and

---

[8]Wilde uses several names that were close to actual place names, but not exactly. Victorian London had a Hoxton Street (not Road) in the East End, and a Holburn Theatre Royal (not Royal Theatre) that had burned down in 1880. The Bell was a common name for Victorian taverns.

[9]The color of the wrappers in which French novels were sold; it became the cult color of Victorian decadence, later enshrined in the title of the premier decadent journal, *The Yellow Book*.

[10]Possibly because the honeycomb of ordinary bees is hexagonal, so that Dorian imagines that this octagonal table must be the work of "strange . . . bees."

taking up the volume, flung himself into an arm-chair, and began to turn over the leaves. After a few minutes he became absorbed. It was the strangest book that he had ever read. It seemed to him that in exquisite raiment, and to the delicate sound of flutes, the sins of the world were passing in dumb show before him. Things that he had dimly dreamed of were suddenly made real to him. Things of which he had never dreamed were gradually revealed.

It was a novel without a plot, and with only one character, being, indeed, simply a psychological study of a certain young Parisian, who spent his life trying to realize in the nineteenth century all the passions and modes of thought that belonged to every century except his own, and to sum up, as it were, in himself the various moods through which the world-spirit had ever passed, loving for their mere artificiality those renunciations that men have unwisely called virtue, as much as those natural rebellions that wise men still call sin.[11] The style in which it was written was that curious jewelled style, vivid and obscure at once, full of *argot* and of archaisms, of technical expressions and of elaborate paraphrases, that characterizes the work of some of the finest artists of the French school of *Symbolistes*.[12] There were in it metaphors as monstrous as orchids, and as subtle in colour. The life of the senses was described in the terms of mystical philosophy. One hardly knew at times whether one was reading the spiritual ecstasies of some mediæval saint or the morbid confessions of a modern sinner. It was a poisonous book. The heavy odour of incense seemed to cling about its pages and to trouble the brain. The mere cadence of the sentences, the subtle monotony of their music, so full as it was of complex refrains and movements elaborately repeated, produced in the mind of the lad, as he passed from chapter to chapter, a form of reverie, a malady of dreaming, that made him unconscious of the falling day and creeping shadows.

[11]This book is based on *À Rebours* (*Against the Grain*) (1884) by the French novelist Joris-Karl Huysmans (1848–1907), although Wilde alters some details to avoid too exact a correspondence. He also leaves out the important fact that the hero of *À Rebours*, des Esseintes, suffers excruciatingly from the effects of venereal disease; many of his decadent adventures are attempts to distract himself from bodily agony.

[12]A group of late 19th-c. French poets known for anti-realist, formally experimental, impressionistic lyrics, drawing for effect on nuance and suggestion rather than on overt statement.

Cloudless, and pierced by one solitary star, a copper-green sky gleamed through the windows. He read on by its wan light till he could read no more. Then, after his valet had reminded him several times of the lateness of the hour, he got up, and, going into the next room, placed the book on the little Florentine table that always stood at his bedside, and began to dress for dinner.

It was almost nine o'clock before he reached the club, where he found Lord Henry sitting alone, in the morning-room, looking very much bored.

"I am so sorry, Harry," he cried, "but really it is entirely your fault. That book you sent me so fascinated me that I forgot how the time was going."

"Yes: I thought you would like it," replied his host, rising from his chair.

"I didn't say I liked it, Harry. I said it fascinated me. There is a great difference."

"Ah, you have discovered that?" murmured Lord Henry. And they passed into the dining-room.

Chapter 11[1]

For years, Dorian Gray could not free himself from the influence of this book. Or perhaps it would be more accurate to say that he never sought to free himself from it. He procured from Paris no less than nine large-paper copies of the first edition, and had them bound in different colours, so that they might suit his various moods and the changing fancies of a nature over which he seemed, at times, to have almost entirely lost control. The hero, the wonderful young Parisian, in whom the romantic and the scientific temperaments were so strangely blended, became to him a kind of prefiguring type of himself. And, indeed, the whole book seemed to him to contain the story of his own life, written before he had lived it.

In one point he was more fortunate than the novel's fantastic hero. He never knew—never, indeed, had any cause to know—that somewhat grotesque dread of mirrors, and polished metal surfaces, and still water, which came upon the young Parisian so early in his life, and was occasioned by the sudden decay of a beauty that had once, apparently, been so remarkable. It was with an almost cruel joy—and perhaps in nearly every joy, as certainly in every pleasure, cruelty has its place—that he used to read the latter part of the book, with its really tragic, if somewhat over-emphasized, account of the sorrow and despair of one who had himself lost what in others, and in the world, he had most dearly valued.

For the wonderful beauty that had so fascinated Basil Hallward, and many others besides him, seemed never to leave him. Even those who had heard the most evil things against him, and from time to time strange rumours about his mode of life crept through London and became the chatter of the clubs, could not believe anything to his dishonour when they saw him. He had always the look of one who had kept himself unspotted from the world. Men who talked grossly became silent when Dorian Gray entered the room. There was something in the purity of his face that rebuked them. His mere presence seemed to recall to them the memory of the innocence that they had tarnished. They wondered how one so charming and graceful as he was could have escaped the stain of an age that was at once sordid and sensual.

---

[1]See the discussion and annotation of this chapter in "Textual Issues," p. 232.

Often, on returning home from one of those mysterious and prolonged absences that gave rise to such strange conjecture among those who were his friends, or thought that they were so, he himself would creep upstairs to the locked room, open the door with the key that never left him now, and stand, with a mirror, in front of the portrait that Basil Hallward had painted of him, looking now at the evil and aging face on the canvas, and now at the fair young face that laughed back at him from the polished glass. The very sharpness of the contrast used to quicken his sense of pleasure. He grew more and more enamoured of his own beauty, more and more interested in the corruption of his own soul. He would examine with minute care, and sometimes with a monstrous and terrible delight, the hideous lines that seared the wrinkling forehead or crawled around the heavy sensual mouth, wondering sometimes which were the more horrible, the signs of sin or the signs of age. He would place his white hands beside the coarse bloated hands of the picture, and smile. He mocked the misshapen body and the failing limbs.

There were moments, indeed, at night, when, lying sleepless in his own delicately-scented chamber, or in the sordid room of the little ill-famed tavern near the Docks,[2] which, under an assumed name, and in disguise, it was his habit to frequent, he would think of the ruin he had brought upon his soul, with a pity that was all the more poignant because it was purely selfish. But moments such as these were rare. That curiosity about life which Lord Henry had first stirred in him, as they sat together in the garden of their friend, seemed to increase with gratification. The more he knew, the more he desired to know. He had mad hungers that grew more ravenous as he fed them.

Yet he was not really reckless, at any rate in his relations to society. Once or twice every month during the winter, and on each Wednesday evening while the season lasted, he would throw open to the world his beautiful house and have the most celebrated musicians of the day to charm his guests with the wonders of their art. His little dinners, in the settling of which Lord Henry always

---

[2]Shipping area running "through shabby, slatternly places, by low and poor houses, amid shiftless riverside loungers, with the shipping-littered Thames on the right" (Doré and Jerrold 29).

assisted him, were noted as much for the careful selection and placing of those invited, as for the exquisite taste shown in the decoration of the table, with its subtle symphonic arrangements of exotic flowers, and embroidered cloths, and antique plate of gold and silver. Indeed, there were many, especially among the very young men, who saw, or fancied that they saw, in Dorian Gray the true realization of a type of which they had often dreamed in Eton or Oxford days, a type that was to combine something of the real culture of the scholar with all the grace and distinction and perfect manner of a citizen of the world. To them he seemed to be of the company of those whom Dante describes as having sought to "make themselves perfect by the worship of beauty."[3] Like Gautier, he was one for whom "the visible world existed."[4]

And, certainly, to him Life itself was the first, the greatest, of the arts, and for it all the other arts seemed to be but a preparation. Fashion, by which what is really fantastic becomes for a moment universal, and Dandyism, which, in its own way, is an attempt to assert the absolute modernity of beauty, had, of course, their fascination for him. His mode of dressing, and the particular styles that from time to time he affected, had their marked influence on the young exquisites of the Mayfair balls and Pall Mall club windows,[5] who copied him in everything that he did, and tried to reproduce the accidental charm of his graceful, though to him only half-serious, fopperies.

For, while he was but too ready to accept the position that was almost immediately offered to him on his coming of age, and found, indeed, a subtle pleasure in the thought that he might really become to the London of his own day what to imperial Neronian Rome the author of the "Satyricon"[6] once had been, yet in his inmost heart he

---

[3]Not Dante; the source is Walter Pater's *Marius the Epicurean*: Marius is one of those "who, in the words of a poet who came long after, must be 'made perfect by the love of visible beauty'" (the poet is unidentified).

[4]For Gautier, see ch. 9, n. 2. Discussing his critics, Gautier claimed, "All my value, they've never spoken of that; it's that *I am a man for whom the visible world exists*" (Bristow 396).

[5]For Mayfair, see ch. 4, n. 1. Pall Mall "is a street of palaces . . . Hansom cabs in number come and go, dropping their occupants at the doors of one or other of the great club houses, and about dinner-time quite a stream of quiet well-dressed men stroll down the street and are absorbed in these immense buildings" (Dickens 194).

[6]Petronius (d. 66 C.E.), an intimate of notoriously cruel Roman emperor Nero (37–68 C.E.); his *Satyricon* features an array of sexual behaviors, displaying Roman excess.

desired to be something more than a mere *arbiter elegantiarum*,[7] to be consulted on the wearing of a jewel, or the knotting of a necktie, or the conduct of a cane. He sought to elaborate some new scheme of life that would have its reasoned philosophy and its ordered principles, and find in the spiritualizing of the senses its highest realization. The worship of the senses has often, and with much justice, been decried, men feeling a natural instinct of terror about passions and sensations that seem stronger than themselves, and that they are conscious of sharing with the less highly organized forms of existence. But it appeared to Dorian Gray that the true nature of the senses had never been understood, and that they had remained savage and animal merely because the world had sought to starve them into submission or to kill them by pain, instead of aiming at making them elements of a new spirituality, of which a fine instinct for beauty was to be the dominant characteristic. As he looked back upon man moving through History, he was haunted by a feeling of loss. So much had been surrendered! and to such little purpose! There had been mad wilful rejections, monstrous forms of self-torture and self-denial, whose origin was fear, and whose result was a degradation infinitely more terrible than that fancied degradation from which, in their ignorance, they had sought to escape, Nature, in her wonderful irony, driving out the anchorite to feed with the wild animals of the desert and giving to the hermit the beasts of the field as his companions.

Yes: there was to be, as Lord Henry had prophesied, a new Hedonism that was to recreate life, and to save it from that harsh uncomely puritanism that is having, in our own day, its curious revival. It was to have its service of the intellect, certainly; yet, it was never to accept any theory or system that would involve the sacrifice of any mode of passionate experience. Its aim, indeed, was to be experience itself, and not the fruits of experience, sweet or bitter as they might be. Of the asceticism that deadens the senses, of the vulgar profligacy that dulls them, it was to know nothing. But it was to teach man to concentrate himself upon the moments of a life that is itself but a moment.

There are few of us who have not sometimes wakened before dawn, either after one of those dreamless nights that make us almost

---

[7]An authority on matters of taste (Latin).

enamoured of death, or one of those nights of horror and misshapen joy, when through the chambers of the brain sweep phantoms more terrible than reality itself, and instinct with that vivid life that lurks in all grotesques, and that lends to Gothic art its enduring vitality,[8] this art being, one might fancy, especially the art of those whose minds have been troubled with the malady of reverie. Gradually white fingers creep through the curtains, and they appear to tremble. In black fantastic shapes, dumb shadows crawl into the corners of the room, and crouch there. Outside, there is the stirring of birds among the leaves, or the sound of men going forth to their work,[9] or the sigh and sob of the wind coming down from the hills, and wandering round the silent house, as though it feared to wake the sleepers, and yet must needs call forth sleep from her purple cave. Veil after veil of thin dusky gauze is lifted, and by degrees the forms and colours of things are restored to them, and we watch the dawn remaking the world in its antique pattern. The wan mirrors get back their mimic life. The flameless tapers stand where we had left them, and beside them lies the half-cut book[10] that we had been studying, or the wired flower that we had worn at the ball, or the letter that we had been afraid to read, or that we had read too often. Nothing seems to us changed. Out of the unreal shadows of the night comes back the real life that we had known. We have to resume it where we had left off, and there steals over us a terrible sense of the necessity for the continuance of energy in the same wearisome round of stereotyped habits, or a wild longing, it may be, that our eyelids might open some morning upon a world that had been refashioned anew in the darkness for our pleasure, a world in which things would have fresh shapes and colours, and be changed, or have other secrets, a world in which the past would have little or no place, or survive, at any rate, in no conscious form of obligation or regret, the remembrance even of joy having its bitterness, and the memories of pleasure their pain.

It was the creation of such worlds as these that seemed to Dorian Gray to be the true object, or amongst the true objects, of life;

---

[8] In *The Stones of Venice* (1851–53), John Ruskin theorizes the grotesque aesthetics of Gothic (medieval) art as the result of human capability inadequate to its inspiration.

[9] "Man goeth forth unto his work and to his labor until the evening" (Psalm 104.23).

[10] With some of its pages still folded together.

and in his search for sensations that would be at once new and delightful, and possess that element of strangeness that is so essential to romance, he would often adopt certain modes of thought that he knew to be really alien to his nature, abandon himself to their subtle influences, and then, having, as it were, caught their colour and satisfied his intellectual curiosity, leave them with that curious indifference that is not incompatible with a real ardour of temperament, and that, indeed, according to certain modern psychologists, is often a condition of it.

It was rumoured of him once that he was about to join the Roman Catholic communion, and certainly the Roman ritual had always a great attraction for him. The daily sacrifice, more awful really than all the sacrifices of the antique world, stirred him as much by its superb rejection of the evidence of the senses as by the primitive simplicity of its elements and the eternal pathos of the human tragedy that it sought to symbolize. He loved to kneel down on the cold marble pavement, and watch the priest, in his stiff flowered dalmatic, slowly and with white hands moving aside the veil of the tabernacle, or raising aloft the jewelled lantern-shaped monstrance with that pallid wafer that at times, one would fain think, is indeed the *"panis cælestis,"* the bread of angels, or, robed in the garments of the Passion of Christ, breaking the Host into the chalice, and smiting his breast for his sins. The fuming censers, that the grave boys, in their lace and scarlet, tossed into the air like great gilt flowers, had their subtle fascination for him. As he passed out, he used to look with wonder at the black confessionals, and long to sit in the dim shadow of one of them and listen to men and women whispering through the worn grating the true story of their lives.

But he never fell into the error of arresting his intellectual development by any formal acceptance of creed or system, or of mistaking, for a house in which to live, an inn that is but suitable for the sojourn of a night, or for a few hours of a night in which there are no stars and the moon is in travail. Mysticism, with its marvellous power of making common things strange to us, and the subtle antinomianism[11] that always seems to accompany it, moved him for a season; and for a season he inclined to the materialistic doctrines of

---

[11]Belief that existing moral laws no longer apply to those in God's grace.

the *Darwinismus* movement in Germany[12] and found a curious pleasure in tracing the thoughts and passions of men to some pearly cell in the brain, or some white nerve in the body, delighting in the conception of the absolute dependence of the spirit on certain physical conditions, morbid or healthy, normal or diseased. Yet, as has been said of him before, no theory of life seemed to him to be of any importance compared with life itself. He felt keenly conscious of how barren all intellectual speculation is when separated from action and experiment. He knew that the senses, no less than the soul, have their spiritual mysteries to reveal.

And so he would now study perfumes, and the secrets of their manufacture, distilling heavily-scented oils, and burning odorous gums from the East. He saw that there was no mood of the mind that had not its counterpart in the sensuous life, and set himself to discover their true relations, wondering what there was in frankincense that made one mystical, and in ambergris that stirred one's passions, and in violets that woke the memory of dead romances, and in musk that troubled the brain, and in champak that stained the imagination; and seeking often to elaborate a real psychology of perfumes, and to estimate the several influences of sweet-smelling roots and scented pollen-laden flowers, of aromatic balms, and of dark and fragrant woods, of spikenard that sickens, of hovenia that makes men mad, and of aloes that are said to be able to expel melancholy from the soul.

At another time he devoted himself entirely to music, and in a long latticed room, with a vermilion-and-gold ceiling and walls of olive-green lacquer, he used to give curious concerts in which mad gipsies tore wild music from little zithers, or grave yellow-shawled Tunisians plucked at the strained strings of monstrous lutes, while grinning negroes beat monotonously upon copper drums, and, crouching upon scarlet mats, slim turbaned Indians blew through long pipes of reed or brass, and charmed, or feigned to charm, great hooded snakes and horrible horned adders. The harsh intervals and shrill discords of barbaric music stirred him at times when Schubert's grace, and Chopin's beautiful sorrows, and the mighty harmonies of Beethoven himself, fell unheeded on his ear. He collected together from all parts of the world the strangest instruments

[12]German reception of Darwin's scientific theory of evolution.

that could be found, either in the tombs of dead nations or among the few savage tribes that have survived contact with Western civilizations, and loved to touch and try them. He had the mysterious *juruparis* of the Rio Negro Indians, that women are not allowed to look at, and that even youths may not see till they have been subjected to fasting and scourging, and the earthen jars of the Peruvians that have the shrill cries of birds, and flutes of human bones such as Alfonso de Ovalle heard in Chile, and the sonorous green jaspers that are found near Cuzco and give forth a note of singular sweetness. He had painted gourds filled with pebbles that rattled when they were shaken; the long *clarin* of the Mexicans, into which the performer does not blow, but through which he inhales the air; the harsh *ture* of the Amazon tribes, that is sounded by the sentinels who sit all day long in high trees, and can be heard, it is said, at a distance of three leagues; the *teponaztli*, that has two vibrating tongues of wood, and is beaten with sticks that are smeared with an elastic gum obtained from the milky juice of plants; the *yotl*-bells of the Aztecs, that are hung in clusters like grapes; and a huge cylindrical drum, covered with the skins of great serpents, like the one that Bernal Diaz saw when he went with Cortes into the Mexican temple, and of whose doleful sound he has left us so vivid a description. The fantastic character of these instruments fascinated him, and he felt a curious delight in the thought that Art, like Nature, has her monsters, things of bestial shape and with hideous voices. Yet, after some time, he wearied of them, and would sit in his box at the Opera, either alone or with Lord Henry, listening in rapt pleasure to "Tannhäuser," and seeing in the prelude to that great work of art a presentation of the tragedy of his own soul.

On one occasion he took up the study of jewels, and appeared at a costume ball as Anne de Joyeuse, Admiral of France, in a dress covered with five hundred and sixty pearls. This taste enthralled him for years, and, indeed, may be said never to have left him. He would often spend a whole day settling and resettling in their cases the various stones that he had collected, such as the olive-green chrysoberyl that turns red by lamplight, the cymophane with its wire-like line of silver, the pistachio-coloured peridot, rose-pink and wine-yellow topazes, carbuncles of fiery scarlet with tremulous four-rayed stars, flame-red cinnamon-stones, orange and violet spinels, and amethysts with their alternate layers of ruby and sapphire. He loved the red gold of the sunstone, and the moonstone's pearly whiteness, and the broken rainbow of the milky opal. He procured from Amsterdam three emeralds of extraordinary size and richness of colour, and had a turquoise *de la vieille roche* that was the envy of all the connoisseurs.

He discovered wonderful stories, also, about jewels. In Alphonso's "Clericalis Disciplina" a serpent was mentioned with eyes of real jacinth, and in the romantic history of Alexander, the Conqueror of Emathia was said to have found in the vale of Jordan snakes "with collars of real emeralds growing on their backs." There was a gem in the brain of the dragon, Philostratus told us, and "by the exhibition of golden letters and a scarlet robe" the monster could be thrown into a magical sleep and slain. According to the great alchemist, Pierre de Boniface, the diamond rendered a man invisible, and the agate of India made him eloquent. The cornelian appeased anger, and the hyacinth provoked sleep, and the amethyst drove away the fumes of wine. The garnet cast out demons, and the hydropicus deprived the moon of her colour. The selenite waxed and waned with the moon, and the meloceus, that discovers thieves, could be affected only by the blood of kids. Leonardus Camillus had seen a white stone taken from the brain of a newly-killed toad, that was a certain antidote against poison. The bezoar, that was found in the heart of the Arabian deer, was a charm that could cure the plague. In the nests of Arabian birds was the aspilates, that, according to Democritus, kept the wearer from any danger by fire.

The King of Ceilan rode through his city with a large ruby in his hand, at the ceremony of his coronation. The gates of the palace of John the Priest were "made of sardius, with the horn of the horned snake inwrought, so that no man might bring poison within." Over the gable were "two golden apples, in which were two carbuncles," so that the gold might shine by day, and the carbuncles by night. In Lodge's strange romance "A Margarite of America" it was stated that in the chamber of the queen one could behold "all the chaste ladies of the world, inchased out of silver, looking through fair mirrours of chrysolites, carbuncles, sapphires, and greene emeraults." Marco Polo had seen the inhabitants of Zipangu place rose-coloured pearls in the mouths of the dead. A sea-monster had been enamoured of the pearl that the diver brought to King Perozes, and had slain the thief, and mourned for seven moons over its loss. When the Huns lured the king into the great pit, he flung it away—Procopius tells the story—nor was it ever found again, though the Emperor Anastasius offered five hundredweight of gold pieces for it. The King of Malabar had shown to a certain Venetian a rosary of three hundred and four pearls, one for every god that he worshipped.

When the Duke de Valentinois, son of Alexander VI, visited Louis XII of France, his horse was loaded with gold leaves, according to Brantôme, and his cap had double rows of rubies that threw out a great light. Charles of England had ridden in stirrups hung with four hundred and twenty-one diamonds. Richard II had a coat, valued at thirty thousand marks, which was covered with balas rubies. Hall described Henry VIII, on his way to the Tower previous to his coronation, as wearing "a jacket of raised gold, the placard embroidered with diamonds and other rich stones, and a great bauderike about his neck of large balasses." The favourites of James I wore earrings of emeralds set in gold filigrane. Edward II gave to Piers Gaveston a suit of red-gold armour studded with jacinths, a collar of gold roses set with turquoise-stones, and a skull-cap parsemé[13] with pearls. Henry II wore jewelled gloves reaching to the elbow, and had a hawk-glove sewn with twelve rubies and fifty-two great orients. The ducal hat of Charles the Rash, the last Duke of Burgundy of his race, was hung with pear-shaped pearls and studded with sapphires.

How exquisite life had once been! How gorgeous in its pomp and decoration! Even to read of the luxury of the dead was wonderful.

Then he turned his attention to embroideries, and to the tapestries that performed the office of frescoes in the chill rooms of the Northern nations of Europe. As he investigated the subject—and he always had an extraordinary faculty of becoming absolutely absorbed for the moment in whatever he took up—he was almost saddened by the reflection of the ruin that Time brought on beautiful and wonderful things. He, at any rate, had escaped that. Summer followed summer, and the yellow jonquils bloomed and died many times, and nights of horror repeated the story of their shame, but he was unchanged. No winter marred his face or stained his flower-like bloom. How different it was with material things!

---

[13]Sprinkled (French).

Where had they passed to? Where was the great crocus-coloured robe, on which the gods fought against the giants, that had been worked by brown girls for the pleasure of Athena? Where, the huge velarium that Nero had stretched across the Colosseum at Rome, that Titan sail of purple on which was represented the starry sky, and Apollo driving a chariot drawn by white gilt-reined steeds? He longed to see the curious table-napkins wrought for the Priest of the Sun, on which were displayed all the dainties and viands that could be wanted for a feast; the mortuary cloth of King Chilperic, with its three hundred golden bees; the fantastic robes that excited the indignation of the Bishop of Pontus, and were figured with "lions, panthers, bears, dogs, forests, rocks, hunters—all, in fact, that a painter can copy from nature"; and the coat that Charles of Orleans once wore, on the sleeves of which were embroidered the verses of a song beginning "*Madame, je suis tout joyeux,*" the musical accompaniment of the words being wrought in gold thread, and each note, of square shape in those days, formed with four pearls. He read of the room that was prepared at the palace at Rheims for the use of Queen Joan of Burgundy, and was decorated with "thirteen hundred and twenty-one parrots, made in broidery, and blazoned with the king's arms, and five hundred and sixty-one butterflies, whose wings were similarly ornamented with the arms of the queen, the whole worked in gold." Catherine de Médicis had a mourning-bed made for her of black velvet powdered with crescents and suns. Its curtains were of damask, with leafy wreaths and garlands, figured upon a gold and silver ground, and fringed along the edges with broideries of pearls, and it stood in a room hung with rows of the queen's devices in cut black velvet upon cloth of silver. Louis XIV had gold embroidered caryatides[14] fifteen feet high in his apartment. The state bed of Sobieski, King of Poland, was made of Smyrna gold brocade embroidered in turquoises with verses from the Koran. Its supports were of silver gilt, beautifully chased, and profusely set with enamelled and jewelled medallions. It had been taken from the Turkish camp before Vienna, and the standard of Mohammed had stood beneath the tremulous gilt of its canopy.

And so, for a whole year, he sought to accumulate the most exquisite specimens that he could find of textile and embroidered

---

[14]Pillars in the form of draped female figures.

work, getting the dainty Delhi muslins, finely wrought with gold-thread palmates and stitched over with iridescent beetles' wings; the Dacca gauzes, that from their transparency are known in the East as "woven air," and "running water," and "evening dew"; strange figured cloths from Java; elaborate yellow Chinese hangings; books bound in tawny satins or fair blue silks, and wrought with *fleurs de lys*, birds, and images; veils of *lacis* worked in Hungary point; Sicilian brocades, and stiff Spanish velvets; Georgian work, with its gilt coins, and Japanese *Foukousas* with their green-toned golds and their marvellously plumaged birds.

He had a special passion, also, for ecclesiastical vestments, as indeed he had for everything connected with the service of the Church. In the long cedar chests that lined the west gallery of his house he had stored away many rare and beautiful specimens of what is really the raiment of the Bride of Christ, who must wear purple and jewels and fine linen that she may hide the pallid macerated[15] body that is worn by the suffering that she seeks for, and wounded by self-inflicted pain. He possessed a gorgeous cope of crimson silk and gold-thread damask, figured with a repeating pattern of golden pomegranates set in six-petalled formal blossoms, beyond which on either side was the pine-apple device wrought in seed-pearls. The orphreys were divided into panels representing scenes from the life of the Virgin, and the coronation of the Virgin was figured in coloured silks upon the hood. This was Italian work of the fifteenth century. Another cope was of green velvet, embroidered with heart-shaped groups of acanthus-leaves, from which spread long-stemmed white blossoms, the details of which were picked out with silver thread and coloured crystals. The morse bore a seraph's head in gold-thread raised work. The orphreys were woven in a diaper of red and gold silk, and were starred with medallions of many saints and martyrs, among whom was St. Sebastian. He had chasubles, also, of amber-coloured silk, and blue silk and gold brocade, and yellow silk damask and cloth of gold, figured with representations of the Passion and Crucifixion of Christ, and embroidered with lions and peacocks and other emblems; dalmatics of white satin and pink silk damask, decorated with tulips and dolphins and *fleurs de lys*; altar frontals of crimson velvet and blue

---

[15]Wasted away.

linen; and many corporals, chalice-veils, and sudaria. In the mystic offices to which such things were put, there was something that quickened his imagination.

For these treasures, and everything that he collected in his lovely house, were to be to him means of forgetfulness, modes by which he could escape, for a season, from the fear that seemed to him at times to be almost too great to be borne. Upon the walls of the lonely locked room where he had spent so much of his boyhood, he had hung with his own hands the terrible portrait whose changing features showed him the real degradation of his life, and in front of it had draped the purple-and-gold pall as a curtain. For weeks he would not go there, would forget the hideous painted thing, and get back his light heart, his wonderful joyousness, his passionate absorption in mere existence. Then, suddenly, some night he would creep out of the house, go down to dreadful places near Blue Gate Fields,[16] and stay there, day after day, until he was driven away. On his return he would sit in front of the picture, sometimes loathing it and himself, but filled, at other times, with that pride of individualism that is half the fascination of sin, and smiling, with secret pleasure at the misshapen shadow that had to bear the burden that should have been his own.

After a few years he could not endure to be long out of England, and gave up the villa that he had shared at Trouville[17] with Lord Henry, as well as the little white walled-in house at Algiers[18] where they had more than once spent the winter. He hated to be separated from the picture that was such a part of his life, and was also afraid that during his absence some one might gain access to the room, in spite of the elaborate bars that he had caused to be placed upon the door.

He was quite conscious that this would tell them nothing. It was true that the portrait still preserved, under all the foulness and ugliness of the face, its marked likeness to himself; but what could they learn from that? He would laugh at any one who tried to taunt him. He had not painted it. What was it to him how vile and full of shame it looked? Even if he told them, would they believe it?

---

[16]Near the London Docks, noted for opium dens.
[17]Elegant French resort town, on the Normandy coast.
[18]Capital of Algeria, a homosexual playground.

Yet he was afraid. Sometimes when he was down at his great house in Nottinghamshire,[19] entertaining the fashionable young men of his own rank who were his chief companions, and astounding the county by the wanton luxury and gorgeous splendour of his mode of life, he would suddenly leave his guests and rush back to town to see that the door had not been tampered with, and that the picture was still there. What if it should be stolen? The mere thought made him cold with horror. Surely the world would know his secret then. Perhaps the world already suspected it.

For, while he fascinated many, there were not a few who distrusted him. He was very nearly blackballed[20] at a West End club of which his birth and social position fully entitled him to become a member, and it was said that on one occasion, when he was brought by a friend into the smoking-room of the Churchill,[21] the Duke of Berwick and another gentleman got up in a marked manner and went out. Curious stories became current about him after he had passed his twenty-fifth year. It was rumoured that he had been seen brawling with foreign sailors in a low den in the distant parts of Whitechapel,[22] and that he consorted with thieves and coiners and knew the mysteries of their trade. His extraordinary absences became notorious, and, when he used to reappear again in society, men would whisper to each other in corners, or pass him with a sneer, or look at him with cold searching eyes, as though they were determined to discover his secret.

Of such insolences and attempted slights he, of course, took no notice, and in the opinion of most people his frank debonnair manner, his charming boyish smile, and the infinite grace of that wonderful youth that seemed never to leave him, were in themselves a sufficient answer to the calumnies, for so they termed them, that were circulated about him. It was remarked, however, that some of those who had been most intimate with him appeared, after a time, to shun him. Women who had wildly adored him, and for his sake had braved all social censure and set convention at defiance, were seen to grow pallid with shame or horror if Dorian Gray entered the room.

[19]County in central England, site of many aristocratic estates, including Byron's Newstead Abbey.

[20]Received enough negative votes (originally cast as black balls) to deny admission.

[21]A fictitious club (most of the ones mentioned in the novel are real).

[22]Seedy London district.

Yet these whispered scandals only increased in the eyes of many, his strange and dangerous charm. His great wealth was a certain element of security. Society, civilized society at least, is never very ready to believe anything to the detriment of those who are both rich and fascinating. It feels instinctively that manners are of more importance than morals, and, in its opinion, the highest respectability is of much less value than the possession of a good *chef*. And, after all, it is a very poor consolation to be told that the man who has given one a bad dinner, or poor wine, is irreproachable in his private life. Even the cardinal virtues cannot atone for half-cold *entrées* as Lord Henry remarked once, in a discussion on the subject; and there is possibly a good deal to be said for his view. For the canons of good society are, or should be, the same as the canons of art. Form is absolutely essential to it. It should have the dignity of a ceremony, as well as its unreality, and should combine the insincere character of a romantic play with the wit and beauty that make such plays delightful to us. Is insincerity such a terrible thing? I think not. It is merely a method by which we can multiply our personalities.

Such, at any rate, was Dorian Gray's opinion. He used to wonder at the shallow psychology of those who conceive the Ego in man as a thing simple, permanent, reliable, and of one essence. To him, man was a being with myriad lives and myriad sensations, a complex multiform creature that bore within itself strange legacies of thought and passion, and whose very flesh was tainted with the monstrous maladies of the dead. He loved to stroll through the gaunt cold picture-gallery of his country house and look at the various portraits of those whose blood flowed in his veins. Here was Philip Herbert described by Francis Osborne, in his "Memoires on the Reigns of Queen Elizabeth and King James," as one who was "caressed by the Court for his handsome face, which kept him not long company." Was it young Herbert's life that he sometimes led? Had some strange poisonous germ crept from body to body till it had reached his own? Was it some dim sense of that ruined grace that had made him so suddenly, and almost without cause, give utterance, in Basil Hallward's studio, to the mad prayer that had so changed his life? Here, in gold-embroidered red doublet, jewelled surcoat, and gilt-edged ruff and wristbands, stood Sir Anthony Sherard, with his silver-and-black armour piled at his feet. What had this man's legacy been? Had the lover of Giovanna of Naples bequeathed him some inheritance of sin and shame? Were his own actions merely the dreams that the dead man had not dared to realize? Here, from the fading canvas, smiled Lady Elizabeth Devereux, in her gauze hood, pearl stomacher, and pink slashed sleeves. A flower was in her right hand, and her left clasped an enamelled collar of white and damask roses. On a table by her side lay a mandolin and an apple. There were large green rosettes upon her little pointed shoes. He knew her life, and the strange stories that were told about her lovers. Had he something of her temperament in him? These oval heavy-lidded eyes seemed to look curiously at him. What of George Willoughby, with his powdered hair and fantastic patches? How evil he looked! The face was saturnine and swarthy, and the sensual lips seemed to be twisted with disdain. Delicate lace ruffles fell over the lean yellow hands that were so overladen with rings. He had been a macaroni of the eighteenth century, and the friend, in his youth, of Lord Ferrars. What of the second Lord Beckenham, the companion of the Prince Regent in his wildest days, and one of the witnesses at the secret marriage with Mrs. Fitzherbert? How proud and handsome he was, with his chestnut curls and insolent pose! What passions had he bequeathed? The world had looked upon him as infamous. He had led the orgies at Carlton House. The star of the Garter glittered upon his breast. Beside him hung the portrait of his wife, a pallid, thin-lipped woman in black. Her blood, also, stirred within him. How curious it all seemed! And his mother with her Lady Hamilton face, and her moist wine-dashed lips—he knew what he had got from her. He had got from her his beauty, and his passion for the beauty of others. She laughed at him in her loose Bacchante dress. There were vine leaves in her hair. The purple spilled from the cup she was holding. The carnations of the painting had withered, but the eyes were still wonderful in their depth and brilliancy of colour. They seemed to follow him wherever he went.

Yet one had ancestors in literature, as well as in one's own race, nearer perhaps in type and temperament, many of them, and certainly with an influence of which one was more absolutely conscious. There were times when it appeared to Dorian Gray that the whole of history was merely the record of his own life, not as he had lived it in act and circumstance, but as his imagination had created it for him, as it had been in his brain and in his passions. He felt that he had known them all, those strange terrible figures that had passed across the stage of the world and made sin so marvellous and evil so full of subtlety. It seemed to him that in some mysterious way their lives had been his own.

The hero of the wonderful novel that had so influenced his life had himself known this curious fancy. In the seventh chapter he tells how, crowned with laurel, lest lightning might strike him, he had sat, as Tiberius, in a garden at Capri, reading the shameful books of Elephantis, while dwarfs and peacocks strutted round him and the flute-player mocked the swinger of the censer; and, as Caligula, had caroused with the green-shirted jockeys in their stables, and supped in an ivory manger with a jewel-frontleted horse; and, as Domitian, had wandered through a corridor lined with marble mirrors, looking round with haggard eyes for the reflection of the dagger that was to end his days, and sick with that ennui, that terrible *tædium vitæ*,[23] that comes on those to whom life denies nothing; and had peered through a clear emerald at the red shambles of the Circus, and then, in a litter of pearl and purple drawn by silver-shod mules, been carried through the Street of Pomegranates to a House of Gold, and heard men cry on Nero Cæsar as he passed by; and, as Elagabalus, had painted his face with colours, and plied the distaff among the women, and brought the Moon from Carthage, and given her in mystic marriage to the Sun.

Over and over again Dorian used to read this fantastic chapter, and the two chapters immediately following, in which, as in some curious tapestries or cunningly-wrought enamels, were pictured the awful and beautiful forms of those whom Vice and Blood and Weariness had made monstrous or mad: Filippo, Duke of Milan, who slew his wife, and painted her lips with a scarlet poison that her lover might suck death from the dead thing he fondled; Pietro Barbi, the Venetian, known as Paul the Second, who sought in his vanity to assume the title of Formosus, and whose tiara, valued at two hundred thousand florins, was bought at the price of a terrible sin; Gian Maria Visconti, who used hounds to chase living men, and whose murdered body was covered with roses by a harlot who

[23]Weariness with life (Latin).

Charles Ricketts, "[Sleeping Faun]" (1891). An example of decadent, homoerotic imagery. Ricketts, a gay artist and friend of Wilde, was a model for Basil Hallward (Ellman 313). From illustrations for A. C. Swinburne's "A Nympholept," *Black and White* (May 23, 1891): 515. (Courtesy of Wilson Library, University of Minnesota.)

had loved him; the Borgia on his white horse, with Fratricide riding beside him, and his mantle stained with the blood of Perotto; Pietro Riario, the young Cardinal Archbishop of Florence, child and minion of Sixtus IV, whose beauty was equalled only by his debauchery, and who received Leonora of Aragon in a pavilion of white and crimson silk, filled with nymphs and centaurs, and gilded a boy that he might serve at the feast as Ganymede or Hylas; Ezzelin, whose melancholy could be cured only by the spectacle of death, and who had a passion for red blood, as other men have for red wine—the son of the Fiend, as was reported, and one who had cheated his father at dice when gambling with him for his own soul; Giambattista Cibo, who in mockery took the name of Inno-

cent, and into whose torpid veins the blood of three lads was infused by a Jewish doctor; Sigismondo Malatesta, the lover of
Isotta, and the lord of Rimini, whose effigy was burned at Rome as
the enemy of God and man, who strangled Polyssena with a napkin, and gave poison to Ginevra d'Este in a cup of emerald, and in
honour of a shameful passion built a pagan church for Christian
worship; Charles VI, who had so wildly adored his brother's wife
that a leper had warned him of the insanity that was coming on
him, and who, when his brain had sickened and grown strange,
could only be soothed by Saracen cards painted with the images of
Love and Death and Madness; and, in his trimmed jerkin and jewelled cap and acanthus-like curls, Grifonetto Baglioni, who slew
Astorre with his bride, and Simonetto with his page, and whose
comeliness was such that, as he lay dying in the yellow piazza of Perugia, those who had hated him could not choose but weep, and
Atalanta, who had cursed him, blessed him.

There was a horrible fascination in them all. He saw them at
night, and they troubled his imagination in the day. The Renaissance knew of strange manners of poisoning—poisoning by a hel-
met and a lighted torch, by an embroidered glove and a jewelled
fan, by a gilded pomander[24] and by an amber chain. Dorian Gray
had been poisoned by a book. There were moments when he
looked on evil simply as a mode through which he could realize his
conception of the beautiful.

[24]A perforated ball filled with herbs and spices used to perfume a room.

Chapter 12

It was on the ninth of November, the eve of his own thirty-eighth birthday, as he often remembered afterwards.

He was walking home about eleven o'clock from Lord Henry's, where he had been dining, and was wrapped in heavy furs, as the night was cold and foggy. At the corner of Grosvenor Square and South Audley Street,[1] a man passed him in the mist, walking very fast, and with the collar of his grey ulster[2] turned up. He had a bag in his hand. Dorian recognized him. It was Basil Hallward. A strange sense of fear, for which he could not account, came over him. He made no sign of recognition, and went on quickly, in the direction of his own house.

But Hallward had seen him. Dorian heard him first stopping on the pavement and then hurrying after him. In a few moments, his hand was on his arm.

"Dorian! What an extraordinary piece of luck! I have been waiting for you in your library ever since nine o'clock. Finally I took pity on your tired servant, and told him to go to bed, as he let me out. I am off to Paris by the midnight train, and I particularly wanted to see you before I left. I thought it was you, or rather your fur coat, as you passed me. But I wasn't quite sure. Didn't you recognize me?"

"In this fog, my dear Basil? Why, I can't even recognize Grosvenor Square. I believe my house is somewhere about here, but I don't feel at all certain about it. I am sorry you are going away, as I have not seen you for ages. But I suppose you will be back soon?"

"No: I am going to be out of England for six months. I intend to take a studio in Paris, and shut myself up till I have finished a great picture I have in my head. However, it wasn't about myself I wanted to talk. Here we are at your door. Let me come in for a moment. I have something to say to you."

"I shall be charmed. But won't you miss your train?" said Dorian Gray, languidly, as he passed up the steps and opened the door with his latch-key.

[1]Since the 1750s, "the most fashionable place of residence in London" (Hare 2.89).
[2]Long, loose overcoat.

The lamplight struggled out through the fog, and Hallward looked at his watch. "I have heaps of time," he answered. "The train doesn't go till twelve-fifteen, and it is only just eleven. In fact, I was on my way to the club to look for you, when I met you. You see, I sha'n't have any delay about luggage, as I have sent on my heavy things. All I have with me is in this bag, and I can easily get to Victoria[3] in twenty minutes."

Dorian looked at him and smiled. "What a way for a fashionable painter to travel! A Gladstone bag,[4] and an ulster! Come in, or the fog will get into the house. And mind you don't talk about anything serious. Nothing is serious nowadays. At least nothing should be."

Hallward shook his head, as he entered, and followed Dorian into the library. There was a bright wood fire blazing in the large open hearth. The lamps were lit, and an open Dutch silver spirit-case[5] stood, with some siphons of soda-water and large cut-glass tumblers, on a little marqueterie table.[6]

"You see your servant made me quite at home, Dorian. He gave me everything I wanted, including your best gold-tipped cigarettes. He is a most hospitable creature. I like him much better than the Frenchman you used to have. What has become of the Frenchman, by the bye?"

Dorian shrugged his shoulders. "I believe he married Lady Radley's maid, and has established her in Paris as an English dress-maker. *Anglomanie*[7] is very fashionable over there now, I hear. It seems silly of the French, doesn't it? But—do you know?—he was not at all a bad servant. I never liked him, but I had nothing to complain about. One often imagines things that are quite absurd. He was really very devoted to me, and seemed quite sorry when he went away. Have another brandy-and-soda? Or would you like hock-and-seltzer?[8] I always take hock-and-seltzer myself. There is sure to be some in the next room."

"Thanks, I won't have anything more," said the painter, taking his cap and coat off, and throwing them on the bag that he had

---

[3]Basil is planning to take the train from Victoria Station to the eastern coastal port of Dover, cross the Channel to Calais, and continue by train to Paris.

[4]A light valise, named for the liberal politician William E. Gladstone (1808–98).

[5]For bottles of liquor; Sherlock Holmes, another bachelor hero of the 1890s, also owns one. The Dutch were famous silversmiths.

[6]Inlaid with wood or ivory.

[7]French term for enthusiasm for things English.

[8]Rhine wine and carbonated water.

BVE O'CLOCK P.M. : THE FASHIONABLE CLUB.

William M'Connell, "Five O'Clock P.M.: The Fashionable Club" (1858–59). From George Augustus Sala, *Twice Round the Clock; Or, the Hours of the Day and Night in London*, illus. William M'Connell (1859) (London: John and Robert Maxwell, 1878), p. 212. (Courtesy of Wilson Library, University of Minnesota.)

placed in the corner. "And now, my dear fellow, I want to speak to you seriously.[9] Don't frown like that. You make it so much more difficult for me."

"What is it all about?" cried Dorian, in his petulant way, flinging himself down on the sofa. "I hope it is not about myself. I am tired of myself to-night. I should like to be somebody else."

"It is about yourself," answered Hallward, in his grave, deep voice, "and I must say it to you. I shall only keep you half an hour."

Dorian sighed, and lit a cigarette. "Half an hour!" he murmured.

"It is not much to ask of you, Dorian, and it is entirely for your own sake that I am speaking. I think it right that you should know that the most dreadful things are being said against you in London."

---

[9]The version in *Lippincott's*, from this sentence to "What gentleman would associate with him?" (p. 149), was quoted at Wilde's trials to argue that the novel was about sodomy (Holland 100–02).

"I don't wish to know anything about them. I love scandals about other people, but scandals about myself don't interest me. They have not got the charm of novelty."

"They must interest you, Dorian. Every gentleman is interested in his good name. You don't want people to talk of you as something vile and degraded. Of course you have your position, and your wealth, and all that kind of thing. But position and wealth are not everything. Mind you, I don't believe these rumours at all. At least, I can't believe them when I see you. Sin is a thing that writes itself across a man's face. It cannot be concealed. People talk sometimes of secret vices. There are no such things. If a wretched man has a vice, it shows itself in the lines of his mouth, the droop of his eyelids, the moulding of his hands even. Somebody—I won't mention his name, but you know him—came to me last year to have his portrait done. I had never seen him before, and had never heard anything about him at the time, though I have heard a good deal since. He offered an extravagant price. I refused him. There was something in the shape of his fingers that I hated. I know now that I was quite right in what I fancied about him. His life is dreadful. But you, Dorian, with your pure, bright, innocent face, and your marvellous untroubled youth—I can't believe anything against you. And yet I see you very seldom, and you never come down to the studio now, and when I am away from you, and I hear all these hideous things that people are whispering about you, I don't know what to say. Why is it, Dorian, that a man like the Duke of Berwick leaves the room of a club when you enter it? Why is it that so many gentlemen in London will neither go to your house nor invite you to theirs? You used to be a friend of Lord Staveley. I met him at dinner last week. Your name happened to come up in conversation, in connection with the miniatures you have lent to the exhibition at the Dudley.[10] Staveley curled his lip, and said that you might have the most artistic tastes, but that you were a man whom no pureminded girl should be allowed to know, and whom no chaste woman should sit in the same room with. I reminded him that I was a friend of yours, and asked him what he meant. He told me. He told me right out before everybody. It was horrible! Why is your friendship so fatal to young men? There was that wretched boy in

[10]An exhibition gallery in Egyptian Hall, an entertainment center in Piccadilly.

the Guards[11] who committed suicide. You were his great friend. There was Sir Henry Ashton, who had to leave England, with a tarnished name. You and he were inseparable. What about Adrian Singleton, and his dreadful end? What about Lord Kent's only son, and his career? I met his father yesterday in St. James's Street.[12] He seemed broken with shame and sorrow. What about the young Duke of Perth? What sort of life has he got now? What gentleman would associate with him?"

"Stop, Basil. You are talking about things of which you know nothing," said Dorian Gray, biting his lip, and with a note of infinite contempt in his voice. "You ask me why Berwick leaves a room when I enter it. It is because I know everything about his life, not because he knows anything about mine. With such blood as he has in his veins, how could his record be clean? You ask me about Henry Ashton and young Perth. Did I teach the one his vices, and the other his debauchery? If Kent's silly son takes his wife from the streets, what is that to me? If Adrian Singleton writes his friend's name across a bill, am I his keeper?[13] I know how people chatter in England. The middle classes air their moral prejudices over their gross dinner-tables, and whisper about what they call the profligacies of their betters in order to try and pretend that they are in smart society, and on intimate terms with the people they slander. In this country it is enough for a man to have distinction and brains for every common tongue to wag against him. And what sort of lives do these people, who pose as being moral, lead themselves? My dear fellow, you forget that we are in the native land of the hypocrite."

"Dorian," cried Hallward, "that is not the question. England is bad enough I know, and English society is all wrong. That is the reason why I want you to be fine. You have not been fine. One has a right to judge of a man by the effect he has over his friends. Yours seem to lose all sense of honour, of goodness, of purity. You have filled them with a madness for pleasure. They have gone down into the depths. You led them there. Yes: you led them there, and yet you

[11]General name for the oldest, most prestigious regiments in the British army, originally soldiers who guarded the royal family (Pool 110).

[12]A district with prestigious gentlemen's clubs (Baedeker 220).

[13]Singleton has forged a promissory note; to being asked the whereabouts of his brother, whom he has killed, Cain retorts, "Am I my brother's keeper?" (Genesis 4.9).

can smile, as you are smiling now. And there is worse behind. I know you and Harry are inseparable. Surely for that reason, if for none other, you should not have made his sister's name a by-word."

"Take care, Basil. You go too far."

"I must speak, and you must listen. You shall listen. When you met Lady Gwendolen, not a breath of scandal had ever touched her. Is there a single decent woman in London now who would drive with her in the Park? Why, even her children are not allowed to live with her. Then there are other stories—stories that you have been seen creeping at dawn out of dreadful houses and slinking in disguise into the foulest dens in London. Are they true? Can they be true? When I first heard them, I laughed. I hear them now, and they make me shudder. What about your country house, and the life that is led there? Dorian, you don't know what is said about you. I won't tell you that I don't want to preach to you. I remember Harry saying once that every man who turned himself into an amateur curate[14] for the moment always began by saying that, and then proceeded to break his word. I do want to preach to you. I want you to lead such a life as will make the world respect you. I want you to have a clean name and a fair record. I want you to get rid of the dreadful people you associate with. Don't shrug your shoulders like that. Don't be so indifferent. You have a wonderful influence. Let it be for good, not for evil. They say that you corrupt every one with whom you become intimate, and that it is quite sufficient for you to enter a house, for shame of some kind to follow after. I don't know whether it is so or not. How should I know? But it is said of you. I am told things that it seems impossible to doubt. Lord Gloucester was one of my greatest friends at Oxford. He showed me a letter that his wife had written to him when she was dying alone in her villa at Mentone.[15] Your name was implicated in the most terrible confession I ever read. I told him that it was absurd—that I knew you thoroughly, and that you were incapable of anything of the kind. Know you? I wonder do I know you? Before I could answer that, I should have to see your soul."

"To see my soul!" muttered Dorian Gray, starting up from the sofa and turning almost white from fear.

---

[14]Parish assistants, not usually preachers.

[15]Resort on the border between Italy and France, popular with British tourists.

"Yes," answered Hallward, gravely, and with deep-toned sorrow in his voice—"to see your soul. But only God can do that."

A bitter laugh of mockery broke from the lips of the younger man. "You shall see it yourself, to-night!" he cried, seizing a lamp from the table. "Come: it is your own handiwork. Why shouldn't you look at it? You can tell the world all about it afterwards, if you choose. Nobody would believe you. If they did believe you, they would like me all the better for it. I know the age better than you do, though you will prate about it so tediously. Come, I tell you. You have chattered enough about corruption. Now you shall look on it face to face."[16]

There was the madness of pride in every word he uttered. He stamped his foot upon the ground in his boyish insolent manner. He felt a terrible joy at the thought that some one else was to share his secret, and that the man who had painted the portrait that was the origin of all his shame was to be burdened for the rest of his life with the hideous memory of what he had done.

"Yes," he continued, coming closer to him, and looking steadfastly into his stern eyes, "I shall show you my soul. You shall see the thing that you fancy only God can see."

Hallward started back. "This is blasphemy, Dorian!" he cried. "You must not say things like that. They are horrible, and they don't mean anything."

"You think so?" He laughed again.

"I know so. As for what I said to you to-night, I said it for your good. You know I have been always a staunch friend to you."

"Don't touch me. Finish what you have to say."

A twisted flash of pain shot across the painter's face. He paused for a moment, and a wild feeling of pity came over him. After all, what right had he to pry into the life of Dorian Gray? If he had done a tithe of what was rumoured about him, how much he must have suffered! Then he straightened himself up, and walked over to the fireplace, and stood there, looking at the burning logs with their frost-like ashes and their throbbing cores of flame.

"I am waiting, Basil," said the young man, in a hard, clear voice.

He turned round. "What I have to say is this," he cried. "You must give me some answer to these horrible charges that are made

[16]Anticipating the second coming of Jesus, Paul writes, "For now we see through a glass, darkly; but then face to face" (1 Corinthians 13.12).

against you. If you tell me that they are absolutely untrue from be-ginning to end, I shall believe you. Deny them, Dorian, deny them! Can't you see what I am going through? My God! don't tell me that you are bad, and corrupt, and shameful."

Dorian Gray smiled. There was a curl of contempt in his lips. "Come upstairs, Basil," he said, quietly. "I keep a diary of my life from day to day, and it never leaves the room in which it is written. I shall show it to you if you come with me."

"I shall come with you, Dorian, if you wish it. I see I have missed my train. That makes no matter. I can go to-morrow. But don't ask me to read anything to-night. All I want is a plain answer to my question."

"That shall be given to you upstairs. I could not give it here. You will not have to read long."

Chapter 13

He passed out of the room, and began the ascent, Basil Hallward following close behind. They walked softly, as men do instinctively at night. The lamp cast fantastic shadows on the wall and staircase. A rising wind made some of the windows rattle.

When they reached the top landing, Dorian set the lamp down on the floor, and taking out the key, turned it in the lock. "You insist on knowing, Basil?" he asked, in a low voice.

"Yes."

"I am delighted," he answered, smiling. Then he added, somewhat harshly, "You are the one man in the world who is entitled to know everything about me. You have had more to do with my life than you think:" and, taking up the lamp, he opened the door and went in. A cold current of air passed them, and the light shot up for a moment in a flame of murky orange. He shuddered. "Shut the door behind you," he whispered, as he placed the lamp on the table.

Hallward glanced round him, with a puzzled expression. The room looked as if it had not been lived in for years. A faded Flemish tapestry, a curtained picture, an old Italian *cassone*, and an almost empty book-case—that was all that it seemed to contain, besides a chair and a table. As Dorian Gray was lighting a half-burned candle that was standing on the mantelshelf, he saw that the whole place was covered with dust, and that the carpet was in holes. A mouse ran scuffling behind the wainscoting. There was a damp odour of mildew.

"So you think that it is only God who sees the soul, Basil? Draw that curtain back, and you will see mine."

The voice that spoke was cold and cruel. "You are mad, Dorian, or playing a part," muttered Hallward, frowning.

"You won't? Then I must do it myself," said the young man; and he tore the curtain from its rod, and flung it on the ground.

An exclamation of horror broke from the painter's lips as he saw in the dim light the hideous face on the canvas grinning at him. There was something in its expression that filled him with disgust and loathing. Good heavens! it was Dorian Gray's own face that he was looking at! The horror, whatever it was, had not yet entirely spoiled that marvellous beauty. There was still some gold in the thinning hair and some scarlet on the sensual mouth. The sodden eyes had kept something of the loveliness of their blue, the noble curves had not yet completely passed away from chiselled nostrils and from plastic[1] throat. Yes, it was Dorian himself. But who had done it? He seemed to recognize his own brush-work, and the frame was his own design. The idea was monstrous, yet he felt afraid. He seized the lighted candle, and held it to the picture. In the left-hand corner was his own name, traced in long letters of bright vermilion.

It was some foul parody, some infamous, ignoble satire. He had never done that. Still, it was his own picture. He knew it, and he felt as if his blood had changed in a moment from fire to sluggish ice. His own picture! What did it mean? Why had it altered? He turned, and looked at Dorian Gray with the eyes of a sick man. His mouth twitched, and his parched tongue seemed unable to articulate. He passed his hand across his forehead. It was dank with clammy sweat.

The young man was leaning against the mantel-shelf, watching him with that strange expression that one sees on the faces of those who are absorbed in a play when some great artist is acting. There was neither real sorrow in it nor real joy. There was simply the passion of the spectator, with perhaps a flicker of triumph in his eyes. He had taken the flower out of his coat, and was smelling it, or pretending to do so.

"What does this mean?" cried Hallward, at last. His own voice sounded shrill and curious in his ears.

"Years ago, when I was a boy," said Dorian Gray, crushing the flower in his hand, "you met me, flattered me, and taught me to be vain of my good looks. One day you introduced me to a friend of yours, who explained to me the wonder of youth, and you finished a portrait of me that revealed to me the wonder of beauty. In a mad moment, that, even now, I don't know whether I regret or not, I made a wish, perhaps you would call it a prayer . . ."

"I remember it! Oh, how well I remember it! No! the thing is impossible. The room is damp. Mildew has got into the canvas. The paints I used had some wretched mineral poison in them. I tell you the thing is impossible."

[1]Pliant, supple.

"Ah, what is impossible?" murmured the young man, going over to the window, and leaning his forehead against the cold, mist-stained glass.

"You told me you had destroyed it."

"I was wrong. It has destroyed me."

"I don't believe it is my picture."

"Can't you see your ideal in it?" said Dorian, bitterly.

"My ideal, as you call it . . ."

"As you called it."

"There was nothing evil in it, nothing shameful. You were to me such an ideal as I shall never meet again. This is the face of a satyr."[2]

"It is the face of my soul."

"Christ! what a thing I must have worshipped! It has the eyes of a devil."

"Each of us has Heaven and Hell in him,[3] Basil," cried Dorian, with a wild gesture of despair.

Hallward turned again to the portrait, and gazed at it. "My God! If it is true," he exclaimed, "and this is what you have done with your life, why, you must be worse even than those who talk against you fancy you to be!" He held the light up again to the canvas, and examined it. The surface seemed to be quite undisturbed, and as he had left it. It was from within, apparently, that the foulness and horror had come. Through some strange quickening of inner life the leprosies of sin were slowly eating the thing away. The rotting of a corpse in a watery grave was not so fearful.

His hand shook, and the candle fell from its socket on the floor, and lay there sputtering. He placed his foot on it and put it out. Then he flung himself into the rickety chair that was standing by the table and buried his face in his hands.

"Good God, Dorian, what a lesson! what an awful lesson!" There was no answer, but he could hear the young man sobbing at the window. "Pray, Dorian, pray," he murmured. "What is it that one was taught to say in one's boyhood? 'Lead us not into temptation.

---

[2]Lustful woodland god, companion of Bacchus, the god of wine.

[3]Milton's Satan boasts, "The mind is its own place, and in itself / Can make a Heav'n of Hell, a Hell of Heav'n" (*Paradise Lost* 1.254–55).

Forgive us our sins. Wash away our iniquities.'[4] Let us say that together. The prayer of your pride has been answered. The prayer of your repentance will be answered also. I worshipped you too much. I am punished for it. You worshipped yourself too much. We are both punished."

Dorian Gray turned slowly around, and looked at him with tear-dimmed eyes. "It is too late, Basil," he faltered.

"It is never too late, Dorian. Let us kneel down and try if we cannot remember a prayer. Isn't there a verse somewhere, 'Though your sins be as scarlet, yet I will make them as white as snow'?"[5]

"Those words mean nothing to me now."

"Hush! don't say that. You have done enough evil in your life. My God! don't you see that accursed thing leering at us?"

Dorian Gray glanced at the picture, and suddenly an uncontrollable feeling of hatred for Basil Hallward came over him, as though it had been suggested to him by the image on the canvas, whispered into his ear by those grinning lips. The mad passions of a hunted animal stirred within him, and he loathed the man who was seated at the table, more than in his whole life he had ever loathed anything. He glanced wildly around. Something glimmered on the top of the painted chest that faced him. His eye fell on it. He knew what it was. It was a knife that he had brought up, some days before, to cut a piece of cord, and had forgotten to take away with him. He moved slowly towards it, passing Hallward as he did so. As soon as he got behind him, he seized it and turned round. Hallward stirred in his chair as if he was going to rise. He rushed at him, and dug the knife into the great vein that is behind the ear, crushing the man's head down on the table, and stabbing again and again.

There was a stifled groan, and the horrible sound of some one choking with blood. Three times the outstretched arms shot up convulsively, waving grotesque stiff-fingered hands in the air. He stabbed him twice more, but the man did not move. Something be-

---

[4]"Forgive us our trespasses, / As we forgive them that trespass against us. / And lead us not into temptation" (Luke 11.4, from *Book of Common Prayer* [1662]); "Wash me thoroughly from mine iniquity, and cleanse me from my sin" (Psalm 51.2; recited by Catholic priests in mass ritual).

[5]"Come now, and let us reason together, saith the Lord: though your sins be as scarlet, they shall be as white as snow; though they be red like crimson, they shall be as wool" (Isaiah 1.18).

gan to trickle on the floor. He waited for a moment, still pressing the head down. Then he threw the knife on the table, and listened.

He could hear nothing, but the drip, drip on the threadbare carpet. He opened the door and went out on the landing. The house was absolutely quiet. No one was about. For a few seconds he stood bending over the balustrade, and peering down into the black seething well of darkness. Then he took out the key and returned to the room, locking himself in as he did so.

The thing was still seated in the chair, straining over the table with bowed head, and humped back, and long fantastic arms. Had it not been for the red jagged tear in the neck, and the clotted black pool that was slowly widening on the table, one would have said that the man was simply asleep.

How quickly it had all been done! He felt strangely calm, and, walking over to the window, opened it, and stepped out on the balcony. The wind had blown the fog away, and the sky was like a monstrous peacock's tail, starred with myriads of golden eyes. He looked down, and saw the policeman going his rounds and flashing the long beam of his lantern on the doors of the silent houses. The crimson spot of a prowling hansom gleamed at the corner, and then vanished. A woman in a fluttering shawl was creeping slowly by the railings, staggering as she went. Now and then she stopped, and peered back. Once, she began to sing in a hoarse voice. The policeman strolled over and said something to her. She stumbled away, laughing. A bitter blast swept across the Square. The gas-lamps flickered, and became blue, and the leafless trees shook their black iron branches to and fro. He shivered, and went back, closing the window behind him.

Having reached the door, he turned the key, and opened it. He did not even glance at the murdered man. He felt that the secret of the whole thing was not to realize the situation. The friend who had painted the fatal portrait to which all his misery had been due, had gone out of his life. That was enough.

Then he remembered the lamp. It was a rather curious one of Moorish workmanship,[6] made of dull silver inlaid with arabesques of burnished steel, and studded with coarse turquoises. Perhaps it might be missed by his servant, and questions would be asked. He

---

[6]In the style of Moorish Spain (8th–15th c.) and northern Africa.

hesitated for a moment, then he turned back and took it from the table. He could not help seeing the dead thing. How still it was! How horribly white the long hands looked! It was like a dreadful wax image.

Having locked the door behind him, he crept quietly downstairs. The woodwork creaked, and seemed to cry out as if in pain. He stopped several times and waited. No: everything was still. It was merely the sound of his own footsteps.

When he reached the library, he saw the bag and coat in the corner. They must be hidden away somewhere. He unlocked a secret press that was in the wainscoting, a press in which he kept his own curious disguises, and put them into it. He could easily burn them afterwards. Then he pulled out his watch. It was twenty minutes to two.

He sat down and began to think. Every year—every month, almost—men were strangled in England for what he had done. There had been a madness of murder in the air. Some red star had come too close to the earth. . . . And yet what evidence was there against him? Basil Hallward had left the house at eleven. No one had seen him come in again. Most of the servants were at Selby Royal. His valet had gone to bed. . . . Paris! Yes. It was to Paris that Basil had gone, and by the midnight train, as he had intended. With his curious reserved habits, it would be months before any suspicions would be roused. Months! Everything could be destroyed long before then.

A sudden thought struck him. He put on his fur coat and hat, and went out into the hall. There he paused, hearing the slow heavy tread of the policeman on the pavement outside, and seeing the flash of the bull's-eye[7] reflected in the window. He waited, and held his breath.

After a few moments he drew back the latch, and slipped out, shutting the door very gently behind him. Then he began ringing the bell. In about five minutes his valet appeared, half-dressed, and looking very drowsy.

"I am sorry to have had to wake you up, Francis,"[8] he said, stepping in; "but I had forgotten my latch-key. What time is it?"

---

[7]Policeman's lantern.

[8]A small joke: Dorian has replaced Victor, his servant from France, with an English servant named Francis.

"Ten minutes past two, sir," answered the man, looking at the clock and blinking.

"Ten minutes past two? How horribly late! You must wake me at nine to-morrow. I have some work to do."

"All right, sir."

"Did any one call this evening?"

"Mr. Hallward, sir. He stayed here till eleven, and then he went away to catch his train."

"Oh! I am sorry I didn't see him. Did he leave any message?"

"No, sir, except that he would write to you from Paris, if he did not find you at the club."

"That will do, Francis. Don't forget to call me at nine to-morrow."

"No, sir."

The man shambled down the passage in his slippers.

Dorian Gray threw his hat and coat upon the table, and passed into the library. For a quarter of an hour he walked up and down the room biting his lip, and thinking. Then he took down the Blue Book[9] from one of the shelves, and began to turn over the leaves. "Alan Campbell, 152, Hertford Street, Mayfair."[10] Yes; that was the man he wanted.

[9] A social register.

[10] A short walk south from Dorian's house in Grosvenor Square.

Chapter 14

At nine o'clock the next morning his servant came in with a cup of chocolate on a tray, and opened the shutters. Dorian was sleeping quite peacefully, lying on his right side, with one hand underneath his cheek. He looked like a boy who had been tired out with play, or study.

The man had to touch him twice on the shoulder before he woke, and as he opened his eyes a faint smile passed across his lips, as though he had been lost in some delightful dream. Yet he had not dreamed at all. His night had been untroubled by any images of pleasure or of pain. But youth smiles without any reason. It is one of its chiefest charms.

He turned round, and, leaning upon his elbow, began to sip his chocolate. The mellow November sun came streaming into the room. The sky was bright, and there was a genial warmth in the air. It was almost like a morning in May.

Gradually the events of the preceding night crept with silent blood-stained feet into his brain, and reconstructed themselves there with terrible distinctness. He winced at the memory of all that he had suffered, and for a moment the same curious feeling of loathing for Basil Hallward, that had made him kill him as he sat in the chair, came back to him, and he grew cold with passion. The dead man was still sitting there, too, and in the sunlight now. How horrible that was! Such hideous things were for the darkness, not for the day.

He felt that if he brooded on what he had gone through he would sicken or grow mad. There were sins whose fascination was more in the memory than in the doing of them, strange triumphs that gratified the pride more than the passions, and gave to the intellect a quickened sense of joy, greater than any joy they brought, or could ever bring, to the senses. But this was not one of them. It was a thing to be driven out of the mind, to be drugged with poppies, to be strangled lest it might strangle one itself.

When the half-hour struck, he passed his hand across his forehead, and then got up hastily, and dressed himself with even more than his usual care, giving a good deal of attention to the choice of his necktie and scarf-pin, and changing his rings more than once. He spent a long time also over breakfast, tasting the various dishes, talking to his valet about some new liveries that he was thinking of getting made for the servants at Selby, and going through his correspondence. At some of the letters he smiled. Three of them bored him. One he read several times over, and then tore up with a slight look of annoyance in his face. "That awful thing, a woman's memory!" as Lord Henry had once said.

After he had drunk his cup of black coffee, he wiped his lips slowly with a napkin, motioned to his servant to wait, and going over to the table sat down and wrote two letters. One he put in his pocket, the other he handed to the valet.

"Take this round to 152, Hertford Street, Francis, and if Mr. Campbell is out of town, get his address."

As soon as he was alone, he lit a cigarette, and began sketching upon a piece of paper, drawing first flowers, and bits of architecture, and then human faces. Suddenly he remarked that every face that he drew seemed to have a fantastic likeness to Basil Hallward. He frowned, and, getting up, went over to the bookcase and took out a volume at hazard. He was determined that he would not think about what had happened until it became absolutely necessary that he should do so.

When he had stretched himself on the sofa, he looked at the title-page of the book. It was Gautier's "Émaux et Camées," Charpentier's Japanese-paper edition, with the Jacquemart etching.[1] The binding was of citron-green leather, with a design of gilt trellis-work and dotted pomegranates. It had been given to him by Adrian Singleton. As he turned over the pages his eye fell on the poem about the hand of Lacenaire, the cold yellow hand *"du supplice encore mal lavée,"* with its downy red hairs and its *"doigts de faune."*[2] He glanced at his own white taper fingers, shuddering

[1]*Enamels and Cameos* (1852; later expanded) by Théophile Gautier (1811–72), a pioneer of Aestheticism; see ch. 9, n. 2. Charpentier was a French publisher; Japanese paper is made by hand from mulberry tree bark; Jules-Ferdinand Jacquemart (1837–80) was a major French etcher, illustrator, and watercolorist. Dorian's edition was published in 1872 (Bristow 421).

[2]"Lacenaire" is the second part of a two-part poem, "Étude de mains" ("Study of Hands"). The first describes a sculpture of a beautiful female hand; the second, that of Pierre Lacenaire, a murderer who had been guillotined and whose hand had been preserved. The French phrases mean "not yet cleansed of its tortures" and "faun-like fingers."

slightly in spite of himself, and passed on, till he came to those lovely stanzas upon Venice:

> "*Sur une gamme chromatique,*
> *Le sein de perles ruisselant,*
> *La Vénus de l'Adriatique*
> *Sort de l'eau son corps rose et blanc.*
>
> *Les dômes, sur l'azur des ondes*
> *Suivant la phrase au pur contour,*
> *S'enflent comme des gorges rondes*
> *Que soulève un soupir d'amour.*
>
> *L'esquif aborde et me dépose,*
> *Jetant son amarre au pilier,*
> *Devant une façade rose,*
> *Sur le marbre d'un escalier.*"[3]

How exquisite they were! As one read them, one seemed to be floating down the green waterways of the pink and pearl city, seated in a black gondola with silver prow and trailing curtains. The mere lines looked to him like those straight lines of turquoise-blue that follow one as one pushes out to the Lido.[4] The sudden flashes of colour reminded him of the gleam of the opal-and-iris-

---

[3]These stanzas are from "Sur les lagunes" (On the Lagoons), the second part of a four-part poem, "Variations sur le Carnaval de Venise" ("Variations on 'The Carnival of Venice'"). The poet describes a vision of Venice that comes to him while listening to a familiar song about the city:

Her breast a chromatic scale
   Of pearly droplets,
The Venus of the Adriatic
   Emerges from the water, her body pink and white.

The domes, on the azure waves
   Following the pure outline of the phrase,
Swell like rounded breasts
   Stirred by a sigh of love.

The skiff reaches land and I alight,
   Its mooring line thrown about a piling
In front of a rose-colored façade,
   Upon a marble staircase. (trans. Daniel Brewer)

[4]Famous beach resort near Venice.

throated birds that flutter round the tall honey-combed Campanile,[5] or stalk, with such stately grace, through the dim, dust-stained arcades. Leaning back with half-closed eyes, he kept saying over and over to himself:—

"*Devant une façade rose,*
Sur le marbre d'un escalier."

The whole of Venice was in those two lines. He remembered the autumn that he had passed there, and a wonderful love that had stirred him to mad, delightful follies. There was romance in every place. But Venice, like Oxford, had kept the background for romance, and, to the true romantic, background was everything, or almost everything. Basil had been with him part of the time, and had gone wild over Tintoret.[6] Poor Basil! what a horrible way for a man to die!

He sighed, and took up the volume again, and tried to forget. He read of the swallows that fly in and out of the little café at Smyrna where the Hadjis sit counting their amber beads and the turbaned merchants smoke their long tasselled pipes and talk gravely to each other;[7] he read of the Obelisk in the Place de la Concorde that weeps tears of granite in its lonely sunless exile, and longs to be back by the hot lotus-covered Nile, where there are Sphinxes, and rose-red ibises, and white vultures with gilded claws, and crocodiles, with small beryl eyes, that crawl over the green steaming mud;[8] he began to brood over those verses which, drawing music from kiss-stained marble, tell of that curious statue that Gautier compares to a contralto voice, the "*monstre charmant*"

[5]Lofty bell-tower in Venice's St. Mark's Square.

[6]Jacopo Tintoretto (1519–94), prolific Venetian painter, whose reputation, after long neglect, had been resurrected by John Ruskin.

[7]Gautier's "Ce que disent les hirondelles: chanson d'automne" ("What the Swallows Say: An Autumn Song"); Smyrna is a Turkish port and the Hadjis are Muslims who have made the greater pilgrimage to Mecca (on the 8th to 10th day of the 12th month of the Muslim year).

[8]Gautier's "Nostalgies d'obélisques," a two-part poem contrasting the famous Egyptian obelisk located in the center of Paris (on the Place de la Concorde) with an obelisk at Egypt's Temple of Luxor. In the first part, the Parisian obelisk longs to return to ancient Egypt; in the second, the obelisk at Luxor dreams of going to Paris. Dorian concentrates on the first poem, but takes some Egyptian details from the second.

that couches in the porphyry-room of the Louvre.[9] But after a time the book fell from his hand. He grew nervous, and a horrible fit of terror came over him. What if Alan Campbell should be out of England? Days would elapse before he could come back. Perhaps he might refuse to come. What could he do then? Every moment was of vital importance.

They had been great friends once, five years before—almost inseparable, indeed. Then the intimacy had come suddenly to an end. When they met in society now, it was only Dorian Gray who smiled: Alan Campbell never did.

He was an extremely clever young man, though he had no real appreciation of the visible arts, and whatever little sense of the beauty of poetry he possessed he had gained entirely from Dorian. His dominant intellectual passion was for science. At Cambridge he had spent a great deal of his time working in the Laboratory,[10] and had taken a good class in the Natural Science Tripos[11] of his year. Indeed, he was still devoted to the study of chemistry, and had a laboratory of his own, in which he used to shut himself up all day long, greatly to the annoyance of his mother, who had set her heart on his standing for Parliament and had a vague idea that a chemist was a person who made up prescriptions.[12] He was an excellent musician, however, as well, and played both the violin and the piano better than most amateurs. In fact, it was music that had first brought him and Dorian Gray together—music and that indefinable attraction that Dorian seemed to be able to exercise whenever he wished—and, indeed, exercised often without being conscious of it. They had met at Lady Berkshire's the night that Rubinstein[13] played there, and after that used to be always seen together at the Opera, and wherever good music was going on. For eighteen months their intimacy lasted. Campbell was always either at Selby Royal or in Grosvenor Square. To him, as to many others, Dorian

---

[9]The "curious statue" in Gautier's "Contralto" is the Louvre's double-sexed statue of Hermaphroditus, an icon for Victorian writers interested in same-sex eroticism; "monstre charmant" means "sweet monster."

[10]Cambridge University, a center for math and science, opened a laboratory for chemistry in 1887 (Bristow 423).

[11]Course of study.

[12]"Chemist" used to mean "druggist."

[13]Anton Rubinstein (1829–94), virtuosic Russian-Jewish pianist and composer.

Gray was the type of everything that is wonderful and fascinating in life. Whether or not a quarrel had taken place between them no one ever knew. But suddenly people remarked that they scarcely spoke when they met, and that Campbell seemed always to go away early from any party at which Dorian Gray was present. He had changed, too—was strangely melancholy at times, appeared almost to dislike hearing music, and would never himself play, giving as his excuse, when he was called upon, that he was so absorbed in science that he had no time left in which to practise. And this was certainly true. Every day he seemed to become more interested in biology, and his name appeared once or twice in some of the scientific reviews, in connection with certain curious experiments.

This was the man Dorian Gray was waiting for. Every second he kept glancing at the clock. As the minutes went by he became horribly agitated. At last he got up, and began to pace up and down the room, looking like a beautiful caged thing. He took long stealthy strides. His hands were curiously cold.

The suspense became unbearable. Time seemed to him to be crawling with feet of lead, while he by monstrous winds was being swept towards the jagged edge of some black cleft of precipice. He knew what was waiting for him there; saw it indeed, and, shuddering, crushed with dank hands his burning lids as though he would have robbed the very brain of sight, and driven the eyeballs back into their cave. It was useless. The brain had its own food on which it battened, and the imagination, made grotesque by terror, twisted and distorted as a living thing by pain, danced like some foul puppet on a stand, and grinned through moving masks. Then, suddenly, Time stopped for him. Yes: that blind, slow-breathing thing crawled no more, and horrible thoughts, Time being dead, raced nimbly on in front, and dragged a hideous future from its grave, and showed it to him. He stared at it. Its very horror made him stone.

At last the door opened, and his servant entered. He turned glazed eyes upon him.

"Mr. Campbell, sir," said the man.

A sigh of relief broke from his parched lips, and the colour came back to his cheeks.

"Ask him to come in at once, Francis." He felt that he was himself again. His mood of cowardice had passed away.

The man bowed, and retired. In a few moments Alan Campbell walked in, looking very stern and rather pale, his pallor being intensified by his coal-black hair and dark eyebrows.

"Alan! this is kind of you. I thank you for coming."

"I had intended never to enter your house again, Gray. But you said it was a matter of life and death." His voice was hard and cold. He spoke with slow deliberation. There was a look of contempt in the steady searching gaze that he turned on Dorian. He kept his hands in the pockets of his Astrakhan[14] coat, and seemed not to have noticed the gesture with which he had been greeted.

"Yes: it is a matter of life and death, Alan, and to more than one person. Sit down."

Campbell took a chair by the table, and Dorian sat opposite to him. The two men's eyes met. In Dorian's there was infinite pity. He knew that what he was going to do was dreadful.

After a strained moment of silence, he leaned across and said, very quietly, but watching the effect of each word upon the face of him he had sent for, "Alan, in a locked room at the top of this house, a room to which nobody but myself has access, a dead man is seated at a table. He has been dead ten hours now. Don't stir, and don't look at me like that. Who the man is, why he died, how he died, are matters that do not concern you. What you have to do is this—"

"Stop, Gray. I don't want to know anything further. Whether what you have told me is true or not true doesn't concern me. I entirely decline to be mixed up in your life. Keep your horrible secrets to yourself. They don't interest me any more."

"Alan, they will have to interest you. This one will have to interest you. I am awfully sorry for you, Alan. But I can't help myself. You are the one man who is able to save me. I am forced to bring you into the matter. I have no option. Alan, you are scientific. You know about chemistry, and things of that kind. You have made experiments. What you have got to do is to destroy the thing that is upstairs—to destroy it so that not a vestige of it will be left. Nobody saw this person come into the house. Indeed, at the present moment he is supposed to be in Paris. He will not be missed for months. When he is missed, there must be no trace of him found

---

[14]A soft, luxurious leather, from the skin of unborn or newborn lambs.

here. You, Alan, you must change him, and everything that belongs to him, into a handful of ashes that I may scatter in the air."

"You are mad, Dorian."

"Ah! I was waiting for you to call me Dorian."

"You are mad, I tell you—mad to imagine that I would raise a finger to help you, mad to make this monstrous confession. I will have nothing to do with this matter, whatever it is. Do you think I am going to peril my reputation for you? What is it to me what devil's work you are up to?"

"It was suicide, Alan."

"I am glad of that. But who drove him to it? You, I should fancy."

"Do you still refuse to do this for me?"

"Of course I refuse. I will have absolutely nothing to do with it. I don't care what shame comes on you. You deserve it all. I should not be sorry to see you disgraced, publicly disgraced. How dare you ask me, of all men in the world, to mix myself up in this horror? I should have thought you knew more about people's characters. Your friend Lord Henry Wotton can't have taught you much about psychology, whatever else he has taught you. Nothing will induce me to stir a step to help you. You have come to the wrong man. Go to some of your friends. Don't come to me."

"Alan, it was murder. I killed him. You don't know what he had made me suffer. Whatever my life is, he had more to do with the making or the marring of it than poor Harry has had. He may not have intended it, the result was the same."

"Murder! Good God, Dorian, is that what you have come to? I shall not inform upon you. It is not my business. Besides, without my stirring in the matter, you are certain to be arrested. Nobody ever commits a crime without doing something stupid. But I will have nothing to do with it."

"You must have something to do with it. Wait, wait a moment; listen to me. Only listen, Alan. All I ask of you is to perform a certain scientific experiment. You go to hospitals and dead-houses, and the horrors that you do there don't affect you. If in some hideous dissecting-room or fetid laboratory you found this man lying on a leaden table with red gutters scooped out in it for the blood to flow through, you would simply look upon him as an admirable subject. You would not turn a hair. You would not believe that you were doing anything wrong. On the contrary, you would probably feel that you were benefiting the human race, or increasing the sum of knowledge in the world, or gratifying intellectual curiosity, or something of that kind. What I want you to do is merely what you have often done before. Indeed, to destroy a body must be far less horrible than what you are accustomed to work at. And, remember, it is the only piece of evidence against me. If it is discovered, I am lost; and it is sure to be discovered unless you help me."

"I have no desire to help you. You forget that. I am simply indifferent to the whole thing. It has nothing to do with me."

"Alan, I entreat you. Think of the position I am in. Just before you came I almost fainted with terror. You may know terror yourself some day. No! don't think of that. Look at the matter purely from the scientific point of view. You don't inquire where the dead things on which you experiment come from. Don't inquire now. I have told you too much as it is. But I beg of you to do this. We were friends once, Alan."

"Don't speak about those days, Dorian: they are dead."

"The dead linger sometimes. The man upstairs will not go away. He is sitting at the table with bowed head and outstretched arms. Alan! Alan! if you don't come to my assistance I am ruined. Why, they will hang me, Alan! Don't you understand? They will hang me for what I have done."

"There is no good in prolonging this scene. I absolutely refuse to do anything in the matter. It is insane of you to ask me."

"You refuse?"

"Yes."

"I entreat you, Alan."

"It is useless."

The same look of pity came into Dorian Gray's eyes. Then he stretched out his hand, took a piece of paper, and wrote something on it. He read it over twice, folded it carefully, and pushed it across the table. Having done this, he got up, and went over to the window.

Campbell looked at him in surprise, and then took up the paper, and opened it. As he read it, his face became ghastly pale, and he fell back in his chair. A horrible sense of sickness came over him. He felt as if his heart was beating itself to death in some empty hollow.

After two or three minutes of terrible silence, Dorian turned round, and came and stood behind him, putting his hand upon his shoulder.

"I am so sorry for you, Alan," he murmured, "but you leave me no alternative. I have a letter written already. Here it is. You see the address. If you don't help me, I must send it. If you don't help me, I will send it. You know what the result will be. But you are going to help me. It is impossible for you to refuse now. I tried to spare you. You will do me the justice to admit that. You were stern, harsh, offensive. You treated me as no man has ever dared to treat me—no living man, at any rate. I bore it all. Now it is for me to dictate terms."

Campbell buried his face in his hands, and a shudder passed through him.

"Yes, it is my turn to dictate terms, Alan. You know what they are. The thing is quite simple. Come, don't work yourself into this fever. The thing has to be done. Face it, and do it."

A groan broke from Campbell's lips, and he shivered all over. The ticking of the clock on the mantelpiece seemed to him to be dividing Time into separate atoms of agony, each of which was too terrible to be borne. He felt as if an iron ring was being slowly tightened round his forehead, as if the disgrace with which he was threatened had already come upon him. The hand upon his shoulder weighed like a hand of lead. It was intolerable. It seemed to crush him.

"Come, Alan, you must decide at once."

"I cannot do it," he said, mechanically, as though words could alter things.

"You must. You have no choice. Don't delay."

He hesitated a moment. "Is there a fire in the room upstairs?"

"Yes, there is a gas-fire with asbestos."

"I shall have to go home and get some things from the laboratory."

"No, Alan, you must not leave the house. Write out on a sheet of note-paper what you want, and my servant will take a cab and bring the things back to you."

Campbell scrawled a few lines, blotted them, and addressed an envelope to his assistant. Dorian took the note up and read it carefully. Then he rang the bell and gave it to his valet, with orders to return as soon as possible, and to bring the things with him.

As the hall door shut, Campbell started nervously, and, having got up from the chair, went over to the chimney-piece. He was shivering with a kind of ague. For nearly twenty minutes, neither of the men spoke. A fly buzzed noisily about the room, and the ticking of the clock was like the beat of a hammer.

As the chime struck one, Campbell turned round, and, looking at Dorian Gray, saw that his eyes were filled with tears. There was something in the purity and refinement of that sad face that seemed to enrage him. "You are infamous, absolutely infamous!" he muttered.

"Hush, Alan: you have saved my life," said Dorian.

"Your life? Good heavens! what a life that is! You have gone from corruption to corruption, and now you have culminated in crime. In doing what I am going to do, what you force me to do, it is not of your life that I am thinking."

"Ah, Alan," murmured Dorian, with a sigh, "I wish you had a thousandth part of the pity for me that I have for you." He turned away as he spoke, and stood looking out at the garden. Campbell made no answer.

After about ten minutes a knock came to the door, and the servant entered, carrying a large mahogany chest of chemicals, with a long coil of steel and platinum wire and two rather curiously-shaped iron clamps.

"Shall I leave the things here, sir?" he asked Campbell.

"Yes," said Dorian. "And I am afraid, Francis, that I have another errand for you. What is the name of the man at Richmond[15] who supplies Selby with orchids?"

"Harden, sir."[16]

"Yes—Harden. You must go down to Richmond at once, see Harden personally, and tell him to send twice as many orchids as I ordered, and to have as few white ones as possible. In fact, I don't want any white ones. It is a lovely day, Francis, and Richmond is a very pretty place—otherwise I wouldn't bother you about it."

"No trouble, sir. At what time shall I be back?"

Dorian looked at Campbell. "How long will your experiment take, Alan?" he said, in a calm, indifferent voice. The presence of a third person in the room seemed to give him extraordinary courage.

---

[15]One of London's "prettiest and most favorite suburbs," with a large deer park and a good view of the Thames (Dickens 225).

[16]Orchids were a cult flower in the Victorian period because of their beauty and the difficulty of growing them in a British climate. "Orchid" comes from a Greek root meaning testicle; "Harden" may be a joke on this.

Campbell frowned, and bit his lip. "It will take about five hours," he answered.

"It will be time enough, then, if you are back at half-past seven, Francis. Or stay: just leave my things out for dressing. You can have the evening to yourself. I am not dining at home, so I shall not want you."

"Thank you, sir," said the man, leaving the room.

"Now, Alan, there is not a moment to be lost. How heavy this chest is! I'll take it for you. You bring the other things." He spoke rapidly, and in an authoritative manner. Campbell felt dominated by him. They left the room together.

When they reached the top landing, Dorian took out the key and turned it in the lock. Then he stopped, and a troubled look came into his eyes. He shuddered. "I don't think I can go in, Alan," he murmured.

"It is nothing to me. I don't require you," said Campbell, coldly.

Dorian half opened the door. As he did so, he saw the face of his portrait leering in the sunlight. On the floor in front of it the torn curtain was lying. He remembered that the night before he had forgotten, for the first time in his life, to hide the fatal canvas, and was about to rush forward, when he drew back with a shudder.

What was that loathsome red dew that gleamed, wet and glistening, on one of the hands, as though the canvas had sweated blood? How horrible it was!—more horrible, it seemed to him for the moment, than the silent thing that he knew was stretched across the table, the thing whose grotesque misshapen shadow on the spotted carpet showed him that it had not stirred, but was still there, as he had left it.

He heaved a deep breath, opened the door a little wider, and with half-closed eyes and averted head walked quickly in, determined that he would not look even once upon the dead man. Then, stooping down, and taking up the gold-and-purple hanging, he flung it right over the picture.

There he stopped, feeling afraid to turn round, and his eyes fixed themselves on the intricacies of the pattern before him. He heard Campbell bringing in the heavy chest, and the irons, and the other things that he had required for his dreadful work. He began to wonder if he and Basil Hallward had ever met, and, if so, what they had thought of each other.

"Leave me now," said a stern voice behind him.

He turned and hurried out, just conscious that the dead man had been thrust back into the chair, and that Campbell was gazing into a glistening yellow face. As he was going downstairs he heard the key being turned in the lock.

It was long after seven when Campbell came back into the library. He was pale, but absolutely calm. "I have done what you asked me to do," he muttered. "And now, good-bye. Let us never see each other again."

"You have saved me from ruin, Alan. I cannot forget that," said Dorian, simply.

As soon as Campbell had left, he went upstairs. There was a horrible smell of nitric acid in the room. But the thing that had been sitting at the table was gone.[17]

---

[17]Campbell has cremated Hallward's body and dissolved the ashes in nitric acid, rather than leaving them as Dorian has asked.

Chapter 15

That evening, at eight-thirty, exquisitely dressed, and wearing a large buttonhole of Parma violets,[1] Dorian Gray was ushered into Lady Narborough's drawing-room by bowing servants. His forehead was throbbing with maddened nerves, and he felt wildly excited, but his manner as he bent over his hostess's hand was as easy and graceful as ever. Perhaps one never seems so much at one's ease as when one has to play a part. Certainly no one looking at Dorian Gray that night could have believed that he had passed through a tragedy as horrible as any tragedy of our age. Those finely shaped fingers could never have clutched a knife for sin, nor those smiling lips have cried out on God and goodness. He himself could not help wondering at the calm of his demeanour, and for a moment felt keenly the terrible pleasure of a double life.[2]

It was a small party, got up rather in a hurry by Lady Narborough, who was a very clever woman, with what Lord Henry used to describe as the remains of really remarkable ugliness. She had proved an excellent wife to one of our most tedious ambassadors, and having buried her husband properly in a marble mausoleum, which she had herself designed, and married off her daughters to some rich, rather elderly men, she devoted herself now to the pleasures of French fiction, French cookery, and French *esprit*[3] when she could get it.

Dorian was one of her especial favourites, and she always told him that she was extremely glad she had not met him in early life. "I know, my dear, I should have fallen madly in love with you," she used to say, "and thrown my bonnet right over the mills[4] for your sake. It is most fortunate that you were not thought of at the time. As it was, our bonnets were so unbecoming, and the mills were so occupied in trying to raise the wind, that I never had even a flirtation with anybody. However, that was all Narborough's fault. He was dreadfully short-sighted, and there is no pleasure in taking in a husband who never sees anything."

---

[1] A lavender-hued, heavy-scented flower, worn by Des Esseintes, the hero of Huysmans' *À Rebours* (see ch. 10, n. 11).

[2] The "double life" was a keyword in homosexual discourse.

[3] Wit (French).

[4] Slang: thrown discretion to the winds.

Her guests this evening were rather tedious. The fact was, as she explained to Dorian, behind a very shabby fan, one of her married daughters had come up quite suddenly to stay with her, and, to make matters worse, had actually brought her husband with her. "I think it is most unkind of her, my dear," she whispered. "Of course I go and stay with them every summer after I come from Homburg,[5] but then an old woman like me must have fresh air sometimes, and besides, I really wake them up. You don't know what an existence they lead down there. It is pure unadulterated country life. They get up early, because they have so much to do, and go to bed early because they have so little to think about. There has not been a scandal in the neighbourhood since the time of Queen Elizabeth, and consequently they all fall asleep after dinner. You sha'n't sit next either of them. You shall sit by me, and amuse me."

Dorian murmured a graceful compliment and looked round the room. Yes: it was certainly a tedious party. Two of the people he had never seen before, and the others consisted of Ernest Harrowden, one of those middle-aged mediocrities so common in London clubs who have no enemies, but are thoroughly disliked by their friends; Lady Ruxton, an overdressed woman of forty-seven, with a hooked nose, who was always trying to get herself compromised, but was so peculiarly plain that to her great disappointment no one would ever believe anything against her; Mrs. Erlynne, a pushing nobody, with a delightful lisp, and Venetian-red[6] hair; Lady Alice Chapman, his hostess's daughter, a dowdy dull girl, with one of those characteristic British faces that, once seen, are never remembered; and her husband, a red-cheeked, white-whiskered creature who, like so many of his class, was under the impression that inordinate joviality can atone for an entire lack of ideas.

He was rather sorry he had come, till Lady Narborough, looking at the great ormolu[7] gilt clock that sprawled in gaudy curves on the mauve-draped mantelshelf, exclaimed: "How horrid of Henry Wotton to be so late! I sent round to him this morning on chance, and he promised faithfully not to disappoint me."

---

[5]Fashionable German spa, popular with wealthy Britons, known for its casino.

[6]Dark orange-red.

[7]Gilded bronze or a gold-colored alloy of copper, zinc, and tin, typically associated with elaborate furnishings.

It was some consolation that Harry was to be there, and when the door opened and he heard his slow musical voice lending charm to some insincere apology, he ceased to feel bored.

But at dinner he could not eat anything. Plate after plate went away untasted. Lady Narborough kept scolding him for what she called "an insult to poor Adolphe, who invented the *menu* specially for you," and now and then Lord Henry looked across at him, wondering at his silence and abstracted manner. From time to time the butler filled his glass with champagne. He drank eagerly, and his thirst seemed to increase.

"Dorian," said Lord Henry, at last, as the *chaudfroid*[8] was being handed round, "what is the matter with you to-night? You are quite out of sorts."

"I believe he is in love," cried Lady Narborough, "and that he is afraid to tell me for fear I should be jealous. He is quite right. I certainly should."

"Dear Lady Narborough," murmured Dorian, smiling, "I have not been in love for a whole week—not, in fact, since Madame de Ferrol left town."

"How you men can fall in love with that woman!" exclaimed the old lady. "I really cannot understand it."

"It is simply because she remembers you when you were a little girl, Lady Narborough," said Lord Henry. "She is the one link between us and your short frocks."

"She does not remember my short frocks at all, Lord Henry. But I remember her very well at Vienna thirty years ago, and how *décolletée*[9] she was then."

"She is still *décolletée*," he answered, taking an olive in his long fingers; "and when she is in a very smart gown she looks like an *édition de luxe* of a bad French novel. She is really wonderful, and full of surprises. Her capacity for family affection is extraordinary. When her third husband died, her hair turned quite gold from grief."

"How can you, Harry!" cried Dorian.

"It is a most romantic explanation," laughed the hostess. "But her third husband, Lord Henry! You don't mean to say Ferrol is the fourth?"

[8]Cooked meat or fish, coated with brown or white sauce and served cold in aspic jelly.
[9]In a low-necked gown (French).

"Certainly, Lady Narborough."

"I don't believe a word of it."

"Well, ask Mr. Gray. He is one of her most intimate friends."

"Is it true, Mr. Gray?"

"She assures me so, Lady Narborough," said Dorian. "I asked her whether, like Marguerite de Navarre,[10] she had their hearts embalmed and hung at her girdle. She told me she didn't, because none of them had had any hearts at all."

"Four husbands! Upon my word that is *trop de zêle.*"

"*Trop d'audace,*[11] I tell her," said Dorian.

"Oh! she is audacious enough for anything, my dear. And what is Ferrol like? I don't know him."

"The husbands of very beautiful women belong to the criminal classes," said Lord Henry, sipping his wine.

Lady Narborough hit him with her fan. "Lord Henry, I am not at all surprised that the world says that you are extremely wicked."

"But what world says that?" asked Lord Henry, elevating his eyebrows. "It can only be the next world. This world and I are on excellent terms."

"Everybody I know says you are very wicked," cried the old lady, shaking her head.

Lord Henry looked serious for some moments. "It is perfectly monstrous," he said, at last, "the way people go about nowadays saying things against one behind one's back that are absolutely and entirely true."

"Isn't he incorrigible?" cried Dorian, leaning forward in his chair.

"I hope so," said his hostess, laughing. "But really if you all worship Madame de Ferrol in this ridiculous way, I shall have to marry again so as to be in the fashion."

"You will never marry again, Lady Narborough," broke in Lord Henry. "You were far too happy. When a woman marries again, it is because she detested her first husband. When a man marries again, it is because he adored his first wife. Women try their luck; men risk theirs."

---

[10]Margaret of Valois (see ch. 4, n. 2), not the Marguerite de Navarre who wrote *The Heptameron*. Wilde took this image from Victor Hugo's *La Reine Margot* (*Queen Margot*) (1847), in which Margaret is supposed to keep her former lovers' (not husbands') hearts embalmed in a gold box (Bristow 449).

[11]Too much zeal; too much daring (French).

"Narborough wasn't perfect," cried the old lady.

"If he had been, you would not have loved him, my dear lady," was the rejoinder. "Women love us for our defects. If we have enough of them they will forgive us everything, even our intellects. You will never ask me to dinner again, after saying this, I am afraid, Lady Narborough; but it is quite true."

"Of course it is true, Lord Henry. If we women did not love you for your defects, where would you all be? Not one of you would ever be married. You would be a set of unfortunate bachelors. Not, however, that that would alter you much. Nowadays all the married men live like bachelors, and all the bachelors like married men."

"*Fin de siècle*," murmured Lord Henry.

"*Fin du globe*,"[12] answered his hostess.

"I wish it were *fin du globe*," said Dorian, with a sigh. "Life is a great disappointment."

"Ah, my dear," cried Lady Narborough, putting on her gloves, "don't tell me that you have exhausted Life. When a man says that one knows that Life has exhausted him. Lord Henry is very wicked, and I sometimes wish that I had been; but you are made to be good—you look so good. I must find you a nice wife. Lord Henry, don't you think that Mr. Gray should get married?"

"I am always telling him so, Lady Narborough," said Lord Henry, with a bow.

"Well, we must look out for a suitable match for him. I shall go through Debrett[13] carefully to-night, and draw out a list of all the eligible young ladies."

"With their ages, Lady Narborough?" asked Dorian.

"Of course, with their ages, slightly edited. But nothing must be done in a hurry. I want it to be what *The Morning Post*[14] calls a suitable alliance, and I want you both to be happy."

"What nonsense people talk about happy marriages!" exclaimed Lord Henry. "A man can be happy with any woman, as long as he does not love her."

"Ah! what a cynic you are!" cried the old lady, pushing back her chair and nodding to Lady Ruxton. "You must come and dine with

[12]End of the century; end of the world (French). During the 1890s, "*fin de siècle*" was synonymous with "decadent."

[13]Book listing British aristocratic families.

[14]Daily paper, with conservative sympathies (Curtis 109).

me soon again. You are really an admirable tonic, much better than what Sir Andrew prescribes for me. You must tell me what people you would like to meet, though. I want it to be a delightful gathering."

"I like men who have a future, and women who have a past," he answered. "Or do you think that would make it a petticoat party?"

"I fear so," she said, laughing, as she stood up. "A thousand pardons, my dear Lady Ruxton," she added, "I didn't see you hadn't finished your cigarette."

"Never mind, Lady Narborough. I smoke a great deal too much. I am going to limit myself, for the future."

"Pray don't, Lady Ruxton," said Lord Henry. "Moderation is a fatal thing. Enough is as bad as a meal. More than enough is as good as a feast."

Lady Ruxton glanced at him curiously. "You must come and explain that to me some afternoon, Lord Henry. It sounds a fascinating theory," she murmured, as she swept out of the room.

"Now, mind you don't stay too long over your politics and scandal," cried Lady Narborough from the door. "If you do, we are sure to squabble upstairs."

The men laughed, and Mr. Chapman got up solemnly from the foot of the table and came up to the top. Dorian Gray changed his seat, and went and sat by Lord Henry. Mr. Chapman began to talk in a loud voice about the situation in the House of Commons. He guffawed at his adversaries. The word *doctrinaire*—word full of terror to the British mind—reappeared from time to time between his explosions. An alliterative prefix served as an ornament of oratory. He hoisted the Union Jack[15] on the pinnacles of Thought. The inherited stupidity of the race—sound English common sense he jovially termed it—was shown to be the proper bulwark for Society.

A smile curved Lord Henry's lips, and he turned round and looked at Dorian.

"Are you better, my dear fellow?" he asked. "You seemed rather out of sorts at dinner."

"I am quite well, Harry. I am tired. That is all."

"You were charming last night. The little Duchess is quite devoted to you. She tells me she is going down to Selby."

"She has promised to come on the twentieth."

[15]British flag.

"Is Monmouth to be there too?"

"Oh, yes, Harry."

"He bores me dreadfully, almost as much as he bores her. She is very clever, too clever for a woman. She lacks the indefinable charm of weakness. It is the feet of clay that make the gold of the image precious. Her feet are very pretty, but they are not feet of clay. White porcelain feet, if you like. They have been through the fire, and what fire does not destroy, it hardens. She has had experiences."

"How long has she been married?" asked Dorian.

"An eternity, she tells me. I believe, according to the peerage, it is ten years, but ten years with Monmouth must have been like eternity, with time thrown in. Who else is coming?"

"Oh, the Willoughbys, Lord Rugby and his wife, our hostess, Geoffrey Clouston, the usual set. I have asked Lord Grotrian."

"I like him," said Lord Henry. "A great many people don't, but I find him charming. He atones for being occasionally somewhat over-dressed, by being always absolutely over-educated. He is a very modern type."

"I don't know if he will be able to come, Harry. He may have to go to Monte Carlo with his father."

"Ah! what a nuisance people's people are! Try and make him come. By the way, Dorian, you ran off very early last night. You left before eleven. What did you do afterwards? Did you go straight home?"

Dorian glanced at him hurriedly, and frowned.

"No, Harry," he said at last, "I did not get home till nearly three."

"Did you go to the club?"

"Yes," he answered. Then he bit his lip. "No, I don't mean that. I didn't go to the club. I walked about. I forget what I did. . . . How inquisitive you are, Harry! You always want to know what one has been doing. I always want to forget what I have been doing. I came in at half-past two, if you wish to know the exact time. I had left my latch-key at home, and my servant had to let me in. If you want any corroborative evidence on the subject you can ask him."

Lord Henry shrugged his shoulders. "My dear fellow, as if I cared! Let us go up to the drawing-room. No sherry, thank you, Mr. Chapman. Something has happened to you, Dorian. Tell me what it is. You are not yourself to-night."

"Don't mind me, Harry. I am irritable, and out of temper. I shall come round and see you to-morrow, or next day. Make my excuses to Lady Narborough. I sha'n't go upstairs. I shall go home. I must go home."

"All right, Dorian. I dare say I shall see you to-morrow at tea-time. The Duchess is coming."

"I will try to be there, Harry," he said, leaving the room. As he drove back to his own house he was conscious that the sense of terror he thought he had strangled had come back to him. Lord Henry's casual questioning had made him lose his nerves for the moment, and he wanted his nerve still. Things that were dangerous had to be destroyed. He winced. He hated the idea of even touching them.

Yet it had to be done. He realized that, and when he had locked the door of his library, he opened the secret press into which he had thrust Basil Hallward's coat and bag. A huge fire was blazing. He piled another log on it. The smell of the singeing clothes and burning leather was horrible. It took him three-quarters of an hour to consume everything. At the end he felt faint and sick, and having lit some Algerian pastilles[16] in a pierced copper brazier, he bathed his hands and forehead with a cool musk-scented vinegar.

Suddenly he started. His eyes grew strangely bright, and he gnawed nervously at his underlip. Between two of the windows stood a large Florentine cabinet,[17] made out of ebony, and inlaid with ivory and blue lapis.[18] He watched it as though it were a thing that could fascinate and make afraid, as though it held something that he longed for and yet almost loathed. His breath quickened. A mad craving came over him. He lit a cigarette and then threw it away. His eyelids drooped till the long fringed lashes almost touched his cheek. But he still watched the cabinet. At last he got up from the sofa on which he had been lying, went over to it, and, having unlocked it, touched some hidden spring. A triangular drawer passed slowly out. His fingers moved instinctively towards it, dipped in, and closed on something. It was a small Chinese box of black and gold-dust lacquer, elaborately wrought,

[16]Small pellets burned as incense; an Ottoman indulgence, often from Algeria.

[17]With many small drawers or pigeonholes, a favorite for aristocratic collectors of *objets*.

[18]Lapis lazuli, a bright-blue mineral.

the sides patterned with curved waves, and the silken cords hung with round crystals and tasselled in plaited metal threads. He opened it. Inside was a green paste[19] waxy in lustre, the odour curiously heavy and persistent.

He hesitated for some moments, with a strangely immobile smile upon his face. Then shivering, though the atmosphere of the room was terribly hot, he drew himself up, and glanced at the clock. It was twenty minutes to twelve. He put the box back, shutting the cabinet doors as he did so, and went into his bedroom.

As midnight was striking bronze blows upon the dusky air, Dorian Gray, dressed commonly, and with a muffler wrapped round his throat, crept quietly out of his house. In Bond Street[20] he found a hansom with a good horse. He hailed it, and in a low voice gave the driver an address.

The man shook his head. "It is too far for me," he muttered.

"Here is a sovereign for you," said Dorian. "You shall have another if you drive fast."

"All right, sir," answered the man, "you will be there in an hour,"[21] and after his fare had got in he turned his horse round, and drove rapidly towards the river.

---

[19]Opium; the paste was lit and the smoke inhaled. In this pure form, it was supposed to be available only to chemists and druggists (Milligan 141).

[20]Site of fashionable shops and galleries, such as the Grosvenor (see p. 6).

[21]An hour ride usually cost 2½ shillings (Baedeker 28); a sovereign is 20 shillings.

Chapter 16

A cold rain began to fall, and the blurred street-lamps looked ghastly in the dripping mist. The public-houses were just closing, and dim men and women were clustering in broken groups round their doors. From some of the bars came the sound of horrible laughter. In others, drunkards brawled and screamed.

Lying back in the hansom, with his hat pulled over his forehead, Dorian Gray watched with listless eyes the sordid shame of the great city, and now and then he repeated to himself the words that Lord Henry had said to him on the first day they had met, "To cure the soul by means of the senses, and the senses by means of the soul." Yes, that was the secret. He had often tried it, and would try it again now. There were opium-dens,[1] where one could buy oblivion, dens of horror where the memory of old sins could be destroyed by the madness of sins that were new.

The moon hung low in the sky like a yellow skull. From time to time a huge misshapen cloud stretched a long arm across and hid it. The gas-lamps grew fewer, and the streets more narrow and gloomy. Once the man lost his way, and had to drive back half a mile. A steam rose from the horse as it splashed up the puddles. The side-windows of the hansom were clogged with a grey-flannel mist.

"To cure the soul by means of the senses, and the senses by means of the soul!" How the words rang in his ears! His soul, certainly, was sick to death. Was it true that the senses could cure it? Innocent blood had been spilt. What could atone for that? Ah! for that there was no atonement; but though forgiveness was impossible, forgetfulness was possible still, and he was determined to forget, to stamp the thing out, to crush it as one would crush the adder that had stung one. Indeed, what right had Basil to have spoken to him as he had done? Who had made him a judge over others? He had said things that were dreadful, horrible, not to be endured.

On and on plodded the hansom, going slower, it seemed to him, at each step. He thrust up the trap,[2] and called to the man to drive faster. The hideous hunger for opium began to gnaw at him. His

---

[1] Usually in the London dock district east of the Tower of London.
[2] Roof-door.

A WEST-END HANSOM.

[Anon.], "A West-End Hansom" (1896). From *Windsor Magazine* 4 (1896): 152. (Courtesy of Wilson Library, University of Minnesota.)

throat burned, and his delicate hands twitched nervously together. He struck at the horse madly with his stick. The driver laughed, and whipped up. He laughed in answer, and the man was silent.

The way seemed interminable, and the streets like the black web of some sprawling spider. The monotony became unbearable, and, as the mist thickened, he felt afraid.

Then they passed by lonely brickfields.[3] The fog was lighter here, and he could see the strange bottle-shaped kilns with their orange fanlike tongues of fire. A dog barked as they went by, and far away in the darkness some wandering sea-gull screamed. The horse stumbled in a rut, then swerved aside, and broke into a gallop.

After some time they left the clay road, and rattled again over rough-paven streets. Most of the windows were dark, but now and then fantastic shadows were silhouetted against some lamp-lit blind. He watched them curiously. They moved like monstrous marionettes, and made gestures like live things. He hated them. A

---

[3]Where clay was dug out and used to make bricks for kilns.

dull rage was in his heart. As they turned a corner a woman yelled something at them from an open door, and two men ran after the hansom for about a hundred yards. The driver beat at them with his whip.

It is said that passion makes one think in a circle. Certainly with hideous iteration the bitten lips of Dorian Gray shaped and reshaped those subtle words that dealt with soul and sense, till he had found in them the full expression, as it were, of his mood, and justified, by intellectual approval, passions that without such justification would still have dominated his temper. From cell to cell of his brain crept the one thought; and the wild desire to live, most terrible of all man's appetites, quickened into force each trembling nerve and fibre. Ugliness that had once been hateful to him because it made things real, became dear to him now for that very reason. Ugliness was the one reality. The coarse brawl, the loathsome den, the crude violence of disordered life, the very vileness of thief and outcast, were more vivid, in their intense actuality of impression, than all the gracious shapes of Art, the dreamy shadows of Song. They were what he needed for forgetfulness. In three days he would be free.

Suddenly the man drew up with a jerk at the top of a dark lane. Over the low roofs and jagged chimney-stacks of the houses rose the black masts of ships. Wreaths of white mist clung like ghostly sails to the yards.

"Somewhere about here, sir, ain't it?" he asked huskily through the trap.

Dorian started and peered round. "This will do," he answered, and, having got out hastily, and given the driver the extra fare he had promised him, he walked quickly in the direction of the quay. Here and there a lantern gleamed at the stern of some huge merchantman. The light shook and splintered in the puddles. A red glare came from an outward-bound steamer that was coaling. The slimy pavement looked like a wet mackintosh.[4]

He hurried on towards the left, glancing back now and then to see if he was being followed. In about seven or eight minutes he reached a small shabby house, that was wedged in between two gaunt factories. In one of the top-windows stood a lamp. He stopped, and gave a peculiar knock.

---

[4]Rubber raincoat.

After a little time he heard steps in the passage, and the chain being unhooked. The door opened quietly, and he went in without saying a word to the squat misshapen figure that flattened itself into the shadow as he passed. At the end of the hall hung a tattered green curtain that swayed and shook in the gusty wind which had followed him in from the street. He dragged it aside, and entered a long, low room which looked as if it had once been a third-rate dancing-saloon. Shrill flaring gas-jets, dulled and distorted in the fly-blown mirrors that faced them, were ranged round the walls. Greasy reflectors of ribbed tin backed them, making quivering disks of light. The floor was covered with ochre-coloured sawdust, trampled here and there into mud, and stained with dark rings of spilt liquor. Some Malays[5] were crouching by a little charcoal stove playing with bone counters, and showing their white teeth as they chattered. In one corner with his head buried in his arms, a sailor sprawled over a table, and by the tawdrily-painted bar that ran across one complete side stood two haggard women mocking an old man who was brushing the sleeves of his coat with an expression of disgust. "He thinks he's got red ants on him," laughed one of them, as Dorian passed by. The man looked at her in terror, and began to whimper.

At the end of the room there was a little staircase, leading to a darkened chamber. As Dorian hurried up its three ricketty steps, the heavy odour of opium met him. He heaved a deep breath, and his nostrils quivered with pleasure. When he entered, a young man with smooth yellow hair, who was bending over a lamp lighting a long thin pipe, looked up at him, and nodded in a hesitating manner.

"You here, Adrian?" muttered Dorian.

"Where else should I be?" he answered, listlessly. "None of the chaps will speak to me now."

"I thought you had left England."

"Darlington is not going to do anything. My brother paid the bill at last. George doesn't speak to me either. . . . I don't care," he added, with a sigh. "As long as one has this stuff, one doesn't want friends. I think I have had too many friends."

Dorian winced, and looked round at the grotesque things that lay in such fantastic postures on the ragged mattresses. The twisted

[5]From southeast Asia.

limbs, the gaping mouths, the staring lustreless eyes, fascinated him. He knew in what strange heavens they were suffering, and what dull hells were teaching them the secret of some new joy. They were better off than he was. He was prisoned in thought. Memory, like a horrible malady, was eating his soul away. From time to time he seemed to see the eyes of Basil Hallward looking at him. Yet he felt he could not stay. The presence of Adrian Singleton troubled him. He wanted to be where no one would know who he was. He wanted to escape from himself.

"I am going on to the other place," he said, after a pause.

"On the wharf?"

"Yes."

"That mad-cat is sure to be there. They won't have her in this place now."

Dorian shrugged his shoulders. "I am sick of women who love one. Women who hate one are much more interesting. Besides, the stuff is better."

"Much the same."

"I like it better. Come and have something to drink. I must have something."

"I don't want anything," murmured the young man.

"Never mind."

Adrian Singleton rose up wearily and followed Dorian to the bar. A half-caste,[6] in a ragged turban and a shabby ulster, grinned a hideous greeting as he thrust a bottle of brandy and two tumblers in front of them. The women sidled up, and began to chatter. Dorian turned his back on them, and said something in a low voice to Adrian Singleton.

A crooked smile, like a Malay crease,[7] writhed across the face of one of the women. "We are very proud to-night," she sneered.

"For God's sake don't talk to me," cried Dorian, stamping his foot on the ground. "What do you want? Money? Here it is. Don't ever talk to me again."

Two red sparks flashed for a moment in the woman's sodden eyes, then flickered out, and left them dull and glazed. She tossed

[6]Of European and Asian (usually Indian) heritage.

[7]Often spelled "kris," a wavy-bladed dagger.

her head, and raked the coins off the counter with greedy fingers. Her companion watched her enviously.

"It's no use," sighed Adrian Singleton. "I don't care to go back. What does it matter? I am quite happy here."

"You will write to me if you want anything, won't you?" said Dorian, after a pause.

"Perhaps."

"Good-night, then."

"Good-night," answered the young man, passing up the steps, and wiping his parched mouth with a handkerchief.

Dorian walked to the door with a look of pain in his face. As he drew the curtain aside a hideous laugh broke from the painted lips of the woman who had taken his money. "There goes the devil's bargain!" she hiccoughed, in a hoarse voice.

"Curse you!" he answered, "don't call me that."

She snapped her fingers. "Prince Charming is what you like to be called, ain't it?" she yelled after him.

The drowsy sailor leaped to his feet as she spoke, and looked wildly round. The sound of the shutting of the hall door fell on his ear. He rushed out as if in pursuit.

Dorian Gray hurried along the quay through the drizzling rain. His meeting with Adrian Singleton had strangely moved him, and he wondered if the ruin of that young life was really to be laid at his door, as Basil Hallward had said to him with such infamy of insult. He bit his lip, and for a few seconds his eyes grew sad. Yet, after all, what did it matter to him? One's days were too brief to take the burden of another's errors on one's shoulders. Each man lived his own life, and paid his own price for living it. The only pity was one had to pay so often for a single fault. One had to pay over and over again, indeed. In her dealings with man Destiny never closed her accounts.

There are moments, psychologists tell us, when the passion for sin, or for what the world calls sin, so dominates a nature, that every fibre of the body, as every cell of the brain, seems to be instinct with fearful impulses. Men and women at such moments lose the freedom of their will. They move to their terrible end as automatons move. Choice is taken from them, and conscience is either killed, or, if it lives at all, lives but to give rebellion its fascination, and disobedience its charm. For all sins, as theologians weary not of reminding us, are sins of disobedience. When that high spirit, that morning-star of evil,[8] fell from heaven, it was as a rebel that he fell.

Callous, concentrated on evil, with stained mind, and soul hungry for rebellion, Dorian Gray hastened on, quickening his step as he went, but as he darted aside into a dim archway, that had served him often as a short cut to the ill-famed place where he was going, he felt himself suddenly seized from behind, and before he had time to defend himself he was thrust back against the wall, with a brutal hand round his throat.

He struggled madly for life, and by a terrible effort wrenched the tightening fingers away. In a second he heard the click of a revolver, and saw the gleam of a polished barrel pointing straight at his head, and the dusky form of a short thick-set man facing him.

"What do you want?" he gasped.

"Keep quiet," said the man. "If you stir, I shoot you."

"You are mad. What have I done to you?"

"You wrecked the life of Sibyl Vane," was the answer, "and Sibyl Vane was my sister. She killed herself. I know it. Her death is at your door. I swore I would kill you in return. For years I have sought you. I had no clue, no trace. The two people who could have described you were dead. I knew nothing of you but the pet name she used to call you. I heard it to-night by chance. Make your peace with God, for to-night you are going to die."

Dorian Gray grew sick with fear. "I never knew her," he stammered. "I never heard of her. You are mad."

"You had better confess your sin, for as sure as I am James Vane, you are going to die." There was a horrible moment. Dorian did not know what to say or do. "Down on your knees!" growled the man. "I give you one minute to make your peace—no more. I go on board to-night for India, and I must do my job first. One minute. That's all."

Dorian's arms fell to his side. Paralysed with terror, he did not know what to do. Suddenly a wild hope flashed across his brain. "Stop," he cried. "How long ago is it since your sister died? Quick, tell me!"

---

[8]Satan's name in Heaven, before his rebellion, was Lucifer ("light-bearer"); also the name of the morning star.

"Eighteen years," said the man. "Why do you ask me? What do years matter?"

"Eighteen years," laughed Dorian Gray, with a touch of triumph in his voice. "Eighteen years! Set me under the lamp and look at my face!"

James Vane hesitated for a moment, not understanding what was meant. Then he seized Dorian Gray and dragged him from the archway.

Dim and wavering as was the windblown light, yet it served to show him the hideous error, as it seemed, into which he had fallen, for the face of the man he had sought to kill had all the bloom of boyhood, all the unstained purity of youth. He seemed little more than a lad of twenty summers, hardly older, if older indeed at all, than his sister had been when they had parted so many years ago. It was obvious that this was not the man who had destroyed her life.

He loosened his hold and reeled back. "My God! my God!" he cried, "and I would have murdered you!"

Dorian Gray drew a long breath. "You have been on the brink of committing a terrible crime, my man," he said, looking at him sternly. "Let this be a warning to you not to take vengeance into your own hands."

"Forgive me, sir," muttered James Vane. "I was deceived. A chance word I heard in that damned den set me on the wrong track."

"You had better go home, and put that pistol away, or you may get into trouble," said Dorian, turning on his heel, and going slowly down the street.

James Vane stood on the pavement in horror. He was trembling from head to foot. After a little while a black shadow that had been creeping along the dripping wall, moved out into the light and came close to him with stealthy footsteps. He felt a hand laid on his arm and looked round with a start. It was one of the women who had been drinking at the bar

"Why didn't you kill him?" she hissed out, putting her haggard face quite close to his. "I knew you were following him when you rushed out from Daly's. You fool! You should have killed him. He has lots of money, and he's as bad as bad."

"He is not the man I am looking for," he answered, "and I want no man's money. I want a man's life. The man whose life I want must be nearly forty now. This one is little more than a boy. Thank God, I have not got his blood upon my hands."

The woman gave a bitter laugh. "Little more than a boy!" she sneered. "Why, man, it's nigh on eighteen years since Prince Charming made me what I am."

"You lie!" cried James Vane.

She raised her hand up to heaven. "Before God I am telling the truth," she cried.

"Before God?"

"Strike me dumb if it ain't so. He is the worst one that comes here. They say he has sold himself to the devil for a pretty face. It's nigh on eighteen years since I met him. He hasn't changed much since then. I have, though," she added, with a sickly leer.

"You swear this?"

"I swear it," came in hoarse echo from her flat mouth. "But don't give me away to him," she whined; "I am afraid of him. Let me have some money for my night's lodging."

He broke from her with an oath, and rushed to the corner of the street, but Dorian Gray had disappeared. When he looked back, the woman had vanished also.

Chapter 17

A week later Dorian Gray was sitting in the conservatory at Selby Royal talking to the pretty Duchess of Monmouth, who with her husband, a jaded-looking man of sixty, was amongst his guests. It was tea-time, and the mellow light of the huge lace-covered lamp that stood on the table lit up the delicate china and hammered silver of the service at which the Duchess was presiding. Her white hands were moving daintily among the cups, and her full red lips were smiling at something that Dorian had whispered to her. Lord Henry was lying back in a silk-draped wicker chair, looking at them. On a peach-coloured divan sat Lady Narborough pretending to listen to the Duke's description of the last Brazilian beetle that he had added to his collection. Three young men in elaborate smoking-suits were handing tea-cakes to some of the women. The house-party consisted of twelve people, and there were more expected to arrive on the next day.

"What are you two talking about?" said Lord Henry, strolling over to the table, and putting his cup down. "I hope Dorian has told you about my plan for rechristening everything, Gladys. It is a delightful idea."

"But I don't want to be rechristened, Harry," rejoined the Duchess, looking up at him with her wonderful eyes. "I am quite satisfied with my own name, and I am sure Mr. Gray should be satisfied with his."

"My dear Gladys, I would not alter either name for the world. They are both perfect. I was thinking chiefly of flowers. Yesterday I cut an orchid, for my buttonhole. It was a marvellous spotted thing, as effective as the seven deadly sins. In a thoughtless moment I asked one of the gardeners what it was called. He told me it was a fine specimen of *Robinsoniana*,[1] or something dreadful of that kind. It is a sad truth, but we have lost the faculty of giving lovely names to things. Names are everything. I never quarrel with actions. My one quarrel is with words. That is the reason I hate vulgar realism in literature. The man who could call a spade a spade should be compelled to use one. It is the only thing he is fit for."

"Then what should we call you, Harry?" she asked.

---

[1]Probably not the gardener's term: the *Anemone nemerosa* "Robinsoniana" is not spotted and is not an orchid.

"His name is Prince Paradox," said Dorian.

"I recognize him in a flash," exclaimed the Duchess.

"I won't hear of it," laughed Lord Henry, sinking into a chair. "From a label there is no escape! I refuse the title."

"Royalties may not abdicate," fell as a warning from pretty lips.

"You wish me to defend my throne, then?"

"Yes."

"I give the truths of to-morrow."

"I prefer the mistakes of to-day," she answered.

"You disarm me, Gladys," he cried, catching the wilfulness of her mood.

"Of your shield, Harry: not of your spear."

"I never tilt against Beauty," he said, with a wave of his hand.

"That is your error, Harry, believe me. You value beauty far too much."

"How can you say that? I admit that I think that it is better to be beautiful than to be good. But on the other hand no one is more ready than I am to acknowledge that it is better to be good than to be ugly."

"Ugliness is one of the seven deadly sins, then?" cried the Duchess. "What becomes of your simile about the orchid?"

"Ugliness is one of the seven deadly virtues, Gladys. You, as a good Tory, must not underrate them. Beer, the Bible, and the seven deadly virtues have made our England what she is."

"You don't like your country, then?" she asked.

"I live in it."

"That you may censure it the better."

"Would you have me take the verdict of Europe on it?" he inquired.

"What do they say of us?"

"That Tartuffe has emigrated to England and opened a shop."[2]

"Is that yours, Harry?"

"I give it to you."

"I could not use it. It is too true."

"You need not be afraid. Our countrymen never recognize a description."

---

[2]The religious hypocrite in Molière's *Tartuffe* (1664); Adam Smith referred to the British as a "nation of shopkeepers" in *The Wealth of Nations* (1776), and Napoleon echoed the remark.

"They are practical."

"They are more cunning than practical. When they make up their ledger, they balance stupidity by wealth, and vice by hypocrisy."

"Still, we have done great things."

"Great things have been thrust on us, Gladys."[3]

"We have carried their burden."

"Only as far as the Stock Exchange."

She shook her head. "I believe in the race," she cried.

"It represents the survival of the pushing."[4]

"It has development."

"Decay fascinates me more."

"What of Art?" she asked.

"It is a malady."

"Love?"

"An illusion."

"Religion?"

"The fashionable substitute for Belief."

"You are a sceptic."

"Never! Scepticism is the beginning of Faith."

"What are you?"

"To define is to limit."

"Give me a clue."

"Threads snap. You would lose your way in the labyrinth."[5]

"You bewilder me. Let us talk of some one else."

"Our host is a delightful topic. Years ago he was christened Prince Charming."

"Ah! don't remind me of that," cried Dorian Gray.

"Our host is rather horrid this evening," answered the Duchess, colouring. "I believe he thinks that Monmouth married me on purely scientific principles as the best specimen he could find of a modern butterfly."

"Well, I hope he won't stick pins into you, Duchess," laughed Dorian.

[3]"Some are born great, some achieve greatness, and some have greatness thrust upon them" (Shakespeare, *Twelfth Night* 2.2.145–46).

[4]Parody of Charles Darwin's doctrine of the "survival of the fittest" (Darwin does not actually use this phrase).

[5]Clue: both a key to a riddle and a ball of thread, especially the one given by Ariadne to help Theseus find his way out of the Minotaur's labyrinth.

"Oh! my maid does that already, Mr. Gray, when she is annoyed with me."

"And what does she get annoyed with you about, Duchess?"

"For the most trivial things, Mr. Gray, I assure you. Usually because I come in at ten minutes to nine and tell her that I must be dressed by half-past eight."

"How unreasonable of her! You should give her warning."

"I daren't, Mr. Gray. Why, she invents hats for me. You remember the one I wore at Lady Hilstone's garden-party? You don't, but it is nice of you to pretend that you do. Well, she made if out of nothing. All good hats are made out of nothing."

"Like all good reputations, Gladys," interrupted Lord Henry. "Every effect that one produces gives one an enemy. To be popular one must be a mediocrity."

"Not with women," said the Duchess, shaking her head; "and women rule the world. I assure you we can't bear mediocrities. We women, as some one says, love with our ears, just as you men love with your eyes, if you ever love at all."

"It seems to me that we never do anything else," murmured Dorian.

"Ah! then, you never really love, Mr. Gray," answered the Duchess with mock sadness.

"My dear Gladys!" cried Lord Henry. "How can you say that? Romance lives by repetition, and repetition converts an appetite into an art. Besides, each time that one loves is the only time one has ever loved. Difference of object does not alter singleness of passion. It merely intensifies it. We can have in life but one great experience at best, and the secret of life is to reproduce that experience as often as possible."

"Even when one has been wounded by it, Harry?" asked the Duchess after a pause.

"Especially when one has been wounded by it," answered Lord Henry.

The Duchess turned and looked at Dorian Gray with a curious expression in her eyes. "What do you say to that, Mr. Gray?" she inquired.

Dorian hesitated for a moment. Then he threw his head back and laughed. "I always agree with Harry, Duchess."

"Even when he is wrong?"

"Harry is never wrong, Duchess."

"And does his philosophy make you happy?"

"I have never searched for happiness. Who wants happiness? I have searched for pleasure."

"And found it, Mr. Gray?"

"Often. Too often."

The Duchess sighed. "I am searching for peace," she said, "and if I don't go and dress, I shall have none this evening."

"Let me get you some orchids, Duchess," cried Dorian, starting to his feet, and walking down the conservatory.

"You are flirting disgracefully with him," said Lord Henry to his cousin. "You had better take care. He is very fascinating."

"If he were not, there would be no battle."

"Greek meets Greek, then?"

"I am on the side of the Trojans. They fought for a woman."[6]

"They were defeated."

"There are worse things than capture," she answered.

"You gallop with a loose rein."

"Pace gives life," was the *riposte*.[7]

"I shall write it in my diary to-night."

"What?"

"That a burnt child loves the fire."[8]

"I am not even singed. My wings are untouched."

"You use them for everything, except flight."

"Courage has passed from men to women. It is a new experience for us."

"You have a rival."

"Who?"

He laughed. "Lady Narborough," he whispered. "She perfectly adores him."

"You fill me with apprehension. The appeal to Antiquity is fatal to us who are romanticists."

"Romanticists! You have all the methods of science."

"Men have educated us."

---

[6]Helen, the legendary cause of the Trojan War.

[7]In fencing, a quick thrust after parrying a lunge; hence, a quick and effective comeback.

[8]A riff on the proverb "A burned child dreads the fire."

"But not explained you."

"Describe us as a sex," was her challenge.

"Sphynxes without secrets."

She looked at him, smiling. "How long Mr. Gray is!" she said. "Let us go and help him. I have not yet told him the colour of my frock."

"Ah! you must suit your frock to his flowers, Gladys."

"That would be a premature surrender."

"Romantic Art begins with its climax."

"I must keep an opportunity for retreat."

"In the Parthian[9] manner?"

"They found safety in the desert. I could not do that."

"Women are not always allowed a choice," he answered, but hardly had he finished the sentence before from the far end of the conservatory came a stifled groan, followed by the dull sound of a heavy fall. Everybody started up. The Duchess stood motionless in horror. And with fear in his eyes Lord Henry rushed through the flapping palms, to find Dorian Gray lying face downwards on the tiled floor in a death-like swoon.

He was carried at once into the blue drawing-room, and laid upon one of the sofas. After a short time he came to himself, and looked round with a dazed expression.

"What has happened?" he asked. "Oh! I remember. Am I safe here, Harry?" He began to tremble.

"My dear Dorian," answered Lord Henry, "you merely fainted. That was all. You must have overtired yourself. You had better not come down to dinner. I will take your place."

"No, I will come down," he said, struggling to his feet. "I would rather come down. I must not be alone."

He went to his room and dressed. There was a wild recklessness of gaiety in his manner as he sat at table, but now and then a thrill of terror ran through him when he remembered that, pressed against the window of the conservatory, like a white handkerchief, he had seen the face of James Vane watching him.

---

[9]Inhabitants of Parthia in what is now Iran, notorious for attacking while they pretended to retreat.

Chapter 18

The next day he did not leave the house, and, indeed, spent most of the time in his own room, sick with a wild terror of dying, and yet indifferent to life itself. The consciousness of being hunted, snared, tracked down, had begun to dominate him. If the tapestry did but tremble in the wind, he shook. The dead leaves that were blown against the leaded panes seemed to him like his own wasted resolutions and wild regrets. When he closed his eyes, he saw again the sailor's face peering through the mist-stained glass, and horror seemed once more to lay its hand upon his heart.

But perhaps it had been only his fancy that had called vengeance out of the night, and set the hideous shapes of punishment before him. Actual life was chaos, but there was something terribly logical in the imagination. It was the imagination that set remorse to dog the feet of sin. It was the imagination that made each crime bear its misshapen brood.[1] In the common world of fact the wicked were not punished, nor the good rewarded. Success was given to the strong, failure thrust upon the weak. That was all. Besides, had any stranger been prowling round the house he would have been seen by the servants or the keepers. Had any footmarks been found on the flower-beds, the gardeners would have reported it. Yes: it had been merely fancy. Sibyl Vane's brother had not come back to kill him. He had sailed away in his ship to founder in some winter sea. From him, at any rate, he was safe. Why, the man did not know who he was, could not know who he was. The mask of youth had saved him.

And yet if it had been merely an illusion, how terrible it was to think that conscience could raise such fearful phantoms, and give them visible form, and make them move before one! What sort of life would his be if, day and night, shadows of his crime were to peer at him from silent corners, to mock him from secret places, to whisper in his ear as he sat at the feast, to wake him with icy fingers as he lay asleep! As the thought crept through his brain, he grew pale with terror, and the air seemed to him to have become suddenly colder. Oh! in what a wild hour of madness he had killed his

---

[1]In Milton's *Paradise Lost* (Book 2), Satan copulates with his daughter Sin, who gives birth to Death, who in turn rapes Sin and engenders the hellhounds by which she is eternally tortured.

friend! How ghastly the mere memory of the scene! He saw it all again. Each hideous detail came back to him with added horror. Out of the black cave of Time, terrible and swathed in scarlet, rose the image of his sin. When Lord Henry came in at six o'clock, he found him crying as one whose heart will break.

It was not till the third day that he ventured to go out. There was something in the clear, pine-scented air of that winter morning that seemed to bring him back his joyousness and his ardour for life. But it was not merely the physical conditions of environment that had caused the change. His own nature had revolted against the excess of anguish that had sought to maim and mar the perfection of its calm. With subtle and finely wrought temperaments it is always so. Their strong passions must either bruise or bend. They either slay the man, or themselves die. Shallow sorrows and shallow loves live on. The loves and sorrows that are great are destroyed by their own plenitude. Besides, he had convinced himself that he had been the victim of a terror-stricken imagination, and looked back now on his fears with something of pity and not a little of contempt.

After breakfast he walked with the Duchess for an hour in the garden, and then drove across the park to join the shooting-party. The crisp frost lay like salt upon the grass. The sky was an inverted cup of blue metal. A thin film of ice bordered the flat reed-grown lake.

At the corner of the pine-wood he caught sight of Sir Geoffrey Clouston, the Duchess's brother, jerking two spent cartridges out of his gun. He jumped from the cart, and having told the groom to take the mare home, made his way towards his guest through the withered bracken and rough undergrowth.

"Have you had good sport, Geoffrey?" he asked.

"Not very good, Dorian. I think most of the birds have gone to the open. I dare say it will be better after lunch, when we get to new ground."

Dorian strolled along by his side. The keen aromatic air, the brown and red lights that glimmered in the wood, the hoarse cries of the beaters[2] ringing out from time to time, and the sharp snaps of the guns that followed, fascinated him, and filled him with a

---

[2]Men who rouse game by beating the bushes with sticks.

sense of delightful freedom. He was dominated by the carelessness of happiness, by the high indifference of joy.

Suddenly from a lumpy tussock of old grass, some twenty yards in front of them, with black-tipped ears erect, and long hinder limbs throwing it forward, started a hare. It bolted for a thicket of alders. Sir Geoffrey put his gun to his shoulder, but there was something in the animal's grace of movement that strangely charmed Dorian Gray, and he cried out at once, "Don't shoot it, Geoffrey. Let it live."

"What nonsense, Dorian!" laughed his companion, and as the hare bounded into the thicket he fired. There were two cries heard, the cry of a hare in pain, which is dreadful, the cry of a man in agony, which is worse.

"Good heavens! I have hit a beater!" exclaimed Sir Geoffrey. "What an ass the man was to get in front of the guns! Stop shooting there!" he called out at the top of his voice. "A man is hurt."

The head-keeper came running up with a stick in his hand.

"Where, sir? Where is he?" he shouted. At the same time the firing ceased along the line.

"Here," answered Sir Geoffrey angrily hurrying towards the thicket. "Why on earth don't you keep your men back? Spoiled my shooting for the day."

Dorian watched them as they plunged into the alder-clump, brushing the lithe, swinging branches aside. In a few moments they emerged, dragging a body after them into the sunlight. He turned away in horror. It seemed to him that misfortune followed wherever he went. He heard Sir Geoffrey ask if the man was really dead, and the affirmative answer of the keeper. The wood seemed to him to have become suddenly alive with faces. There was the trampling of myriad feet, and the low buzz of voices. A great copper-breasted pheasant came beating through the boughs overhead.

After a few moments, that were to him, in his perturbed state, like endless hours of pain, he felt a hand laid on his shoulder. He started, and looked round.

"Dorian," said Lord Henry, "I had better tell them that the shooting is stopped for to-day. It would not look well to go on."

"I wish it were stopped for ever, Harry," he answered bitterly. "The whole thing is hideous and cruel. Is the man . . . ?"

He could not finish the sentence.

"I am afraid so," rejoined Lord Henry. "He got the whole charge of shot in his chest. He must have died almost instantaneously. Come; let us go home."

They walked side by side in the direction of the avenue for nearly fifty yards without speaking. Then Dorian looked at Lord Henry, and said, with a heavy sigh, "It is a bad omen, Harry, a very bad omen."

"What is?" asked Lord Henry. "Oh! this accident, I suppose. My dear fellow, it can't be helped. It was the man's own fault. Why did he get in front of the guns? Besides, it is nothing to us. It is rather awkward for Geoffrey, of course. It does not do to pepper beaters. It makes people think that one is a wild shot. And Geoffrey is not; he shoots very straight. But there is no use talking about the matter."

Dorian shook his head. "It is a bad omen, Harry. I feel as if something horrible were going to happen to some of us. To myself, perhaps," he added, passing his hand over his eyes, with a gesture of pain.

The elder man laughed. "The only horrible thing in the world is *ennui*,[3] Dorian. That is the one sin for which there is no forgiveness. But we are not likely to suffer from it, unless these fellows keep chattering about this thing at dinner. I must tell them that the subject is to be tabooed. As for omens, there is no such thing as an omen. Destiny does not send us heralds. She is too wise or too cruel for that. Besides, what on earth could happen to you, Dorian? You have everything in the world that a man can want. There is no one who would not be delighted to change places with you."

"There is no one with whom I would not change places, Harry. Don't laugh like that. I am telling you the truth. The wretched peasant who has just died is better off than I am. I have no terror of Death. It is the coming of Death that terrifies me. Its monstrous wings seem to wheel in the leaden air around me. Good heavens! don't you see a man moving behind the trees there, watching me, waiting for me?"

Lord Henry looked in the direction in which the trembling gloved hand was pointing. "Yes," he said, smiling, "I see the gardener waiting for you. I suppose he wants to ask you what flowers

[3]Profound boredom (French), a decadent world-weariness.

you wish to have on the table to-night. How absurdly nervous[4] you are, my dear fellow! You must come and see my doctor, when we get back to town."

Dorian heaved a sigh of relief as he saw the gardener approaching. The man touched his hat, glanced for a moment at Lord Henry in a hesitating manner, and then produced a letter, which he handed to his master. "Her Grace told me to wait for an answer," he murmured.

Dorian put the letter into his pocket. "Tell her Grace that I am coming in," he said, coldly. The man turned round, and went rapidly in the direction of the house.

"How fond women are of doing dangerous things!" laughed Lord Henry. "It is one of the qualities in them that I admire most. A woman will flirt with anybody in the world as long as other people are looking on."

"How fond you are of saying dangerous things, Harry! In the present instance you are quite astray. I like the Duchess very much, but I don't love her."

"And the Duchess loves you very much, but she likes you less, so you are excellently matched."

"You are talking scandal, Harry, and there is never any basis for scandal."

"The basis of every scandal is an immoral certainty," said Lord Henry, lighting a cigarette.

"You would sacrifice anybody, Harry, for the sake of an epigram."

"The world goes to the altar of its own accord," was the answer.

"I wish I could love," cried Dorian Gray, with a deep note of pathos in his voice. "But I seem to have lost the passion, and forgotten the desire. I am too much concentrated on myself. My own personality has become a burden to me. I want to escape, to go away, to forget. It was silly of me to come down here at all. I think I shall send a wire to Harvey to have the yacht got ready. On a yacht one is safe."

"Safe from what, Dorian? You are in some trouble. Why not tell me what it is? You know I would help you."

"I can't tell you, Harry," he answered, sadly. "And I dare say it is only a fancy of mine. This unfortunate accident has upset me. I

[4]Hypersensitive.

have a horrible presentiment that something of the kind may happen to me."

"What nonsense!"

"I hope it is, but I can't help feeling it. Ah! here is the Duchess, looking like Artemis[5] in a tailor-made gown. You see we have come back, Duchess."

"I have heard all about it, Mr. Gray," she answered. "Poor Geoffrey is terribly upset. And it seems that you asked him not to shoot the hare. How curious!"

"Yes, it was very curious. I don't know what made me say it. Some whim, I suppose. It looked the loveliest of little live things. But I am sorry they told you about the man. It is a hideous subject."

"It is an annoying subject," broke in Lord Henry. "It has no psychological value at all. Now if Geoffrey had done the thing on purpose, how interesting he would be! I should like to know some one who had committed a real murder."

"How horrid of you, Harry!" cried the Duchess. "Isn't it, Mr. Gray? Harry, Mr. Gray is ill again. He is going to faint."

Dorian drew himself up with an effort, and smiled. "It is nothing, Duchess," he murmured; "my nerves are dreadfully out of order. That is all. I am afraid I walked too far this morning. I didn't hear what Harry said. Was it very bad? You must tell me some other time. I think I must go and lie down. You will excuse me, won't you?"

They had reached the great flight of steps that led from the conservatory on to the terrace. As the glass door closed behind Dorian, Lord Henry turned and looked at the Duchess with his slumberous eyes. "Are you very much in love with him?" he asked.

She did not answer for some time, but stood gazing at the landscape. "I wish I knew," she said at last.

He shook his head. "Knowledge would be fatal. It is the uncertainty that charms one. A mist makes things wonderful."

"One may lose one's way."

"All ways end at the same point, my dear Gladys."

"What is that?"

"Disillusion."

"It was my *début*[6] in life," she sighed.

---

[5]Greek virgin goddess of the hunt.

[6]One's formal introduction to society and, therefore, availability for courtship.

"It came to you crowned."

"I am tired of strawberry leaves."[7]

"They become you."

"Only in public."

"You would miss them," said Lord Henry.

"I will not part with a petal."

"Monmouth has ears."

"Old age is dull of hearing."

"Has he never been jealous?"

"I wish he had been."

He glanced about as if in search of something. "What are you looking for?" she inquired.

"The button from your foil,"[8] he answered. "You have dropped it."

She laughed. "I have still the mask."

"It makes your eyes lovelier," was his reply.

She laughed again. Her teeth showed like white seeds in a scarlet fruit.

Upstairs, in his own room, Dorian Gray was lying on a sofa, with terror in every tingling fibre of his body. Life had suddenly become too hideous a burden for him to bear. The dreadful death of the unlucky beater, shot in the thicket like a wild animal, had seemed to him to prefigure death for himself also. He had nearly swooned at what Lord Henry had said in a chance mood of cynical jesting.

At five o'clock he rang his bell for his servant and gave him orders to pack his things for the night-express to town, and to have the brougham at the door by eight-thirty. He was determined not to sleep another night at Selby Royal. It was an ill-omened place. Death walked there in the sunlight. The grass of the forest had been spotted with blood.

Then he wrote a note to Lord Henry, telling him that he was going up to town to consult his doctor, and asking him to entertain his guests in his absence. As he was putting it into the envelope, a knock came to the door, and his valet informed him that the head-keeper wished to see him. He frowned, and bit his lip. "Send him in," he muttered, after some moments' hesitation.

---

[7]Decoration for aristocrat's coronet.

[8]Fencing terms; the button is placed on the end of a foil (a short sword) to blunt it.

As soon as the man entered Dorian pulled his cheque-book[9] out of a drawer, and spread it out before him.

"I suppose you have come about the unfortunate accident of this morning, Thornton?" he said, taking up a pen.

"Yes, sir," answered the gamekeeper.

"Was the poor fellow married? Had he any people dependent on him?" asked Dorian, looking bored. "If so, I should not like them to be left in want, and will send them any sum of money you may think necessary."

"We don't know who he is, sir. That is what I took the liberty of coming to you about."

"Don't know who he is?" said Dorian, listlessly. "What do you mean? Wasn't he one of your men?"

"No, sir. Never saw him before. Seems like a sailor, sir."

The pen dropped from Dorian Gray's hand, and he felt as if his heart had suddenly stopped beating. "A sailor?" he cried out. "Did you say a sailor?"

"Yes, sir. He looks as if he had been a sort of sailor; tattooed on both arms, and that kind of thing."

"Was there anything found on him?" said Dorian, leaning forward and looking at the man with startled eyes. "Anything that would tell his name?"

"Some money, sir—not much, and a six-shooter.[10] There was no name of any kind. A decent-looking man, sir, but rough-like. A sort of sailor we think."

Dorian started to his feet. A terrible hope fluttered past him. He clutched at it madly. "Where is the body?" he exclaimed. "Quick! I must see it at once."

"It is in an empty stable in the Home Farm,[11] sir. The folk don't like to have that sort of thing in their houses. They say a corpse brings bad luck."

"The Home Farm! Go there at once and meet me. Tell one of the grooms to bring my horse round. No. Never mind. I'll go to the stables myself. It will save time."

[9]An accounting ledger.

[10]Six-chambered revolver.

[11]The farm for Dorian's estate (as opposed to tenant farms on his land).

In less than a quarter of an hour Dorian Gray was galloping down the long avenue as hard as he could go. The trees seemed to sweep past him in spectral procession, and wild shadows to fling themselves across his path. Once the mare swerved at a white gate-post and nearly threw him. He lashed her across the neck with his crop. She cleft the dusky air like an arrow. The stones flew from her hoofs.

At last he reached the Home Farm. Two men were loitering in the yard. He leapt from the saddle and threw the reins to one of them. In the farthest stable a light was glimmering. Something seemed to tell him that the body was there, and he hurried to the door, and put his hand upon the latch.

There he paused for a moment, feeling that he was on the brink of a discovery that would either make or mar his life. Then he thrust the door open, and entered.

On a heap of sacking in the far corner was lying the dead body of a man dressed in a coarse shirt and a pair of blue trousers. A spotted handkerchief had been placed over the face. A coarse candle, stuck in a bottle, sputtered beside it.

Dorian Gray shuddered. He felt that his could not be the hand to take the handkerchief away, and called out to one of the farm-servants to come to him.

"Take that thing off the face. I wish to see it," he said, clutching at the door-post for support.

When the farm-servant had done so, he stepped forward. A cry of joy broke from his lips. The man who had been shot in the thicket was James Vane.

He stood there for some minutes looking at the dead body. As he rode home, his eyes were full of tears, for he knew he was safe.

Chapter 19[1]

"There is no use your telling me that you are going to be good," cried Lord Henry, dipping his white fingers into a red copper bowl filled with rose-water. "You are quite perfect. Pray, don't change."

Dorian Gray shook his head. "No, Harry, I have done too many dreadful things in my life. I am not going to do any more. I began my good actions yesterday."

"Where were you yesterday?"

"In the country, Harry. I was staying at a little inn by myself."

"My dear boy," said Lord Henry, smiling, "anybody can be good in the country. There are no temptations there. That is the reason why people who live out of town are so absolutely uncivilized. Civilization is not by any means an easy thing to attain to. There are only two ways by which man can reach it. One is by being cultured, the other by being corrupt. Country people have no opportunity of being either, so they stagnate."

"Culture and corruption," echoed Dorian. "I have known something of both. It seems terrible to me now that they should ever be found together. For I have a new ideal, Harry. I am going to alter. I think I have altered."

"You have not yet told me what your good action was. Or did you say you had done more than one?" asked his companion, as he spilt into his plate a little crimson pyramid of seeded strawberries and, through a perforated, shell-shaped spoon, snowed white sugar upon them.

"I can tell you, Harry. It is not a story I could tell to any one else. I spared somebody. It sounds vain, but you understand what I mean. She was quite beautiful, and wonderfully like Sibyl Vane. I think it was that which first attracted me to her. You remember Sibyl, don't you? How long ago that seems! Well, Hetty was not one of our own class of course. She was simply a girl in a village. But I really loved her. I am quite sure that I loved her. All during this wonderful May that we have been having, I used to run down and see her two or three times a week. Yesterday she met me in a little orchard. The apple-blossoms kept tumbling down on her hair, and she was laughing. We were to have gone away together this

[1]The scene has shifted to Lord Henry's London home.

morning at dawn. Suddenly I determined to leave her as flower-like as I had found her."

"I should think the novelty of the emotion must have given you a thrill of real pleasure, Dorian," interrupted Lord Henry. "But I can finish your idyll for you. You gave her good advice, and broke her heart. That was the beginning of your reformation."

"Harry, you are horrible! You mustn't say these dreadful things. Hetty's heart is not broken. Of course she cried and all that. But there is no disgrace upon her. She can live, like Perdita, in her garden of mint and marigold."[2]

"And weep over a faithless Florizel,"[3] said Lord Henry, laughing, as he leant back in his chair. "My dear Dorian, you have the most curiously boyish moods. Do you think this girl will ever be really content now with any one of her own rank? I suppose she will be married some day to a rough carter or a grinning ploughman. Well, the fact of having met you, and loved you, will teach her to despise her husband, and she will be wretched. From a moral point of view, I cannot say that I think much of your great renunciation. Even as a beginning, it is poor. Besides, how do you know that Hetty isn't floating at the present moment in some star-lit mill-pond, with lovely water-lilies round her, like Ophelia?"[4]

"I can't bear this, Harry! You mock at everything, and then suggest the most serious tragedies. I am sorry I told you now. I don't care what you say to me. I know I was right in acting as I did. Poor Hetty! As I rode past the farm this morning, I saw her white face at the window, like a spray of jasmine. Don't let us talk about it any more, and don't try to persuade me that the first good action I have done for years, the first little bit of self-sacrifice I have ever known, is really a sort of sin. I want to be better. I am going to be better. Tell me something about yourself. What is going on in town? I have not been to the club for days."

"The people are still discussing poor Basil's disappearance."

---

[2]Perdita, the "lost girl," is the heroine of Shakespeare's *The Winter's Tale*; she is raised in a pastoral setting, ignorant of her royal origins. Brides in ancient Greece carried wreaths of mint and marigold, both aphrodisiacs.

[3]The prince who falls in love with Perdita.

[4]Lord Henry prettifies the actual description of mad, suicidal Ophelia's death in *Hamlet* (4.7.166–83).

"I should have thought they had got tired of that by this time," said Dorian, pouring himself out some wine, and frowning slightly.

"My dear boy, they have only been talking about it for six weeks, and the British public are really not equal to the mental strain of having more than one topic every three months. They have been very fortunate lately, however. They have had my own divorce-case, and Alan Campbell's suicide. Now they have got the mysterious disappearance of an artist. Scotland Yard[5] still insists that the man in the grey ulster who left for Paris by the midnight train on the ninth of November was poor Basil, and the French police declare that Basil never arrived in Paris at all. I suppose in about a fortnight we shall be told that he has been seen in San Francisco. It is an odd thing, but every one who disappears is said to be seen at San Francisco.[6] It must be a delightful city, and possess all the attractions of the next world."

"What do you think has happened to Basil?" asked Dorian, holding up his Burgundy against the light, and wondering how it was that he could discuss the matter so calmly.

"I have not the slightest idea. If Basil chooses to hide himself, it is no business of mine. If he is dead, I don't want to think about him. Death is the only thing that ever terrifies me. I hate it."

"Why?" said the younger man, wearily.

"Because," said Lord Henry, passing beneath his nostrils the gilt trellis of an open vinaigrette box, "one can survive everything nowadays except that. Death and vulgarity are the only two facts in the nineteenth century that one cannot explain away. Let us have our coffee in the music-room, Dorian. You must play Chopin[7] to me. The man with whom my wife ran away played Chopin exquisitely. Poor Victoria! I was very fond of her. The house is rather lonely without her. Of course, married life is merely a habit, a bad habit. But then one regrets the loss even of one's worst habits. Perhaps one regrets them the most. They are such an essential part of one's personality."

---

[5]The detective department of the Metropolitan Police force.

[6]Such as Terrence Bellew McManus (1811/12–61), a member of the Young Ireland movement who, having been convicted of treason and transported to Van Dieman's Land, escaped to San Francisco. Wilde's mother, Lady Jane Francesca Wilde, was closely involved with the Young Ireland movement and the trials of its leaders.

[7]See Contexts, p. 234.

Dorian said nothing, but rose from the table, and, passing into the next room, sat down to the piano and let his fingers stray across the white and black ivory of the keys. After the coffee had been brought in, he stopped, and looking over at Lord Henry, said, "Harry, did it ever occur to you that Basil was murdered?"

Lord Henry yawned. "Basil was very popular, and always wore a Waterbury watch.[8] Why should he have been murdered? He was not clever enough to have enemies. Of course he had a wonderful genius for painting. But a man can paint like Velasquez[9] and yet be as dull as possible. Basil was really rather dull. He only interested me once, and that was when he told me, years ago, that he had a wild adoration for you, and that you were the dominant motive of his art."

"I was very fond of Basil," said Dorian, with a note of sadness in his voice. "But don't people say that he was murdered?"

"Oh, some of the papers do. It does not seem to me to be at all probable. I know there are dreadful places in Paris, but Basil was not the sort of man to have gone to them. He had no curiosity. It was his chief defect."

"What would you say, Harry, if I told you that I had murdered Basil?" said the younger man. He watched him intently after he had spoken.

"I would say, my dear fellow, that you were posing for a character that doesn't suit you. All crime is vulgar, just as all vulgarity is crime. It is not in you, Dorian, to commit a murder. I am sorry if I hurt your vanity by saying so, but I assure you it is true. Crime belongs exclusively to the lower orders. I don't blame them in the smallest degree. I should fancy that crime was to them what art is to us, simply a method of procuring extraordinary sensations."

"A method of procuring sensations? Do you think, then, that a man who has once committed a murder could possibly do the same crime again? Don't tell me that."

"Oh! anything becomes a pleasure if one does it too often," cried Lord Henry, laughing. "That is one of the most important secrets of life. I should fancy, however, that murder is always a mistake. One should never do anything that one cannot talk about af-

[8]Inexpensive pocket watch from Connecticut's Waterbury Watch Company.

[9]This 17th-c. painter, known for loose, expressive brushwork, was a major influence on Wilde's contemporaries James McNeil Whistler and John Singer Sargent.

ter dinner. But let us pass from poor Basil. I wish I could believe that he had come to such a really romantic end as you suggest; but I can't. I dare say he fell into the Seine off an omnibus, and that the conductor hushed up the scandal. Yes: I should fancy that was his end. I see him lying now on his back under those dull-green waters with the heavy barges floating over him, and long weeds catching in his hair. Do you know, I don't think he would have done much more good work. During the last ten years his painting had gone off very much."

Dorian heaved a sigh, and Lord Henry strolled across the room and began to stroke the head of a curious Java parrot, a large grey-plumaged bird, with pink crest and tail, that was balancing itself upon a bamboo perch.[10] As his pointed fingers touched it, it dropped the white scurf of crinkled lids over black glass-like eyes and began to sway backwards and forwards.

"Yes," he continued, turning round, and taking his handkerchief out of his pocket; "his painting had quite gone off. It seemed to me to have lost something. It had lost an ideal. When you and he ceased to be great friends, he ceased to be a great artist. What was it separated you? I suppose he bored you. If so, he never forgave you. It's a habit bores have. By the way, what has become of that wonderful portrait he did of you? I don't think I have ever seen it since he finished it. Oh! I remember your telling me years ago that you had sent it down to Selby, and that it had got mislaid or stolen on the way. You never got it back? What a pity! It was really a masterpiece. I remember I wanted to buy it. I wish I had now. It belonged to Basil's best period. Since then, his work was that curious mixture of bad painting and good intentions that always entitles a man to be called a representative British artist. Did you advertise for it? You should."

"I forget," said Dorian. "I suppose I did. But I never really liked it. I am sorry I sat for it. The memory of the thing is hateful to me. Why do you talk of it? It used to remind me of those curious lines in some play—'Hamlet,' I think—how do they run?—

> "'*Like the painting of a sorrow,*
> *A face without a heart.*'"[11]

---

[10] A Wildean fantasy; no actual parrots conform to this description.

[11] Claudius challenging Laertes about the sincerity of his grief for his father (*Hamlet* 4.7.108–9).

"Yes: that is what it was like."

Lord Henry laughed. "If a man treats life artistically, his brain is his heart," he answered, sinking into an arm-chair.

Dorian Gray shook his head and struck some soft chords on the piano. "'Like the painting of a sorrow,'" he repeated, "'a face without a heart.'"

The elder man lay back and looked at him with half-closed eyes. "By the way, Dorian," he said after a pause, "'what does it profit a man if he gain the whole world and lose—how does the quotation run?—his own soul'?"[12]

The music jarred, and Dorian Gray started and stared at his friend. "Why do you ask me that, Harry?"

"My dear fellow," said Lord Henry, elevating his eyebrows in surprise, "I asked you because I thought you might be able to give me an answer. That is all. I was going through the Park last Sunday, and close by the Marble Arch there stood a little crowd of shabby-looking people listening to some vulgar street-preacher. As I passed by, I heard the man yelling out that question to his audience.[13] It struck me as being rather dramatic. London is very rich in curious effects of that kind. A wet Sunday, an uncouth Christian in a mackintosh, a ring of sickly white faces under a broken roof of dripping umbrellas, and a wonderful phrase flung into the air by shrill hysterical lips—it was really very good in its way, quite a suggestion. I thought of telling the prophet that Art had a soul, but that man had not. I am afraid, however, he would not have understood me."

"Don't, Harry. The soul is a terrible reality. It can be bought, and sold, and bartered away. It can be poisoned, or made perfect. There is a soul in each one of us. I know it."

"Do you feel quite sure of that, Dorian?"

"Quite sure."

"Ah! then it must be an illusion. The things one feels absolutely certain about are never true. That is the fatality of Faith, and the lesson of Romance. How grave you are! Don't be so serious. What have you or I to do with the superstitions of our age? No: we have

[12]Jesus to his followers: "For what shall it profit a man, if he shall gain the whole world, and lose his own soul?" (Mark 8.36; see also Matthew 16.26; Luke 9.25).

[13]At Speaker's Corner in the northeast corner of Hyde Park; since 1872, a site for public speaking.

given up our belief in the soul. Play me something. Play me a nocturne,[14] Dorian, and, as you play, tell me, in a low voice, how you have kept your youth. You must have some secret. I am only ten years older than you are, and I am wrinkled, and worn, and yellow. You are really wonderful, Dorian. You have never looked more charming than you do to-night. You remind me of the day I saw you first. You were rather cheeky, very shy, and absolutely extraordinary. You have changed, of course, but not in appearance. I wish you would tell me your secret. To get back my youth I would do anything in the world, except take exercise, get up early, or be respectable. Youth! There is nothing like it. It's absurd to talk of the ignorance of youth. The only people to whose opinions I listen now with any respect are people much younger than myself. They seem in front of me. Life has revealed to them her latest wonder. As for the aged, I always contradict the aged. I do it on principle. If you ask them their opinion on something that happened yesterday, they solemnly give you the opinions current in 1820, when people wore high stocks,[15] believed in everything, and knew absolutely nothing. How lovely that thing you are playing is! I wonder did Chopin write it at Majorca,[16] with the sea weeping round the villa, and the salt spray dashing against the panes? It is marvellously romantic. What a blessing it is that there is one art left to us that is not imitative! Don't stop. I want music to-night. It seems to me that you are the young Apollo, and that I am Marsyas[17] listening to you. I have sorrows, Dorian, of my own, that even you know nothing of. The tragedy of old age is not that one is old, but that one is young. I am amazed sometimes at my own sincerity. Ah, Dorian, how happy you are! What an exquisite life you have had! You have drunk deeply of everything. You have crushed the grapes against your palate.[18] Nothing has been hidden from you. And it has all been to you no more than the sound of music. It has not marred you. You are still the same."

[14]Night music; Chopin was the most famous composer in this genre.

[15]Stiff neck-cloths.

[16]Extremely ill, Chopin had a miserable time on this western Mediterranean island, despite the company of his lover Aurore Dupin ("George Sand").

[17]The satyr who challenged the god Apollo to a contest at flute playing and was skinned alive upon losing.

[18]In Keats's "Ode on Melancholy," the elect worshipper of Melancholy "can burst Joy's grape against his palate fine" (l. 28); the ode was a favorite among the aesthetes.

"I am not the same, Harry."

"Yes: you are the same. I wonder what the rest of your life will be. Don't spoil it by renunciations. At present you are a perfect type. Don't make yourself incomplete. You are quite flawless now. You need not shake your head: you know you are. Besides, Dorian, don't deceive yourself. Life is not governed by will or intention. Life is a question of nerves, and fibres, and slowly built-up cells in which thought hides itself and passion has its dreams. You may fancy yourself safe, and think yourself strong. But a chance tone of colour in a room or a morning sky, a particular perfume that you had once loved and that brings subtle memories with it, a line from a forgotten poem that you had come across again, a cadence from a piece of music that you had ceased to play—I tell you, Dorian, that it is on things like these that our lives depend. Browning writes about that somewhere;[19] but our own senses will imagine them for us. There are moments when the odour of *lilas blanc*[20] passes suddenly across me, and I have to live the strangest month of my life over again. I wish I could change places with you, Dorian. The world has cried out against us both, but it has always worshipped you. It always will worship you. You are the type of what the age is searching for, and what it is afraid it has found. I am so glad that you have never done anything, never carved a statue, or painted a picture, or produced anything outside of yourself! Life has been your art. You have set yourself to music. Your days are your sonnets."

Dorian rose up from the piano, and passed his hand through his hair. "Yes, life has been exquisite," he murmured, "but I am not going to have the same life, Harry. And you must not say these extravagant things to me. You don't know everything about me. I think that if you did, even you would turn from me. You laugh. Don't laugh."

"Why have you stopped playing, Dorian? Go back and give me the nocturne over again. Look at that great honey-coloured moon that hangs in the dusky air. She is waiting for you to charm

[19]In "Bishop Blougram's Apology" (1855) by Robert Browning (1812–89), a Roman Catholic Bishop describes how, in the midst of "unbelief," events such as "a sunset-touch, / A fancy from a flower-bell, someone's death, / A chorus ending in Euripedes" (182–84) tempt the renewal of faith.

[20]White lilacs (French).

her, and if you play she will come closer to the earth. You won't? Let us go to the club, then. It has been a charming evening, and we must end it charmingly. There is some one at White's[21] who wants immensely to know you—young Lord Poole, Bournemouth's eldest son. He has already copied your neckties, and has begged me to introduce him to you. He is quite delightful, and rather reminds me of you."

"I hope not," said Dorian, with a sad look in his eyes. "But I am tired to-night, Harry. I sha'n't go to the club. It is nearly eleven, and I want to go to bed early."

"Do stay. You have never played so well as to-night. There was something in your touch that was wonderful. It had more expression than I had ever heard from it before."

"It is because I am going to be good," he answered, smiling. "I am a little changed already."

"You cannot change to me, Dorian," said Lord Henry. "You and I will always be friends."

"Yet you poisoned me with a book once. I should not forgive that. Harry, promise me that you will never lend that book to any one. It does harm."

"My dear boy, you are really beginning to moralize. You will soon be going about like the converted, and the revivalist, warning people against all the sins of which you have grown tired. You are much too delightful to do that. Besides, it is no use. You and I are what we are, and will be what we will be. As for being poisoned by a book, there is no such thing as that. Art has no influence upon action. It annihilates the desire to act. It is superbly sterile. The books that the world calls immoral are books that show the world its own shame. That is all. But we won't discuss literature. Come round to-morrow. I am going to ride at eleven. We might go together, and I will take you to lunch afterwards with Lady Branksome. She is a charming woman, and wants to consult you about some tapestries she is thinking of buying. Mind you come. Or shall we lunch with our little Duchess? She says she never sees you now. Perhaps you are tired of Gladys? I thought you would be. Her clever tongue gets on one's nerves. Well, in any case, be here at eleven."

[21]Exclusive West End Tory club.

"Must I really come, Harry?"

"Certainly. The Park is quite lovely now. I don't think there have been such lilacs since the year I met you."

"Very well. I shall be here at eleven," said Dorian. "Good-night, Harry." As he reached the door, he hesitated for a moment, as if he had something more to say. Then he sighed and went out.

Chapter 20

It was a lovely night, so warm that he threw his coat over his arm, and did not even put his silk scarf round his throat. As he strolled home, smoking his cigarette, two young men in evening dress passed him. He heard one of them whisper to the other, "That is Dorian Gray." He remembered how pleased he used to be when he was pointed out, or stared at, or talked about. He was tired of hearing his own name now. Half the charm of the little village where he had been so often lately was that no one knew who he was. He had often told the girl whom he had lured to love him that he was poor, and she had believed him. He had told her once that he was wicked, and she had laughed at him, and answered that wicked people were always very old and very ugly. What a laugh she had!—just like a thrush singing. And how pretty she had been in her cotton dresses and her large hats! She knew nothing, but she had everything that he had lost.

When he reached home, he found his servant waiting up for him. He sent him to bed, and threw himself down on the sofa in the library, and began to think over some of the things that Lord Henry had said to him.

Was it really true that one could never change? He felt a wild longing for the unstained purity of his boyhood—his rose-white boyhood, as Lord Henry had once called it. He knew that he had tarnished himself, filled his mind with corruption and given horror to his fancy; that he had been an evil influence to others, and had experienced a terrible joy in being so; and that of the lives that had crossed his own it had been the fairest and the most full of promise that he had brought to shame. But was it all irretrievable? Was there no hope for him?

Ah! in what a monstrous moment of pride and passion he had prayed that the portrait should bear the burden of his days, and he keep the unsullied splendour of eternal youth! All his failure had been due to that. Better for him that each sin of his life had brought its sure, swift penalty along with it. There was purification in punishment. Not "Forgive us our sins"[1] but "Smite us for our iniquities" should be the prayer of man to a most just God.

[1] Part of the Lord's Prayer (Luke 11.4).

The curiously-carved mirror that Lord Henry had given to him, so many years ago now, was standing on the table, and the white-limbed Cupids laughed round as of old. He took it up, as he had done on that night of horror, when he had first noted the change in the fatal picture, and with wild tear-dimmed eyes looked into its polished shield. Once, some one who had terribly loved him, had written to him a mad letter, ending with these idolatrous words: "The world is changed because you are made of ivory and gold. The curves of your lips rewrite history." The phrases came back to his memory, and he repeated them over and over to himself. Then he loathed his own beauty, and flinging the mirror on the floor crushed it into silver splinters beneath his heel. It was his beauty that had ruined him, his beauty and the youth that he had prayed for. But for those two things, his life might have been free from stain. His beauty had been to him but a mask, his youth but a mockery. What was youth at best? A green, an unripe time, a time of shallow moods, and sickly thoughts. Why had he worn its livery? Youth had spoiled him.

It was better not to think of the past. Nothing could alter that. It was of himself, and of his own future, that he had to think. James Vane was hidden in a nameless grave in Selby churchyard. Alan Campbell had shot himself one night in his laboratory, but had not revealed the secret that he had been forced to know. The excitement, such as it was, over Basil Hallward's disappearance would soon pass away. It was already waning. He was perfectly safe there. Nor, indeed, was it the death of Basil Hallward that weighed most upon his mind. It was the living death of his own soul that troubled him. Basil had painted the portrait that had marred his life. He could not forgive him that. It was the portrait that had done everything. Basil had said things to him that were unbearable, and that he had yet borne with patience. The murder had been simply the madness of a moment. As for Alan Campbell, his suicide had been his own act. He had chosen to do it. It was nothing to him.

A new life! That was what he wanted. That was what he was waiting for. Surely he had begun it already. He had spared one innocent thing, at any rate. He would never again tempt innocence. He would be good.

As he thought of Hetty Merton, he began to wonder if the portrait in the locked room had changed. Surely it was not still so horrible as it had been? Perhaps if his life became pure, he would be able to expel every sign of evil passion from the face. Perhaps the signs of evil had already gone away. He would go and look.

He took the lamp from the table and crept upstairs. As he unbarred the door, a smile of joy flitted across his strangely younglooking face and lingered for a moment about his lips. Yes, he would be good, and the hideous thing that he had hidden away would no longer be a terror to him. He felt as if the load had been lifted from him already.

He went in quietly, locking the door behind him, as was his custom, and dragged the purple hanging from the portrait. A cry of pain and indignation broke from him. He could see no change, save that in the eyes there was a look of cunning, and in the mouth the curved wrinkle of the hypocrite. The thing was still loathsome—more loathsome, if possible, than before—and the scarlet dew that spotted the hand seemed brighter, and more like blood newly spilt. Then he trembled. Had it been merely vanity that had made him do his one good deed? Or the desire for a new sensation, as Lord Henry had hinted, with his mocking laugh? Or that passion to act a part that sometimes makes us do things finer than we are ourselves? Or, perhaps, all these? And why was the red stain larger than it had been? It seemed to have crept like a horrible disease over the wrinkled fingers. There was blood on the painted feet, as though the thing had dripped—blood even on the hand that had not held the knife. Confess? Did it mean that he was to confess? To give himself up, and be put to death? He laughed. He felt that the idea was monstrous. Besides, even if he did confess, who would believe him? There was no trace of the murdered man anywhere. Everything belonging to him had been destroyed. He himself had burned what had been below-stairs. The world would simply say that he was mad. They would shut him up if he persisted in his story. . . . Yet it was his duty to confess, to suffer public shame, and to make public atonement. There was a God who called upon men to tell their sins to earth as well as to heaven. Nothing that he could do would cleanse him till he had told his own sin. His sin? He shrugged his shoulders. The death of Basil Hallward seemed very little to him. He was thinking of Hetty Merton. For it was an unjust mirror, this mirror of his soul that he was looking at. Vanity? Curiosity? Hypocrisy? Had there been nothing more in his renunciation than that? There had been something more. At least he thought so. But who could tell? . . . No. There had been nothing more. Through vanity he had spared her. In hypocrisy he had worn the mask of goodness. For curiosity's sake he had tried the denial of self. He recognized that now.

But this murder—was it to dog him all his life? Was he always to be burdened by his past? Was he really to confess? Never. There was only one bit of evidence left against him. The picture itself— that was evidence. He would destroy it. Why had he kept it so long? Once it had given him pleasure to watch it changing and growing old. Of late he had felt no such pleasure. It had kept him awake at night. When he had been away, he had been filled with terror lest other eyes should look upon it. It had brought melancholy across his passions. Its mere memory had marred many moments of joy. It had been like conscience to him. Yes, it had been conscience. He would destroy it.

He looked round and saw the knife that had stabbed Basil Hallward. He had cleaned it many times, till there was no stain left upon it. It was bright, and glistened. As it had killed the painter, so it would kill the painter's work, and all that that meant. It would kill the past, and when that was dead he would be free. It would kill this monstrous soul-life, and without its hideous warnings, he would be at peace. He seized the thing, and stabbed the picture with it.

There was a cry heard, and a crash. The cry was so horrible in its agony that the frightened servants woke, and crept out of their rooms. Two gentlemen, who were passing in the Square below, stopped and looked up at the great house. They walked on till they met a policeman, and brought him back. The man rang the bell several times, but there was no answer. Except for a light in one of the top windows, the house was all dark. After a time, he went away, and stood in an adjoining portico and watched.

"Whose house is that, constable?" asked the elder of the two gentlemen.

"Mr. Dorian Gray's, sir," answered the policeman.

They looked at each other, as they walked away, and sneered. One of them was Sir Henry Ashton's uncle.

Inside, in the servants' part of the house, the half-clad domestics were talking in low whispers to each other. Old Mrs. Leaf was crying, and wringing her hands. Francis was as pale as death.

After about a quarter of an hour, he got the coachman and one of the footmen and crept upstairs. They knocked, but there was no reply. They called out. Everything was still. Finally, after vainly trying to force the door, they got on the roof, and dropped down on to the balcony. The windows yielded easily: their bolts were old.

When they entered, they found hanging upon the wall a splendid portrait of their master as they had last seen him, in all the wonder of his exquisite youth and beauty. Lying on the floor was a dead man, in evening dress, with a knife in his heart. He was withered, wrinkled, and loathsome of visage. It was not till they had examined the rings that they recognized who it was.

CONTEXTS

Textual Issues

The Two Versions of
The Picture of Dorian Gray

Wilde initially published *The Picture of Dorian Gray* in the American *Lippincott's Magazine* at the invitation of its editor, J. M. Stoddart. Stoddart had a substantial hand not only in commissioning the work from Wilde but also in editing it; he adapted Wilde's punctuation for an American audience and toned down sexual references, both homo- and heterosexual. Wilde received £200 for his work, which sold well at the cheap price of one shilling.

Wilde had already been thinking of lengthening the story into a substantial novel. But publishers worried that the story was too scandalous. Even before negative reviews of the first version appeared, the proposed novel was turned down by the prestigious publisher Macmillan's. Bookseller W. H. Smith refused to stock the *Lippincott's* version.

Not to be defeated, Wilde took the flood of negative reviews as a chance to defend and advertise his work in the press. Yet the publicity did not allay publishers' fears, and Wilde had to settle for the small firm of Ward, Lock, and Co., the British publishers of *Lippincott's*. They offered him a standard deal of £125, although he had hoped for more. Wilde lengthened the original (ominous) thirteen chapters to twenty by adding new ones (3, 5, 15, 16, 17), expanding the initial concluding chapter into two chapters, and adding a preface. He did not comply with the publisher's moralizing suggestion to conclude with Dorian having to live miserably with his true, ugly face or repenting and leading a better life. Wilde also revised, deleted, and added throughout. His changes, while often small, cumulatively make the 1891 version significantly different from the 1890 version, and the two versions, like the two versions of Shelley's *Frankenstein*, should be understood as different works. Ward, Lock, and Co. issued the new version in two editions: 3,000 small-paper copies at 6 shillings, and a deluxe large-paper edition at a guinea (22 shillings). Neither sold well, possibly because the cheap *Lippincott's* version had already exhausted interest. *The Picture of Dorian Gray* that was best known during Wilde's lifetime was not the 1891 version, the standard in the twentieth century.

Compelling aesthetic arguments can be made for both the 1890 and 1891 versions. The 1890 version brings a concentrated focus to Dorian and his story, and, despite Stoddart's editing, its language is more overtly homoerotic. The 1891 version widens the cultural scope with episodes: Lord Henry's dialogue with his uncle, with its telling evocation of Dorian's ancestry; the Vane household; Dorian's visit to the opium den and his encounter with James Vane; and the later country house scenes, with their brilliant dialogues—his first audition of the conversations he perfected in his stage comedies. And paradoxically, Wilde's efforts to veil the homoerotic aspects of the 1890 text make the 1891 text seem even more homoerotic: veiling increases attention to what is being veiled.

The full 1890 text, available both online and in hard copy, is important to the full history of the novel. This section presents a few samples of Wilde's revisions, particularly with regard to sexuality.

from Chapter 1, Dialogue between Lord Henry and Basil Hallward

1890 Text	1891 Text
"I have always been my own master; had at least always been so, till I met Dorian Gray. Then—but I don't know how to explain it to you. Something seemed to tell me that I was on the verge of a terrible crisis in my life. I had a strange feeling that	"I have always been my own master; had at least always been so, till I met Dorian Gray. Then—but I don't know how to explain it to you. Something seemed to tell me that I was on the verge of a terrible crisis in my life. I had a strange feeling that

Fate had in store for me exquisite joys and exquisite sorrows. I knew that if I spoke to Dorian I would become absolutely devoted to him, and that I ought not to speak to him. I grew afraid, and turned to quit the room. It was not conscience that made me do so: it was cowardice. I take no credit to myself for trying to escape.

. . .

Our eyes met again. It was mad of me, but I asked Lady Brandon to introduce me to him. Perhaps it was not so mad, after all. It was simply inevitable. We would have spoken to each other without any introduction. I am sure of that. Dorian told me so afterwards. He, too, felt that we were destined to know each other."

. . .

"Tell me more about Dorian Gray. How often do you see him?"

"Every day. I couldn't be happy if I didn't see him every day. Of course sometimes it is only for a few minutes. But a few minutes with somebody one worships mean a great deal."

"But you don't really worship him?"

"I do."

"How extraordinary! I thought you would never care for anything but your painting,—

Fate had in store for me exquisite joys and exquisite sorrows.

I grew afraid, and turned to quit the room. It was not conscience that made me do so: it was a sort of cowardice. I take no credit to myself for trying to escape.

. . .

Our eyes met again. It was reckless of me, but I asked Lady Brandon to introduce me to him. Perhaps it was not so reckless, after all. It was simply inevitable. We would have spoken to each other without any introduction. I am sure of that. Dorian told me so afterwards. He, too, felt that we were destined to know each other."

. . .

"Tell me more about Mr. Dorian Gray. How often do you see him?"

"Every day. I couldn't be happy if I didn't see him every day. He is absolutely necessary to me."

"How extraordinary! I thought you would never care for anything but your art."

your art, I should say. Art
sounds better, doesn't it?"

"He is all my art to me now.
I sometimes think, Harry,
that there are only two eras
of any importance in the
history of the world. The first is
the appearance of a new medium
for art, and the second is the
appearance of a new personality
for art also."

"He is all my art to me now,"
said the painter, gravely. "I sometimes think, Harry, that there are
only two eras of any importance
in the world's history. The first is
the appearance of a new medium
for art, and the second is the
appearance of a new personality
for art also."

from Chapter 7 (1890) and Chapter 9 (1891), Dialogue between Basil Hallward and Dorian Gray

1890 Text

"Basil," he said, coming
over quite close, and looking
him straight in the face, "we
have each of us a secret. Let me
know yours, and I will tell you
mine. What was your reason for
refusing to exhibit my picture?"

Hallward shuddered in
spite of himself. "Dorian, if I
told you, you might like me less
than you do, and you would
certainly laugh at me. I could
not bear your doing either of
those two things. If you wish me
never to look at your picture
again, I am content. I have
always you to look at. If you
wish the best work I have ever
done to be hidden from the
world, I am satisfied. Your
friendship is dearer to me than
any fame or reputation."

1891 Text

"Basil," he said, coming
over quite close, and looking
him straight in the face, "we
have each of us a secret. Let me
know yours, and I shall tell you
mine. What was your reason for
refusing to exhibit my picture?"

The painter shuddered in
spite of himself. "Dorian, if I
told you, you might like me less
than you do, and you would
certainly laugh at me. I could
not bear your doing either of
those two things. If you wish me
never to look at your picture
again, I am content. I have
always you to look at. If you
wish the best work I have ever
done to be hidden from the
world, I am satisfied. Your
friendship is dearer to me than
any fame or reputation."

"No, Basil, you must tell me," murmured Dorian Gray. "I think I have a right to know." His feeling of terror had passed away, and curiosity had taken its place. He was determined to find out Basil Hallward's mystery.

"Let us sit down, Dorian," said Hallward, looking pale and pained. "Let us sit down. I will sit in the shadow, and you shall sit in the sunlight. Our lives are like that. Just answer me one question. Have you noticed in the picture something that you did not like?—something that probably at first did not strike you, but that revealed itself to you suddenly?"

"Basil!" cried the lad, clutching the arms of his chair with trembling hands, and gazing at him with wild, startled eyes.

"I see you did. Don't speak. Wait till you hear what I have to say. It is quite true that I have worshipped you with far more romance of feeling than a man usually gives to a friend. Somehow, I had never loved a woman. I suppose I never had time. Perhaps, as Harry says, a really 'grande passion' is the privilege of those who have nothing to do, and that is the use of the idle classes in a country. Well, from the moment I met you, your personality had the most extra-

"No, Basil, you must tell me," insisted Dorian Gray. "I think I have a right to know." His feeling of terror had passed away, and curiosity had taken its place. He was determined to find out Basil Hallward's mystery.

"Let us sit down, Dorian," said the painter, looking troubled. "Let us sit down.

And just answer me one question. Have you noticed in the picture something curious?—something that probably at first did not strike you, but that revealed itself to you suddenly?"

"Basil!" cried the lad, clutching the arms of his chair with trembling hands and gazing at him with wild, startled eyes.

"I see you did. Don't speak. Wait till you hear what I have to say.

Dorian, from the moment I met you, your personality had the most extraordinary influence over me. I quite admit that I adored you madly, extravagantly, absurdly.

ordinary influence over me. I was dominated, soul, brain, and power by you. You became to me the visible incarnation of that unseen ideal whose memory haunts us artists like an exquisite dream. I worshipped you.

I was jealous of every one to whom you spoke. I wanted to have you all to myself. I was only happy when I was with you. When I was away from you, you were still present in my art. It was all wrong and foolish. It is all wrong and foolish still. Of course I never let you know anything about this. It would have been impossible. You would not have understood it; I did not understand it myself. One day I determined to paint a wonderful portrait of you. It was to have been my masterpiece. It is my masterpiece. But, as I worked at it, every flake and film of color seemed to me to reveal my secret. I grew afraid that the world would know of my idolatry. I felt, Dorian, that I had told too much. Then it was that I resolved never to allow the picture to be exhibited."

I grew jealous of every one to whom you spoke. I wanted to have you all to myself. I was only happy when I was with you. When you were away from me, you were still present in my art. . . .

Of course, I never let you know anything about this. It would have been impossible. You would not have understood it. I hardly understood it myself."

from Chapter 10 (1890) and Chapter 12 (1891), Dialogue between Basil Hallward and Dorian Gray

1890 Text

"What about Lord Kent's only son, and his career? I met

1891 Text

"What about Lord Kent's only son, and his career? I met

his father yesterday in St. James Street. He seemed broken with shame and sorrow. What about the young Duke of Perth? What sort of life has he got now? What gentleman would associate with him? Dorian, Dorian, your reputation is infamous.

his father yesterday in St. James's Street. He seemed broken with shame and sorrow. What about the young Duke of Perth? What sort of life has he got now? What gentleman would associate with him?"

"Stop, Basil. You are talking about things of which you know nothing," said Dorian Gray, biting his lip, and with a note of infinite contempt in his voice. "You ask me why Berwick leaves a room when I enter it. It is because I know everything about his life, not because he knows anything about mine. With such blood as he has in his veins, how could his record be clean? You ask me about Henry Ashton and young Perth. Did I teach the one his vices, and the other his debauchery? If Kent's silly son takes his wife from the streets, what is that to me? If Adrian Singleton writes his friend's name across a bill, am I his keeper? I know how people chatter in England. The middle classes air their moral prejudices over their gross dinner-tables, and whisper about what they call the profligacies of their betters in order to try and pretend that they are in smart society, and on intimate terms with the people they slander. In this country it is enough for a man to have distinction and brains for every common tongue to wag against him. And what sort of lives do these people, who pose as being moral, lead themselves? My dear fellow, you forget that we are in the native land of the hypocrite."

"Dorian," cried Hallward, "that is not the question. England is bad enough I know, and English society is all wrong. That is the reason why I want you to be fine. You have not been fine. One has a right to judge of a man by the effect he has over his friends. Yours seem to lose all sense of honour, of goodness, of purity. You have filled them with a madness for pleasure. They have gone down into the depths. You led them there. Yes: you led them there, and yet you can smile, as you are smiling now. And there is

I know you and Harry are great friends. I say nothing about that now, but surely you need not have made his sister's name a by-word.

worse behind. I know you and Harry are inseparable. Surely for that reason, if for none other, you should not have made his sister's name a byword."

"Take care, Basil. You go too far."

"I must speak, and you must listen. You shall listen.

When you met Lady Gwendolen, not a breath of scandal had ever touched her. Is there a single decent woman in London

When you met Lady Gwendolen, not a breath of scandal had ever touched her. Is there a single decent woman in London

now who would drive with her
in the Park? Why, even her
children are not allowed to live
with her."

now who would drive with her
in the Park? Why, even her
children are not allowed to live
with her."

**from Chapter 13 (1890) and Chapter 20 (1891),
Dorian's Internal Monologue**

1890 Text

It was an unjust mirror,
this mirror of his soul that he was
looking at. Vanity? Curiosity?
Hypocrisy? Had there been
nothing more in his renunciation than that? There had been
something more. At least he
thought so. But who could tell?

And this murder,—was it to
dog him all his life? Was he
never to get rid of the past?
Was he really to confess?
No. There was only one bit
of evidence left against him. The
picture itself,—that was evidence.

He would destroy it. Why
had he kept it so long? It had
given him pleasure once to watch
it changing and growing old. Of
late he had felt no such pleasure.
It had kept him awake at night.
When he had been away, he had
been filled with terror lest other

1891 Text

For it was an unjust mirror,
this mirror of his soul that he was
looking at. Vanity? Curiosity?
Hypocrisy? Had there been
nothing more in his renunciation than that? There had been
something more. At least he
thought so. But who could tell?
. . . No. There had been nothing
more. Through vanity he had
spared her. In hypocrisy he had
worn the mask of goodness. For
curiosity's sake he had tried the
denial of self. He recognized
that now.

But this murder—was it to
dog him all his life? Was he
always to be burdened by his
past? Was he really to confess?
Never. There was only one bit
of evidence left against him. The
picture itself—that was evidence.

He would destroy it. Why
had he kept it so long? Once it
had given him pleasure to watch
it changing and growing old. Of
late he had felt no such pleasure.
It had kept him awake at night.
When he had been away, he had
been filled with terror lest other

eyes should look upon it. It had brought melancholy across his passions. Its mere memory had marred many moments of joy. It had been like conscience to him. Yes, it had been conscience. He would destroy it.

He looked round, and saw the knife that had stabbed Basil Hallward. He had cleaned it many times, till there was no stain left upon it. It was bright, and glistened. As it had killed the painter, so it would kill the painter's work, and all that that meant. It would kill the past, and when that was dead he would be free.

He seized it, and stabbed the canvas with it, ripping the thing right up from top to bottom.

eyes should look upon it. It had brought melancholy across his passions. Its mere memory had marred many moments of joy. It had been like conscience to him. Yes, it had been conscience. He would destroy it.

He looked round and saw the knife that had stabbed Basil Hallward. He had cleaned it many times, till there was no stain left upon it. It was bright, and glistened. As it had killed the painter, so it would kill the painter's work, and all that that meant. It would kill the past, and when that was dead he would be free. It would kill this monstrous soul-life, and without its hideous warnings, he would be at peace. He seized the thing, and stabbed the picture with it.

Chapter 11: Further Annotations

Chapter 11 (Chapter 9 in the 1890 version) has long been one of the most controversial in an already controversial book. Wilde's early reviewers attacked it for what the *Daily Chronicle* called its "obtrusively cheap scholarship."[1] As later scholars have found, Wilde did his homework for this chapter: he gathered obscure information from a variety of sources, including his own book reviews, museum catalogues, popular handbooks, and classical and contemporary history (see Bristow 398–419). Yet it is more than

---

[1]Anonymous, Review of *The Picture of Dorian Gray*, *Daily Chronicle*, reprinted in *Oscar Wilde: The Critical Heritage*, ed. Karl Beckson (London: Routledge, 1970), 72.

just a compendium: it is the heart of the book, literally and figuratively, because the chapter separates the work's two chief time periods by giving us an overview of Dorian's search to realize his personality. In terms of its imagery, it condenses and recapitulates images of exotic times, people, objects, and places that radiate throughout the book.

Rhetorically, the chapter is a dazzling exercise in the mode of the catalogue or list. Wilde's lists are carefully arranged for variety. Some move to climaxes, others deliberately avoid them; some objects are passed over briefly, while others get lovingly detailed descriptions. For the first-time reader, these catalogues may feel overwhelming. Much of their effect arises from their obscurity: Wilde depends on his reader not knowing what he is describing, so that the reader may develop a sequence of fantasy images to accompany his words. As a result, annotating the chapter works against its hard-won glamour and aura of esoteric knowledge; detailed notes also create a distracting "up and down" for readers, who have to move back and forth between text and footnotes, when the text is after the effect of inundation.

Even so, some may find themselves wanting to know more about the items in the catalogues. I have moved the annotations out of footnotes to satisfy the integrity of Wilde's rhetoric of inundation and to supply information for the curious reader.

P. 131, paragraph beginning *It was rumoured of him*: Not just in aesthetic beauty but also in its intense homoerotic culture, Catholicism was an attractive alternative to Protestantism's perceived repressiveness (Roden); "dalmatic": a shin-length tunic with sleeves worn while celebrating mass; "monstrance": a receptacle for displaying the Host (the communion wafer).

P. 132, paragraph beginning *And so he would now study perfumes*: A study modeled, like many of Dorian's obsessions, on des Esseintes in Huysmans' *À Rebours*; "frankincense": aromatic gum resin burned as incense, one of the gifts of the Magi; "ambergris": perfume made from a sperm-whale's secretion; "musk": perfume made from male musk deer; "champak": Asian evergreen tree sacred to the Hindu god Vishnu; "spikenard": from an Indian plant—see Mark 14.3; "hovenia": from the Japanese raisin-tree; "aloes": not the bitter plant but a spicy perfume—see Psalms 45.8 and Song of Songs 4.14.

P. 132, paragraph beginning *At another time he devoted himself entirely to music*: "Schubert's grace": Franz Schubert (1797–1828), tragically short-lived Austrian Romantic composer; "Chopin's sorrows": Frédéric Chopin (1810–49), Polish-born pianist and composer; "mighty harmonies of Beethoven": Ludwig van Beethoven (1770–1827), greatest German Romantic composer who eventually went completely deaf. None married; Chopin had a legendary romance with the cross-dressing female novelist George Sand. "*juruparis*": wooden trumpet whose name means "devils" or "demons"; "Alfonso de Ovalle": actually Alonso de Ovalle (1601–51), author of *A Historical Account of the Kingdom of Chile* (1646); "Cuzco": capital of the Incan empire until the Spanish conquest in 1533; "*clarin*": bugle; "*ture*": bamboo trumpet; "*teponaztli*": percussion instrument used in Aztec ceremonies; "*yotl*-bells": resembling horse- or sleigh-bells; "Bernal Diaz": Bernal Díaz del Castillo (1495/6–1584), author of *The True History of the Conquest of New Spain* (pub. 1632) and an officer of Hernando Cortés (1485–1547), Spanish conquistador who destroyed the Aztec empire; "Tannhaüser": opera (1844) by Richard Wagner whose overture depicts a conflict between Christian asceticism and sensual abandon.

P. 133, paragraph beginning *On one occasion he took up the study of jewels*: "Anne de Joyeuse": the Duke de Joyeuse, Admiral of France (1561–87), a male favorite of France's Henry III; "chrysoberyl": yellowish-green gem; "cymophane": chrysoberyl cat's-eye; "peridot": green semiprecious stone; "topazes": usually a dark yellow color; "carbuncles": general term for red stones; "cinnamon-stones": brown and yellow garnets; "spinels": typically dark red, resembling rubies; "amethysts": usually clear purple or blue-violet; "sunstone": aventurine felspar, with small spangles that reflect light; "moonstone": milky-colored minerals; "opal": iridescent stone; "Amsterdam": center in the gem trade; "*de la vieille roche*": "of the old rock" (French), from an exhausted mine.

P. 134, paragraph beginning *He discovered wonderful stories*: "Alphonso's 'Clericalis Disciplina'": Petrus Alfonsi (1062–1110?), Spanish physician and author of *Disciplina Clericalis* (c. 1106); "Alexander, the Conqueror of Emathia": legends of Alexander the Great (4th c. B.C.E.), King of Macedonia (called "Emathia" by Homer), conqueror of the Persian Empire; "Philostratus": Greek sophist and author (c. 170–c. 247 C.E.); the quotation is from *Life of Apollonius*; "Pierre de Boniface": medieval alchemist (d. 1323) whose claims about gems were quoted by French prophet Nostradamus (1506–66); "Leonardus Camillus": Italian author of the *Speculum Lapidum* (Mirror of Stones) (1502); "bezoar": any stone used as an antidote; "Democritus": Greek philosopher and geometrician (c. 460–c. 370 B.C.E.).

P. 134, paragraph beginning *The King of Ceilan*: "Ceilan": Ceylon (Sri Lanka); "John the Priest": legendary Eastern priest and king, often known as Prester John; "sardius": dark-red chalcedony; "Margarite of America": prose tale (1596) by Thomas Lodge; "Marco Polo": Venetian author (c. 1254–c. 1324) who wrote of his travels in central Asia; "Zipangu": Japan; "King Perozes": King of Persia (457–84 C.E.); "Procopius": Byzantine historian (fl. mid-6th c. C.E.); "Emperor Anastasius": Roman emperor (c. 430–518); "Malabar": on the west coast of India; "certain Venetian": Marco Polo.

P. 135, paragraph beginning *When the Duke de Valentinois*: The duke is Cesare Borgia (1475–1507), anti-hero of Machiavelli's *Prince* on the basis of his ruthless drive to power in central Italy; "Alexander VI": pope from 1431 to 1503; "Louis XII": king of France (1462–1515), who gave Borgia his dukedom; "Brantôme": French historian (c. 1540–1614); "Charles of England": king of Great Britain and Ireland (1630–85); "Richard II": king of England (1367–1400); "Hall": English historian (1498–1547), major source for Shakespeare's history plays; "Henry VIII": king of England (1491–1547); "James I": king of England (1566–1625), also known as James VI, King of Scotland, notorious for his same-sex relationships with his favorites; "Edward II": king of England (1284–1327) who angered barons because of privileges given to his favorite, Piers Gaveston (Gaveston was executed, and Edward himself was eventually imprisoned and murdered; their relationship is the subject of Christopher Marlowe's *Edward II*); "Henry II": first Plantagenet king of England (1154–89); "orients": pearls from the seas around India; "Charles the Rash": usually known as Charles the Bold (1433–77).

P. 135, paragraph beginning *Then he turned his attention to embroideries*: "Athena": Greek goddess of wisdom; "velarium": large awning; "Apollo": Greek god of the sun and homoerotic icon;

"Priest of the Sun": Elagabalus, Roman Emperor (3rd c. C.E.), notorious for his excesses, an icon for Decadent art; "Chilperic": Childeric, Merovingian king (c. 436–481); "Bishop of Pontus": Asterius (c. 400) of Amasea in Pontus, now part of Turkey; "Charles of Orleans": French poet (1391–1465) who wrote poetry in England after being captured at Agincourt; "Queen Joan of Burgundy": queen (d. c. 1349) of Philip VI de Valois, King of France (1293–1350); "Catherine de Médicis": queen of France (1519–89); her husband Henry II died in 1559; "Sobieski": John III, King of Poland (1629–96); "Smyrna": city on the Aegean coast, now Izmir, Turkey; "Turkish camp before Vienna": in 1683, Sobieski's cavalry defeated the Turks, who were about to conquer Vienna.

P. 136, paragraph beginning *And so, for a whole year*: "*fleurs de lys*": a stylized lily, part of the former royal arms of France; "Hungary point": elaborate embroidery; "Georgian work": from Georgia on the shores of the Black Sea; "*Foukousas*": textiles used for gift wrapping.

P. 137, paragraph beginning *He had a special passion*: "cope": ceremonial cloak; "orphreys": border on an ecclesiastical vestment; "acanthus": frequent decoration on classical architecture; "morse": fastening for a cope; "St. Sebastian": late 3rd-c. Roman martyr, shot to death with arrows and thus a popular subject for Renaissance artists, who established him as a homoerotic icon; "chasubles": ceremonial vestments; "corporals": vessels holding consecrated bread and wine; "chalice-veils": used to cover chalice and patten; "sudaria": cloth supposedly impressed with the image of Jesus.

P. 140, paragraph beginning *Such, at any rate, was Dorian Gray's opinion*: "Philip Herbert": 4th Earl of Pembroke (1584–1650), the first of James I's English favorites and the only actual historical figure among Dorian's ancestors; "Francis Osborne": his *Historical Memoires* (1658) is a major historical source for knowledge about Elizabeth I and James I (Watkins); "Giovanna of Naples": possibly Giovanna II di Durazzo, Queen of Naples (1371–1435), although dates seem early for this Tudor-Stuart section of Dorian's portrait gallery; "stomacher": V-shaped ornamental panel worn over the breasts and stomach of a woman's dress; "macaroni": dandies, known for imitating Continental fashions, spoofed in American ballad "Yankee Doodle Dandy"; "Prince Regent": later George IV (1762–1830), notorious for his rakish living in his youth; "Mrs. Fitzherbert": Roman Catholic widow (1756–1837), whom the prince married illegally in 1784; "Carlton House": lavish London residence, 1783–1826; "Garter": see ch. 1, n. 22; "Lady Hamilton": English beauty (1765–1815), mistress of British naval hero Horatio Nelson; "Bacchante": frenzied worshipper of Bacchus, the Greek god of wine.

P. 142, paragraph beginning *The hero of the wonderful novel*: "Tiberius": Roman emperor (42 B.C.E.–37 C.E.), unpopular in Rome, who moved to Capri, where he led a decadent life; "Elephantis": female poet who wrote a book of sexual techniques; "Caligula": 1st-c. Roman emperor famous for his dictatorial style; "Domitian": 1st-c. Roman emperor who was obsessed with conspiracies against him and, like Caligula, was assassinated; "Circus": Roman arena, site of chariot races and gladiatorial combat.

P. 142, paragraph beginning *Over and over again Dorian used to read*: "Filippo, Duke of Milan": Filippo Maria Visconti (1392–1447), 3rd duke of Milan, executed his wife Beatrice on a trumped-up charge of adultery. Wilde took much of his information about the Renaissance from John Addington Symonds's *The Age of the Despots* (1875), the first volume of *The Renaissance in Italy*, 7 vols. (1875–98), which plays up male homoeroticism in Renaissance political history; "Paul the Second": (1417–71), ordered the imprisonment and torture of the humanist historian Platina; "Gian Maria Visconti": 2nd duke of Milan (1389–1412), notorious for cruelty; "the Borgia": Cesare Borgia (see p. 235), suspected of murdering his brother Juan and Perotto (Pedro Calderon), a Spanish chamberlain who supposedly had impregnated his sister Lucrezia; "Riario": (1445–74), notorious for sexual and financial profligacy; "Sixtus IV": pope from 1414 to 1484; "Leonora of Aragon": wife of Ercole d'Este (1431–1505), Duke of Ferrara; "Ganymede or Hylas": Ganymede is cupbearer to the Olympian gods, and Hylas, companion of Hercules, was drowned by water nymphs who had fallen in love with him—both figures had become icons of homoerotic attraction; "Ezzelin": tyrannical Duke of Padua (1194–1259) whom Dante placed in Canto XII of the *Inferno*; "Cibo": the openly corrupt Pope Innocent VIII (1432–92); "Sigismondo Malatesta": ruler of Rimini (1417–68), supposed to have murdered his wives Ginevra d'Este and Polissena Sforza and then married his lover, Isotta degli Atti (Alberti designed for him the temple of San Francesco at Rimini, whose classical design created suspicions of impiety); "Charles VI": king of France (1368–1422), known as "Charles the Mad"; "Baglioni": in 1500, Carlo and Grifonetto Baglioni conspired to murder the other members of their family, including Astorre and Simonetto, in a struggle for control over Perugia; Grifonetto was in turn murdered. Atalanta, Grifonetto's mother, commissioned Raphael's *Entombment* (1507) to honor him.

Victorian Reactions to The Picture of Dorian Gray

Reviews

The initial 1890 publication of Wilde's novel in *Lippincott's* occasioned a storm of controversy; the work became a scandalous success, with a whirl of reactions in the press. Reviews appeared not only in quarterly periodicals but in newspapers as well. In this medium, Wilde was able to respond quickly. His response to a hostile review in the *St. James's Gazette* touched off a print war, a volley of commentaries between Wilde and the paper. Responding to his critics, Wilde formulated statements on the autonomy of art soon crystallized in the famous preface to the 1891 novel.

Ward, Lock, and Co.

Ward, Lock, and Co. circulated the following advertisement for Wilde's novel, evidently without his knowledge, to London's newspaper editors.

Lippincott's Advertisement for *The Picture of Dorian Gray* (1890)[1]

Mr. Oscar Wilde will contribute to the July number of *Lippincott's Magazine* a complete novel, entitled "The Picture of Dorian Gray," which, as the first venture in fiction of one of the most prominent

---

[1]Quoted in the *St. James's Gazette* (June 28, 1890), 5.

personalities and artistic influences of the day, will be everywhere read with wide interest and curiosity. But the story is in itself so strong and strange, and so picturesque and powerful in style, that it must inevitably have created a sensation in the literary world, even if published without Mr. Wilde's name on the title-page. Viewed merely as a romance, it is—from the opening paragraph down to the tragic and ghastly climax—full of strong and sustained interest; as a study in psychology it is phenomenal; and, judged even purely as a piece of literary workmanship, it is one of the most brilliant and remarkable productions of the year.

Samuel Henry Jeyes (1857–1911)

> *Victorian journalist and biographer Samuel Henry Jeyes wrote a guide to studying for the Oxford entrance exams, as well as a biography of the conservative prime minister Robert Cecil, Marquess of Salisbury. But he came to notice for his attacks on the Aesthetic movement. The* St. James's Gazette *was a fashionable, conservative newspaper, mentioned in* The Picture of Dorian Gray *itself. An evening publication, it catered to the gentleman's clubs that form a significant part of the novel's action. This review launched a war of words between the paper and Wilde, included here after Jeyes's review.*

"A Study in Puppydom," *St. James's Gazette* 20 (June 24, 1890): 3–4

Time was (it was in the '70s) when we talked about Mr. Oscar Wilde; time came (it came in the '80s) when he tried to write poetry and, more adventurous, we tried to read it; time is when we had forgotten him, or only remember him as the late editor of the *Woman's World*[1]—a part for which he was singularly unfitted, if we are to judge him by the work which he has been allowed to publish in *Lippincott's Magazine* and which Messrs. Ward, Lock and Co. have not been ashamed to circulate in Great Britain. Not being curious in ordure, and not wishing to offend the nostrils of decent persons, we do not propose to analyse "The Picture of Dorian Gray:"

---

[1]Periodical that Wilde edited from 1887 to 1889.

that would be to advertise the developments of an esoteric pruri- ence. Whether the Treasury or the Vigilance Society[2] will think it worth while to prosecute Mr. Oscar Wilde or Messrs. Ward, Lock and Co., we do not know; but on the whole we hope they will not. The puzzle is that a young man of decent parts, who enjoyed (when he was at Oxford) the opportunity of associating with gen- tlemen, should put his name (such as it is) to so stupid and vulgar a piece of work. Let nobody read it in the hope of finding witty paradox or racy wickedness. The writer airs his cheap research among the garbage of French *Décadents* like any drivelling pedant, and he bores you unmercifully with his prosy rigmaroles about the beauty of the Body and the corruption of the Soul. The grammar is better than Ouida's;[3] the erudition equal; but in every other respect we prefer the talented lady who broke off with "pious aposiopesis"[4] when she touched upon "the horrors which are described in the pages of Suetonius and Livy"[5]—not to men- tion the yet worse infamies believed by many scholars to be accu- rately portrayed in the lost works of Plutarch, Venus, and Nicodemus, especially Nicodemus.[6]

Let us take one peep at the young men in Mr. Oscar Wilde's story. Puppy No. 1 is the painter of the picture of Dorian Gray; Puppy No. 2 is the critic (a courtesy lord, skilled in all the knowl- edge of the Egyptians and a-weary of all the sins and pleasures of London); Puppy No. 3 is the original, cultivated by Puppy No. 1 with a "romantic friendship." The Puppies fall a-talking. Puppy No. 1 about his Art, Puppy No. 2 about his sins and pleasures and the pleasures of sin, and Puppy No. 3 about himself—always about himself, and generally about his face, which is "brainless and beau- tiful." The Puppies appear to fill up the intervals of talk by plucking daisies and playing with them, and sometimes by drinking "some- thing with strawberry in it." The youngest Puppy is told that he is

[2]The Director of Public Prosecutions, who would have handled obscenity charges, was also the Treasury Solictor; the Vigilance Society was devoted to moral reform.

[3]Pen name of Marie Louise de la Ramée (1839–1908), popular late Victorian novel- ist and major influence on Wilde.

[4]In rhetoric, the sudden breaking off of speech.

[5]Classical Roman historians, whose works describe the homosexual behavior of Rome's emperors.

[6]Plutarch (c. 40–c. 120 C.E.), Greek author of *Parallel Lives*; "Venus" is unidentified; Nicodemus of Hereclea (?300 B.C.E.), Greek poet.

charming; but he mustn't sit in the sun for fear of spoiling his complexion. When he is rebuked for being a naughty, wilful boy, he makes a pretty *moue*—this man of twenty! This is how he is addressed by the Blasé Puppy at their first meeting:—

"Yes, Mr. Gray, the gods have been good to you. But what the gods give they quickly take away . . . When your youth goes, your beauty will go with it, and then you will suddenly discover that there are no triumphs left for you. . . . Time is jealous of you, and wars against your lilies and roses. You will become sallow, and hollow-cheeked, and dull-eyed. You will suffer horribly."

Why, bless our souls! haven't we read something of this kind somewhere in the classics? Yes, of course we have! But in what recondite author? Ah—yes—no—yes, it *was* in Horace![7] What an advantage it is to have received a classical education! And how it will astonish the Yankees! But we must not forget our Puppies, who have probably occupied their time in lapping "something with strawberry in it." Puppy No. 1 (the Art Puppy) has been telling Puppy No. 3 (the Doll Puppy) how much he admires him. What is the answer? "I am less to you than your ivory Hermes or your silver Faun. You will like them always. How long will you like me? Till I have my first wrinkle, I suppose. I know now that when one loses one's good looks, whatever they may be, one loses everything. . . . I am jealous of the portrait you have painted of me. Why should it keep what I must lose? . . . Oh, if it was only the other way! If the picture could only change, and I could be always what I am now!"

No sooner said than done! The picture *does* change: the original doesn't. Here's a situation for you! Théophile Gautier[8] could have made it romantic, entrancing, beautiful. Mr. Stevenson[9] could have made it convincing, humorous, pathetic. Mr. Anstey[10] could have made it screamingly funny. It has been reserved for Mr. Oscar Wilde to make it dull and nasty. The promising youth plunges into every kind of mean depravity, and ends in being "cut" by fast women and vicious men. He finishes with murder: the New Voluptuousness always leads up to blood-shedding—that is part of the

---

[7]*Ode* 1.11, "Tu ne quaesieris," famous for its advice to seize the day (*carpe diem*).

[8]Théophile Gautier (1811–72), leading French author and aesthete.

[9]Robert Louis Stevenson (1850–94), Scottish novelist whose *The Strange Case of Dr. Jekyll and Mr. Hyde* (1886) was a source for Wilde.

[10]Thomas Anstey Guthrie (1856–1934), comic writer in *Punch*.

cant. The gore and gashes wherein Mr. Rider Haggard[11] takes a chaste delight are natural diet for a cultivated palate which is tired of mere licentiousness. And every wickedness or filthiness committed by Dorian Gray is faithfully registered upon his face in the picture; but his living features are undisturbed and unmarred by his inward vileness. This is the story which Mr. Oscar Wilde has tried to tell; a very lame story it is, and very lamely it is told.

Why has he told it? There are two explanations; and, so far we can see, not more than two. Not to give pleasure to his readers: the thing is too clumsy, too tedious, and—alas! that we should say it— too stupid. Perhaps it was to shock his readers, in order that they might cry Fie! upon him and talk about him, much as Mr. Grant Allen recently tried in *The Universal Review* to arouse, by a licentious theory of the sexual relations, an attention which is refused to his popular chatter about other men's science.[12] Are we then to suppose that Mr. Oscar Wilde has yielded to the craving for a notoriety which he once earned by talking fiddle faddle about other men's art, and sees his only chance of recalling it by making himself obvious at the cost of being obnoxious, and by attracting the notice which the olfactory sense cannot refuse to the presence of certain self-asserting organisms? That is an uncharitable hypothesis, and we would gladly abandon it. It may be suggested (but is it more charitable?) that he derives pleasure from treating a subject merely because it is disgusting. The phenomenon is not unknown in recent literature; and it takes two forms, in appearance widely separate—in fact, two branches from the same root, a root which draws its life from malodorous putrefaction. One development is found in the Puritan prurience which produced Tolstoi's "Kreutzer Sonata" and Mr. Stead's famous outbursts.[13] That is odious enough and mischievous enough, and it is rightly execrated, because it is tainted with an hypocrisy and the less culpable because charitable persons may believe it to be unconscious. But is it more odious or more mischievous than the "frank Paganism" (that is the word, is it not?) which

[11]Henry Rider Haggard (1856–1925), famous for African adventure stories.

[12]"The Girl of the Future" (*Universal Review* 7 [May 1890]: 49–64) by Allen (1848–99) criticized traditional marriage.

[13]In Tolstoy's "The Kreutzer Sonata" (1891), a jealous husband murders his wife; William Thomas Stead's "The Maiden Tribute of Modern Babylon" (1885) is a sensational exposé of child prostitution.

delights in dirtiness and confesses its delight? Still they are both chip from the same block—"The Maiden Tribute of Modern Babylon" and "The Picture of Dorian Gray"—and both of them ought to be chucked into the fire. Not so much because they are dangerous and corrupt (they are corrupt but not dangerous) as because they are incurably silly, written by simpleton *poseurs* (whether they call themselves Puritan or Pagan) who know nothing about the life which they affect to have explored, and because they are mere catch penny revelations of the non-existent, which, if they reveal anything at all, are revelations only of the singularly unpleasant minds from which they emerge.

Wilde: Letter to the *St. James's Gazette* 20 (June 26, 1890): 4

Mr. Oscar Wilde's "Bad Case"

To the EDITOR *of the* St. JAMES'S GAZETTE[1]

SIR,—I have read your criticism of my story, "The Picture of Dorian Gray;" and I need hardly say that I do not propose to discuss its merits or demerits, its personalities or its lack of personality. England is a free country, and ordinary English criticism is perfectly free and easy. Besides, I must admit that, either from temperament or taste, or from both, I am quite incapable of understanding how any work of art can be criticised from a moral standpoint. The sphere of art and the sphere of ethics are absolutely distinct and separate; and it is to the confusion between the two that we owe the appearance of Mrs. Grundy,[2] that amusing old lady who represents the only original form of humour that the middle classes of this country have been able to produce. What I do object to most strongly is that you should have placarded the town with posters on which was printed in large letters:—MR. OSCAR WILDE'S LATEST ADVERTISEMENT; A BAD CASE.

---

[1]Sidney Low (1857–1932), editor of the *St. James's Gazette*, solicited the "criticism" (by Jeyes).

[2]The personification of prudish social opinion, originally from Thomas Morton's play *Speed the Plough* (1798).

Whether the expression "A Bad Case" refers to my book or to the present position of the Government, I cannot tell. What was silly and unnecessary was the use of the term "advertisement."

I think I may say without vanity—though I do not wish to appear to run vanity down—that of all men in England I am the one who requires least advertisement. I am tired to death of being advertised. I feel no thrill when I see my name in a paper. The chronicle does not interest me any more. I wrote this book entirely for my own pleasure, and it gave me very great pleasure to write it. Whether it becomes popular or not is a matter of absolute indifference to me. I am afraid, Sir, that the real advertisement is your cleverly written article. The English public, as a mass, takes no interest in a work of art until it is told that the work in question is immoral, and your *réclame*[3] will, I have no doubt, largely increase the sale of the magazine; in which sale I may mention with some regret, I have no pecuniary interest.—I remain, Sir, your obedient servant, OSCAR WILDE.

16, *Tite-street, Chelsea, June 25*

Jeyes: Response in the *St. James's Gazette* 20 (June 26, 1890): 4

[The following note appeared in the column next to Wilde's letter.]

In the preceding column will be found the best reply which Mr. Oscar Wilde can make to our recent criticism of his mawkish and nauseous story, "The Picture of Dorian Gray." Mr. Wilde tells us that he is constitutionally unable to understand how any work of art can be criticized from a moral standpoint. We were quite aware that ethics and aesthetics are different matters, and that is why the greater part of our criticism was devoted not so much to the nastiness of "The Picture of Dorian Gray," but to its dulness and stupidity. Mr. Wilde pretends that we have advertised it. So we have, if any readers are attracted to a book which, we have warned them, will bore them insufferably. That the story is corrupt cannot be denied; but we added, and assuredly believe, that it is not danger-

---

[3]Publicity (French).

ous, because, as we said, it tedious and stupid. Mr. Wilde tells us that he wrote the story for his own pleasure, and found great pleasure in writing it. We congratulate him; there is no triumph more precious to your "aesthete" than the discovery of a delight which outsiders cannot share or even understand. The author of "The Picture of Dorian Gray" is the only person likely to find pleasure in it.

Wilde: Letter to the *St. James's Gazette* 20 (June 27, 1890): 5

Mr. Oscar Wilde continues to carry on the defense of his novelette "The Picture of Dorian Gray." Writing to us under yesterday's date, he says:[1]—In your issue of today you state that my brief letter published in your columns is the "best reply" I can make to your article upon "Dorian Gray." This is not so. I do not propose to discuss fully the matter here, but I feel bound to say that your article contains the most unjustifiable attack that has been made upon any man of letters for many years. The writer of it, who is quite incapable of concealing his personal malice, and so in some measure destroys the effect he wishes to produce, seems not to have the slightest idea of the temper in which a work of art should be approached. To say that such a book as mine should be "chucked into the fire" is silly. That is what one does with newspapers.

Of the value of pseudo-ethical criticism in dealing with artistic work I have spoken already. But as your writer has ventured into the perilous grounds of literary criticism I ask you to allow me, in fairness not merely to myself but to all men to whom literature is a fine art, to say a few words about his critical method.

He begins by assailing me with much ridiculous virulence because the chief personages in my story are "puppies." They *are* puppies. Does he think that literature went to the dogs when Thackeray wrote about puppydom?[2] I think that puppies are extremely interesting from an artistic as well as from a psychological point of view. They seem to me to be certainly far more

[1]The newspaper editor introduced Wilde's letter.

[2]In this context, "puppies" are conceited young men; the type is frequent in the novels and sketches of William Makepeace Thackeray (1811–63).

interesting than prigs; and I am of opinion that Lord Henry Wotton is an excellent corrective of the tedious ideal shadowed forth in the semi theological novels of our age.

He then makes vague and fearful insinuations about my grammar and my erudition. Now, as regards grammar, I hold that, in prose at any rate, correctness should always be subordinate to artistic effect and musical cadence; and any peculiarities of syntax that may occur in "Dorian Gray" are deliberately intended, and are introduced to show the value of the artistic theory in question. Your writer gives no instance of any such peculiarity. This I regret, because I do not think that any such instances occur.

As regards erudition, it is always difficult, even for the most modest of us, to remember that other people do not know quite as much as one does oneself. I myself frankly admit I cannot imagine how a casual reference to Suetonius and Petronius Arbiter can be construed into evidence of a desire to impress an unoffending and ill-educated public by an assumption of superior knowledge. I should fancy that the most ordinary of scholars is perfectly well acquainted with the "Lives of the Cæsars" and with the "Satyricon." The "Lives of the Cæsars," at any rate, forms part of the curriculum at Oxford for those who take the Honour School of "Literæ Humaniores;" and as for the "Satyricon," it is popular even among passmen, though I suppose they are obliged to read it in translations.

The writer of the article then suggests that I, in common with that great and noble artist Count Tolstoi, take pleasure in a subject because it is dangerous. About such a suggestion there is this to be said. Romantic art deals with the exception and with the individual. Good people, belonging as they do to the normal, and so commonplace, type, are artistically uninteresting. Bad people are, from the point of view of art, fascinating studies. They represent colour, variety and strangeness. Good people exasperate one's reason; bad people stir one's imagination. Your critic, if I must give him so honourable a title, states that the people in my story have no counterpart in life; that they are, to use his vigorous if somewhat vulgar phrase, "mere catchpenny revelations of the non-existent." Quite so. If they existed they would not be worth writing about. The function of the artist is to invent, not to chronicle. There are no such people. If there were, I would not write about them. Life by its realism is always spoiling the subject-matter of art. The supreme pleasure in literature is to realize the non-existent.

And, finally, let me say this. You have reproduced, in a journalistic form, the comedy of "Much Ado about Nothing," and have, of course, spoiled it in your reproduction. The poor public, hearing, from an authority so high as your own, that this is a wicked book that should be coerced and suppressed by a Tory Government, will, no doubt, rush to it and read it. But, alas! they will find that it is a story with a moral. And the moral is this: All excess, as well as all renunciation, brings its own punishment. The painter, Basil Hallward, worshipping physical beauty far too much, as most painters do, dies by the hand of one in whose soul he has created a monstrous and absurd vanity. "Dorian Gray," having led a life of mere sensation and pleasure, tries to kill conscience, and at that moment kills himself. Lord Henry Wotton seeks to be merely the spectator of life. He finds that those who reject the battle are more deeply wounded than those who take part in it. Yes; there is a terrible moral in "Dorian Gray"—a moral which the prurient will not be able to find in it, but it will be revealed to all whose minds are healthy. Is this an artistic error? I fear it is. It is the only error in the book.

Jeyes: Response in the *St. James's Gazette* 20 (June 27, 1890): 4

[Jeyes included this note; it, strangely, appears on the page before Wilde's letter does.]

Mr. Oscar Wilde may perhaps be excused for being angry at the remarks which we allowed ourselves to make concerning his "moral tale" of the Three Puppies and the Magic Picture; but he should not misrepresent us. He says we suggested that his novel was a "wicked book which should be coerced and suppressed by a Tory Government." We did nothing of the kind. The authors of books of much less questionable character have been proceeded against by the Treasury or the Vigilance Society; but we expressly said that we hope Mr. Wilde's masterpiece would be left alone. Then, Mr. Wilde (like any young lady who has published her first novel "at the request of numerous friends") falls back on the theory of the critic's "personal malice." This is unworthy of so experienced a literary gentleman. We can assure Mr. Wilde that the writer of that article had, and has, no "personal malice" or personal feeling towards him. We can surely censure a work which we believe to be silly, and know to be offensive, without the imputation of malice—especially when that book is written by one who is so clearly capable of better things.

As for the critical question, Mr. Wilde is beating the air when he defends idealism and "romantic art" in literature. In the words of Mrs. Harris to Mrs. Gamp, "Who's a-deniging of it?"[1] Heaven forbid that we should refuse to an author the "supreme pleasure of realizing the nonexistent;" or that we should judge the "aesthetic" from the purely "ethical" standpoint. No; our criticism starts from lower ground. Mr. Wilde says that his story is a moral tale, because the wicked persons in it come to a bad end. We will not be so rude as to quote a certain remark about morality which Mr. Charles Surface made to Mr. Joseph Surface.[2] We simply say that every critic has the right to point out that a work of art or literature is dull and incompetent in its treatment—as "The Picture of Dorian Gray" is; and that its dullness and incompetence are not redeemed because it constantly hints, not obscurely, at disgusting sins and abominable crimes—as "The Picture of Dorian Gray" does.

Wilde: Letter to the *St. James's Gazette* 20 (June 28, 1890): 5

Mr. Oscar Wilde's Defense

To the EDITOR *of the* ST. JAMES'S GAZETTE

Sir, As you still keep up, though in a somewhat milder form than before, your attacks on me and my book, you not only confer on me the right, but you impose upon me the duty, of reply.

[1] In Dickens's *Life and Adventures of Martin Chuzzlewit* (1844), nurse Sairey Gamp invents a companion, Mrs. Harris, who praises her constantly (though not in this exact phrase).

[2] In Richard Brinsley Sheridan's *The School for Scandal* (1777), Charles Surface tells his hypocritical brother Joseph that he "should be obliged to borrow a little of [his] Morality" if he were interested in another man's wife. Jeyes is probably misattributing to Charles the words of Sir Oliver Surface about Joseph: "If he salutes me with a scrap sentence of morality in his mouth I shall be sick directly."

You state, in your issue of to-day, that I misrepresented you when I said that you suggested that a book so wicked as mine should be "suppressed and coerced by a Tory Government." Now you did not propose this, but you did suggest it. When you declare that you do not know whether or not the Government will take action about my book, and remark that the authors of books much less wicked have been proceeded against in law, the suggestion is quite obvious. In your complaint of misrepresentation you seem to me, Sir, to have been not quite candid. However, as far as I am concerned, the suggestion is of no importance. What is of importance is that the editor of a paper like yours should appear to countenance the monstrous theory that the Government of a country should exercise a censorship over imaginative literature. This is a theory against which I, and all men of letters of my acquaintance, protest most strongly; and any critic who admits the reasonableness of such a theory shows at once that he is quite incapable of understanding what literature is, and what are the rights that literature possesses. A Government might just as well try to teach painters how to paint, or sculptors how to model, as attempt to interfere with the style, treatment and subject-matter of the literary artist; and no writer, however eminent or obscure, should ever give his sanction to a theory that would degrade literature far more than any didactic or so-called immoral book could possibly do.

You then express your surprise that "so experienced a literary gentleman" as myself should imagine that your critic was animated by any feeling of personal malice towards him. The phrase "literary gentleman" is a vile phrase; but let that pass. I accept quite readily your assurance that your critic was simply criticising a work of art in the best way that he could; but I feel that I was fully justified in forming the opinion of him that I did. He opened his article by a gross personal attack on myself. This, I need hardly say, was an absolutely unpardonable error of critical taste. There is no excuse for it, except personal malice; and you, Sir, should not have sanctioned it. A critic should be taught to criticise a work of art without making any reference to the personality of the author. This, in fact, is the beginning of criticism. However, it was not merely his personal attack on me that made me imagine that he was actuated by malice. What really confirmed me in my first impression was his reiterated assertion that my book was tedious and dull. Now, if I were criticising my book, which I have some thoughts of doing, I think I would consider it my duty to point out that it is far too crowded with sensational incident, and far too paradoxical in style, as far, at any rate, as the dialogue goes. I feel that from a standpoint of art these are two defects in the book. But tedious and dull the book is not. Your critic has cleared himself of the charge of personal malice, his denial and yours being quite sufficient in the matter; but he has done so only by a tacit admission that he has really no critical instinct about literature and literary work, which, in one who writes about literature, is, I need hardly say, a much graver fault than malice of any kind.

Finally, Sir, allow me to say this. Such an article as you have published really makes me despair of the possibility of any general culture in England. Were I a French author, and my book brought out in Paris, there is not a single literary critic in France, on any paper of high standing, who would think for a moment of criticising it from an ethical standpoint. If he did so, he would stultify himself, not merely in the eyes of all men of letters, but in the eyes of the majority of the public. You have yourself often spoken against Puritanism. Believe me, Sir, Puritanism is never so offensive and destructive as when it deals with art matters. It is there that it is radically wrong. It is this Puritanism, to which your critic has given expression, that is always marring the artistic instinct of the English. So far from encouraging it, you should set yourself against it, and should try to teach your critics to recognize the essential difference between art and life. The gentleman who criticised my book is in a perfectly hopeless confusion about it, and your attempt to help him out by proposing that the subject-matter of art should be limited does not mend matters. It is proper that limitations should be placed on action. It is not proper that limitations should be placed on art. To art belong all things that are and all things that are not, and even the editor of a London paper has no right to restrain the freedom of art in the selection of subject-matter.

I now trust, Sir, that these attacks on me and on my book will cease. There are forms of advertisement that are unwarranted and unwarrantable.—I am, Sir, your obedient servant,

Oscar Wilde.

16, Tite-street, Chelsea, June 27

Jeyes: Response in the *St. James's Gazette* 20 (June 28, 1890): 4

[Once again, Jeyes responds to Wilde's letter on the page before the letter itself appeared.]

Mr. Oscar Wilde makes his third and, we presume, his final reply to the criticism which we published on "The Picture of Dorian Gray." Somewhat grudgingly, but in sufficiently explicit terms, he withdraws the charge of "personal malice" which he brought against the critic, and which, we may again assure him is absolutely unfounded. But he adheres to the other charge of critical incapacity. Mr. Wilde assures us that his book, so far from being dull and tedious, is full of interest; an opinion which is shared (see the letter we print on page 5 to-day) by his publishers' advertising agent-in-advance. Well, we can only repeat that we disagree with Mr. Wilde and his publishers' paragraphist. Quite apart from "ethical" considerations, the book seems to us a feeble and ineffective attempt at a kind of allegory which in the hands of abler writers (writers like Mr. Stevenson and Mr. Anstey, for instance) can be made striking or amusing.

Mr. Wilde also says that we suggested that the author and publishers of "The Picture of Dorian Gray" ought to be prosecuted by the "Tory Government," by which we presume he means the Treasury. No; we consider that such prosecutions are ill-advised, and expressly suggested that such action ought not to be taken against a book which we believed to be rendered innocuous by the tedious and stupid qualities which the critic discovered and explained. Secondly, Mr. Oscar Wilde hints that the "rights of literature" include a right to say what it pleases, how it pleases, and where it pleases. That is a right not only not recognized by the law of the land, but expressly denied by penalties which have been repeatedly enforced. Then what does Mr. Oscar Wilde mean by talking about the "rights of literature"? We will not insult an artist, who is by his own account un-moral or supra-moral, by suggesting that he means "moral rights." But he tells us that limitations may be set on action but ought not to be set on art. Quite so. But art becomes action where the work of art is published. It is offensive publications which we object to, not the offensive imaginings of such minds as find their pleasure therein.

[In the same issue, the *St. James's Gazette* published a letter from "A London Editor" (p. 8) that quoted Ward, Lock, and Co.'s advertisement for Wilde's novel. The "London Editor" used this advertisement to sneer at Wilde's claim in his first letter to the newspaper that he needed and desired no advertisement.]

Wilde: Letter to the *St. James's Gazette* 20 (June 30, 1890): 5

Mr. Oscar Wilde's Defence

To the EDITOR *of the* ST. JAMES'S GAZETTE

SIR,—In your issue of this evening you publish a letter from "A London Editor" which clearly insinuates in the last paragraph that I have in some way sanctioned the circulation of an expression of opinion, on the part of the proprietors of *Lippincott's Magazine*, of the literary and artistic value of my story of "The Picture of Dorian Gray."

Allow me, Sir, to state that there are no grounds for this insinuation. I was not aware that any such document was being circulated; and I have written to the agents, Messrs. Ward and Lock—who cannot, I feel sure, be primarily responsible for its appearance—to ask them to withdraw it at once.[1] No publisher should ever express an opinion of the value of what he publishes. That is a matter entirely for the literary critic to decide. I must admit, as one to whom contemporary literature is constantly submitted for criticism, that the only thing that ever prejudices me against a book is the lack of literary style; but I can quite understand how any ordinary critic would be strongly prejudiced against a work that was accompanied by a premature and unnecessary panegyric from the publisher. A publisher is simply a useful middleman. It is not for him to anticipate the verdict of criticism.

I may, however, while expressing my thanks to the "London Editor" for drawing my attention to this, I trust, purely American method of procedure, venture to differ from him in one of his criticisms. He states that he regards the expression "complete," as

[1]Wilde kept his word (*Letters* 433).

applied to a story, as a specimen of the "adjectival exuberance of the puffer"! Here, it seems to me, he sadly exaggerates. What my story is, is an interesting problem. What my story is not is a "novelette"—a term which you have more than once applied to it. There is no such word in the English language as novelette. It should not be used. It is merely part of the slang of Fleet Street.[2]

In another part of your paper, Sir, you state that I received your assurance of the lack of malice in your critic "somewhat grudgingly." This is not so. I frankly said that I accepted that assurance "quite readily," and that your own denial and that of your own critic were "sufficient." Nothing more generous could have been said. What I did feel was that you saved your critic from the charge of malice by convicting him of the unpardonable crime of lack of literary instinct. I still feel that. To call my book an ineffective attempt at allegory that, in the hands of Mr. Anstey, might have been made striking, is absurd. Mr. Anstey's sphere in literature, and my sphere, are different—very widely different.

You then gravely ask me what rights I imagine literature possesses. That is really an extraordinary question for the editor of a newspaper such as yours to ask. The rights of literature, Sir, are the rights of intellect.

I remember once hearing M. Renan[3] say that he would sooner live under a military despotism than under the despotism of the Church, because the former merely limited the freedom of action, while the latter limited the freedom of mind. You say that a work of art is a form of action. It is not. It is the highest mode of thought.

In conclusion, Sir, let me ask you not to force on me this continued correspondence by daily attacks. It is a trouble and a nuisance. As you assailed me first, I have a right to the last word. Let that last word be the present letter, and leave my book, I beg you, to the immortality that it deserves.—I am, Sir, your obedient servant,

OSCAR WILDE.

16, *Tite-street, Chelsea, June 28*

[Wilde's correspondence ended here, though Jeyes once again commented on the letter to note that "we do not consider that he has

---

[2]London location of the major newspapers.

[3]Ernest Renan (1823–92), French historian and theologian whose *Life of Jesus* (1863) rejected the supernatural element in Jesus's life.

satisfactorily met our arguments and our objections" (p. 4) and continued to throw small barbs at Wilde in the ensuing months.]

Walter Pater (1839–1894)

Wilde's 1891 revision also received reviews, though far fewer than the 1890 edition did. The most detailed was by Walter Pater, who read The Picture of Dorian Gray *as a work of aesthetic criticism. In 1890, Pater had refused to review the first version because he felt it was too dangerous, but he agreed to review the revision for* The Bookman. *During his libel trial against the Marquess of Queensberry, Wilde claimed that a comment Pater had made to him in person actually inspired his revision.*

"A Novel by Mr. Oscar Wilde," *The Bookman* 1 (Nov. 1891): 59–60

THERE is always something of an excellent talker about the writing of Mr. Oscar Wilde; and in his hands, as happens so rarely with those who practise it, the form of dialogue is justified by its being really alive. His genial, laughter-loving sense of life and its enjoyable intercourse, goes far to obviate any crudity there may be in the paradox, with which, as with the bright and shining truth which often underlies it, Mr. Wilde, startling his "countrymen," carries on, more perhaps than any other writer, the brilliant critical work of Matthew Arnold. *The Decay of Lying*, for instance, is all but unique in its half-humorous, yet wholly convinced, presentment of certain valuable truths of criticism. Conversational ease, the fluidity of life, felicitous expression, are qualities which have a natural alliance to the successful writing of fiction; and side by side with Mr. Wilde's *Intentions* (so he entitles his critical efforts) comes a novel, certainly original, and affording the reader a fair opportunity of comparing his practise as a creative artist with many a precept he has enounced as critic concerning it.

A wholesome dislike of the common-place, rightly or wrongly identified by him with the *bourgeois,* with our middle-class—its habits and tastes—leads him to protest emphatically against so-called "realism" in art; life, as he argues, with much plausibility, as a matter of fact, when it is really awake, following art—the fashion an effective artist sets; while art, on the other hand, influential and effective art, has never taken its cue from actual life. In *Dorian Gray* he is true certainly, on the whole, to the æsthetic philosophy of his *Intentions*; yet not infallibly, even on this point: there is a certain amount of the intrusion of real life and its sordid aspects—the low theatre, the pleasures and griefs, the faces of some very unrefined people, managed, of course, cleverly enough. The interlude of Jim Vane, his half-sullen but wholly faithful care for his sister's honour, is as good as perhaps anything of the kind, marked by a homely but real pathos, sufficiently proving a versatility in the writer's talent, which should make his books popular. Clever always, this book, however, seems to set forth anything but a homely philosophy of life for the middle-class—a kind of dainty Epicurean[1] theory, rather—yet fails, to some degree, in this; and one can see why. A true Epicureanism aims at a complete though harmonious development of man's entire organism. To lose the moral sense therefore, for instance, the sense of sin and righteousness, as Mr. Wilde's hero—his heroes are bent on doing as speedily, as completely as they can, is to lose, or lower, organisation, to become less complex, to pass from a higher to a lower degree of development. As a story, however, a partly supernatural story, it is first-rate in artistic management; those Epicurean niceties only adding to the decorative colour of its central figure, like so many exotic flowers, like the charming scenery and the perpetual, epigrammatic, surprising, yet so natural, conversations, like an atmosphere all about it. All that pleasant accessory detail, taken straight from the culture, the intellectual and social interests, the conventionalities, of the moment, have, in fact, after all, the effect of the better sort of realism, throwing into relief the adroitly-devised supernatural element after the manner of Poe,[2] but with a grace he never reached, which supersedes that earlier didactic purpose, and makes the quite sufficing interest of an excellent story.

We like the hero, and in spite of his, somewhat unsociable devotion to his art, Hallward, better than Lord Henry Wotton. He has

---

[1]Devotion to sensual enjoyment; a popular oversimplification of the Greek philosopher Epicurus.

[2]Edgar Allan Poe (1809–49), famed for horror and detective fiction.

too much of a not very really refined world in and about him, and
his somewhat cynical opinions, which seem sometimes to be those
of the writer, who may, however, have intended Lord Henry as a
satiric sketch. Mr. Wilde can hardly have intended him, with his
cynic amity of mind and temper, any more than the miserable end
of Dorian himself, to figure the motive and tendency of a true Cyre-
naic or Epicurean doctrine of life. In contrast with Hallward, the
artist, whose sensibilities idealise the world around him, the personality of Dorian Gray, above all, into something magnificent and
strange, we might say that Lord Henry, and even more the, from the
first, suicidal hero, loses too much in life to be a true Epicurean—
loses so much in the way of impressions, of pleasant memories, and
subsequent hopes, which Hallward, by a really Epicurean economy,
manages to secure. It should be said, however, in fairness, that the
writer is impersonal: seems not to have identified himself entirely
with any one of his characters: and Wotton's cynicism, or whatever
it be, at least makes a very clever story possible. He becomes the
spoiler of the fair young man, whose bodily form remains un-aged;
while his picture, the *chef d'œuvre* of the artist Hallward, changes
miraculously with the gradual corruption of his soul. How true,
what a light on the artistic nature, is the following on actual personalities and their revealing influence in art. We quote it as an example of Mr. Wilde's more serious style.

"I sometimes think that there are only two eras of any importance in the world's history. The first is the appearance of a new
medium for art, and the second is the appearance of new personality for art also. What the invention of oil-painting was to the Venetians, the face of Antinous was to late Greek sculpture, and the face
of Dorian Gray will some day be to me. It is not merely that I paint
from him, draw from him, sketch from him. Of course I have done
all that. But he is much more to me than a model or a sitter. I won't
tell you that I am dissatisfied with what I have done of him, or that
his beauty is such that art cannot express it. There is nothing that
Art cannot express, and I know that the work I have done, since I
met Dorian Gray, is good work, is the best work of my life. But in
some curious way his personality has suggested to me an entirely
new manner in art, an entirely new mode of style. I see things differently, I think of them differently. I can now recreate life in a way
that was hidden from me before."

Dorian himself, though certainly a quite unsuccessful experiment in Epicureanism, in life as a fine art, is (till his inward spoiling takes visible effect suddenly, and in a moment, at the end of his story) a beautiful creation. But his story is also a vivid, though carefully considered, exposure of the corruption of a soul, with a very plain moral, pushed home, to the effect that vice and crime make people coarse and ugly. General readers, nevertheless, will probably care less for this moral, less for the fine, varied, largely appreciative culture of the writer, in evidence from page to page, than for the story itself, with its adroitly managed supernatural incidents, its almost equally wonderful applications of natural science; impossible, surely, in fact, but plausible enough in fiction. Its interest turns on that very old theme, old because based on some inherent experience or fancy of the human brain, of a double life: of Döppelgänger—not of two *persons*, in this case, but of the man and his portrait; the latter of which, as we hinted above, changes, decays, is spoiled, while the former, through a long course of corruption, remains, to the outward eye, unchanged, still in all the beauty of a seemingly immaculate youth—"the devil's bargain." But it would be a pity to spoil the reader's enjoyment by further detail. We need only emphasise, once more, the skill, the real subtlety of art, the ease and fluidity withal of one telling a story by word of mouth, with which the consciousness of the supernatural is introduced into, and maintained amid, the elaborately conventional, sophisticated, disabused world Mr. Wilde depicts so cleverly, so mercilessly. The special fascination of the piece is, of course, just there—at that point of contrast. Mr. Wilde's work may fairly claim to go with that of Edgar Poe, and with some good French work of the same kind, done, probably, in more or less conscious imitation of it.

Parodies

It might seem that a writer as ironically self-aware as Wilde would preempt parodies, but he was subject to them almost before his career had started. Gilbert and Sullivan's *Patience* is the most famous, written long before *The Picture of Dorian Gray*. The most intriguing parodies of Wilde seem inspired by the scenes between Lord Henry Wotton and the Duchess of Monmouth, a Wilde-like character in opposition to an intelligent woman more than able to hold her own.

Robert Smythe Hichens (1864–1950)

Journalist Robert Smythe Hichens met Lord Alfred Douglas in Egypt. Back in London, Douglas introduced Hichens to Wilde himself. Shortly thereafter, Hichens published The Green Carnation *anonymously. Wilde appears as Esmé Amarinth, and Douglas as his protégé Lord Reginald Hastings. The title derives from Wilde's attending the theater, with five admirers, sporting green carnations—soon, a code for homosexuals. Although* The Green Carnation *is often described as a satire, much of it is unnervingly accurate: at times, with an appropriately Wildean logic, Amarinth is a better Oscar Wilde than Wilde was. Wilde even had to write to the press to deny rumors that he was the author. In the excerpt below, Hastings talks with Lady Locke, an older woman whose interest teeters between the maternal and the romantic.*

from *The Green Carnation* (1894)

"So I have. We none of us live up to our ideals, I suppose. But really I have none. I agree with Esmé that nothing is so limited as to have an ideal."

"And yet you look sometimes as if you might have many," she said, as if half to herself. The curious motherly feeling had come upon her again, a kind of tenderness that often leads to preaching.

Reggie glanced up at her quickly, and with a pleased expression. A veiled tribute to his good looks delighted him, whether it came from man or woman. Only an unveiled one surpassed it in his estimation.

"Ah! but that means nothing," he said. "It is quite a mistake to believe, as many people do, that the mind shows itself in the face. Vice may sometimes write itself in lines and changes of contour, but that is all. Our faces are really masks given to us to conceal our minds with. Of course occasionally the mask slips partly off, generally when we are stupid and emotional. But that is an inartistic accident. Outward revelations of what is going on inside of us take place far more seldom than silly people suppose. No more preposterous theory has ever been put forward than that of the artist revealing himself in his art. The writer, for instance, has at least three minds—his Society mind, his writing mind, and his real mind. They are all quite separate and distinct, or they ought to be. When his writing mind and his real mind get mixed up together, he ceases to be an artist. That is why Swinburne has gone off so much. If you want to write really fine erotic poetry, you must live an absolutely rigid and entirely respectable life. The 'Laus Veneris'[1] could only have been produced by a man who had a Nonconformist conscience. I am certain that Mrs. Humphrey Ward is the most strictly orthodox Christian whom we have. Otherwise, her books against the accepted Christianity could never have brought her in so many thousands of pounds.[2] I never read her, of course. Life is far too long and lovely for that sort of thing; but a bishop once told me that she was a great artist, and that if she had a sense of gravity, she would rival George Eliot. Dickens had probably no sense of humour. That is why he makes second-rate people die of laughing. Oscar Wilde was utterly mistaken when he wrote the 'Picture of Dorian Gray.' After Dorian's act of cruelty, the picture ought to have grown more sweet, more saintly, more angelic in expression."

"I never read that book."

"Then you have gained a great deal. Poor Oscar! He is terribly truthful. He reminds me so much of George Washington."

George Slythe Street (1867–1936)

Now largely forgotten, George Slythe Street was a prominent essayist and man of letters during the late Victorian and Edwardian periods; he later gained a degree of notoriety as the official reader (i.e., censor) of plays. His second book, The Autobiography of a Boy, *one of his*

---

[1]Algernon Charles Swinburne (1837–1909), leading Victorian poet whose "*Laus Veneris*" ("Praise of Venus," 1866) describes the sadomasochistic devotion to Venus of the medieval knight Tannhäuser.

[2]Mary Ward (1851–1920), Victorian and Edwardian novelist whose bestseller *Robert Elsemere* (1888) concerns a clergyman's crisis of faith.

most prominent literary successes, is a satire of Wilde. It is written in the voice of Tubby (an unflattering reference to Wilde's weight), a pretentious young man who unwittingly reveals his own crassness and stupidity. After graduating from Oxford, Tubby moves to London and strives to adopt an aesthetic lifestyle by writing poems like "Ballad of Shameful Kisses" and "A Dirge of Desire Dead." Tubby longs to be known as "a man to whom no chaste woman should be allowed to speak." He is roundly laughed at; no one prints his poems; and, overwhelmed by debt, he flees to Canada. In the following selection from the chapter "A Feminine Question," he meets the cousin of his friend Hughy.

from *The Autobiography of a Boy: Passages Selected by His Friends* (1894)

She began by quoting some foolish question Hughy had just put to her, showing the poor fellow's complete lack of all reading. "Ah," I said, gaily, "to be in the Guards covers a multitude of ignorances: Hughy looks sweet in his tunic.[1] You must not expect too much!" "I expect," she answered, "a great deal of you, because he says you're very philosophical. I want so much somebody to explain to me this theory of ———." She mentioned some horrid German name which I had never heard. I do not attempt to follow all the vagaries of modern philosophy; there are so many things to do in life, and mere book-learning is so futile. I do not at all value my reputation for philosophy, which is surely secure with those who can discriminate, but I thought it a social duty to continue the subject this pedantic girl had chosen. "Which theory?" I asked her. She told me; there was nothing charming in it, and I have forgotten it now. "It is not worth explaining," I said; "what germ of truth there is in it simply amounts to the only practical outcome of all sound philosophy." "What is that?" she asked me, smiling for some reason, thinking perhaps I would make some silly joke, as Hughy would. "It is," I said, folding my hands and speaking slowly, "that you must live your life."

There was never such a literal and persistent girl. She caught me up at once. "Surely that is obvious: of course I must live my life." "Obvious indeed," I said sadly, "but how difficult!" "But what *do*

---

[1]Splendid uniform of the Royal Guards, the household soldiers of the British sovereign.

you mean? You might as well say I must dine on my dinner." A hopeless girl, but I tried to make her see a minute particle of my meaning. "I mean you must be free and joyous, not tyrannized over by foolish dogmas of altruism, but fulfilling your own instincts and desires." "Do just what I please? Be thoroughly selfish? But that *wouldn't* be *my* life. Why should you say that is more my life than acting naturally, as one is accustomed to act? One has certain inherited tendencies"—I smiled at the foolish catchword—"and education forms them into habits, and one's natural life is to act as they direct." "Dear lady," I said, desperately, "don't let us quarrel about it. When you have had my experience you will see what a beautiful thing egotism is. Then you will live your life; until then not." "What *do* you—" she began, but broke off, and asked, with a laugh, this utterly irrelevant question: "Do *you* wear a tunic too? And do you look sweet in it?" How women care for these trifles!

A quite irrelevant question, but the only feminine thing she had said. I suppose she was posing; but she was an uncomfortable girl, and I do not want to meet her again.

Wilde's Trials

The events leading to the notorious trials that ruined Wilde began when John Sholto Douglas, the ninth Marquess of Queensberry and the father of Lord Alfred Douglas, sent Wilde a hastily scrawled note, "For Oscar Wilde posing somdomite [*sic*]." In many ways, Wilde was a model of Victorian propriety next to Queensberry, who had divorced his first wife after a series of affairs, had his second marriage annulled on the grounds of impotence and supposed deformity, and been thrown out of respectable society because of his reputation as a free thinker and secularist. He also shared some prominent features with Wilde, only ten years his junior: he was deeply influenced by the thought of Herbert Spencer and Thomas Henry Huxley, had written poetry, and reveled in the London club scene. Unlike Wilde, however, he had spent his youth with the navy and was fond of hunting and boxing (the "Queensberry rules" are named after him).

Probably because his eldest son had committed suicide in a homosexual scandal regarding Lord Rosebery, the future prime minister, Queensberry was infuriated by Wilde's relationship with Douglas. Although Wilde had charmed Queensberry during their initial meetings, Queensberry grew hostile to Wilde's involvement with his son and even went to Wilde's home threatening to beat him up. Queensberry's note, which Wilde received on February 18, 1895, was the last straw. If his decision to prosecute Queensberry for libel has seemed deliberately self-destructive to some later biographers, it also seems an attempt to rid himself of a dangerous, violent bully.

Queensberry had not accused Wilde of being a sodomite, only of posing as one. The burden of his defense, undertaken by the brilliant lawyer Edward Carson, was to show that Wilde had both committed sodomy and paraded as a person who might be thought to do so. To prove the first charge, the defense searched out the so-called rent boys, the prostitutes whom Wilde patronized; to prove the second, Carson concentrated on Wilde's writings, especially *The Picture of Dorian Gray*. This second gambit was hardly successful: Wilde parried him point by point. But the first charge was sustained by such convincing evidence that Wilde's lawyer, Sir Edward Clarke, virtually gave up, hoping only that if Wilde agreed to accept the charge of "posing," he could avoid prosecution for actual sodomy. The judge refused, and Wilde lost the trial.

Almost immediately, Wilde and Alfred Taylor, one of his associates, were both arrested for gross indecency under Section 11 of the 1885 Criminal Law Amendment Act (the Labouchère Amendment):

> Any male person who, in public or private, commits, or is a party to the commission of, or procures, or attempts to procure the commission by any male person of, any act of gross indecency shall be guilty of misdemeanour, and being convicted shall be liable at the discretion of the Court to be imprisoned for any term not exceeding two years, with or without hard labour.

The first trial ended with a hung jury, and the matter could have ended there. But the government insisted on a second trial, partly concerned that the first one had dredged up rumors about the sexuality of Lord Rosebery, the prime minister. Wilde and Taylor were both found guilty and given the maximum sentence: two years, with hard labor.

Regina (Oscar Wilde) vs. John Douglas (Marquess of Queensberry)

In a mystery of British law, the official transcripts of the Wilde trials have disappeared. Various versions have been published, cobbled together from personal reminiscences and press reports. In 2003, Merlin Holland, Wilde's grandson, published what appears to be the most detailed transcript of the first trial in The Real Trial of Oscar Wilde. *It reveals that the discussion of* The Picture of Dorian Gray *was more extensive than had been known. Much of the lengthy discussion hinged on the differences between the two versions; Carson cited the 1890 edition and the fact that it had been revised to argue that Wilde had posed as a sodomite. The excerpt presented here is not a verbatim transcription but a condensed overview, modified in light of Holland's transcript. The examination occurred on the afternoon of Wednesday, April 3, 1895.*

from *Regina (Oscar Wilde) vs. John Douglas (Marquess of Queensberry)* (1895)

CARSON: This is in your introduction to *Dorian Gray*: "There is no such thing as a moral or an immoral book. Books are well written, or badly written." That expresses your view?

WILDE: My view of art, yes.

CARSON: Then, I take it, that no matter how immoral a book may be, if it is well written, it is, in your opinion, a good book?

WILDE: Yes; if it were well written so as to produce a sense of beauty, which is the highest sense of which a human being can be capable. If it were badly written, it would produce a sense of disgust.

CARSON: Then a well-written book putting forward sodomitical views may be a good book?

WILDE: No work of art ever puts forward views. Views belong to people who are not artists.

CARSON: A sodomitical novel might be a good book?

WILDE: I don't know what you mean by a sodomitical novel.

CARSON: Then I will suggest *Dorian Gray* as open to the interpretation of being such a novel?

WILDE: That could only be to brutes and illiterates.

CARSON: An illiterate person reading *Dorian Gray* might consider it such a novel?

WILDE: The views of illiterates on art are unaccountable. I am concerned only with my view of art. I don't care twopence what other people think of it.

CARSON: The majority of persons would come under your definition of Philistines and illiterates?

WILDE: I have found wonderful exceptions.

CARSON: Do you think that the majority of people live up to the position you are giving us?

WILDE: I am afraid they are not cultivated enough.

CARSON: Not cultivated enough to draw the distinction between a good book and a bad book?

WILDE: Certainly not.

CARSON: The affection and love of the artist of Dorian Gray might lead an ordinary individual to believe that it might have a sodomitical tendency?

WILDE: I have no knowledge of the views of ordinary individuals.

CARSON: You did not prevent the ordinary individual from buying your book?

WILDE: I have never discouraged them.

[A discussion then followed between Carson and Wilde's lawyer Sir Edward Clarke about which version of *The Picture of Dorian Gray* was to be used in court, the 1890 or the 1891. Wilde told Clarke that he was indifferent; evidently, both were present in the courtroom. Carson then read from the dialogue between Lord Henry and Basil in the 1890 version:

"I want you to explain to me why you won't exhibit Dorian Gray's picture. I want the real reason."

"I told you the real reason."

"No, you did not. You said it was because there was too much of yourself in it. Now, that is childish."

"Harry," said Basil Hallward, looking him straight in the face, "every portrait that is painted with feeling is a portrait of the artist, not of the sitter. The sitter is merely the accident, the occasion. It is not he who is revealed by the painter; it is rather the painter who, on the colored canvas, reveals himself. The reason I will not exhibit this picture is that I am afraid that I have shown with it the secret of my own soul."

Lord Harry laughed. "And what is that?" he asked.

"I will tell you," said Hallward; and an expression of perplexity came over his face.

"I am all expectation, Basil," murmured his companion, looking at him.

"Oh, there is really very little to tell, Harry," answered the young painter; "and I am afraid you will hardly understand it. Perhaps you will hardly believe it."

Lord Henry smiled, and, leaning down, plucked a pink-petalled daisy from the grass, and examined it. "I am quite sure I shall understand it," he replied, gazing intently at the little golden white-feathered disk, "and I can believe anything, provided that it is incredible."

"Well, this is incredible," repeated Hallward, rather bitterly,— "incredible to me at times. I don't know what it means. The story is simply this. Two months ago I went to a crush at Lady Brandon's. You know we poor painters have to show ourselves in society from time to time, just to remind the public that we are not savages. With an evening coat and a white tie, as you told me once, anybody, even a stock-broker, can gain a reputation for being civilized. Well, after I had been in the room about ten minutes, talking to huge overdressed dowagers and tedious Academicians, I suddenly became conscious that some one was looking at me. I turned half-way round, and saw Dorian Gray for the first time. When our eyes met, I felt that I was growing pale. A curious instinct of terror came over me. I knew that I had come face to face with some one whose mere personality was so fascinating that, if I allowed it to do so, it would absorb my whole nature, my whole soul, my very art itself. I did not want any external influence in my life. You know yourself, Harry, how independent I am by nature. My father destined me for the army. I insisted on going to Oxford. Then he made me enter my name at the Middle Temple. Before I had eaten half a dozen dinners I gave up the Bar, and announced my intention of becoming a painter.

Carson continued reading from the 1890 version until the words "He, too, felt that we were destined to know each other"; for the rest of the passage, and the changes that Wilde made to it in the 1891 version, see the first excerpt in the "Textual Issues" section.]

CARSON: Now I ask you, Mr. Wilde, do you consider that that description of the feeling of one man towards another, a youth just grown up, was a proper or an improper feeling?

WILDE: I think it is the most perfect description of what an artist would feel on meeting a beautiful personality that was in some way necessary to his art and life.

CARSON: You think that is a feeling a young man should have towards another?

WILDE: Yes, as an artist.

[The examination then moved to a discussion of Basil's confession to Dorian himself. Carson claimed, "I believe it was left out in the purged edition"; Wilde answered, "I do not call it purged." Carson responded, "Yes, I know that; but we will see." After some more discussion of the exact page number, Carson read the dialogue between Basil and Dorian in Chapter 7 of the 1890 text. For this passage in the 1890 and 1891 versions, see the second excerpt in the "Textual Issues" section.]

CARSON: Do you mean to say that that passage describes the natural feeling of one man towards another?

WILDE: It would be the influence produced by a beautiful personality.

CARSON: A beautiful person?

WILDE: I said a "beautiful personality." You can describe it as you like. Dorian Gray's was a most remarkable personality.

CARSON: May I take it that you, as an artist, have never known the feeling described here?

WILDE: I have never allowed any personality to dominate my art.

CARSON: Then you have never known the feeling you described?

WILDE: No; it is a work of fiction.

CARSON: So far as you are concerned you have no experience as to its being a natural feeling?

WILDE: I think it is perfectly natural for any artist to admire intensely and love a young man. It is an incident in the life of almost every artist.

CARSON: But let us go over it phrase by phrase.[1] "I quite admit that I adored you madly." What do you say to that? Have you ever adored a young man madly?

WILDE: No, not madly. I prefer love—that is a higher form.

CARSON: Never mind about that. Let us keep down to the level we are at now.

WILDE: I have never given adoration to anybody except myself.

CARSON: I suppose you think that a very smart thing?

WILDE: Not at all.

CARSON: Then you have never had that feeling?

WILDE: No. The whole idea was borrowed from Shakespeare, I regret to say; yes, from Shakespeare's sonnets.

CARSON: "I have adored you extravagantly"?—Do you mean financially?

WILDE: Oh, yes, financially.

CARSON: Do you think we are talking about finance?

WILDE: I don't know what you are talking about.

CARSON: Don't you? Well, I hope I shall make myself very plain before I have done. "I was jealous of every one to whom you spoke." Have you ever been jealous of a young man?

WILDE: Never in my life.

CARSON: "I wanted to have you all to myself." Did you ever have that feeling?

WILDE: No; I should consider it an intense nuisance, an intense bore.

CARSON: I believe you have written an article to show that Shakespeare's sonnets were practically sodomitical?

WILDE: On the contrary I have written an article to show that they are not. I objected to such a perversion being put upon Shakespeare.

CARSON: "I grew afraid that the world would know of my idolatry." Why should he grow afraid that the world should know of it?

---

[1]Carson actually began the phrase-by-phrase approach at Wilde's request (Holland 2003, 90).

WILDE: Because there are people in the world who cannot understand the intense devotion, affection, and admiration that an
artist can feel for a wonderful and beautiful personality. These
are the conditions under which we live. I regret them.

CARSON: These unfortunate people, that have not the high understanding that you have, might put it down to something wrong?

WILDE: Undoubtedly; to any point they chose. I am not concerned
with the ignorance of others.

Aestheticism

Aestheticism encompasses a variety of developments in late Victorian culture that arose not solely from the world of art but also from science, philology, economics, and politics. At its core is the doctrine of "art for art's sake," in defiance of the measures of popularity, moral value, political stance, religious teachings, or other benefits to the reader. The value of self-contained perfection flouted such Victorian predecessors as Charles Dickens, George Eliot, Elizabeth Barrett Browning, and Alfred Tennyson, all of whom infused their writing with moral, political, and religious issues, above all the power of art to respond to and analyze culture. Freed from this demand, aestheticism embraced the casual, the trivial, the unrepresentative, the fleeting, the boring, the ephemeral, the bizarre, and the inauthentic. If Victorian realism found its icon in the enormous, triple-decker novel, aestheticism favored the lyric, the romance, the short story, the epigram, and the well-crafted essay.

Yet the anti-realism of aestheticism was always something of a pose. For one thing, aestheticism quickly developed an intimate, complicated relationship to the marketplace. While its works submit middle-class mores to unrelenting scorn and rarely refer overtly to production and marketing, aestheticism proved a good business, influencing advertisements and interior decoration and underwriting Wilde's popular lecture tour of the United States and Canada. Moreover, writers in the aesthetic mode were not indifferent to politics. William Morris, writer of some of the most otherworldly romances of the Victorian period, was also a fiery socialist; Algernon Charles Swinburne wrote exquisitely decadent lyrics but also verse denouncing political tyranny; and even Wilde wrote "The

Simeon Solomon, *Allegorical Self-Portrait* (1873). Solomon, a gay, Jewish painter, codes his self-portrait in a mysterious allegory. (Courtesy of the Minneapolis Institute of Arts.)

Soul of Man Under Socialism" the same year that he revised *The Picture of Dorian Gray*. Women writers such as Michael Field and Vernon Lee found in aestheticism a vehicle for new social and sexual thought and contested the mythologization of female beauty in male aesthetic writers. In all these adventures, Victorian aestheticism was in love with paradox: engaged otherworldliness; professional dilettantism; beautiful ugliness; normative transgressions; and innovative clichés.

Walter Pater (1839–1894)

Walter Pater, universally acknowledged leading philosopher of Victorian aestheticism, had a quiet, academic life, but one that put him in a position of considerable influence. Lecturing in classics at Oxford's Brasenose College, Oxford, Pater shaped some of the brightest minds in late Victorian Britain. Wilde learned much from him while he was a student in the 1870s, though Wilde never actually attended Pater's lectures. But Pater, having nearly lost his position because of an affair with a male undergraduate, closeted his homosexuality in ways that put him at odds with Wilde's flamboyance.

His most famous book was Studies in the History of the Renaissance *(1873), with its famous, lyric, controversial "Conclusion" (presented here as published in 1893, in the last version that Pater corrected). Pater's* Renaissance *was wide ranging, moving from twelfth-century France to the German historian Winckelmann in the eighteenth century. Where John Ruskin privileged medieval art for its devotional sincerity and aspirations to greatness, Pater turned to the art of the Italian Renaissance and crafted his prose to convey its effect on the viewer. His famous rhapsody on Leonardo da Vinci's* Mona Lisa *is a set piece in this mode. Pater's chapter on Winckelmann celebrated the Greeks' admiration of male beauty and popularized Hellenism as a mode for exploring same-sex desire.*

The "Conclusion" to The Renaissance *first appeared in a review of the poems of William Morris. When it appeared in* The Renaissance, *the controversy that ensued convinced Pater to delete it from the second edition. He thought again and restored it in the third edition (1888), explaining that he had given in to worries that its raptures "might possibly mislead some of those young men into whose hands it might fall."*

"Conclusion" to *The Renaissance* (1893)

Λέγει που Ἡράκλειτος ὅτι πάντα χωρεῖ καὶ οὐδὲν μένει[1]

To regard all things and principles of things as inconstant modes or fashions has more and more become the tendency of modern thought. Let us begin with that which is without—our physical life. Fix upon it in one of its more exquisite intervals, the moment, for instance, of delicious recoil from the flood of water in summer heat. What is the whole physical life in that moment but a combination of natural elements to which science gives their names? But those elements, phosphorus and lime and delicate fibres, are present not in the human body alone: we detect them in places most remote from it. Our physical life is a perpetual motion of them—the passage of the blood, the waste and repairing of the lenses of the eye, the modification of the tissues of the brain under every ray of light and sound—processes which science reduces to simpler and more elementary forces. Like the elements of which we are composed, the action of these forces extends beyond us: it rusts iron and ripens corn. Far out on every side of us those elements are broadcast, driven in many currents; and birth and gesture and death and the springing of violets from the grave are but a few out of ten thousand resultant combinations. That clear, perpetual outline of face and limb is but an image of ours, under which we group them—a design in a web, the actual threads of which pass out beyond it. This at least of flamelike our life has, that it is but the concurrence, renewed from moment to moment, of forces parting sooner or later on their ways.

Or if we begin with the inward world of thought and feeling, the whirlpool is still more rapid, the flame more eager and devouring. There it is no longer the gradual darkening of the eye, the gradual fading of colour from the wall—movements of the shore-side, where the water flows down indeed, though in apparent rest—but the race of the mid-stream, a drift of momentary acts of sight and passion and thought. At first sight experience seems to bury us under a flood of external objects, pressing upon us with a sharp and importunate reality, calling us out of ourselves in a thousand forms of action. But when reflexion begins to play upon these objects they

[1]Heraclitus says, "All things give way; nothing remaineth" (Pater's translation, from Plato's *Cratylus*).

are dissipated under its influence; the cohesive force seems suspended like some trick of magic; each object is loosed into a group of impressions—colour, odour, texture—in the mind of the observer. And if we continue to dwell in thought on this world, not of objects in the solidity with which language invests them, but of impressions, unstable, flickering, inconsistent, which burn and are extinguished with our consciousness of them, it contracts still further: the whole scope of observation is dwarfed into the narrow chamber of the individual mind. Experience, already reduced to a group of impressions, is ringed round for each one of us by that thick wall of personality through which no real voice has ever pierced on its way to us, or from us to that which we can only conjecture to be without. Every one of those impressions is the impression of the individual in his isolation, each mind keeping as a solitary prisoner its own dream of a world. Analysis goes a step farther still, and assures us that those impressions of the individual mind to which, for each one of us, experience dwindles down, are in perpetual flight; that each of them is limited by time, and that as time is infinitely divisible, each of them is infinitely divisible also; all that is actual in it being a single moment, gone while we try to apprehend it, of which it may ever be more truly said that it has ceased to be than that it is. To such a tremulous wisp constantly re-forming itself on the stream, to a single sharp impression, with a sense in it, a relic more or less fleeting, of such moments gone by, what is real in our life fines itself down. It is with this movement, with the passage and dissolution of impressions, images, sensations, that analysis leaves off—that continual vanishing away, that strange, perpetual, weaving and unweaving of ourselves.

Philosophiren, says Novalis, *ist dephlegmatisiren, vivificiren.*[2] The service of philosophy, of speculative culture, towards the human spirit, is to rouse, to startle it to a life of constant and eager observation. Every moment some form grows perfect in hand or face; some tone on the hills or the sea is choicer than the rest; some mood of passion or insight or intellectual excitement is irresistibly real and attractive to us,—for that moment only. Not the fruit of experience, but experience itself, is the end. A counted number of pulses only is given to us of a variegated, dramatic life. How may

---

[2]"To philosophize is to become unphlegmatic, to become alive"; Novalis is Baron Friedrich von Hardenberg (1772–1801), a German Romantic writer.

we see in them all that is to seen in them by the finest senses? How shall we pass most swiftly from point to point, and be present always at the focus where the greatest number of vital forces unite in their purest energy? To burn always with this hard, gemlike flame, to maintain this ecstasy, is success in life. In a sense it might even be said that our failure is to form habits: for, after all, habit is relative to a stereotyped world, and meantime it is only the roughness of the eye that makes any two persons, things, situations, seem alike. While all melts under our feet, we may well grasp at any exquisite passion, or any contribution to knowledge that seems by a lifted horizon to set the spirit free for a moment, or any stirring of the senses, strange dyes, strange colours, and curious odours, or work of the artist's hands, or the face of one's friend. Not to discriminate every moment some passionate attitude in those about us, and in the very brilliancy of their gifts some tragic dividing of forces on their ways, is, on this short day of frost and sun, to sleep before evening. With this sense of the splendour of our experience and of its awful brevity, gathering all we are into one desperate effort to see and touch, we shall hardly have time to make theories about the things we see and touch. What we have to do is to be for ever curiously testing new opinions and courting new impressions, never acquiescing in a facile orthodoxy of Comte, or of Hegel,[3] or of our own. Philosophical theories or ideas, as points of view, instruments of criticism, may help us to gather up what might otherwise pass unregarded by us. "Philosophy is the microscope of thought."[4] The theory or idea or system which requires of us the sacrifice of any part of this experience, in consideration of some interest into which we cannot enter, or some abstract theory we have not identified with ourselves, or of what is only conventional, has no real claim upon us.

One of the most beautiful passages of Rousseau is that in the sixth book of the *Confessions*,[5] where he describes the awakening in him of the literary sense. An undefinable taint of death had clung always about him, and now in early manhood he believed himself

[3] Auguste Comte (1798–1857), founder of positivism; Georg W. F. Hegel (1770–1831), leading German philosopher of history and art.

[4] From *Les Misérables* (1862) by Victor Hugo (1802–85).

[5] Autobiography of Jean-Jacques Rousseau (1712–78), French writer and philosopher.

smitten by mortal disease. He asked himself how he might make as much as possible of the interval that remained; and he was not biassed by anything in his previous life when he decided that it must be by intellectual excitement, which he found just then in the clear, fresh writings of Voltaire. Well! we are all *condamnés*, as Victor Hugo says: we are all under sentence of death but with a sort of indefinite reprieve—*les hommes sont tous condamnés mort avec des sursis indéfinis*:[6] we have an interval, and then our place knows us no more. Some spend this interval in listlessness, some in high passions, the wisest, at least among "the children of this world,"[7] in art and song. For our one chance lies in expanding that interval, in getting as many pulsations as possible into the given time. Great passions may give us this quickened sense of life, ecstasy and sorrow of love, the various forms of enthusiastic activity, disinterested or otherwise, which come naturally to many of us. Only be sure it is passion—that it does yield you this fruit of a quickened, multiplied consciousness. Of such wisdom, the poetic passion, the desire of beauty, the love of art for its own sake, has most. For art comes to you proposing frankly to give nothing but the highest quality to your moments as they pass, and simply for those moments' sake.

Matthew Arnold (1822–1888)

Matthew Arnold was the son of educational theorist Thomas Arnold, famous for his model reforms at Rugby school. Although Arnold did less well on his exams than Wilde would, he was awarded a fellowship to Oriel College and began to publish poetry. In 1851, he became a school inspector, an exhausting job that involved extensive travel. He also was elected to the Professorship of Poetry at Oxford in 1857, though by this time he was writing less poetry than cultural criticism, especially on religion in modern life. He was the first to lecture in English rather than in Latin.

Culture and Anarchy, Arnold's most famous work, began as a series of essays for Cornhill Magazine, *one of the great Victorian peri-*

---

[6]From *The Last Day of a Condemned Man* (1832).

[7]"For the children of this world are wiser in their generation than the children of light" (Luke 16.8).

odicals noted for high intellectual distinction. Arnold's essays mount a devastating attack on the smugness, complacency, and what he calls the "Hebraism" of contemporary British culture. In the section presented here, Arnold divides the British population into the Barbarians (the aristocracy), the Philistines (the middle class), and the Populace (the working class). All are guilty of the ethos of "doing what one likes," instead of striving to realize their "best" self. Yet in every class there are "aliens" capable of transcending class prejudices. With these, Arnold contends, lies the greatest hope for the perfection of culture.

Arnold, who did not subscribe to "art for art's sake," may seem an unusual writer to include in a section on aestheticism: his criterion was the moral seriousness that Wilde refuted and frequently satirized. Yet Wilde's career doubled Arnold's in many respects. Both studied "Greats" at Oxford; both won the Newdigate Prize for their poems; both admired French literature; both gave lecture tours in America; and both disdained the narrowness and parochialism of British culture. And in prose style, Wilde's sophisticated irony owes far more to Arnold than to Pater.

from *Culture and Anarchy* (1869, rev. 1882)

All of us, so far as we are Barbarians, Philistines, or Populace, imagine happiness to consist in doing what one's ordinary self likes. What one's ordinary self likes differs according to the class to which one belongs, and has its severer and its lighter side; always, however, remaining machinery, and nothing more. The graver self of the Barbarian likes honours and consideration; his more relaxed self, field-sports and pleasure. The graver self of one kind of Philistine likes fanaticism, business, and money-making; his more relaxed self, comfort and tea-meetings. Of another kind of Philistine, the graver self likes rattening;[1] the relaxed self, deputations, or hearing Mr. Odger[2] speak. The sterner self of the Populace likes bawling, hustling, and smashing; the lighter self, beer. But in each class there are born a certain number of natures with a curiosity about their best self, with a bent for seeing things as they are, for disentangling themselves from machinery, for simply concerning themselves with reason and the will of God, and doing their best to make these prevail;—for the pursuit, in a word, of perfection. To certain manifes-

[1]Destroying equipment to enforce compliance with trade union rules.
[2]George Odger (1820–77), trade union leader.

tations of this love for perfection mankind have accustomed themselves to give the name of genius; implying, by this name, something original and heaven-bestowed in the passion. But the passion is to be found far beyond those manifestations of it to which the world usually gives the name of genius, and in which there is, for the most part, a *talent* of some kind or other, a special and striking faculty of execution, informed by the heaven-bestowed ardour, or genius. It is to be found in many manifestations besides these, and may best be called, as we have called it, the love and pursuit of perfection; culture being the true nurse of the pursuing love, and sweetness and light the true character of the pursued perfection. Natures with this bent emerge in all classes,—among the Barbarians, among the Philistines, among the Populace. And this bent always tends to take them out of their class, and to make their distinguishing characteristic not their Barbarianism or their Philistinism, but their *humanity*. They have, in general, a rough time of it in their lives; but they are sown more abundantly than one might think, they appear where and when one least expects it, they set up a fire which enfilades,[3] so to speak, the class with which they are ranked; and, in general, by the extrication of their best self as the self to develop, and by the simplicity of the ends fixed by them as paramount, they hinder the unchecked predominance of that class-life which is the affirmation of our ordinary self, and seasonably disconcert mankind in their worship of machinery.

Therefore, when we speak of ourselves as divided into Barbarians, Philistines, and Populace, we must be understood always to imply that within each of these classes there are a certain number of *aliens*, if we may so call them,—persons who are mainly led, not by their class spirit, but by a general *humane* spirit, by the love of human perfection; and that this number is capable of being diminished or augmented. I mean, the number of those who will succeed in developing this happy instinct will be greater or smaller, in proportion both to the force of the original instinct within them, and to the hindrance or encouragement which it meets with from without. In almost all who have it, it is mixed with some infusion of the spirit of an ordinary self, some quantity of class-instinct, and even, as has been shown, of more than one class-instinct at the same

---

[3]Sweeps from one end to the other.

time; so that, in general, the extrication of the best self, the predominance of the *humane* instinct, will very much depend upon its
meeting, or not, with what is fitted to help and elicit it. At a
moment, therefore, when it is agreed that we want a source of
authority, and when it seems probable that the right source is our
best self, it becomes of vast importance to see whether or not the
things around us are, in general, such as to help and elicit our best
self, and if they are not, to see why they are not, and the most
promising way of mending them.

Oscar Wilde (1854–1900)

Wilde thought The Decay of Lying *the best of his dialogues. It was first
published in the* Nineteenth Century *in 1889, then collected in* Intentions *(1891). The interlocutors Cyril and Vivian are named after
Wilde's sons. Cyril is the naïve questioner; Vivian, the sophisticated
critic who refuses the elevation of realism and nature to argue for art's
independence from these conventional measures. This passage is from
the conclusion.*

from *The Decay of Lying* (1891)

CYRIL.   But in order to avoid making any error I want you to tell
me briefly the doctrines of the new aesthetics.

VIVIAN.   Briefly, then, they are these. Art never expresses anything but itself. It has an independent life, just as Thought has, and
develops purely on its own lines. It is not necessarily realistic in an
age of realism, nor spiritual in an age of faith. So far from being the
creation of its time, it is usually in direct opposition to it, and the
only history that it preserves for us is the history of its own
progress. Sometimes it returns upon its footsteps, and revives some
antique form, as happened in the archaistic movement of late Greek
Art, and in the pre-Raphaelite movement[1] of our own day. At other
times it entirely anticipates its age, and produces in one century

[1]The Pre-Raphaelite Brotherhood, founded in 1848 by D. G. Rossetti and others,
aimed to free painting from academic conventions; its later members embraced a
neo-medieval style.

work that it takes another century to understand, to appreciate, and to enjoy. In no case does it reproduce its age. To pass from the art of a time to the time itself is the great mistake that all historians commit.

The second doctrine is this. All bad art comes from returning to Life and Nature, and elevating them into ideals. Life and Nature may sometimes be used as part of Art's rough material, but before they are of any real service to art they must be translated into artistic conventions. The moment Art surrenders its imaginative medium it surrenders everything. As a method Realism is a complete failure, and the two things that every artist should avoid are modernity of form and modernity of subject-matter. To us, who live in the nineteenth century, any century is a suitable subject for art except our own. The only beautiful things are the things that do not concern us. It is, to have the pleasure of quoting myself, exactly because Hecuba is nothing to us that her sorrows are so suitable a motive for a tragedy.[2] Besides, it is only the modern that ever becomes old-fashioned. M. Zola[3] sits down to give us a picture of the Second Empire. Who cares for the Second Empire now? It is out of date. Life goes faster than Realism, but Romanticism is always in front of Life.

The third doctrine is that Life imitates Art far more than Art imitates Life. This results not merely from Life's imitative instinct, but from the fact that the self-conscious aim of Life is to find expression, and that Art offers it certain beautiful forms through which it may realize that energy. It is a theory that has never been put forward before, but it is extremely fruitful, and throws an entirely new light upon the history of Art.

It follows, as a corollary from this, that external Nature also imitates Art. The only effects that she can show us are effects that we have already seen through poetry, or in paintings. This is the secret of Nature's charm, as well as the explanation of Nature's weakness.

The final revelation is that Lying, the telling of beautiful untrue things, is the proper aim of Art. But of this I think I have spoken at sufficient length. And now let us go out on the terrace, where

[2] Hamlet is amazed at an actor's real tears for a fictional character: "What's Hecuba to him or he to Hecuba, / That he should weep for her?" (2.2.559–60).

[3] Émile Zola (1840–1902), French naturalistic novelist.

"droops the milkwhite peacock like a ghost,"[4] while the evening star "washes the dusk with silver."[5] At twilight nature becomes a wonderfully suggestive effect, and is not without loveliness, though perhaps its chief use is to illustrate quotations from the poets. Come! We have talked long enough.

Joris-Karl Huysmans (1848–1907)

À Rebours *(Against the Grain) by Joris-Karl Huysmans is the inspiration for the "poisonous" book Dorian reads in Chapter 10; Wilde called it "a fantastic variation on Huysmans's over-realistic study of the artistic temperament in our inartistic age" (Letters 524). In this selection from Chapter 8 of Huysmans' book, the hero Des Esseintes, suffering from ill health, decides to give up reading for gardening. Bored with ordinary flowers, he seeks the ugliest, especially those that look artificial.*

from À *Rebours (Against the Grain)* (1884)

The gardeners brought still other varieties which had the appearance of artificial skin ridged with false veins, and most of them looked as though consumed by syphilis and leprosy, for they exhibited livid surfaces of flesh veined with scarlet rash and damasked with eruptions. Some had the deep red hue of scars that have just closed or the dark tint of incipient scabs. Others were marked with matter raised by scaldings. There were forms which exhibited shaggy skins hollowed by ulcers and relieved by cankers. And a few appeared embossed with wounds, covered with black mercurial hog lard, with green unguents of belladonna smeared with grains of dust and the yellow micas of iodoforme.

Collected in his home, these flowers seemed to Des Esseintes more monstrous than when he had beheld them, confused with others among the glass rooms of the conservatory.

"*Sapristi!*"[1] he exclaimed enthusiastically.

[4]Alfred, Lord Tennyson, "Now Sleeps the Crimson Petal," a song from *The Princess* (1847), l. 5.
[5]William Blake, "To the Evening Star" (1783), l. 10.

[1]Exclamation of astonishment (French).

A new plant, modelled like the Caladiums, the *Alocasia Metallica*, excited him even more. It was coated with a layer of bronze green on which glanced silver reflections. It was the masterpiece of artificiality. It could be called a piece of stove pipe, cut by a chimney-maker into the form of a pike head.

The men next brought clusters of leaves, lozenge-like in shape and bottle-green in color. In the center rose a rod at whose end a varnished ace of hearts swayed. As though meaning to defy all conceivable forms of plants, a fleshy stalk climbed through the heart of this intense vermilion ace—a stalk that in some specimens was straight, in others showed ringlets like a pig's tail.

It was the *Anthurium*, an aroid recently imported into France from Columbia; a variety of that family to which also belonged an *Amorphophallus*, a Cochin China plant with leaves shaped like fish-knives, with long dark stems seamed with gashes, like lambs flecked with black.

Des Esseintes exulted.

They brought a new batch of monstrosities from the wagon: *Echinopses*, issuing from padded compresses with rose-colored flowers that looked like the pitiful stumps; gaping *Nidularia* revealing skinless foundations in steel plates; *Tillandsia Lindeni*, the color of wine must, with jagged scrapers; *Cypripedia*, with complicated contours, a crazy piece of work seemingly designed by a crazy inventor. They looked like sabots or like a lady's work-table on which lies a human tongue with taut filaments, such as one sees designed on the illustrated pages of works treating of the diseases of the throat and mouth; two little side-pieces, of a red jujube color, which appeared to have been borrowed from a child's toy mill completed this singular collection of a tongue's underside with the color of slate and wine lees, and of a glossy pocket from whose lining oozed a viscous glue.

He could not remove his eyes from this unnatural orchid which had been brought from India. Then the gardeners, impatient at his procrastinations, themselves began to read the labels fastened to the pots they were carrying in.

Bewildered, Des Esseintes looked on and listened to the cacophonous sounds of the names: the *Encephalartos horridus*, a gigantic iron rust-colored artichoke, like those put on portals of chateaux to foil wall climbers; the *Cocos Micania*, a sort of notched and slender palm surrounded by tall leaves resembling paddles and oars; the *Zamia Lehmanni*, an immense pineapple, a wondrous Chester leaf, planted in sweet-heather soil, its top bristling with barbed javelins and jagged arrows; the *Cibotium Spectabile*, surpassing the others by the craziness of its structure, hurling a defiance to reverie, as it darted, through the palmated foliage, an enormous orang-outang tail, a hairy dark tail whose end was twisted into the shape of a bishop's cross.

But he gave little heed, for he was impatiently awaiting the series of plants which most bewitched him, the vegetable ghouls, the carnivorous plants; the *Antilles Fly-Trap*, with its shaggy border, secreting a digestive liquid, armed with crooked prickles coiling around each other, forming a grating about the imprisoned insect; the *Drosera* of the peat-bogs, provided with glandular hair; the *Sarracena* and the *Cephalothus*, opening greedy horns capable of digesting and absorbing real meat; lastly, the *Nepenthes*, whose capricious appearance transcends all limits of eccentric forms.

He never wearied of turning in his hands the pot in which this floral extravagance stirred. It imitated the gum-tree whose long leaf of dark metallic green it possessed, but it differed in that a green string hung from the end of its leaf, an umbilic cord supporting a greenish urn, streaked with jasper, a sort of German porcelain pipe, a strange bird's nest which tranquilly swung about, revealing an interior covered with hair.

"This is really something worth while," Des Esseintes murmured.

He was forced to tear himself away, for the gardeners, anxious to leave, were emptying the wagons of their contents and depositing, without any semblance of order, the tuberous *Begonias* and black *Crotons* stained like sheet iron with Saturn red.

Then he perceived that one name still remained on his list. It was the *Cattleya* of New Granada. On it was designed a little winged bell of a faded lilac, an almost dead mauve. He approached, placed his nose above the plant and quickly recoiled. It exhaled an odor of toy boxes of painted pine; it recalled the horrors of a New Year's Day.

He felt that he would do well to mistrust it and he almost regretted having admitted, among the scentless plants, this orchid which evoked the most disagreeable memories.

As soon as he was alone his gaze took in this vegetable tide which foamed in the vestibule. Intermingled with each other, they crossed their swords, their krisses and stanchions, taking on a resemblance to a green pile of arms, above which, like barbaric penons, floated flowers with hard dazzling colors.

The air of the room grew rarefied. Then, in the shadowy dimness of a corner, near the floor, a white soft light crept.

He approached and perceived that the phenomenon came from the *Rhizomorphes* which threw out these night-lamp gleams while respiring.

"These plants are amazing," he reflected. Then he drew back to let his eye encompass the whole collection at a glance. His purpose was achieved. Not one single specimen seemed real; the cloth, paper, porcelain and metal seemed to have been loaned by man to nature to enable her to create her monstrosities. When unable to imitate man's handiwork, nature had been reduced to copying the inner membranes of animals, to borrowing the vivid tints of their rotting flesh, their magnificent corruptions.

Science

The Victorians witnessed spectacular developments in science that challenged long-held beliefs about the universe and humanity's place in it. Scientific methodology also shifted. At the beginning of the nineteenth century, "science" was not a unified field with shared practices and protocols. Inquiries into such subjects as natural history, geology, chemistry, and others were pursued in a somewhat haphazard fashion by a range of amateurs, many of whom made brilliant discoveries.

By the end of the century, scientific study had become professionalized, especially in such institutions as the universities. The Royal Commission on Scientific Instruction and the Advancement of Science (the "Devonshire Commission") was established in the 1870s, and Francis Galton's *English Men of Science: Their Nature and Nurture* (1872) gave the character type of the ideal scientist. And the public was curious. Scientific developments were regularly reported in newspapers and periodicals and could command a wide readership.

For all the talk of "art for art's sake," many self-declared aesthetes were paying attention to contemporary science, from Darwinian evolution to analytical psychology. Wilde's notebooks include numerous quotations from such writers as Thomas Henry Huxley, Herbert Spencer, and W. K. Clifford, all of whom explored the implications of Darwin's theories. *The Picture of Dorian Gray* is threaded with references to contemporary science, from Lord Henry's "vivisection" of Dorian, to Dorian's experimentation on himself in Chapter 11 with his range of sensations, to Alan Campbell's chemical removal of Basil Hallward's body.

Charles Darwin (1809–1882)

> *Though Charles Darwin's theory of evolution is famed for undermin-*
> *ing the authority of scripture, much of the early opposition came from*
> *other scientists. At the same time, Darwin's own rhetoric drew heavily*
> *on the tradition of natural theology, which had attempted to reconcile*
> *science and Christianity. Darwin's Victorian champions—famously,*
> *Thomas Henry Huxley—were more prone to agnosticism.*
>   *In* The Descent of Man *(1871), Darwin applies his theories of evo-*
> *lution to human development. The most notorious argument was the*
> *descent of man from early primates, but no less troubling to the Victo-*
> *rians was the argument for nature as a world of fierce competitiveness*
> *in the struggle for existence, which existed in tension with the forma-*
> *tion of cooperative social communities. A key element in nurturing the*
> *formation of such communities is mental stimulation, a mode we can*
> *see in Pater's call for a romance of multiplied consciousness and*
> *Dorian Gray's pursuit of sensation.*

"General Summary and Conclusion," from *The Descent of Man* (1871)

The development of the moral qualities is a more interesting problem. The foundation lies in the social instincts, including under this
term the family ties. These instincts are highly complex, and in the
case of the lower animals give special tendencies towards certain
definite actions; but the more important elements are love, and the
distinct emotion of sympathy. Animals endowed with the social
instincts take pleasure in one another's company, warn one
another of danger, defend and aid one another in many ways.
These instincts do not extend to all the individuals of the species,
but only to those of the same community. As they are highly bene-
ficial to the species, they have in all probability been acquired
through natural selection.

A moral being is one who is capable of reflecting on his past
actions and their motives—of approving of some and disapproving
of others; and the fact that man is the one being who certainly
deserves this designation, is the greatest of all distinctions between
him and the lower animals. But in the fourth chapter I have
endeavoured to shew that the moral sense follows, firstly, from the
enduring and ever-present nature of the social instincts; secondly,
from man's appreciation of the approbation and disapprobation of

his fellows; and thirdly, from the high activity of his mental faculties, with past impressions extremely vivid; and in these latter respects he differs from the lower animals. Owing to this condition of mind, man cannot avoid looking both backwards and forwards, and comparing past impressions. Hence after some temporary desire or passion has mastered his social instincts, he reflects and compares the now weakened impression of such past impulses with the ever-present social instincts; and he then feels that sense of dissatisfaction which all unsatisfied instincts leave behind them, he therefore resolves to act differently for the future,—and this is conscience. Any instinct, permanently stronger or more enduring than another, gives rise to a feeling which we express by saying that it ought to be obeyed. A pointer dog, if able to reflect on his past conduct, would say to himself, I ought (as indeed we say of him) to have pointed at that hare and not have yielded to the passing temptation of hunting it.

Social animals are impelled partly by a wish to aid the members of their community in a general manner, but more commonly to perform certain definite actions. Man is impelled by the same general wish to aid his fellows; but has few or no special instincts. He differs also from the lower animals in the power of expressing his desires by words, which thus become a guide to the aid required and bestowed. The motive to give aid is likewise much modified in man: it no longer consists solely of a blind instinctive impulse, but is much influenced by the praise or blame of his fellows. The appreciation and the bestowal of praise and blame both rest on sympathy; and this emotion, as we have seen, is one of the most important elements of the social instincts. Sympathy, though gained as an instinct, is also much strengthened by exercise or habit. As all men desire their own happiness, praise or blame is bestowed on actions and motives, according as they lead to this end; and as happiness is an essential part of the general good, the greatest-happinesss principle indirectly serves as a nearly safe standard of right and wrong. As the reasoning powers advance and experience is gained, the remoter effects of certain lines of conduct on the character of the individual, and on the general good, are perceived; and then the self-regarding virtues come within the scope of public opinion, and receive praise, and their opposites blame. But with the less civilised nations reason often errs, and many bad customs and base superstitions come within the same scope, and are then esteemed as high virtues, and their breach as heavy crimes. The moral faculties are generally and justly esteemed as of higher value than the intellectual powers. But we should bear in mind that the activity of the mind in vividly recalling past impressions is one of the fundamental though secondary bases of conscience. This affords the strongest argument for educating and stimulating in all possible ways the intellectual faculties of every human being. No doubt a man with a torpid mind, if his social affections and sympathies are well developed, will be led to good actions, and may have a fairly sensitive conscience. But whatever renders the imagination more vivid and strengthens the habit of recalling and comparing past impressions, will make the conscience more sensitive, and may even somewhat compensate for weak social affections and sympathies.

William Kingdon Clifford (1845–1879)

In his short life, William Kingdon Clifford made major contributions to Victorian math and science. He was also a popular lecturer. In "Right and Wrong: The Scientific Ground of their Distinction," Clifford examines human ethical behavior in light of Darwin's theories of evolution (Huxley disapproved). The following passage extends Darwin's discussion of conscience presented in the previous selection.

from "*Right and Wrong*: The Scientific Ground of their Distinction" (1875)

Now to my mind the simplest and clearest and most profound philosophy that was every written upon the subject is to be found in the 2nd and 3rd chapters of Mr. Darwin's *Descent of Man*. In these chapters it appears that just as most physical characteristics of organisms have been evolved and preserved because they were useful to the individual in the struggle for existence against other individuals and other species, so this particular feeling has been evolved and preserved because it is useful to the tribe or community in the struggle for existence against other tribes, and against the environment as a whole. The function of conscience is the preservation of the tribe as a tribe. And we shall rightly train our consciences if we learn to approve those actions which tend to the advantage of the community in the struggle for existence. . . .

The first principles of natural ethics, then, is the sole and supreme allegiance of conscience to the community. I venture to call this *piety* in accordance with the older meaning of the word. Even if it should turn out impossible to sever it from the unfortunate associations which have clung to its later meaning, still it seems worth while to try.

An immediate deduction from our principle is that there are no self-regarding virtues properly so called; those qualities which tend to the advantage and preservation of the individual being only morally *right* in so far as they make him a more useful citizen. And this conclusion is in some cases of great practical importance. The virtue of purity, for example, attains in this way a fairly exact definition: purity in a man is that course of conduct which makes him to be a good husband and father, in a woman that which makes her to be a good wife and mother, or which helps other people so to prepare and keep themselves. It is easy to see how many false ideas and pernicious precepts are swept away by even so simple a definition as that.

Thomas Henry Huxley (1825–1895)

One of the most vigorous popularizers of Darwin's work in the Victorian era, Thomas Henry Huxley also defended scientific education. Against such upholders of the classical curriculum as Matthew Arnold, Huxley contended that modern educated man needed science, not classics. Wilde quoted Huxley extensively in his commonplace book. "Science and Culture" was Huxley's inaugural speech at Josiah Mason's Science College in Birmingham.

from "Science and Culture" (1880)

This distinctive character of our own times lies in the vast and constantly increasing part which is played by natural knowledge. Not only is our daily life shaped by it, not only does the prosperity of millions of men depend upon it, but our whole theory of life has long been influenced, consciously or unconsciously, by the general conceptions of the universe, which have been forced upon us by physical science.

In fact, the most elementary acquaintance with the results of scientific investigation shows us that they offer a broad and striking contradiction to the opinion so implicitly credited and taught in the middle ages. The notions of the beginning and the end of the world entertained by our forefathers are no longer credible. It is very certain that the earth is not the chief body in the material universe, and that the world is not subordinated to man's use. It is even more certain that nature is the expression of a definite order with which nothing interferes, and that the chief business of mankind is to learn that order and govern themselves accordingly. Moreover this scientific "criticism of life" presents itself to us with different credentials from any other. It appeals not to authority, nor to what anybody may have thought or said, but to nature. It admits that all our interpretations of natural fact are more or less imperfect and symbolic, and bids the learner seek for truth not among words but among things. It warns us that the assertion which outstrips evidence is not only a blunder but a crime.

Henry Maudsley (1835–1918)

Henry Maudsley represents another branch of Victorian science heavily influenced by Darwin: psychology. Maudsley was the leading theorist of insanity, working as a university lecturer, private clinician, and writer. His books included The Physiology and Pathology of Mind *(1867),* Body and Mind *(1870),* Responsibility in Mental Disease *(1874),* Natural Causes and Supernatural Seemings *(1886), and* Organic to Human: Psychological and Sociological *(1916). Like other Victorian psychologists, Maudsley argued for the inseparability of body and mind and the force of heredity in the development of the mind. Both ideas color* The Picture of Dorian Gray. *The excerpt presented here aligns madness with genius, a proximity that reflects Victorian anxieties about the kind of exceptional individuals praised, ambivalently, by Arnold as "aliens" (Victorian psychologists were known as "alienists").*

from *The Physiology and Pathology of the Mind* (1867)

from "Varieties of Insanity"

The Insane Temperament, or Neurosis spasmodica.—It is characterized by singularities or eccentricities of thought, feeling, and action. It cannot truly be said of any one so constituted that he is mad, but he is certainly strange, or "queer," or, as it is said, "not quite right." What he does he must often do in a different way from all the rest of the world. If he thinks about anything, he is apt to think about it under strange and novel relations, which would not have occurred to an ordinary person; his feeling of an event is unlike that which other people have of it. He is sometimes impressionable to subtle and usually unrecognized influences; and now and then he does whimsical and apparently quite purposeless acts. There is in the constitution an innate tendency to act independently as an element in the social system, and there is a personal gratification in the indulgence of such disposition, which to lookers-on seems to mark great self-feeling and vanity. Such a one, therefore, is deemed, by the automatic beings who perform their duties in the social system with equable regularity, as odd, queer, strange, or not quite right.

This peculiarity of temperament, which undoubtedly predisposes to insanity, does nevertheless in some instances border very closely upon genius; it is the condition of the talent or wit which is allied to madness, only divided from it by thin partitions. The novel mode of looking at things may be an actual advance upon the accepted system of thought; the individual may be in a minority of one, not because he sees less than, or not so well as, all the world, but because he happens to see deeper, or to be favoured with a flash of intuitive insight. He may differ from all the world, not because he is wrong, and all the world is right, but because he is right, and all the world is wrong. Of necessity every new truth is at first in a minority of one; it is a rebellion against the existing system of belief; accordingly the existing system, ever thinking itself a finality, strives with all the weight of its established organization to crush it out. But by the nature of things that must happen, whether the novelty be a truth or an error. After all, it is only through the appearance of rebels in the social system that progress is effected; and precisely because individuality is a reproach, and sneered at as an eccentricity, is it well for the world, as Mr. J. S. Mill has said, that individuality or eccentricity should exist.[1]

---

[1]John Stuart Mill's *On Liberty* (1859) argued for defending individuality from the tyranny of mass opinion.

Love between Men

There had long been homosexual subcultures in Great Britain, although documentation before the nineteenth century is spotty. For the most part, knowledge before the first half of the nineteenth century comes from legal documents of men who were prosecuted. Sodomy had been a capital offense from 1533 until 1861, when it became punishable by imprisonment from ten years to life. The 1885 Labouchère Amendment to the Criminal Law Amendment Act specifically singled out "gross indecency" between men, either in public or private. As early as the writings of Jeremy Bentham, prominent intellectuals had argued against the criminalization of homosexuality, but with little impact during the Victorian period.

In the second half of the nineteenth century some spaces for male homosexual desire emerged, such as the revival of Catholicism in the Oxford movement and the reinvention of Hellenism by Walter Pater and his circle at Oxford. These cultures were not so much codes for homosexuality as they were intellectual movements and institutions that offered an alternative to traditional sex/gender roles. And, in all events, homosexuality remained closeted and subject to intense social, legal, and religious sanctions. A Victorian cult of manliness, associated with militarism, imperialism, heterosexuality, and self-discipline, flourished in opposition to qualities that had become stereotypically associated with men who loved men, though the cult of manliness itself was never as far from male–male desire as it may have liked to pretend.

Amid this repression, writing that defended male homosexuality became increasingly possible by the end of the nineteenth century, though usually in coterie circulation. Some of this work was highly coded, as in the Hellenic writings of Pater; other work was more open, as in the writings of the sexologist Havelock Ellis and social activist Edward Carpenter.

John Addington Symonds (1840–1893)

John Addington Symonds, prolific Victorian classicist and historian, struggled for years with his homosexuality. He married and had four daughters, but did not find happiness until he and his wife agreed to live separately, enabling Symonds to pursue homosexual relationships. He was best known during his life for his multivolume History of the Renaissance in Italy, *on which Wilde drew extensively for* The Picture of Dorian Gray. *In 1873, Symonds printed ten copies of "A Problem in Greek Ethics," an extensive essay on erotic relations between older and younger men in ancient Greek culture. Symonds struggles with how to understand and evaluate the physical aspects of these relationships. In the excerpt presented here, he ponders sexual relations between Spartan men, traditionally viewed as the most masculine and military. Ellis (see p. 297) reprinted Symonds's essay as an appendix to his* Sexual Inversion.

from "A Problem in Greek Ethics" (1873)

A considerable majority of the legends which have been related in the preceding section are Dorian,[1] and the Dorians gave the earliest and most marked encouragement to Greek love. Nowhere else, indeed, except among the Dorians, who were an essentially military race, living like an army of occupation in the countries they had seized, herding together in barracks and at public messes, and submitting to martial drill and discipline, do we meet with paiderastia[2] developed as an institution. In Crete and Lacedæmon[3] it became a potent instrument of education. What I have to say, in the first instance on this matter is derived almost entirely

---

[1]Greek-speaking people who invaded and conquered Greece in the 12th c. B.C.E.

[2]Love between men and youths.

[3]Sparta and its surroundings.

from C. O. Müller's *Dorians*,[4] to which work I refer my readers for the authorities cited in illustration of each detail. Plato says that the law of Lycurgus[5] in respect to love was ποικίλος,[6] by which he means that it allowed the custom under certain restrictions. It would appear that the lover was called Εἰσπνήλας, or inspirer, at Sparta, while the youth he loved was named Ἀΐτας, or hearer. These local phrases sufficiently indicate the relation which subsisted between the pair. The lover taught, the hearer learned; and so from man to man was handed down the tradition of heroism, the peculiar tone and temper of the state to which, in particular among the Greeks, the Dorians clung with obstinate pertinacity. Xenophon[7] distinctly states that love was maintained among the Spartans with a view to education; and when we consider the customs of the state, by which boys were separated early from their homes and the influences of the family were almost wholly wanting, it is not difficult to understand the importance of the paiderastic institution. The Lacedæmonian lover might represent his friend in the Assembly. He was answerable for his good conduct, and stood before him as a pattern of manliness, courage, and prudence. Of the nature of his teaching we may form some notion from the precepts addressed by the Megarian Theognis to the youth Kurnus.[8] In battle the lovers fought side by side;[9] and it is worthy of notice that before entering into an engagement the Spartans sacrificed to Erôs.[10] It was reckoned a disgrace if a youth found no man to be his lover. Consequently we find that the most illustrious Spartans are mentioned by their biographers in connection with their comrades. Agesilaus heard Lysander; Archidamus, his son loved Cleonymus; Cleomenes III. was the hearer of Xenares and the inspirer of Panteus.[11] The

---

[4]Trans. by Sir G. C. Lewis, vol. ii, pp. 306–313 [Symonds's note, referring to Karl Ottfried Müller's *The History and Antiquities of the Doric Race*].

[5]Founder of Spartan law and military regime, 9th c. B.C.E.

[6]Symp. 182 A [Symonds's note, referring to Plato's *Symposium*].

[7]Greek historian and military leader c. 435–c. 354 B.C.E., author of the *Anabasis* and *Hellenica*.

[8]Greek elegiac poet (6th c. B.C.E.), to whom are attributed short poems to the boy Cyrnus.

[9]Hence the name παραστάτης [Symonds's note].

[10]God of love.

[11]Series of Spartan kings and their male lovers.

affection of Pausanias, on the other hand, for the boy Argilus, who betrayed him according to the account of Thucydides,[12] must not be reckoned among these nobler loves. In order to regulate the moral conduct of both parties, Lycurgus made it felony, punishable with death or exile, for the lover to desire the person of a boy in lust; and, on the other hand, it was accounted exceedingly disgraceful for the younger to meet the advances of the elder with a view to gain. Honest affection and manly self-respect were exacted on both sides; the bond of union implied no more of sensuality than subsists between a father and a son, a brother and a brother. At the same time great license of intercourse was permitted. Cicero, writing long after the great age of Greece, but relying probably upon sources to which we have no access, asserts that "Lacedæmonii ipsi cum omnia concedunt in amore juvenum *præter stuprum* tenui sane muro dissæpiunt id quod excipiunt: *complexus enim concubitusque permittunt.*"[13] "The Lacedemonians, while they permit all things except outrage in the love of youths, certainly distinguish the forbidden by a thin wall of partition from the sanctioned, for they allow embraces and a common couch to lovers."

Richard St. John Tyrwhitt (1827–1895)

Clergyman, art historian, and admirer of Ruskin, Richard St. John Tyrwhitt was also something of a rival to Symonds. In "The Greek Spirit in Modern Literature," he admires Arnold but is unsettled by Symonds's emphasis on male–male desire in his Studies of Greek Poets.

from "The Greek Spirit in Modern Literature" (1877)

These pages are a rebellion against nature as she is here, in the name of nature as described in Athens. And the word nature now brings us unavoidably on awkward ground. Mr. Symonds is probably the most innocent of men; we certainly cannot look upon him in any

---

[12]i.132 [Symonds's note, referring to Thucidydes's great *History of the Peloponnesian War*].

[13]De Rep., iv, 4 [Symonds's note, referring to *De Republica* by the Roman author and orator Cicero].

other light. He might not return the compliment, for everybody who objects to suggestive passages of a certain character is now called prurient by their authors, and this reproach we propose to incur. The emotions of Socrates at sight of the beauty of young Charmides are described for him by Plato, in the dialogue which bears the name of the latter. Socrates's purity, and indeed his asceticism of life are freely and fully vindicated elsewhere by Plato, and will never be disputed here. The expressions put in his mouth are, no doubt, typically Hellenic. But they are not natural: and it is well known that Greek love of nature and beauty went frequently against nature. The word is used equivocally in this book—for the outward shows of creation, and for the inward impulses of man; and it is assumed that because the former are generally beautiful, the latter are invariably to be followed. Neither are good, for what is good? They are both here, and must be taken for what they are.

Other assertions seem to be made rather, it must be said, in the spirit of the persecutor; that is to say, in order to inflict moral outrage instead of physical. Such are the passage about a phallic ecstasy perfectly free from pruriency (we have explained that this is the Anglo-Byzantine for decency); the talk about the frank sensuality of Priapus[1] as a right object of Greek sculpture, and the concluding exhortation to follow Walt Whitman[2] as far as our Hebraistic training and imperfect nature will enable us. . . . And we must say again, that he cannot know his historians as well as he does his poets; or he would have remembered that unnatural practices between men were foreign intrusions from Greece into Asia.

Havelock Ellis (1859–1939)

The revolutionary move of Sexual Inversion, one of the first serious studies of homosexuality, was its basis in actual interviews with gays and lesbians to find out about their lives. Originally published in German in 1896, when it appeared in London in 1897, it was condemned

---

[1]Greek god of fertility, represented as a misshapen man with a huge, erect penis.
[2]Whitman's *Leaves of Grass* (1855) included revelatory celebrations of desire between men.

as obscene and suppressed. Havelock Ellis made sure that his future studies were published instead in the United States. In the following excerpt, Ellis demolishes the widespread assumption that homosexuals were either deeply ashamed of their lives or completely indifferent to moral codes. He also notes their regret at their double lives, a phrase used by Wilde in The Picture of Dorian Gray.

from *Sexual Inversion* (1897)

from Chapter 5, "The Nature of Sexual Inversion"[1]

Moral Attitude of the Invert.—There is some interest in tracing the invert's own attitude toward his anomaly, and his estimate of its morality. As my cases are not patients seeking to be cured of their perversion, this attitude cannot be taken for granted. I have noted the moral attitude in twenty-nine cases. In three the subjects loathe themselves, and have fought in vain against their perversion. Six or seven are doubtful, and have little to say in justification of their condition, which they regard as perhaps morbid. The remainder, a large majority (including all the women) are, on the other hand, emphatic in their assertion that their moral position is precisely the same as that of the normally constituted individual; one or two even regard inverted love as nobler than ordinary sexual love; a few add the proviso that there should be consent and understanding on both sides, and no attempt at seduction. The chief regret of one or two is the double life they are obliged to lead.

When inverts have clearly faced and realized their own nature it is not so much, it seems, their conscience that worries them, or even the fear of the police, as the attitude of the world. An American correspondent writes: "It is the fear of public opinion that hangs above them like the sword of Damocles.[2] This fear is the heritage of all of us. It is not the fear of conscience and is not engendered by a feeling of wrongdoing. Rather, it is a silent submission to prejudices that meet us on every side. The true normal attitude of the sexual invert (and I have known hundreds) with

---

[1] "Sexual Inversion" is Ellis's attempt to find a neutral term to describe homosexuality; he regarded "homosexual" as a "barbarously hybrid word."

[2] According to legend, a courtier who extravagantly praised the happiness of Dionysius I; to show him how precarious this happiness was, Dionysius seated him at a banquet with a sword hung by a single hair over his head.

regard to his particular passion is not essentially different from that of the normal man with regard to his."

It will be seen that my conclusions under this head are in striking contrast to those of Westphal,[3] who believed that every invert regarded himself as morbid, and probably show a much higher proportion of self-approving inverts than any previous series. This is due partly to the way in which the cases were obtained, and partly to the fact that they may be said, on the whole to represent in some degree the intellectual aristocracy of inversion, including individuals who, often not without severe struggles, have found consolation in the example of the Greeks, or elsewhere, and have succeeded in attaining a *modus vivendi* with the moral world, as they have come to conceive it.

from Chapter 7, "Conclusions"

The existing law in England is severe but simple. Carnal knowledge *per anum* of either a man or a woman or an animal is a felony (under 24 and 25 Vict., c. 100, sec. 61) punishable by a sentence of penal servitude for life as a maximum and for ten years as a minimum; the attempt at such carnal knowledge is punishable by ten years penal servitude. The Criminal Law Amendment Act of 1885 goes beyond this and makes even "gross indecency" between males, however privately committed, a penal offence.[4] The Criminal Law Amendment Act is in many respects an admirable enactment: to it we owe the raising of the age at which it becomes lawful for a woman to consent to sexual intercourse from over twelve to over sixteen. But this Act appears to have been somewhat hastily carried through, and many of its provisions, as well as its omissions, have been justly subjected to severe criticism. The clause from which I have quoted is specially open to criticism. With the omission of the words "or private," the clause would be sound and in harmony with the most enlightened European legislation; but it must be pointed out that an act only becomes indecent when those who perform it or witness it regard it as indecent. The act which brought each of us into the world is not indecent; it would become so if

---

[3]Karl Westphal (1833–90), German sexologist who argued that homosexuality was a pathology caused by "contrary sexual feeling."

[4]The Act used to convict Wilde in 1895.

carried on in public. If two male persons, who have reached years of discretion, consent together to perform some act of sexual intimacy in private, no indecency has been committed. If one of the consenting parties subsequently proclaims the act, indecency may doubtless be created, as may happen also in the case of normal sexual intercourse, but it seems contrary to good policy that such proclamation should convert the act itself into a penal offense. Moreover, "gross indecency" between males usually means some form of mutual masturbation; no penal code regards masturbation as an offense, and there seems to be no sufficient reason why mutual masturbation should be so regarded. The main point to be ensured is that no boy or girl who has not reached years of discretion should be seduced or abused by an older person, and this point is equally well guaranteed on the basis introduced by the *Code Napoléon*.[5] However shameful, disgusting, personally immoral, and indirectly anti-social it may be for two adult persons of the same sex, men or women, to consent together to perform an act of sexual intimacy in private, there is no sound or adequate ground for constituting such act a penal offense by law.

---

[5]Codification of French law under Napoleon, which decriminalized sodomy.

Works Cited in the Notes

I have also drawn on such standard reference works as the *Oxford English Dictionary*, the *Oxford Dictionary of National Biography*, and the *Grove Dictionary of Music and Musicians*.

Baedeker, K. *London and Its Environs: A Handbook for Travellers.* 7th rev. ed. Dulau and Co., 1889.

Bennett, Alfred Rosling. *London and Londoners in the Eighteen-Fifties and Sixties.* Unwin, 1924.

Bristow, Joseph, ed. *The Picture of Dorian Gray: The 1890 and 1891 Texts.* Vol. 3 of *The Complete Works of Oscar Wilde.* Ed. Ian Small. Oxford Univ. Press, 2005.

Brown, Lucy. *Victorian News and Newspapers.* Clarendon, 1985.

Burke, Edmund. *Reflections on the Revolution in France* (1790). Ed. Conor Cruise O'Brien. Penguin, 1968.

Cowen, Anne, and Roger Cowen, ed. *Victorian Jews through British Eyes.* Oxford Univ. Press, 1986.

Curtis, L. Perry. *Jack the Ripper and the London Press.* Yale Univ. Press, 2001.

Dickens, Charles (not the famous novelist). *Dickens's Dictionary of London, 1877: An Unconventional Handbook.* London: Charles Dickens, 1879.

Doré, Gustave, and Blanchard Jerrold. *London: A Pilgrimage* (1872). Dover, 1970.

Ellman, Richard. *Oscar Wilde.* Random House, 1987.

Guy, Josephine M., and Ian Small. *Oscar Wilde's Profession: Writing and the Culture Industry in the Late Nineteenth Century.* Oxford Univ. Press, 2001.

Hare, Augustus J. C. *Walks in London.* 2 vols. in 1. George Routledge, 1880.

Holland, Merlin, ed. *The Real Trial of Oscar Wilde*. HarperCollins, 2003.

Lang, Andrew. "Lady Book Lovers." *Fortnightly Review* 16 (1886): 633–40.

Milligan, Barry. *Pleasures and Pains: Opium and the Orient in Nineteenth-Century British Culture*. Univ. of Virginia Press, 1995.

Mogg, Edward S. *Mogg's New Picture of London, or, Strangers' Guide to the British Metropolis*. E. Mogg, 1846.

Montagu, Stephen Williams. *Round London: Down East and Up West*. Macmillan, 1894.

Newbery, Timothy J., et al. *The Italian Renaissance Frames*. Metropolitan Museum of Art, 1990.

Page, Norman, ed. *The Picture of Dorian Gray by Oscar Wilde*. Broadview, 1998.

Pater, Walter. "Giordano Bruno." *Fortnightly Review* 46 (1889): 234–44.

Pool, Daniel. *What Jane Austen Ate and Charles Dickens Knew: From Fox Hunting to Whist—The Facts of Daily Life in Nineteenth-Century England*. Touchstone, 1993.

Roden, Frederick S. *Same-Sex Desire in Victorian Religious Culture*. Palgrave, 2002.

Shakespeare, William. *The Riverside Shakespeare*. 2nd ed. Ed. G. Blakemore Evans et al. Houghton Mifflin, 1997.

Spencer, Herbert. "Introduction: From Freedom to Bondage." In *A Plea for Liberty: An Argument Against Socialism and Socialistic Legislation*. Ed. Thomas Mackay. D. Appleton and Co., 1891, 1–26.

Sutherland, John. *Is Heathcliff a Murderer? Great Puzzles in Nineteenth-Century Literature*. Oxford Univ. Press, 1996.

Symonds, John Addington. "Preface" to *The Sonnets of Michael Angelo Buonarroti and Tomasso Campanella*. Smith, Elder, & Co., 1878.

———. *The Renaissance in Italy*. 6 vols. Smith, Elder, & Co., 1875–86.

———. *Sketches and Studies in Italy and Greece*. 3rd ser. Smith, Elder, & Co., 1898.

Vigar-Harris, Henry. *London at Midnight*. General Publishing, 1885.

Watkins, John. *Representing Elizabeth in Stuart England: Literature, History, Sovereignty.* Cambridge Univ. Press, 2002.

Wheatley, Henry Benjamin. *London, Past and Present: Its History, Associations, and Traditions.* 3 vols. John Murray, 1891.

Yates, Edmund. *Fifty Years of London Life: Memoirs of a Man of the World.* Harper and Brothers, 1885.

Further Reading

Oscar Wilde's Writings

The Collected Works of Oscar Wilde. Ed. Robert Ross. 13 vols. Methuen, 1908.

The Complete Letters of Oscar Wilde. Ed. Merlin Holland and Rupert Hart-Davis. Henry Holt, 2000.

The Complete Works of Oscar Wilde. Ed. Ian Small. 3 vols. to present. Oxford Univ. Press, 2001–.

Oscar Wilde's Oxford Notebooks: A Portrait of Mind in the Making. Ed. Philip E. Smith II and Michael S. Helfland. Oxford Univ. Press, 1989.

The Picture of Dorian Gray: The 1890 and 1891 Texts. Ed. Joseph Bristow. Vol. 3 of *The Complete Works of Oscar Wilde.* Ed. Ian Small. Oxford Univ. Press, 2005.

The Real Trial of Oscar Wilde. Ed. Merlin Holland. Perennial, 2003.

Biographical Studies

Belford, Barbara. *Oscar Wilde: A Certain Genius.* Random House, 2000.

Bentley, Joyce. *The Importance of Being Constance.* R. Hale, 1983.

Ellman, Richard. *Oscar Wilde.* Random House, 1987.

Holland, Merlin. *The Wilde Album.* Henry Holt, 1998.

Knox, Melissa. *Oscar Wilde: A Long and Lovely Suicide.* Yale Univ. Press, 1994.

McCormack, Jerusha Hull. *The Man Who Was Dorian Gray.* St. Martin's Press, 2000.

McKenna, Neil. *The Secret Life of Oscar Wilde.* Arrow, 2004.

Mikhail, E. H., ed. *Oscar Wilde: Interviews and Recollections.* 2 vols. Barnes and Noble, 1979.

Murray, Douglas. *Bosie: A Biography of Lord Alfred Douglas.* Hyperion, 2000.

Page, Norman. *An Oscar Wilde Chronology.* G. K. Hall, 1991.

Critical Studies

Arata, Stephen. *Fictions of Loss in the Victorian Fin de Siècle.* Cambridge Univ. Press, 1996.

Armstrong, Nancy. *Fiction in the Age of Photography: The Legacy of British Realism.* Harvard Univ. Press, 1999.

Backus, Margot Gayle. *The Gothic Family Romance: Heterosexuality, Child Sacrifice, and the Anglo-Irish Colonial Order.* Duke Univ. Press, 1999.

Baker, Houston A., Jr. "A Tragedy of the Artist: *The Picture of Dorian Gray.*" *Nineteenth-Century Fiction* 24 (1969): 349–55.

Bartlett, Neil. *Who Was That Man? A Present for Mr. Oscar Wilde.* Serpent's Tail, 1988.

Beckson, Karl. *The Oscar Wilde Encyclopedia.* AMS, 1998.

———, ed. *Oscar Wilde: The Critical Heritage.* Routledge, 1997.

Bowlby, Rachel. "Promoting Dorian Gray." *Oxford Literary Review* 9 (1987): 147–62.

Brantlinger, Patrick. *The Reading Lesson: The Threat of Mass Literacy in Nineteenth-Century British Fiction.* Indiana Univ. Press, 1998.

Bristow, Joseph. "Wilde, Dorian Gray, and Gross Indecency." In *Sexual Sameness: Textual Differences*, ed. Joseph Bristow. Routledge, 1992, 44–63.

———, ed. *Wilde Writings: Contextual Conditions.* Univ. of Toronto Press, 2003.

Bruhm, Steven. *Reflecting Narcissus: A Queer Aesthetic.* Univ. of Minnesota Press, 2001.

Buckton, Oliver S. *Secret Selves: Confession and Same-Sex Desire in Victorian Autobiography.* Univ. of North Carolina Press, 1998.

Coakley, Davis. *Oscar Wilde: The Importance of Being Irish.* Town House, 1994.

Cohen, Ed. *Talk on the Wilde Side: Towards a Genealogy of a Discourse on Male Sexualities.* Routledge, 1993.

———. "Writing Gone Wilde: Homoerotic Desire in the Closet of Representation." *PMLA* 102 (1987): 801–13.

Cook, Matt. *London and the Culture of Homosexuality, 1885–1914.* Cambridge Univ. Press, 2003.

Craft, Christopher. "Come See About Me: Enchantment of the Double in *The Picture of Dorian Gray.*" *Representations* 91 (2005): 109–36.

Danson, Lawrence. *Wilde's Intentions: The Artist in His Criticism.* Clarendon, 1997.

Dawson, Terence. *The Effective Protagonist in the Nineteenth-Century British Novel: Scott, Brontë, Eliot, Wilde.* Ashgate, 2004.

Dellamora, Richard. *Apocalyptic Overtures: Sexual Politics and the Sense of an Ending.* Rutgers Univ. Press, 1994.

———. *Masculine Desire: The Sexual Politics of Victorian Aestheticism.* Univ. of North Carolina Press, 1990.

Dollimore, Jonathan. *Sexual Dissidence: Augustine to Wilde, Freud to Foucault.* Oxford Univ. Press, 1991.

Dowling, Linda. *Hellenism and Homosexuality in Victorian Oxford.* Cornell Univ. Press, 1994.

Dryden, Linda. *The Modern Gothic and Literary Doubles: Stevenson, Wilde and Wells.* Palgrave, 2003.

Edelman, Lee. *Homographesis: Essays in Gay Literary and Cultural Theory.* Routledge, 1994.

Elfenbein, Andrew. *Byron and the Victorians.* Cambridge Univ. Press, 1995.

Felski, Rita. *The Gender of Modernity.* Harvard Univ. Press, 1995.

Ferguson, Christine. "Decadence as Scientific Fulfillment." *PMLA* 117 (2002): 465–78.

Gagnier, Regenia, ed. *Critical Essays on Oscar Wilde.* G. K. Hall, 1991.

———. *Idylls of the Marketplace: Oscar Wilde and the Victorian Public.* Stanford Univ. Press, 1986.

———. *The Insatiability of Human Wants: Economics and Aesthetics in Market Society.* Univ. of Chicago Press, 2000.

Gaines, Jane. *Contested Culture: The Image, the Voice, and the Law.* Univ. of North Carolina Press, 1991.

Glick, Elisa. "The Dialectics of Dandyism." *Cultural Critique* 48 (2001): 129–63.

Gomel, Elana. "Oscar Wilde, *The Picture of Dorian Gray*, and the (Un)Death of the Author." *Narrative* 12 (2004): 74–92.

Halberstam, Judith. *Skin Shows: Gothic Horror and the Technology of Monsters*. Duke Univ. Press, 1995.

Hannon, Patrice. "Theatre and Theory in the Language of *Dorian Gray*." *Victorian Literature and Culture* 19 (1991): 143–66.

Haslett, Moyra. *Marxist Literary and Cultural Theories*. St. Martin's Press, 2000.

Jaffe, Audrey. *Scenes of Sympathy: Identity and Representation in Victorian Fiction*. Cornell Univ. Press, 2000.

Joyce, Simon. "Sexual Politics and the Aesthetics of Crime: Oscar Wilde in the Nineties." *ELH* 69 (2002): 501–23.

Kane, Michael. *Modern Men: Mapping Masculinity in English and German Literature, 1880–1930*. Cassell, 1999.

Kaye, Richard A. *The Flirt's Tragedy: Desire without End in Victorian and Edwardian Fiction*. Univ. of Virginia Press, 2002.

Keane, Robert N., ed. *Oscar Wilde: The Man, His Writings, and His World*. AMS, 2003.

Kofman, Sarah. "The Imposture of Beauty: The Uncanniness of Oscar Wilde's *Picture of Dorian Gray*." In *Enigmas: Essays on Kofman*. Ed. Penelope Deutscher and Kelly Oliver. Cornell Univ. Press, 1999, 25–48.

Lane, Christopher. *The Ruling Passion: British Colonial Allegory and the Paradox of Homosexual Desire*. Duke Univ. Press, 1995.

Latham, Sean. *"Am I a snob?": Modernism and the Novel*. Cornell Univ. Press, 2003.

Levine, Caroline. *The Serious Pleasures of Suspense: Victorian Realism and Narrative Doubt*. Univ. of Virginia Press, 2003.

Levy, Anita. *Reproductive Urges: Popular Novel-Reading, Sexuality, and the English Nation*. Univ. of Pennsylvania Press, 1999.

Lloyd, Tom. *Crises of Realism: Representing Experience in the British Novel, 1816–1910*. Bucknell Univ. Press, 1997.

Mahaffey, Vicki. *States of Desire: Wilde, Yeats, Joyce, and the Irish Experiment*. Oxford Univ. Press, 1998.

Maier, Wolfgang. *Oscar Wilde, The Picture of Dorian Gray: Eine Kritische Analyse der Anglistischen Forschung von 1962 bis 1982*. Lang, 1984.

Mason, Stuart [Christopher Millard]. *Art and Morality: A Record of the Discussion Which Followed the Publication of "Dorian Gray."* Rev. ed. Frank Palmer, 1912.

Monsman, Gerald. "The Platonic Eros of Walter Pater and Oscar Wilde: 'Love's Reflected Image' in the 1890s." *English Literature in Transition (1880–1920)* 45 (2002): 26–45.

Nethercot, Arthur H. "Oscar Wilde and the Devil's Advocate." *PMLA* 59 (1944): 833–50.

Nunokawa, Jeff. *Tame Passions of Wilde: The Styles of Manageable Desire.* Princeton Univ. Press, 2003.

Oates, Joyce Carol. "*The Picture of Dorian Gray*: Wilde's Parable of the Fall." *Critical Inquiry* 7 (1980): 419–28.

Powell, Kerry. "Tom, Dick, and Dorian Gray: Magic-Picture Mania in Late Victorian Fiction." *Philological Quarterly* 62 (1983): 147–70.

Psomiades, Kathy Alexis. *Beauty's Body: Femininity and Representation in British Aestheticism.* Stanford Univ. Press, 1997.

Raby, Peter, ed. *The Cambridge Companion to Oscar Wilde.* Cambridge Univ. Press, 1997.

Ragland-Sullivan, Ellie. "The Phenomenon of Aging in Oscar Wilde's *Picture of Dorian Gray*: A Lacanian View." In *Memory and Desire: Aging—Literature—Psychoanalysis.* Ed. Kathleen Woodward and Murray M. Schwartz. Indiana Univ. Press, 1986, 114–33.

Riquelme, John Paul. "Oscar Wilde's Aesthetic Gothic: Walter Pater, Dark Enlightenment, and *The Picture of Dorian Gray*." *Modern Fiction Studies* 46 (2000): 609–31.

Roden, Frederick S., ed. *Palgrave Advances in Oscar Wilde Studies.* Palgrave, 2004.

Seagroatt, Heather. "Hard Science, Soft Psychology, and Amorphous Art in *The Picture of Dorian Gray*." *SEL* 38 (1998): 741–59.

Sedgwick, Eve Kosofsky. *Epistemology of the Closet.* Univ. of California Press, 1990.

Showalter, Elaine. *Sexual Anarchy: Gender and Culture at the Fin de Siècle.* Viking, 1990.

Sinfield, Alan. *The Wilde Century: Effeminacy, Oscar Wilde, and the Queer Movement.* Columbia Univ. Press, 1994.

Sloan, John. *Oscar Wilde.* Oxford Univ. Press, 2003.

Stokes, John. *Oscar Wilde: Myths, Miracles, and Imitations.* Cambridge Univ. Press, 1996.

Tanitch, Robert. *Oscar Wilde on Stage and Screen.* Methuen, 1999.

Thurschwell, Pamela. *Literature, Technology, and Magical Thinking, 1880–1920.* Cambridge Univ. Press, 2001.

Selected Adaptations

The Picture of Dorian Gray (1913), dir. Phillips Smalley.

The Picture of Dorian Gray (1916), dir. Fred W. Durrant.

Das Bildnis des Dorian Gray (1917), dir. Richard Oswald.

The Picture of Dorian Gray (1945), dir. Albert Lewin. By far the most famous film adaptation. Starring Hurd Hatfield and a young Angela Lansbury.

Dorian Gray (1971), dir. Massimo Dallamano.

The Picture of Dorian Gray (1973) (TV), dir. Glenn Jordan.

The Picture of Dorian Gray (1976) (TV), dir. John Gorrie, script by John Osborne.

The Sins of Dorian Gray (1987) (TV), dir. Tony Maylam. Makes Dorian female.

The Picture of Dorian Gray (1988), ballet adapted by Saeko Ichinohe for the Louisville ballet.

The Picture of Dorian Gray (1996), opera by Lowell Liebermann.